SINATRA

'An audience is like a broad – if you're indifferent, endsville'

FRANCIS ALBERT SINATRA

Here at last is the complete Sinatra; here is the rise, the fall and the rise again; here is the man whose performance, image and style in the post-war years has entered the hearts of millions all over the world.

'Brilliantly done...Shaw manages to capture some of the enigma that is Sinatra. A fascinating study of the man who has made and lost fortunes and had more friends and more enemies than any other show-biz figure alive'

Melody Maker

'A fascinating insight of a remarkable man'
Yorkshire Evening Post

'As slick as its subject'
Birmingham Post

'This book is a *must*'
She

'Compulsively readable'
The Scotsman

'Told with rare honesty and understanding, I read it from cover to cover non-stop'
Manchester Evening News

SINATRA

Retreat of the Romantic

ARNOLD SHAW

HODDER PAPERBACKS

© ARNOLD SHAW, 1968

First published by
W. H. ALLEN & CO., LTD., 1968
Hodder Paperback edition 1970

*Printed in Great Britain
for Hodder Paperbacks, Ltd.,
St. Paul's House, Warwick Lane, London E.C.4,
by Richard Clay (The Chaucer Press), Ltd.,
Bungay, Suffolk*

ISBN 0 340 12644 2

To Ghita

for her love, patience and wisdom

CONTENTS

OVERTURE

In May 1970 Sinatra and the Count Basie band gave two concerts at London's Royal Festival Hall. The entire proceeds from both performances were donated to children's charities. Out of his own pocket, Sinatra paid not only his expenses and those of his entourage but of all the members of the Basie aggregation—a bill that ran him well over $25,000.

Not too long ago, to celebrate the twenty-fifth wedding anniversary of Rosalind Russell and Fred Brisson, Frank Sinatra reserved the four top floors of the Sands Hotel in Las Vegas. Thirty guests were transported in a chartered DC9 jet from Los Angeles, receiving the keys to their elegant suites before the plane took off on its caviar-and-champagne flight. Dinner on Friday night was at the luxurious Villa d'Este restaurant where Frank commandeered the entire second floor. At dinner on Saturday night, there were no place cards; guests located their chairs by photographs of themselves in silver frames. As favours, the men received inscribed silver cigarette boxes while the women took home silver lamé bags containing twenty-five silver dollars. The total cost of the party, which lasted seventy-two hours, was borne by Sinatra who reportedly spent $25,000.

Whether one considers his mode of spending, his manner of relaxing, his style of living, his methods of doing business, his loyalty to men, his susceptibility to women, the scope of his career or the magnitude of his achievement, the words for Francis Albert Sinatra are extravagant, at times reckless, if not flamboyant. At one time, his handle might have been bigsville.

The fountainhead of Sinatra's power is his unique and unsurpassed singing. Although he has worn many other hats—screen actor, television impresario, film director, hotel keeper, musical conductor, record and movie producer—the figure that hypnotises even today is the man in the snap-brim at the microphone. His sex appeal stems from it and the high voltage electricity of his personality begins with it. At fifty-four, when most vocalists of his generation are inactive or in semi-retirement, he is still the hitmaker—with single records that top best-seller lists in foreign countries as well as the USA and albums that receive awards as million-copy Gold Records. But apart from Sinatra's longevity as a vocalist, he has always been in the main line of the development of popular singing as an art— not merely as a profession or entertainment.

No pop singer before him sought, or achieved, so complete an identification, both personal and emotional, with his material. Through him, involvement and intensity became the touchstones of popular singing, as they were of folk and blues singing. For him, recording early became autobiography, and though he has no use for method actors, he is, in fact, a 'method singer' who selects songs that fit his emotional states. Like no singer before him, and few since, he has made an art of textual contrast ('timbre' is the technical word) and become master of vocal onomatopoeia. Because of his concern with communicating, he helped give new stature to lyrics, inspiring writers to seek the more evocative image, phrase and rhyme, and the more expressive interplay of word and note. As in a Matisse painting where the surprise juxtaposition of familiar colours produces the effect of new colours, Sinatra's spacing of words imparts new meanings to song lyrics. On one of the rare occasions when he spoke out, Lester Young, founder of the cool school in jazz, said: 'Really, my man is Frank Sinatra.' For it was Sinatra who moved Young and other jazzmen to study the words before they improvised on the notes.

But his achievement as a popular singer goes far beyond influence, output and artistry. It can be said of Sinatra as Archibald MacLeish has said of Hemingway: 'His is the one intrinsic style that our century has produced.' Judy Garland, Nat 'King' Cole and Perry Como can be as heartwarming, as sly and as ingratiating. The divine Sarah and scat-singing Ella can swing, alter, bend and smear their notes better. Andy Williams, Mel Tormé and Peggy Lee can be as insouciantly hip. Tony Bennett, Al Martino and Steve Lawrence can surpass his dramatic intensity. Barbra Streisand can match his ability to uncover unexpected nuances of meaning with her phrasing. But the synthesis of all these elements in a recognisable style is Sinatra's alone. The 'swinging ballad' style he perfected combines pop lyricism with jazz inflections, deep feeling with a driving beat, the sweep of soaring strings and the roar of massive brass, the self-pitying tenderness of the lonely and the improvisational toughness of the flip. It is a unique style. And the style is the man.

From the beginning, however, Sinatra's tremendous appeal stemmed from something more than his singing or his showmanship. He has always been a study in myths and images, some of them carefully constructed. He early became the popular symbol of the sensitive youngster in a hostile world, of the little guy bucking the Establishment, of the insatiable man whose reach always exceeded his grasp.

If Humphrey Bogart stands forth as the existential man, viewing life with a sense of detached irony but living with courage within the human condition, Sinatra is the archetype of the romantic man, raging against the human condition. Bogey always seemed to be saying: 'Cool it,' while Frankie Boy cried: 'Swing it! Make it!' Striving unremittingly to squeeze life dry, Sinatra was a twentieth-century American with an almost Renaissance flair for excitement, lavishness and emotional extravagance.

At a peak of his new-won success some years ago, he is said to have stayed awake constantly through the night, the lights burning brightly in his mountain-top home. Friends had to remain into the daybreak hours to keep him company while he paced his courtyard where a life-size statue of Ava Gardner stood and where he paused at times to scan the skies through a telescope. Despite his vast achievements and commanding position in the entertainment world, he was depicted as an insecure man filled with fears that made each night a nightmare, and a large entourage, an unsatisfactory bulwark against loneliness.

Courage is an elusive quality in our time, even in high circles. Although Sinatra's anxieties and desperate moods appealed to the public rather than repelled it, a more attractive phase of his romanticism was Frankie Boy the Brawler. From the start, he was outspoken, truculently taking minority positions. Unafraid to gamble for high stakes—stakes as big as his career and wealth—he tangled with powerful columnists, influential publications, major movie studios and important TV producers. If he lost his temper and let go with his fists or a million-dollar lawsuit, the admiration he drew from a large section of a timid world more than compensated for the beating he took in the press.

Sinatra's power as a twentieth-century romantic derives from a set of clashing chords. In the hierarchy of our sex symbols and love gods, he has been the tormented lover, vul-

9

nerable as well as triumphant, hurt as well as hurting. Protective in his attitude towards his children and ex-wives, he openly manifested a far-ranging interest in the female of the species. Despite his own culture and wide reading, he associated with men who were barely literate. Liberal in his politics and concerned with the problems of the underprivileged, he did not exclude underworld figures from the circle of his friends. If there was much in Sinatra of Balzac whose walking stick bore the inscription, 'Whatever gets in my way, I crush!' there was also something of Kafka, who carved on his cane: 'Everything that gets in my way, crushes me!' In terms of *The Petrified Forest*, he was both the writer-dreamer played by Leslie Howard and the hood played by Bogart—unrelenting in his search for self-expression, driven by a tendency towards self-destruction, full of a simmering hostility and tense with a feeling for conflict. It is this constant counterpoint of toughness and tenderness that has made Sinatra a magnetic and enigmatic personality. And it was the projection of these polarities in his singing that helped make him the master singer of our time.

Dubbed An American Phenomenon by the *New Yorker* at the start of his career, Sinatra has remained an American original whose newsworthiness has not dimmed with time. John Lardner once observed that Charles A. Lindbergh resisted being interviewed but, nevertheless, possessed an instinct for grabbing space; in Lardner's words, Lindy had a remarkable feeling for 'the rhythm and uses of notoriety'. In spite of his celebrated, and sometimes violent, efforts to guard his privacy, is there any entertainer whose private life is more a matter of public record than Sinatra's? When he celebrated his fiftieth birthday and his twenty-fifth year in show business, he was on the cover of three of the biggest news magazines in the country, and his handling of the press on his CBS-TV profile was not inappropriately characterised as 'the greatest conning of the Fourth Estate in modern times'. Regardless of personal magnetism and abundant talent, the Sinatra charisma is the product of a brilliant and tantalising use of publicity.

While there have been many loves in Sinatra's life, his most sustained affair has been with the public itself. From the beginning, he played an active role in handling his press, fusing his work as a singer and later as an actor with his offstage personality. A number of images have contributed to the Sinatra mystique and to his pre-eminence as a Romantic. Some were carefully nurtured, like the portrayal of his youth as a period of deprivation and delinquency, his position as a libertarian rebel, his concern about underprivileged children, and, most recently, his maturity and dedication as a business executive. Some images like The Bleeder, The Battler and The Swinger were germinated by offstage developments or onstage events, and had to be corrected editorially or underscored musically.

Although adverse publicity hurt his career in the Ava Gardner period, he has displayed a remarkable resilience in riding out a bad press. Neither his strange associates nor his moments of violence, or other negative aspects of his personality have really hurt him with the public. His tremendous popularity has, in fact, launched a new era in public relations: the vogue of the 'talented bastard'. 'He was never much loved', a brochure issued by his own record company states. 'Sinatra has guile and guts and damn it if a lot of people hadn't said right out loud he was the meanest bastard they ever worked for.' The point is that while he wanted to keep aspects of his life private, he did not dissemble with the public. He came through, not in a phony semblance of goodness, but as a contradictory man, multi-dimensional, complex, endlessly interesting. Because of his rashness and candour, attacks seemed after a time to add to his romantic appeal.

Basically, this is a study of a public man as seen through the expressive media of his recordings, the motion picture screen, the TV channel, the night club performance and the press. It is not a couch or a keyhole probe, but an analysis of a unique show business career, viewed in the context of the popular arts of our time. It is neither an etching limned in acid nor a portrait painted in oils, but a black-and-white drawing of a remarkable man and his world.

ARNOLD SHAW
1968

I

LITTLE LORD FAUNTLEROY AND LITTLE CAESAR

It was during the era of the Big Bands in the booming days of the New Deal that Francis Albert Sinatra mastered the art of which he became the most celebrated and most imitated exponent of our time. If Tommy Dorsey and his velvet-voiced trombone fathered Sinatra's singing style, Billie Holiday and her internalised phrasing were the expressive mother. The birth was celebrated in a shrine of the swing bands, the New York Paramount Theatre, where on Columbus Day, 1944, the bobbysoxers shrieked, swooned, waved handkerchiefs and panties and accorded Frankie Boy an involuntary expression of adolescent female ecstasy. In 1936 girls and boys jitterbugged in the aisles of the theatre for the bouncing Benny Goodman band, but in 1944 a war-scarred generation of girls without boys wet their seats.

There was little in Sinatra's background that prepared music business or the world for this liquid benefaction. Considering that Elvis Presley hit in 1954 and the Beatles in 1964, one might almost believe that each generation's moment of release comes every tenth year ending in the number 4. The contrast, however, between the pelvic-twisting, blues-rocking Mr. Presley, ex-Memphis, Tenn., the mop-haired, self-amused Britishers of the Mersey beat, and the Sinatra of the slow, yearning, *messa-di-voce* ballads, suggests that something more basic is involved. Literary and art styles are products of psychology, sociology and changing times. Why not popular song styles and singers?

There were popular vocalists before Sinatra. Just after World War I, the cantor's son in blackface who introduced *Mammy*, gave Gershwin his first big song in *Swanee*, and became co-writer of many hits by contributing third verses to songs that did not have them. Through the '30s and '40s, there was Bing Crosby, who came scat-singing out of Paul Whiteman's Rhythm Boys and scored with his wavering notes on a Gus Arnheim recording of *I Surrender, Dear*. In his earliest press photos, Frankie Boy posed awkwardly in the same kind of yachting cap and multi-coloured sports shirt that the Groaner, later Der Bingle, donned to demonstrate his relaxed personality. But in addition to Al Jolson and Crosby, there was the sleepy-eyed, nasal-voiced ladykiller of the racoon era who made a romantic instrument of the megaphone as Sinatra later did with the microphone.

Hubert Prior Vallee, whose stage name conjured up visions of the then recently deceased Rudolph Valentino but whose chosen name was a tribute to saxophonist Rudy Wiedoeft, came out of a New England background and Yale College. A hit Rodgers and Hart show supplied the handle of his band, *The Connecticut Yankees*, while an engagement at a New York club yielded his radio salutation, '*Heigh-ho*, everybody!' It was radio, still in its infancy, that led to the first theatre frenzy provoked by a singer. The year was 1929 and Rudy Vallee was ensconced at the Versailles, a name its Hungarian owner soon switched to the Villa Vallee. For three days in February, Vallee and his band were booked for a routine personal appearance at Keith's Albee Theatre. Only Rudy was on the air nightly from the club Versailles and on Sunday afternoons for 'Herbert's blue-white diamonds'. Since he did his own announcing while the Connecticut Yankees played long medleys, he vigorously plugged the vaudeville date. The ensuing mêlée brought mounted police and an audience that squealed, yelled and climbed on the seats (but did not swoon). It led to a four-day holdover, then a rarity, a ten-week booking through the Keith chain and to Vallee's glorification as the Vagabond Lover. Soon he occupied the pre-eminent position of host of radio's first hour-long variety show, the Fleischman Hour, launched on the very Thursday of October 1929 when the Stock Market crashed.

Other singers figured in early twentieth-century pop music: minstrel Eddie Leonard in blackface, cakewalker Joe Howard, the Street Singer—Arthur Tracy, the Empress of the Blues— Bessie Smith, and vaudeville headliners like Nora Bayes, Belle Baker and Fanny Brice. But in the days before electrical amplification, the prevailing sound of American popular music was instrumental rather than vocal.

At the turn of the century, Brass Bands, concert and marching, fraternal, funeral and fire-house, multiplied rapidly, as the short lived Spanish–American War left pawnshops stocked with second-hand instruments. (One reason that New Orleans played such a pivotal role in the development of jazz was that it served as an embarkation port for American troops.) The lachrymose ballad *After the Ball* and other song hits were popularised by the famous John Philip Sousa band, which also transported ragtime, the syncopated piano music of an era, to London and the Continent. Later, as New Orleans jazz entered the mainstream of popular music via the Mississippi riverboats, the squealing clarinet, hot trumpet and tailgate trombone of free-wheeling Dixieland combos gave the Jazz Age its characteristic speak-easy sound. After the so-called Great Depression, printed stock orchestrations superseded improvisation, sections replaced single lead instruments, and the small combos grew into large Swing or Sweet Bands.

The era of the Big Bands lasted roughly from the end of the Depression until the end of the World War II. This was the period when Frank embarked on his singing career and came of age musically.

Young Sinatra was an undistinguished graduate of the David E. Rue Junior High School of Hoboken in Jauary 1931, the year that Crosby went solo on the new CBS network. Francis Albert did not contribute to the musical programme of his graduation exercises nor did he receive any rewards. His formal education ended later that year when he dropped out of Demarest High School, also of Hoboken. There is no truth in the tales that he won trophies as a crack athlete, that he was expelled, or that he left in his senior year. *Look* magazine erred, however, when it cut his secondary schooling to forty-seven days. Having graduated from a junior high school, he was in his sophomore year when he left Demarest. Afterwards he attended Drake Business School, perhaps to comply with NJ's statute on compulsory education until the age of sixteen. He has never stopped regretting, or being sensitive about, his limited formal education.

Although *Who's Who in America* and other encyclopaedias still cite the year 1917, Sinatra was born on December 12, 1915, a fact finally confirmed by his fiftieth birthday celebration. It was a snowy Sunday in Hoboken and he was permanently scarred on the left side of his head and neck by a forceps delivery. Weighing a ponderous thirteen and a half pounds, he nearly lost his left ear in the process. The scars are still visible today. His father was Sicilian, born in Catania, while his mother came from Genoa, arriving here with her parents when she was two months old. Both were blue-eyed and easily taken for Irish, which was advantageous in those years of Irish domination of Jersey politics, boxing and the police force.

His mother once said 'I wanted a girl and I bought a lot of pink clothes. When Frank was born, I didn't care. I dressed him in pink anyway. Later, I got my mother to make him Lord Fauntleroy suits.' Deeply embroiled in local politics as a Democratic ward leader, Natalie 'Dolly' Sinatra readily left Frank's upbringing to her mother, in whose nearby apartment he lived for some years, an aunt and a Jewish neighbour. His father, a small, husky, cherubic-faced man, prone to asthmatic attacks, said little then or later. But Martin Sinatra had his own ideas, ideas inspired by three B's of his occupational activities: boxing—he had fought as a bantamweight under the Irish alias of Marty O'Brien; boilermaking—war work in a Hoboken shipyard; and bartending—a tavern he bought with his mother-in-law's money plus Dolly's power as a political leader accounted for the family's rising economic status.

Although Frank was born in a low-income, if not slum area, hard by the yards of the Erie and Lackawanna railroad, the family's subsequent addresses suggest comfort, if not affluence. Sinatra's publicists like to depict him as a 'slum kid', his own phrase as late as 1952. But an accumulation of evidence, including a charge account at a local department store, a fancy wardrobe that led to the nickname of 'Slacks-ey', and his own second-hand Chrysler at fifteen, eliminate the claim that his youth was underprivileged.

When young Sinatra began to display an interest in singing, neither parent showed any sympathy. Martin Sinatra liked to think of his son in a solid he-man's job, or, perhaps, in the ring. Dolly Sinatra wanted her son to attend Stevens Institute of Technology, whose buildings on the Hoboken Palisades at Castle Point were a constant reminder of a more refined way of life. When she found a framed glossy of Bing Crosby in Frank's bedroom and was informed of her son's vocal ambitions, she hurled a shoe at him. 'In your teens,' Sinatra once said, 'there's always someone to spit on your dreams.'

During Sinatra's boyhood, Hoboken was an American Liverpool, a beer-guzzling port-city whose weather-beaten docks, shipyards, factories, freight spurs and railroad yards gave it the sooty, ugly look of some of England's old, industrial cities. A mile-square town of narrow, cobblestone streets and tall, wooden, telegraph poles, it was the port of call of the Hamburg, Holland–American and other ocean-going steamship lines. In the Roaring Twenties, rum-runners made unannounced and unscheduled visits.

Whether or not the tales of a brutal youth, filled with gang fights and bloody beatings, are exaggerated, the fact is that Sinatra and his publicists have depicted it that way. Seeking the role of Maggio in the film *From Here to Eternity*, he said: 'I knew him ... I was beaten up with him on Hoboken.' In a 1952 by-line story, he himself wrote of how two plainclothesmen, suspicious of a new suit he wore, accused him of stealing it and 'beat the stuffing out of me until I was a bleeding mess and my new clothes were ruined'. Other incidents have frequently been retold: a gang fight in which his forehead was lacerated by a broken bottle and another in which he was struck on the side of the head with a tyre chain. Since a draft board later classified him 4F because of a punctured ear drum, there may well be more than fantasy or press-agentry in these memories of 'vicious gang wars'. However, Hoboken neighbours, police and relatives reject the idea that these incidents had any connection with the hoodlum microcosm or dock violence. But just as Bogart had to fight his way out of the name Humphrey as a kid on Manhattan's west side, so it appears that Francis Albert Sinatra had to fight his way out of the natty clothes he early affected and the spindly frame they adorned in tough Hoboken. Adult displays of pent-up fury suggest that he may have been no match for burly opponents.

There was, too, the frustration of being the only child of parents too preoccupied with their own problems to worry about a lonely, troubled youngster. Years later, Sinatra told a reporter who was searching for an explanation of the cut-ups of the so-called Clan: 'I never had any brothers or sisters. In my neighbourhood every family had twelve kids and they fought constantly. But whenever there was a beef or a party, you never saw such closeness. That's exactly what's happening here with us ...'

Music was heard in Hoboken mainly in church or on festive, family, social or political occasions, particularly in the preradio days of Sinatra's boyhood. There were no instruments in the Sinatra home. Frank's musical awakening came comparatively late, emerged intuitively and developed partly as a reaction to an environment that afforded him no other means of expression.

Two 'quirks' manifested themselves early, both coming from his mother, to whom dirt and disorder meant poverty. Members of the Dorsey band later kidded him about 'the Lady Macbeth bit', a reference to his obsessive concern with cleanliness; they said he never stopped washing his hands. Not too long ago, he said: 'I am a symmetrical man, almost to a fault. I demand everything in its place. My clothing must hang just so...' A writer who recently accompanied Sinatra on a long night of partying, noted that at 4 a.m. there were still neat creases in his pants.

The other quirk, perhaps in imitation of his mother's methodology as a Democratic ward leader, was a penchant for giving gifts. In his youth, this took the form of buying clothes for friends, taking them to the movies, or sneaking them into the Palisades Park swimming pool. Frank had a pass. One day the attendant caught him slipping it through the fence to a buddy. He was slapped around and booted out. 'I was hurt,' Frank recalls, 'but I was hurting from something more. All those times I got those guys into the pool! When I am getting clobbered, not one of them comes to help me. They just—scramsville.' Dolly Sinatra has observed 'My son is like me. You cross him, he never forgets.'

Quite early, Frank's concern about his dignity became as basic in his make-up and could be as easily ruffled as, in his own phrase, his 'Sicilian temper'. If the demand for respect was not nurtured in his own home, it could have derived from the mores of the Italian community in which he grew up. His parents were active members of the local Sicilian Cultural League. In Frank's adult tenets of friendship, loyalty and the uses of power, one readily discerns the impact on the Sicilian ethnic concept of *uomini respettati*. In Italian lore 'men of respect' are described in Robin Hood terms as rare individuals, both noble and humble, who are considerate of the weak and unafraid of the strong, quick to punish foes and reward friends, and dedicated to acts of generosity and the redress of wrong. Inflaming the imagination of a growing sentimentalist, these concepts early became themes of Sinatra's romanticism.

Two constitutional Amendments, both passed when he was

17

four, helped shape the environment in which Sinatra spent his boyhood and youth. On August 26, 1920, the ratification of Article XIX gave women the right to vote. Shortly before this, the then Mayor of Hoboken appointed Dolly Sinatra, master of all the dialects spoken in the Italian section, a Democratic ward leader. A post she retained for over twenty years, it left her little time for the home and threw young Frank on his own resources or those of relatives and neighbours. 'I'll never forget that kid,' a neighbour observed in later years, 'leaning against his grandmother's front door, staring into space...'

Early in 1920 the so-called Prohibition Amendment also became effective, conjuring up the complex of speak-easies, hijackers and hood violence that no oceanside municipality like Hoboken could escape. Sinatra's birthplace was no Chicago but it was in gangster Waxey Gordon's territory. Although a neighbourhood thug was killed in front of his Aunt Josie's house, the impact of the silver screen was doubtless more pervasive. In Frank's sixteenth year, Hollywood released more than fifty gangster films. Bogart said at one point 'In my first thirty-four pictures, I was shot in twelve, electrocuted or hanged in eight, and a jailbird in nine.' Nevertheless, hoods came on the screen in romantic, even heroic, terms that made a particular appeal to the young. (Even the intellectuals of the day were not immune to the appeal of the gangster, as *The Petrified Forest* of Pulitzer-prize playwright Robert Sherwood demonstrated.)

That the hood image infiltrated the daydreams of a maladjusted teenager was as inevitable as Frank's discovery of the magic of music. His great movie heroes were then, as for millions of youngsters,* Edward G. Robinson (*Little Caesar*) and Paul Muni (*Scarface*). But the appeal of the image persisted even after he became a celebrity, manifesting itself in the use of gangster epithets, the hint of menace in his manner, the quick resort to fisticuffs and the swaggering way he moved at the head of a male entourage, some of whose members were mugs. 'I think that Sinatra's always nurtured a secret desire to be a hood,' Crosby once remarked. 'But of course he's got too much class to go that route.' Angles, as boyhood friends called him, has credited music with re-directing his aspirations. 'You find that there are just as many angles to figure in being honest as there are in being crooked,' he once said. 'If what you do is honest and you make it, you're a hero. If what you

18

do is crooked and you make it, you're a bum. Me? I grabbed a song.'

Of all the places that a Moon Calf could pick to spend his formative years, Hoboken was surely a dismal 'choice'. But here while the flappers of the day Charlestoned and Black-Bottomed, Francis Albert Sinatra grew up, the toot of Hudson River ferries and tugboats in his ears, the sight of lower Manhattan's skyscrapers in his troubled eyes and a nagging sense of alienation in his heart. Here, caught between his mother's reverence for Little Lord Fauntleroy and his own idealisation of Little Caesar, he first manifested the contradictory impulses that have made him both puzzling and appealing. Here, the feeling for violence and the unrelenting search for expressiveness took shape as the clashing polarities of the great romanticist of our time.

The dream of being a singer emerged unconsciously, perhaps merely as something that intrigued a lonely teenager, seeking in fantasies of fame, a fulfilment and a revenge for what he could not find at home, in school or on the street. It was easy to pick up chords on a ukulele that Uncle Dominick Garavanti gave him and to attract attention on summer nights by crooning the pop songs of the day under a lamp-post. His Hoboken pals were apparently not overwhelmed by his warbling.

Before he embarked on a musical career, Frank worked on a local newspaper. He and his publicists have frequently asserted that he was a cub reporter or sports writer on the *Jersey Observer*. There is no evidence that he went beyond serving as a truck loader and copy boy. It was a short-lived association, for Frank became more and more interested in what he heard over the radio.

The formation of the networks, NBC in 1927 and CBS in 1928, afforded coast-to-coast exposure for singers and gave them new stature as well as greater audiences. Among those vying for public adulation were Gene Austin, who sold a million records of *My Blue Heaven*, Russ Columbo, celebrated for his record of *Prisoner of Love*, and Will Osborne, who boldly imitated Rudy Vallee's megaphone style and accused the Vagabond Lover of copying him.

It was Bing Crosby, however, who ignited Frankie Boy and became his idol. The biggest of the vocal stars by 1932, the

19

year after Sinatra's schooling ended, the Groaner made an appearance in person at the NY theatre that later became Frank's launching pad and racked up a record of twenty consecutive weeks and more than seven hundred record-breaking performances. Everybody was humming *Just One More Chance* and *I've found a Million Dollar Baby (In a Five and Ten Cent Store)*, Bing's big disc. By 1933, as a result of the smash movie musical *The Big Broadcast*, he was Top Ten at the film box-office. During the week of March 3, Crosby appeared in person at a Jersey City vaudeville house, accompanied by a colleague of his Paul Whiteman days, guitarist Eddie Lang. Advertisements in the *Jersey Observer* gave bigger play to Crosby's name than to the stars of the film on the bill. Frankie Boy took the girl who became the first Mrs. Sinatra to hear Bing. He left Loew's Journal Square Theatre vowing that he would make it as a singer. Nancy Barbato agreed.

Today, the road to a successful singing career is frequently a spectacular leap from a demonstration record (demo) to a recording contract. In 1933 the route was more circuitous. It started with an Amateur Contest, might include travelling with a Major Bowes vaudeville unit, involved appearances on local radio and at local roadhouses, and eventually, with talent and luck, a berth with a name band. Thereafter, a songbird might embark on a solo flight. With little parental encouragement but not without his mother's political influence, young Sinatra went the entire route. It took six years of grinding, during part of which the first and future Mrs. Sinatra stuck dollar bills in gloves she conveniently forgot in her boyfriend's pockets.

Amateur Contests were then a regular feature of most movie-vaudeville theatres. At the Central in Jersey City, these occurred on Thursday evenings. Even Hoboken's lone theatre, the Fabian, now the site of a supermarket, had a Future Stars Radio Contest on Wednesdays. It was at The State in JC that Frankie Boy won a contest, which led to an appearance in a contest at a Manhattan vaudeville house.

The Academy of Music on 14th Street, which is today a double-feature movie house, has played a notable role in the history of live entertainment. Built at the turn of the century by impresario Tony Pastor, it helped take variety out of the beer halls, where waitresses in scanties were the main draw, and attracted the carriage and family trade to what became known as *vaudeville*. Standing backstage for his appearance, amateur Frankie Boy heard a raucous crowd interrupt performers and drive them offstage with shouts of 'Get the Hook!' Still in use on amateur nights at the Apollo in Harlem, the Hook was a long pole with a curved end that came out of the wings, fitted around the neck and was used literally to yank ineffective amateurs off the stage.

'I'm standing there shaking,' Sinatra recalled in later years, 'figuring that the moment they announce a guy from Hoboken, he's dead!' But once he was on stage, the gawky guy from Hoboken did not manifest any of the trepidation he was suffering. There were no catcalls, no raspberries, no Bronx cheers and no Hook. But neither was there a prize.

Sinatra's first 'professional' engagement came with a group called the Hoboken Four. It occurred after an arid stretch of more than two years, during which he worked all the local club dates he could muster. Although Dolly Sinatra never gave up plugging for education and Stevens Institute, she footed the bill for a $65 portable public-address system (mike and loudspeaker) that packed away in a rhinestone-studded case. Broadway publishers then had 'professional free lists' and gave gratis pro copies and printed orchestrations (stocks) to bands and vaudeville acts playing well-known clubs and ballrooms. 'Angles' developed a technique of talking counter-boys at various publishers out of free music. Even with the use of his p.a. system and the very necessary library of orchestrations (orks), his return for a night's singing was a meagre $3 to $6.

There are conflicting reports as to how he became a member of the Hoboken Four. Biographies circulated by movie studios and press agents state simply and erroneously that he 'organised the group'. Another tale is that Sinatra, working solo, won a Major Bowes Amateur Hour contest—which he did not—and that he was made lead singer of the quartet when it toured the country as part of a Major Bowes unit. A variant version, which is apparently the truth, is that Major Bowes teamed Sinatra with the trio of singer-instrumentalists, also from Hoboken, when all auditioned for him at about the same time. He apparently dubbed them the Hoboken Four.

There is no question that on September 8, 1935, the quartet with Frank Sinatra as lead singer, appeared on the Major Bowes Amateur Hour, broadcasting from the stage of the

Capitol Theatre in New York. A giant audiometer was used in the theatre to measure audience applause while at-home listeners voted by calling Murray Hill 8–9933. The total tally gave first prize to the group who became part of a Major Bowes travelling unit. While on tour, each member of the Hoboken Four received $50 a week plus meals. The quartet remained on the road for several months, eventually travelling as far as Hollywood where mounting dissension and a fight led to Frank's abruptly leaving the group and returning to New Jersey.

Early in 1936 Frank resumed his grind with the p.a. system and the library of orks. Club work was not difficult to secure. It just seemed to lead nowhere. For some months, he held a steady job at the Union, a local club, where on April 26, 1936, the Sicilian Cultural League of Hoboken, Sam Sinatra, treasurer, presented its second annual ball-and-flag ceremony, with Mr. and Mrs. Martin Sinatra sponsoring an American flag. Located on swank Hudson Street amidst the buildings of Stevens Institute, The Union Club paid Frank $40 a week. Although he was well received, he quit when he could not persuade owner Joseph Samperi to introduce 'a wire', that is, to arrange for broadcasts from the club. While radio stations were willing to foot the bill for 'remotes' from well-known nightspots, smaller clubs were compelled to pay for the telephone lines needed to pick up a programme.

Even at this early stage of his career, Frank tackled problems with the same analytical aggressiveness that later accounted for his great comeback. Cognisant of the vital role radio had played in the rise of Vallee and Crosby, he approached the programme directors of Jersey and New York stations, offering to sing 'for no'—in music-biz lingo, for no remuneration. 'I'd come out of my office,' Jimmy Rich, who was then station accompanist at WNEW, recalls, 'and he'd be standing there to see me or anybody who would listen to him. Somehow he'd get past the receptionist . . . He was a pusher but polite.' Scheduled WNEW singers then included Helen Forrest, Dinah Shore and Barry Wood, later the male vocalist who preceded Sinatra on the Lucky Strike Hit Parade. Whenever the station had an unscheduled open period, Frank seemed available as a filler. Before long, his voice could be heard on every wavelength at all hours of the day and night. Sinatra claims that he was on the air as frequently as eighteen times a week, a demanding schedule that netted him the magnificent sum of 70c. WAAT of Newark gave it to him for his bus fares.

All through this harrowing period, Sinatra's eager blue eyes were fixed on one goal, a berth with a name band. The big break came eventually through the Rustic Cabin, a roadhouse on route 9W near Alpine, NJ, where Frank settled after leaving the Union Club. The Cabin possessed the one thing that caused him to accept a reduction in salary—a radio wire.

There are at least two published accounts of how Frank secured the Cabin job. He himself offered one over his own by-line in the *American Weekly*: 'I got my job when some musician friends brought me to Harold Arden, then the bandleader at the Cabin. Arden gave me my first chance for $15 a week, a sum which I continued to be paid for almost a year and a half.' Another tale credits Dolly Sinatra and her power in New Jersey labour circles with manoeuvring the Cabin job. For his $15 a week, Frank soloed, sang with a group called the Three Flashes or Pages, emceed and sometimes waited on tables.

Two important things happened during his year and a half at the Cabin. One, of course, involved bandleader Harry James. The other, a quiet and unpretentious, olive-skinned brunette named Nancy Barbato, daughter of a Jersey City plasterer. 'In Nancy,' Frank has said, 'I found beauty, warmth and understanding. Being with her was my only escape from what seemed a grim world. All I knew up to that time were tough kids on street corners, gang fights, and parents who were always busy trying to make money ...' Although Frank kept warning her that he was going places and that 'I don't want anyone dragging on my neck', and Nancy kept replying with a reassuring docility, 'I won't get in your way, Frank', their courtship which began at Long Branch where his Aunt Josie had a summer cottage, terminated at the Lady of Sorrows Church in Jersey City.

The ceremony was a double-ring affair on February 4, 1939, shortly after the Rustic Cabin raised his weekly pay to $25. The wedding reception was at the Barbato home. Frank's parents, who were not overjoyed by their son's choice of a bride any more than his choice of a profession, gave the couple their own black Chrysler as a wedding present. On February 13, 1939, on a page titled 'Social Activities throughout Hudson County', the *Jersey Observer* carried a small photo of Nancy in her wedding gown. A short paragraph advised that, after a honeymoon 'in the south', the couple would dwell in their own home at 487 Garfield Avenue in Jersey City. On their return from a four-day auto trip to North Carolina the newly-weds settled in a three-room apartment in Jersey City. The rent was $42 a month.

II

HARRY JAMES AND THE BIG BAND ERA

A legendary story of the Big Band era concerns portly Paul Whiteman whose dance orchestra drew large crowds to the Roof Garden of the New York Biltmore Hotel. One evening, an influential song-plugger arrived with a tall, stately girl whom he introduced as the Duchess. Duly impressed, Whiteman treated her with great deference, as did all the song-pluggers at the dinner table. They were drinking coffee when suddenly Whiteman's face turned crimson, and the hand holding his cup began to shake visibly. The contact men pretended not to notice. But they all knew that the Duchess was at the moment gently running her hand up and down Whiteman's leg. The Duchess was no Duchess but just a lively lady of the evening.

It made for a big laugh when it happened and for an even bigger laugh, even if it didn't happen, in the re-telling. Practical jokes were a staple of the all-male scene that was the music business. To relieve the tedium of long, late hours, characters were in demand. It was an era that had colour and camaraderie. Young Sinatra liked it, found expression in it, and took from it many things that influenced his later off-stage activities. The all-male entourage, variously known as The Varsity (hep), The Rat Pack (hip) and The Clan (that's boss), had its beginnings here. The horseplay, the needling, the glorification of friendship, the sports-oriented slang—a plug that did not materialise was a curve—all were characteristic of an era when broadcasts of the live performance, not recordings, created hit songs.

Many of Sinatra's later locutions originate here: for example, his use of 'ville' as a suffix—'bombsville' for a song that flops, 'scramsville' for 'they ran off,' etc. A 'broad' was a broad among music men long before Frank helped popularise it. Another word of Negro origin, shortened by Frank in public appearances to 'mother', was an accolade of high praise even then.

It was at the Rustic Cabin that Sinatra became intimate with this fringe microcosm of show business, having previously made contact with it through Hank Sanicola, a young song-plugger at Witmark. Boasting only local air-time, the Cabin did not draw the top pluggers who contacted hit-makers like Jimmy Dorsey at the Pennsylvania, Guy Lombardo and his 'business man's bounce' at the Roosevelt, or Glenn Miller at the Glen Island Casino. The lesser pluggers who visited the Cabin were after the small-audience 'sheet shots' that swelled totals during a 'drive', a week in which performances were bunched to make a song No. 1 on plug charts. But like their more successful colleagues, they spoke a brittle lingo—a tab was 'the hot' or 'the third rail'; you got a shock when you touched it—and they worked at mastering the black arts of 'the con', romance and payola. The word 'payola' was current in music biz long before a 1959 congressional investigating committee gave it national currency.

For young Sinatra, the dull, sometimes depressing, eighteen months he spent at the Cabin, were enlivened by the wiry ways of the contact men. Naturally, he 'hyped' the song-pluggers to hype his singing with name bandleaders. Eventually, the combination of broadcasts over WNEW's Dance Parade and plugger word-of-mouth worked. Trumpeter Harry James came one memorable evening to hear him sing.

All through the days of Sinatra's vocalising at the Cabin, big bands were proliferating at such a rate that *Down Beat*'s tabulation of band itineraries included nearly seven hundred aggregations. Best-seller lists of the day consisted almost exclusively of dance discs, with those responsible for vocal choruses receiving no credit on record labels. On bandstands, singers generally posed as instrumentalists, holding guitars with rubber strings or pretending to blow wind instruments. It was a bouncing era, the roar of massive brass providing a joyful accompaniment for a world recovering from depression and trying the togetherness of the New Deal.

The Harry James band was one of several, including Lionel

Hampton's, Teddy Wilson's and Gene Krupa's, that emanated from the Benny Goodman orchestra. Formed in 1939, it was financed by Willard Alexander, an ex-MCA agent, and the Ray himself. (The Ray was a musician's nickname for Goodman, resulting from his piercing glance on the bandstand.) After break-in dates out of town, it played its first major booking at the Pennsylvania Hotel. The notices of March 1939 were friendly but hardly exciting. When James trekked out to Alpine to catch young Sinatra, his band was playing an unspectacular engagement at the NY Paramount, and Frank was manoeuvring to get into the Bob Chester band in which a Jersey City neighbour, Harry Schuchman, played a tenor sax.

'I liked Frank's way of talking a lyric,' James said later, 'and I went back the following night with Gerard Barrett, my manager, and we signed him for $75 a week.' Since the contract was for two years, Sinatra was jubilant as he drove that June night to Jersey City where Nancy Sinatra, who was still holding a $25-a-week secretarial job, waited in their third-floor walk-up.

Sinatra's first appearance with the James band was at the Hippodrome Theatre in Baltimore during the week of June 30, 1939. His vocals on *Wishing* and *My Love for You* went uncelebrated. Thereafter, the band settled at the Roseland Ballroom on Broadway, today the site of the City Squire motel. Except for a seven-day breather on the wind-swept Atlantic City Steel Pier, which developed into a three-week booking, the band remained at Roseland all through the hot summer of the 1939 World's Fair. It was here that Frank's singing received its first critical scrutiny. Writing in *Metronome*, George Simon approved 'the very pleasing vocals of Frank Sinatra whose easy phrasing is especially commendable'. Only recently Simon revealed that Frank's 'need of approbation was reflected in a somewhat unusual routine by James' manager who ... followed me almost to the street as he jockeyed, not for a good review of the band itself, but for good notices for the boy. "He wants a good write-up more than anybody I've ever seen," Gerard Barrett said.'

After Labour Day, the orchestra travelled to Chicago where it opened at the Hotel Sherman. On October 7, a *Billboard* reviewer wrote of Frank at the Panther Room: 'Vocalist Frank Sinatra handles the torchy ballads in a pleasing way in good voice. Only blemish is that he touches the songs with a little too much pash, which is not all convincing...' By contrast, trumpeter Jack Palmer, responsible for the hi-de-ho numbers, knew 'all the angles'. *Variety* made no reference to Sinatra until a month later when a reviewer found 'little appeal' in either side of a new James record *Here Comes the Night* backed with *From the Bottom of My Heart*.

Frank's admiration for Billie Holiday manifested itself in an October *Down Beat*, which ran a photo of James and his vocalist attending a Holiday performance at Chicago's Offbeat Club. Frank then sported a mop of hair combed back in a high pompadour. About the same time, *Down Beat* reported a conversation between James and a staffer that went this way: *Reporter:* 'Who's that skinny little singer? He sings a great song.' *Harry James:* 'Not so loud. The kid's name is Sinatra. He considers himself the greatest vocalist in the business. Get that! No one ever heard of him. He's never had a hit record. He looks like a wet rag. But he says he is the greatest. If he hears you compliment him, he'll demand a raise tonight...'

By this time, James had discovered that his male vocalist was not only confident but strong-minded in other ways. Immediately after signing him, Harry had suggested that Frank change his name, a procedure almost as common among singers as screen stars. Frank rejected the suggestion, pointing out that he had a cousin who was doing quite well 'in spite of' the Sinatra surname. Ray Sinatra was then musical conductor of several of radio's top dramatic series.

After two and a half months at the Panther Room, the James band trekked westward. Unlike the Goodman band in its formative days, James encountered only problems as he travelled towards the California coast. While he himself was extremely popular and was voted No. 1 among the nation's trumpeters in *Down Beat*'s annual poll, his orchestra finished a weak No. 12 in the swing band sweepstakes. That year, largely as a result of *Back Bay Shuffle* and his double-faced recording of *Begin the Beguine*, clarinettist Artie Shaw displaced Goodman as the No. 1 Collegiate Choice of Orchestras, only to be toppled the following year by Glenn Miller, who held the top spot in 1941 and 1942 with *Little Brown Jug*, *In the Mood* and *Moonlight Serenade*.

The trough of the James band's dipping fortune came in Los Angeles where it arrived for a November booking at the

Palomar Ballroom. The famous dance-hall where the Goodman had scored its initial success, was out of business, having burned down during a Charlie Barnett date. Fighting to meet his weekly payroll, James took a substitute booking at Victor Hugo's in Beverly Hills. It was a mistake. 'The chichi crowd didn't dig our "loud" kind of music,' James later lamented, 'and the help outnumbered the customers. After days of complaints and an empty dance floor, the management cancelled us. To make matters worse, they refused to pay us.' (Rudy Vallee, who had just left the Fleischman Hour after five hundred and eighteen consecutive appearances as host, was hastily called to front Garwood Van's mickey-mouse band.) As James and his orchestra headed unhappily back east, a lawsuit resulting from an old accident case led to an attachment of the band's funds. Unable to afford two vocalists, James fired Connie Haines and kept Sinatra.

While Christmas 1939 represented the lowest ebb in the life of the new James band, it had a slightly different meaning for young Sinatra. Nancy, who had travelled with the band for a time, was back in Jersey City awaiting the birth of their first child. And Frank was on the verge of leaving the floundering Harry James orchestra for a job with the band that was No. 1 among the nation's Sweet Bands (*Down Beat*).

Apart from opening the door to the Tommy Dorsey orchestra, the stint with James led to the first hit record of Sinatra's solo career, a hit that did not materialise until almost four years after its initial release. Frank participated in five recording sessions during his tenure with James, the earliest on July 13, 1939, when he sang *From the Bottom of My Heart* and *Melancholy Mood*, and the last on November 8, when he cut *Every Day of My Life* and *Ciribiribin*. The all-important session which yielded *All or Nothing At All* came on August 31. A September *Billboard* advertisement, announcing the release of the record, contains no mention of the Sinatra vocal while *Down Beat* dismissed the disc with the observation that 'the band had a long way to go'. Sales of the record totalled a meagre 8,000 copies, due in part, perhaps, to the deadlock with the broadcasters that kept ASCAP music off the air in 1940. Re-released, however, in 1943, after Sinatra had left Dorsey on his solo career, *All or Nothing At All* became a runaway best-seller. Both *Ciribiribin* and the later ballad hit may be heard in the Columbia album *The Frank Sinatra Story in Music*. They make a curious contrast. In the former, Sinatra is the self-assured band-singer, effortlessly delivering a vocal of sustained tones against the chugging James band; he is relaxed but also emotionally uninvolved. Yet in the torch ballad, recorded months earlier, he displays a sensitivity to texture and an expressive handling of the lyrics, characteristic of the later soloist.

Frank's ride with Harry James, scheduled to last two years, ground to a pleasant but unanticipated halt shortly after Christmas 1939. Tommy Dorsey made an offer and James, who held a contract he could have enforced, permitted his skinny vocalist to leave. 'We dissolved with a handshake,' James has said. 'Frank was expecting a baby then and he needed the extra money. But I never did get around to tearing up the contract. If any of his managers had thought to come to me, Frank later wouldn't have had to pony up all that money to settle with Dorsey. Legally, he was under contract to me.'

Dorsey did not make it easy for Sinatra's predecessor to leave him. Jack Leonard, considered the best band vocalist in the business in 1939, had been responsible for the silver-voiced vocals on Dorsey's hits, including the famous *Marie*. By the autumn of the year, however, the trade press was asking: 'What's this about songbird JL leaving TD?'

Sinatra has said that Dorsey became interested in him as the result of a Harry James disc, perhaps even the *All or Nothing At All* recording, played for the trombone man by a publisher seeking a cover record. Jimmy Hilliard, then music supervisor at CBS in Chicago, remembers Blackie's, a Windy City restaurant, as the spot where Dorsey first became interested in Sinatra. Hilliard, who had played with both Dorseys, was having dinner with the trombonist one night when Tommy spent much of the meal griping about his difficulties with Jack Leonard.

'Have you heard the skinny kid who's singing with Harry James?' Hilliard asked. 'He's nothing to look at, but he's got a sound.' And Hilliard told Dorsey of his experience at the James opening in the Panther Room. 'My back was to the bandstand,' he retorted. 'But when the kid started taking a chorus, I had to turn around. I couldn't resist going back the next night to hear him again. He's got something besides problems with acne. Harry can't be paying him much. Maybe you can take him away.'

Negotiations were carried on by Bobby Burns, manager of the Dorsey band. A note slipped backstage to Frank invited him to phone Dorsey. The following day, Frank auditioned for the man in rimless glasses at the nearby Palmer House where Dorsey was playing. The test was whether he could sing *Marie* in Jack Leonard's style. Sinatra thought he did well. Nevertheless, on November 18, a *Billboard* columnist wrote: 'Now that it's safe to report that Jack Leonard left Dorsey on none too friendly terms, the replacement is Allan DeWitt.' *Billboard* added 'The odd quirk is that TD is holding a personal management contract on JL.' To which Dorsey might have responded with his unmistakable touch: 'Odd, my ass! Do you think I build up a singer, let him use my band as a springboard for his career, and then sit around waiting for a thank-you?' In December, however, *Billboard* reported: 'In spite of the fact that Leonard returns to the band, TD is going to keep Allan DeWitt sharing the lyric assignment.' But then suddenly it was neither Leonard nor DeWitt. In its February issue *Down Beat* advised that Sinatra had left James on January 26, and that DeWitt was going with Bob Chester's band.

Shortly after the pieces came to rest, Jack Leonard appeared as a solo act at the NY Paramount. The usual publicity build-up was started. Stories appeared of how he was mobbed in Times Square by fans. But his attempt to break out of the big-band womb was either premature, or he lacked the qualities that made Sinatra a robust, if emaciated-looking, solo baby three years later. By the end of 1940 Leonard was in uniform.

An interesting sidelight on a twisted skein of relationships is that when Dorsey first hired Leonard in 1936, after spotting him at a Long Beach roadhouse, Jack insisted on bringing Axel Stordahl with him. Stordahl was then an arranger and trumpet-player in the Bert Block band with which Leonard sang. Later, when Sinatra left Dorsey, he took Stordahl with him. It was the blond musician who helped create the lush, woodwind-string sound that became the distinguishing mark of popular ballad music in the '40s and of Sinatra's records *before* the fall.

Frank and Nancy had mixed feelings about his departure from the James band. Frank has said of the snow-filled

January night when he said good-bye 'It was after midnight. There was nobody around and I stood alone with my suitcase in the snow and watched the tail light of the bus disappear. Then the tears started and I tried to run after the bus.' Nancy also remembers the James' days wistfully. Frequently, they ate only onion sandwiches for dinner, or Nancy cooked up a huge pot of spaghetti for all the boys. The band had the camaraderie and the excitement of men on the way up, while for Nancy, the days with Frank were without the complications that the big-time brought.

III

'I REMEMBER TOMMY'

Just before Sinatra arrived for his first appearance with the Dorsey band, the truculent trombonist informed one of his sidemen that he had 'another Italian boy' coming and asked that he 'make the kid feel at home'. Trumpeter Lee Castle, with whom Frank first roomed, has said 'Even then you could see that this boy was tough. If you crossed him, you were dead. And he couldn't stand phonies. But if you were friends, there wasn't anything he wouldn't do for you.' And Dorsey was wont to say 'One thing Frank won't let anyone do is push him around.' Being himself rather expert at pushing, Dorsey unquestionably spoke from first-hand knowledge.

The Dorsey affiliation was, of course, the realisation of a dream. Only recently Frank told of how, in his Harry James days, all the young singers wanted to connect either with Dorsey or Miller. While Miller had the more exciting band, his was not a singer's band. The vocal chorus in a Glenn Miller arrangement was like a side dish between the instrumental courses; the band aroused comment because of a distinctive sound achieved through the use of a clarinet doubling the tenor sax in a higher octave. With Dorsey, however, certain arrangements were written around the vocal chorus and the singer stood forth as the featured talent. While he was with James, Frank had, in fact, tried to attract the trombone man's attention. One evening when he was at the New Yorker listening to the Bob Chester band, he spotted Dorsey in the room with a pretty girl. Frank approached Chester who allowed him to do a vocal with the band. But Dorsey was apparently more interested in his chick than in a new male warbler.

According to Lee Castle, Sinatra sang with the Dorsey band for the first time at the Palmer House in Chicago. Jo Stafford, then one of the Pied Pipers, places Frank's first appearance at Rockford, Illinois, during the last week of January 1940. What we do know is that a *Variety* reviewer caught the Dorsey band at the Lyric Theatre in Indianapolis during the week of February 2, and reported that Frank sang 'in an easy style to a solid hand'. The Sinatra vocals were *My Prayer, Careless, All the Things You Are* and *South of the Border* while *Marie* was a production arrangement in which Frank was joined by the Pied Pipers, three men and a girl.

Jo Stafford's memory of Frank's first performance takes this shape: 'We were on stage when Tommy made the announcement for Sinatra's first appearance. As Frank came up to the mike, I just thought, "Hmm—kinda thin." But by the end of eight bars, I was thinking, "This is the greatest sound I've ever heard." But he had more. Call it talent. You knew he couldn't do a number badly.'

By the middle of March, NY audiences and music business heard Dorsey's new male vocalist at the Paramount. 'Sock all the way,' was *Variety*'s verdict. 'He's sure of himself and it shows in his work.' *Billboard* said: 'He's developing into a first-rate singer. His *South of the Border* is the best thing on the bill.' Nevertheless, Frank's early months with Dorsey were among 'the most miserable', as he later described them, of his performing life. It was not the band but the amazing loyalty that he sensed in audiences to his predecessor, Jack Leonard. Nor did his first year with Dorsey stir any great personal recognition. *Variety* reviews of the band's recordings usually characterised his vocals as 'standout'. Of the May première at the Astor Roof, *Billboard* wrote 'Sinatra, a good ballad singer, is nil on showmanship.' In the publication's annual Collegiate Choice of Male Vocalists, Frank trailed in the low No. 22 position, with Ray Eberle of the Glenn Miller band No. 1, Jack Leonard, ex-Dorsey vocalist No. 2 and Bob Eberly of the Jimmy Dorsey band No. 3.

The Dorsey orchestra was one of the busiest, filling gaps between major engagements at the Meadowbrook, the Astor

Roof and the Hollywood Palladium with highly remunerative one-nighters. In entertainment jargon, a succession of single bookings in different places, one-nighters imposed the gruelling routine of travelling through the night after an engagement, travelling all day, performing all evening, only to spend the night and day travelling to a new location. The Dorsey band used a chauffeured bus. Band members who needed sleep usually took the front seats along with Dorsey who caught his eight hours under any conditions. Sinatra and other night people occupied the rear seats. Apart from the monotony of the grind, one-nighters made it extremely difficult to relax or exercise, to take proper care of simple matters like laundry and clothes, to keep in touch with loved ones, or even to perform well.

One-nighters forced an intimacy upon members of a band, which unavoidably made them familiar with each other's mannerisms and personal habits. Frank left three impressions upon band members. He was regarded as a high-liver. Always ready to pay the check, he insisted on staying at the best hotels, no matter where the rest of the band stayed. Band members were also impressed by his cleanliness. Despite the rigours of travelling and no matter how rushed the trip was, he would not sit down to eat at a dirty table. Nor could band members understand how, after long hours in the bus, Frank would emerge with his clothes immaculate. He insisted on showers, sometimes two or three a day when facilities were available. He washed his hands so frequently it became a joke. Even then, he always asked for his pay and change in new bills. His travelling cases were models of neatness, with each item in place and the clothes precisely folded.

Frank was also known to have a temper better left unprovoked. 'Once in Omaha,' Jo Stafford recalls, 'a man in the audience threw some popcorn while I was singing. Frank flew off the bandstand in a rage. Fortunately, he couldn't pick the man out of the sea of faces. But he was ready to tear him to pieces.'

Band members have never forgotten a party celebrating the opening of the Dorsey Brothers publishing companies. A newspaperman who imbibed a little too freely made an anti-Semitic remark. Although his paper was then influential in music business, Frank dumped him on the floor. 'You'll never get a decent write-up from him as long as you sing,' several bandsmen warned. 'If my career depended on prejudiced guys like that,' Frank said, 'I'd forget it.'

There were other occasions when Frank resorted to violence for less significant reasons. One evening backstage at the Astor Roof, Frank accused drummer Buddy Rich of showing off during one of his vocals. As one word led to another, Frank seized the nearest object, a pitcher filled with water and ice cubes, and hurled it at the drummer. Fortunately, Buddy ducked, but the heavy pitcher shattered against a wall with such force that pieces of the glass were embedded in the plaster. A moment later, Frank was all apologies. Although this was not the last altercation between the two, when Rich launched his own band, Sinatra helped him with a $25,000 loan.

Dorsey's personality had more than a little to do with the short tempers in his band. Disposed to drive hard bargains, the Sentimental Gentlemen of Swing was sharp-tongued, trigger-tempered and loved a fight. The constant war of nerves, which had split the Dorsey Brothers band several years back, provoked feuds and walkouts. Spatting with vivacious Connie Haines, Frank refused for a time to share a microphone with her. Unquestionably, his own truculence and feeling for violence received a fine honing during the Dorsey days.

Before Sinatra completed his first year, the band had a disc that hit the top of best-seller charts. It was an unusual Dorsey record in that, as *Billboard* noted, almost the entire side was taken up by a vocal. 'Tempo is extremely slow,' the reviewer observed, 'with Sinatra and the Pied Pipers singing a prettier-than-average melody beautifully ... A different, arresting record and one with great commercial as well as artistic appeal.' The song was *I'll Never Smile Again* by Ruth Lowe, who had allegedly written it after the sudden death of her husband. The tune so stirred Tommy after Mrs. Lowe auditioned it, he cancelled bookings and drove across country for two days to record it. The date was April 23. Dorsey was obviously dissatisfied with the results, for the song was re-recorded a month later. This version was rushed out, caught on instantly, became No. 1 on the Hit Parade by July 20, 1940, and remained there for a record seven weeks. Much macabre publicity appeared during the period of the song's popularity. But after it became known that another band had made an earlier recording, it seemed clear that the death of the composer's husband had

34

really had nothing to do with the writing of the song. In *Las Vegas Nights*, one of the two short-budget films in which he appeared with the band, Frank was briefly seen and heard singing *I'll Never Smile Again*. George Simon of *Metronome* characterised this film as 'without a doubt the worst this reviewer has seen', but said of Sinatra: 'He sings prettily in an unphotogenic manner.'

Although he was never part of the Pied Pipers, as has sometimes been reported, Frank worked well with the group. In addition to *I'll Never Smile Again*, their first record together —it was cut in April and recut a month later—in 1940 they made memorable discs of *Whispering*, *The One I Love* and *Star Dust* and in the two succeeding years of *There Are Such Things* and *Let's Get Away From It All*. Of the ninety discs Frank cut with Dorsey, the Pied Pipers appeared on twenty-three. Connie Haines also sang on four of these sides, and in 1942, Jo Stafford added her voice on two. On the Stafford sides, Frank doubled melody, singing it an octave below. 'He worked very hard,' Miss Stafford recalls, 'so that his vibrato would match ours. He never stopped working and he blended beautifully with us.'

Besides 'his' first hit record, 1940 brought the birth of Frank's first child. Because of the late hour at which the band finished, presumably Frank had not travelled to the Jersey City apartment. He had just fallen asleep in the Hotel Astor room he occupied with the band's manager, when the phone rang. It was the morning of June 8 and the Margaret Hague Hospital of JC was calling to announce the birth of the girl whom Frank sentimentally dubbed 'Miss Moonbeams' and about whom *Nancy* (*With the Laughing Face*) was later written. Tommy Dorsey became the godfather of the child whose birth temporarily improved but did not cement the relationship between her father and mother.

Shortly after Nancy Sandra's birth, a young song-plugger named Hank Sanicola raised a kitty among members of the MPCE (Music Publishers Contact Employees) for a gift to the newborn child. It is still quite a common practice, although the gesture is today directed mainy at disc jockeys. Sanicola was a counterboy at Witmark when he met Sinatra. A self-taught pianist, he began running over songs with the thin, unknown singer from Hoboken, helping him find his keys (they determine low and high notes in a tune). After a time, Sinatra could rely on Sanicola to get him whatever 'pros' and 'stocks' he wanted from the many publishers in the Brill Building, today still the mother church of Broadway publishers. Probably because of the contrast between spindly Frank and burly Sanicola, Hank became known as Frank's bodyguard. It was said that fights generated by Sinatra's hot temper were frequently settled by Hank. 'Frank does pretty good as a fighter,' Sanicola said on one occasion, 'except he's light and his hands swell.' When Frank opened his first music publishing company after he left Dorsey, Sanicola became a one-third partner. But even before then, when Dorsey launched Embassy Music (BMI) and Dorsey Brothers (ASCAP), Frank helped Sanicola locate with the new firms. The friendship and business relationship between the two lasted through all the stresses of Sinatra's career, coming to an end only in 1963. But even after they had parted, Frank named Sanicola as one of five people who had contributed most to his career. 'Without his encouragement,' he told Ed Sullivan, 'I very easily might have tossed in the sponge.'

During his second year with Dorsey, Frank's popularity began to grow rapidly, giving the bandleader both satisfaction and concern. An early indication was *Billboard*'s annual College Music survey, published as the band opened at the Astor Roof on May 20, 1941. Frank stood at the top of the poll. By the end of the year, *Down Beat* confirmed Sinatra's rising popularity for the first time, he displaced his idol and rival, Bing Crosby, winner of the poll from 1937 to 1940.

Dorsey himself acknowledged Frank's increasing audience by naming him co-author of a book he published on singing. Title: *Tips on Pop Singing*. Authors John Quinlan and Frank Sinatra. Although it has been repeated over and over again that Frank never took singing lessons, Quinlan is one of several vocal teachers with whom Sinatra consulted at various times. Apparently, Frank maintained some contact with Quinlan over a period of years, for in 1948 after he settled on the coast, he sent for him. Quinlan was actually No. 1 on his list of the five people who helped his career. 'You never heard of him,' Frank told Ed Sullivan, 'but he was a former Australian opera singer who became a vocal coach. If it hadn't been for his coaching when my voice was about gone, I'd have had no

36

career. He did it for nothing because I had nothing to give him at the time.'

Dorsey published another Sinatra opus during 1941, a hit song written by Frank in collaboration with Hank Sanicola and a shirt salesman named Sol Parker. A Sinatra perennial, *This Love of Mine* was introduced by him at the Astor opening and recorded by Dorsey a week later—on May 28. Parker is today still associated with Sinatra in his publishing enterprises. Another relationship that has carried over from the Dorsey days involves columnist Earl Wilson of the NY *Post*. As he waited one evening at the Meadowbrook to interview Dorsey, Wilson became involved in conversation with 'a skinny young vocalist'. Although he left without any strong impression of young Sinatra, his wife reacted differently. According to the columnist, who remains Sinatra's main NY news outlet, Mrs. Wilson confidently predicted that Frank would be 'another Crosby'.

By the beginning of 1942, relations between Dorsey and Sinatra were becoming strained. Dorsey could not help noticing that the song-pluggers who came to place new songs in his library almost always sounded Frank's reaction. It appeared that they were happiest when a new tune became part of Sinatra's repertoire rather than a Pied Pipers speciality or a band number. Axel Stordahl, then a Dorsey arranger along with Paul Weston and Sy Oliver, summed up the point of the developing conflict when he said: 'After a while, it was not Tommy's show, but Frank's.'

The results of the *Down Beat* poll of January 1942 did not allay friction between Dorsey and his vocalist. The Dorsey band placed second in the Swing band division where Benny Goodman still was the King; it was also No. 2 among Sweet bands, where Glenn Miller was No. 1. Among Favourite Soloists, Dorsey found himself down the list below Artie Shaw, Harry James and Benny Goodman. But Sinatra scored as No. 1 vocalist, beating such stalwarts as Bob Eberly, Crosby, Ray Eberle and Dick Haymes. Not even Dorsey's receipt of a non-returnable, individually accounted $1,250 for each record he cut at RCA Victor—more than Artie Shaw, Glenn Miller or his brother Jimmy received—seemed to make up for Sinatra's mounting importance.

The record situation also contributed to the tension between Dorsey and his vocalist. At first labels on Dorsey records

37

carried only his name and the vague notation: 'Vocal Chorus.' But letters began coming into the Victor offices asking for the name of Dorsey's singer. Frank Walker, then head of the recording division, suggested that Sinatra be identified. Dorsey balked, then reluctantly yielded. As Walker, who had a wry sense of humour, later summarised developments: 'The type just grew larger.' Before long, Dorsey was faced with the proposition of letting Frank make solo discs. Sinatra was asking and Victor executives were willing, though not too openly. With pressures mounting on all sides, Dorsey finally capitulated.

The four solo sides were cut on January 19, 1942, with Axel Stordahl receiving billing for the orchestral accompaniment on *Night and Day* and *The Night we Called It A Day*, and Tommy Dorsey, for the accompaniment on *The Song Is You* and *Lamplighter's Serenade*. As Victor's west coast Artists and Repertoire chief, Harry Meyerson supervised the historic session. 'Frank was not like a band vocalist at all,' he recalls. 'He came in self-assured, slugging. He knew exactly what he wanted. Watching him from the control booth, I remember thinking how I would have enjoyed seeing a set-to between Frank and Tommy. With their tempers, it would have been something to watch the hot-headed Italian go at the hot-headed Irishman.

'One other thing left an indelible impression. This was my first session with Sinatra and these were his first solo sides. Now, most singers tend to begin with the humble bit. At first, they're licking your hand. Then, the moment they catch a big one, you can't get them on the phone. Popularity didn't really change Sinatra. He started out by having a good opinion of himself. On that first date, he stood his ground and displayed no humility, phony or real.

'What he was not told until after the sessions,' Meyerson continued, 'was that his discs were coming out, not on Victor, but on the subsidiary Bluebird label. Since Bluebird discs sold at 35c as against 75c for Victor, RCA generally did not promote them as hard. It used the subsidiary label to solve difficult problems like Dorsey and Sinatra and to keep other labels from getting big stars. When it acquired Artie Shaw on top of BG, Shaw came out on Bluebird. Trombonist Glenn Miller was Bluebird while Tommy Dorsey was Victor.

'Coming out on the subsidiary label was a kind of slough-off for Sinatra. It was Tommy's way of giving him some rope and letting him hang himself with it. But Sinatra was so good even then, you knew he would be out on his own before long.'

Dorsey arranger Axel Stordahl wrote the 'charts' on all the songs for the solo session. 'I'll never forget when we got the advance dubs on the first two sides,' Stordahl recalled. 'Frank had a room in the Hollywood Plaza on Vine Street opposite the Brown Derby. We sat in it all afternoon of a sunny day, playing the two sides over and over on a portable machine. Frank just couldn't believe his ears. He was so excited, you almost believed he had never recorded before. I think this was a turning point in his career. I think he began to think then what he might do on his own.'

Whether Frank sensed it then or not, he was on his own less than six months later. It was the year in which three men founded a new West Coast record company towards the affluence of which Sinatra later contributed much. The creature of song-writer Johnny Mercer, lyricist Bud DeSylva, then a film producer, and record-store owner Glenn Wallichs, Capitol Records set up shop just about the time that Frank cut his first solo sides. Curiously, its first location was over Wallichs' Music City Store, just a turntable away from where Sinatra and Stordahl sat listening to his solos.

Both *Down Beat* and *Metronome* liked Frank's first two sides better than the second pair. 'Sinatra hits the bull's eye squarely with his relaxed, effortless ways and smart phrasing,' *Down Beat* wrote of *Night and Day*. 'Bluebird has a terrific bet here ... and a potential juke winner.' In *Billboard*'s view, Sinatra sang 'in soulful fashion that rubs so well against fem ears. Taking both in the slow tempo called for, he gives them ample romantic expression.' Of the second disc, *Down Beat* wrote non-committally: 'Very, very pretty singing,' and went on to criticise 'a sloppy falsetto' at the end of *The Song Is You*. *Metronome* was harsher, concluding its comment: 'He is not an impressive singer when he lets out—that's a cinch.' If Sinatra had hoped to make a splash with these discs, he was doomed to disappointment.

Nevertheless, evidence continued to accumulate of Sinatra's growing appeal to audiences. One such omen came with a recording of *There Are Such Things*, cut in July 1942, the last month in which Frank recorded with Dorsey. By December, the tune was No. 1 on the Hit Parade, where it remained for six consecutive weeks. Another was a July booking of the band at the Stanley Theatre in Pittsburgh. Dorsey broke the house record previously held by Kay Kyser. But here is what *Variety* had to say about Sinatra: 'It is unusual for a band vocalist to get the closing spot in a show. But that's the lot of Frank Sinatra. He fills it—and how! Crowd simply wouldn't let him get off and ran the opening performance overtime by at least five minutes.'

Less that a month later, the trade papers were buzzing with rumours of a split between Frank and Tommy. On August 15 *Down Beat* reported that Sinatra was leaving the band in September and that he had been booked for theatre dates and a network radio show by General Artists Corporation (GAC), then the third of the big talent agencies after Music Corporation of America (MCA) and William Morris (WM). Quite recently Sinatra revealed the specific provocation for his leaving Dorsey, as distinguished from his growing desire for independence and larger rewards. 'What really put the clincher on my decision,' he said, 'was when I heard that Bob Eberly was planning to break off with Jimmy Dorsey ... Nobody had broken the ice since Crosby, and I thought that somebody is going to come along and do this any day. If Eberly got out ahead of me, I'd be in trouble.'

Jack Leonard, who had tried the solo route after leaving Dorsey, had not made it. Eberly, who left Jimmy Dorsey later, did not make it. Neither did Dick Haymes, except briefly, who succeeded Sinatra in the Dorsey band. Haymes can be heard paying a tribute to Frank on a widely circulated aircheck of *The Song Is You*, made on September 19, 1942, the occasion of Sinatra's last appearance as Dorsey's male vocalist.

I Remember Tommy, one of the first albums Frank recorded after he founded his own label in 1961, opens with *I'm Getting Sentimental Over You*, Dorsey's theme, and contains eleven other songs that made Frank's association with the trombonist memorable. Reacting to the nostalgia of the occasion, Frank employed the arranging (and conducting) services of Sy Oliver, ex-Dorsey arranger, ex-Jimmy Lunceford trumpeter and arranger, and a key figure in the development of Swing. As one listens to the album, one senses an important source of the rhythmic pulse which Frank imparts to the ballads of the crooning '40s and which became so vital a feature of the mature Capitol Sinatra. In Oliver's approach even to ballads, either the melody itself had to swing or rhythm figures were devised to impart a beat.

Of band singing in general, Frank has recently said: 'It's like lifting weights. You're conditioning yourself.' On another occasion: 'When my son Frankie said he would like to start singing, we thought of his going with the Dorsey band ... He works every night to a different audience. He learns to understand his lyrics a little better...' Add that band vocalists learn how to articulate and phrase, since they must handle words so that accents are right and meaning comes through while they sing at a set dance tempo.

Despite the resentment he felt over the expense of buying out his contract with Dorsey, Frank never minimised his musical debt to the trombonist. 'Tommy taught me everything I knew about singing,' he has said. 'He was my real education.' What Sinatra learned from Dorsey was breath control. Frank early observed that Tommy could play through a long musical phrase, an eight- or sixteen-bar phrase, without apparently taking an audible breath. After a time, he discovered what he has described as 'a sneak pinhole in the corner of Tommy's mouth—not an actual pinhole but a tiny place' where the trombone man was breathing. 'In the middle of a phrase,' Sinatra explains, 'while the tone was still being carried through the trombone, he'd take a quick breath, and play another four bars with that breath.' As a result of this technique, Dorsey solos had a rare mooing smoothness and singing lyricism. According to Frank, it was this flowing quality, rather than his voice, that gave his singing a unique sound.

During Sinatra's tenure with Dorsey, hit song-writer Johnny Mercer became a Sinatra fan and urged all his friends to hear 'the kid who phrased like Tommy and improvised like Berigan'. A trumpeter like the immortal Bix whose lyricism he imitated, Bunny Berigan joined Dorsey soon after Sinatra. It is his appealing horn one hears on the famous April 1940 version of *East of the Sun*. After six months, Berigan, who was an alcoholic, yielded his chair to ex-Goodman trumpeter Ziggy Elman, famous for his solo on *And the Angels Sing*. As he had previously sought to imitate Berigan's elegant melodising, Sinatra slowly mastered Elman's use of vibrato to produce different tonal (and emotional) textures.

Sinatra's debt to Dorsey goes far beyond the realm of music.

Dorsey was one of the first music people who sought to establish an entertainment complex of his own. Starting with publishing companies, he set up his own booking office and approached other artists about joining him. At one point, upset by what trade papers were printing about him, he considered starting his own magazine. Just before his accidental death in 1956—he choked in his sleep on an undigested piece of apple—he was formulating plans to launch his own record company. These projects surely sound like a blueprint for the far-flung enterprises in which Sinatra has involved himself.

Although the two years and eight months with Tommy helped Frank develop musically, they did not apparently improve his relationship with Big Nancy, as she came to be known after the birth of Little Nancy. On several occasions, Frank has said that their marriage began to fall apart just about a year after the ceremony.

There is not much evidence that he worked at being married, even during the first year. This was the period when he was marking time at the Rustic Cabin and impatient to move ahead. Reports have it that he was associated with a high-spirited Hoboken group known as the Azov Club and that on occasion, Nancy would awake in their Jersey City apartment to find that Frank had not come home at all. Not even the birth of Nancy Sinatra apparently changed a situation in which, as Frank has said, he came to feel that he had mistaken friendship for love.

There were additional sources of tension and friction. Nancy, who was even-tempered, nursed hurts quietly but for long periods. Frank was quick to anger, quick to cool off and resentful of Nancy's sulking. Perhaps because she was compelled to work during the first year of their marriage, Nancy tended to handle money with care. Frank's spendthrift ways disturbed her. Nancy did no get along too well with Frank's mother while Frank was not too happy over the many Barbato in-laws that swarmed around his home. Nancy had five sisters; one of them, Tina, moved in with them when they settled in Hollywood.

Once he began travelling with the James and Dorsey bands, the gap between the Sinatras widened steadily. Meeting the poised, smartly dressed and sophisticated women who frequented spots played by name bands made Frank increasingly sensitive to Nancy's limitations. When he returned home, the contrast made for increase tensions and explosions over inconsequential matters. Regardless of crudities and his own limitations, Frank was a dreamer whose driving aspirations ran to extremes. In retrospect years later, he said: 'Nancy is a noble woman. She's done a magnificent job of raising the kids.' And daughter Nancy said: 'In all the years I can remember, Mom has never said an unkind thing about my father.'

IMAGE I

THE VULNERABLE TOUGH

In her autobigraphy Lena Horne tells of how she built a protective wall between herself and audiences, creating an image of 'a woman they can't reach ... They are not getting me—someone they can touch and hurt—but just a singer'. Frank Sinatra was never just a singer. From the start, he was a man sharing his innermost feelings with his listeners. The intimacy of his style transformed mere songs into love letters to a generation of girls.

All Or Nothing At all ... Guess I'll Hang My Tears Out to Dry ... I'll Walk Alone ... Saturday Night Is the Loneliest Night of the Week ...

Singing is a physical as well as emotional relationship. With his hollow cheeks, limp forehead curl, protruding Adam's apple, pencil-thin figure and oversized bow-tie, Frankie Boy was an image of all the hungry and hungering youngsters, all the shy and lonely young people of the time.

Years later, Deborah Kerr, co-star of *From Here to Eternity*, spoke of 'a curiously tender and vulnerable quality' in Sinatra that 'touches you and makes you want to touch back'. In the war-scarred world of the 1940s, bobbysox girls reached out frantically to cuddle the moon calf.

But in the romantic tradition of the American hero, virility came first and vulnerability second. Bogart, Gable and Tracy were basically tough and only subtly tender. Gary Cooper, Marshal Dillon and Palladin were impressively cool and only covertly compassionate, their inner gentleness concealed by a quick, albeit defensive, resort to violence.

After a time, to the soft-focus image of the little boy lost were added the dark shadows of the underprivileged tough and juvenile delinquent. Frankie Boy hated cops. He was beaten by them. He had been in countless gang fights, bloody and vicious. He stole. He was thrown out of school. Underscored by Sinatra's hot temper and excitable fists, this inventive press agentry helped give his image the toughness it needed. Now, the love voice of the bobbysoxers was in the great tradition of the heroic American male.

IV

SINATRAUMA: THE PROCLAMATION OF A NEW ERA

When Bob Weitman, a weary looking, wire-haired man, then managing director of the NY Paramount Theatre, drove out to Newark one evening in November 1942, he little anticipated that he would bring before the entertainment world what the *New Yorker* dubbed 'an American phenomenon'. In making the trip to the Mosque Theatre, Weitman was merely catching another act, an act that was not entirely unknown to him since the thin, young singer had appeared with the Dorsey band at his theatre. Accompanying him was Harry Romm, Sinatra's handler at GAC, who had been pressuring him for weeks to hear Sinatra now that he was on his own.

Although Romm was waxing as enthusiastic as an agent should, the truth is that neither Romm nor GAC was too pleased with the young baritone's progress. While only two months had elapsed since his leaving Dorsey, Frank was not as easy to sell as they had hoped. After his exit from the band, he had gone to the coast to sing *Night and Day* in a Columbia picture *Reveille with Beverly*. (It was an unbilled three-minute spot, but after his success, his name appeared on theatre marquees as if he were the star.) While in Hollywood, he had pitched for the job of staff singer at NBC, a post then held by Johnny Johnson. He was unsuccessful, but the gambit marked the beginning of still-warm, musical friendships with Skitch Henderson, NBC's hollywood staff pianist, and Gordon Jenkins, the station's musical director. Returning east, he appeared on a twice-weekly CBS sustainer, secured for him by Manie Sachs, A & R head at Columbia Records, and the man who had brought him to GAC executive Mike Nidorf. He was riding a new Tommy Dorsey record *There Are Such Things*, which eventually sold a million. But as with *I'll Never Smile Again*, it was listed as a Dorsey hit. His most severe setback was, of course, the strike of recording musicians, initiated on August 1, which prevented him from making new discs.

When Weitman and Romm entered the Mosque Theatre, the cavernous hall was more than half empty. They sat through several acts, Romm uneasy and Weitman bored. 'But then,' Weitman recalls, 'this skinny kid walks out on the stage. He was not much older than the kids in the seats. He looked like he still had milk on his chin. As soon as they saw him, the kids went crazy. And when he started to sing, they stood up and yelled and moaned and carried on until I thought, you should excuse the expression, his pants had fallen down.'

Aware that Sinatra came from Hoboken, Weitman figured that that might explain the audience's excitement. But he was impressed, so impressed that the following day he phoned Benny Goodman, who was the star attraction of the Paramount's New Year's show. Despite Sinatra's years with Dorsey, Goodman's reaction to Weitman's mention of Sinatra was: 'Who's he?'

'He' became an 'Extra Added Attraction' on the show that opened Wednesday, December 30, 1942. Featured with the King of Swing, who received top billing, were Peggy Lee, Jess Stacy (piano) and the BG sextet. Goodman made no attempt to build up the Extra Added Attraction. His introduction was a laconic, 'And now, Frank Sinatra.' But the response from the bobbysoxer audience was another matter. As Frank described it: 'The sound that greeted me was absolutely deafening. It was a tremedous roar ... I was scared stiff ... I couldn't move a muscle. Benny froze too ... He turned around, and looked at the audience and asked, "What the hell is that?" I burst out laughing and gave out with *For Me and My Gal*.'

Almost immediately the Paramount management sensed that something unusual was happening. Business after New Year's, which generally dipped, continued on a festive holiday level. Weitman took to wondering: was the strong box-office due to BG, still the King of Swing, or to the thin singer? After Goodman was gone, Sinatra remained for four additional weeks on bills that included the lesser-known bands of Sonny Dunham and Johnny Long. Instead of diminishing, audience excitement continued to mount, and larger and more hysterical crowds of bobbysoxers flocked to the Paramount. Although actual rioting did not occur at the theatre until the following year, this was the earliest, large-scale manifestation of what movie director Billy Wilder has described as something in Sinatra that is 'beyond talent—it's like some sort of magnetism that goes in higher revolutions'. To historians of popular music, this was, in *Life's* phrase, 'the proclamation of a new era'.

In effect, Sinatra's first Paramount panic marks the onset of the decline of the big bands. By the end of World War II, the Swing Era was no more. Popular music was then in a Sing Era and dominated by the Big Baritones and the Big Ballads. Was it not a prophetic coincidence that Sinatra, who was harbinger of the change, made his first appearance at the Paramount on the same bill as the man who had reigned as King of Swing?

It is doubtless easier to analyse the elements of an entertainment triumph than to determine why it occurs at a given moment. Several American record companies unsuccessfully released recordings by the Beatles more than a year before their raucous acceptance in 1964. The beautiful Rodgers and Hart ballad *Bewitched, Bothered and Bewildered* did not register during the original run of *Pal Joey*, but became a smash ten years later as the result of a piano record by a minor artist. Whatever the elusive explanation, for Francis Sinatra of Hoboken, NJ, the moment of impact was January of the year that saw *Oklahoma* open for a run of 2,248 performances after a hard fight for backers.

The recent Beatlemania and, before that, the hysterical furore over Elvis Presley, have served to rationalise the bewilderment of the adult world over Sinatra's reception by the bobbysoxers. And yet in retrospect, it seems easier to explain the more recent teenage panics than the Sinatra syndrome. Presley was a provocative performer with his choked-up voice, holy-roller eyes, knocking knees and gyrating pelvis. The mop-haired youngsters from Britain were odd-balls from the tips of the pointed, high-heel boots to the bushy tops of their buster-browns.

By contrast young Sinatra was quite tame. The oddest parts

46

of his get-up were his over-sized bow-ties, and a curl straggling across or calculatingly disarranged on his forehead. He did not gesture, swing his hips, stamp his feet or leap in the air. He just stood at a microphone, clutching it as if he were too frail to remain standing without it. But the mike mannerism, the limp curl, the caved-in cheeks, the lean, hungry look, 'the frightened smile', as one reporter put it—all emphasised a boyishness that belied a wife and child and brought him as close as the boy next door. The scenes at the Paramount, and later at broadcasting studios, were the nearest thing to mass hypnosis the country had seen until then, with girls moaning ecstatically, shrieking uncontrollably, waving personal under-clothes at him, and just crying his name in sheer rapture.

During his first appearance at the Paramount, as the fever spread among the bobbysoxers, extra guards had to be re-tained to maintain order. Girls remained in their seats from early morning through Frank's last show at night. Some fainted from hunger, others from excitement. Fearful of losing their precious seats, many would sit through several shows without taking time out for the ladies' room. As his engage-ment lengthened, the windows of his dressing-room had to be blacked out, since the mere sight of him from the street below resulted in traffic jams. Getting him in and out of the theatre, his hotel, a restaurant, developed into an elaborate ritual in which his handlers schemed, and not always successfully, to outwit the fans. When they failed, he did not come away with all of his clothes and belongings. On one occasion, two girls caught hold of the loose ends of his bow tie and, in the pulling match for the momento, almost strangled him to death.

To theatre attendants, Sinatra's impact was evident in one simple fact known to everyone associated with the Paramount, but not previously reported. As one usher put it: 'That Sinatra hit those kids right on the kidneys! At the end of the day, there was more urine on the seats and carpets than in the toilets.' *Time* magazine said it more delicately: 'Not since the days of Rudolph Valentino has American womanhood made such unabashed public love to an entertainer.'

Sinatra remained at the Paramount for eight roaring weeks, a record exceeded only by Bing Crosby when crooning first caught the public's fancy, and equalled only by Rudy Vallee at the peak of his popularity. But audience reactions, as Frank rocketed to fame, far exceeded anything Vallee, or Crosby had elicited, or the world had witnessed, The King of Swing's unhappiness about the notice being showered on the Extra Added Attraction was apparent long before the engagement was over. Benny Goodman's displeasure manifested itself in mid-January when the results of *Down Beat*'s 1942 poll were announced. BG and his Sextet came in first in the Small Combo division while Frank stood at the top of the country's Male Vocalists. To celebrate the occasion, Bob Weitman arranged for Madeleine Carroll to present the winning plaques on the Paramount stage. But Goodman refused the invitation to jitterbug together, as it were. He insisted on receiving his award separately.

Before the end of the month, the top vocal plum in radio fell into Frank's lap. He was signed by George Washington Hill, ardent proponent of the hard sell (LSMFT) on radio, to replace Barry Wood on the all-important, coast-to-coast show *Your Hit Parade*. And before he made his first broadcast on February 6, 1943, he had an RKO picture contract in his pocket. In less than four months, from the position of an aspiring band vocalist, and in less than four years, from a lowly $15-a-week job as a roadhouse singer, he had risen to become 'the biggest name of the moment in the business'. This was *Down Beat*'s mid-April estimate.

There were many, however, who regarded the first of the Paramount panics sceptically. Among these was Arthur Jarwood, who was struggling to keep his Riobamba Club solvent during the wartime scarcity of customers. When the club's press agents Gertrude Bayne and Irving Zussman, suggested that he book Sinatra, the most Jarwood would offer was $750 a week—good money compared to Rustic Cabin standards but less than Jarwood had paid Jane Froman and Benny Fields. As in the case of the Paramount, Sinatra was billed as 'Extra Added Attraction'; the advertised stars of the show were Walter O'Keefe, veteran comic and m.c., and comedienne Sheila Barrett.

Opening night, Frank suffered from a bad case of jitters. Show business was sceptical, and he was uncertain that he could make it with the older, moneyed crowd of the Riobamba. On his closing night four weeks later, Walter O'Keefe told a jam-packed audience: 'When I came into this place, I was the star and a kid named Sinatra, one of the acts,

Then suddenly a steamroller came along and knocked me flat. Ladies and gentlemen, I give you the rightful star—Frank Sinatra!'

By then, 'The Voice that Thrills Millions' had been raised to $1,000 a week and re-signed for an additional three weeks. Frank's stay was extended another three weeks, making ten in all, and his take-home pay rose another five bills to $1,500 a week. Not only did he save a club on the verge of bankruptcy, but he demonstrated, according to *Variety*, that 'what he has to offer is as stirring for Park Avenue as it is among the 10th Avenue coin-machine set'. To one of Sinatra's ringsiders, his boyish self-assurance and sensational acceptance were overwhelming rather than stirring; Dean Martin, then an aspiring baritone, left the club feeling that, perhaps, singing was not the career for him.

From the Riobamba, Sinatra went to Frank Dailey's Meadowbrook in Cedar Grove, NJ, where the name bands played when he was marking time at the Rustic Cabin. Then in mid-May he returned to the Paramount, the scene of his initial triumph. By this time, a *Down Beat* reviewer suggested that 'his spell is not as artless as it looks. He knows his feminine audience and fires romance—moonlight moods—at them with deadly aim.' On his second Paramount appearance, Frank's weekly take rose from $2,100 to $3,100.

When he was booked into the Waldorf's Wedgwood Room, he felt that he had climbed to the top. On opening night, October 1, the audience was heavy not only with the Park Avenue social set but with luminaries from every phase of show business. Frank was so excited that, stepping out of his shower, he slipped, struck his head against the tub and twisted an ankle. Despite the discomfort he went on to face the smug, opulent audience of black ties. Some nights later, one of the patrons who became irritated with his wife's ecstatic cooing, rose in the middle of a song and exclaimed loudly: 'You stink!' Having dreaded the possibility of a humiliating situation from the start, Frank was prepared. He stopped the band, walked quickly to the table, and, as the startled audience strained to see the heckler, did what any outraged Hoboken kid would do—invited his commentator outside for a bit of air. The heckler stared arrogantly through inebriated eyes at Sinatra, but after a moment, plumped down in his chair. Back at the mike, Frank said with a show of self-possession that concealed his vulnerability: 'Ladies and gentlemen, I like to sing. I'm paid to sing. Those who don't like my voice are not compelled to come and surely are under no obligation to stay.' The well-heeled audience applauded. And *Down Beat* approved in a story headlined, even though there were no fisticuffs; 'Don't Say Sinatra Stinks Unless You Can Punch!'

To Earl Wilson, Frank admitted that the engagement kept him on edge. Of opening night, he said: 'If I hadn't been nervous, I'd be a self-satisfied guy and that would stink.' Wilson felt that this was a feigned lack of self-confidence. But Sinatra's entourage of stooges, then known as The Varsity, knew that he was really bugged by Park Avenue hauteur. 'No matter how important they are,' Wilson commented, 'Frank whittled them down to sighs.' In appreciation of both the confidence and the space, the columnist soon was toting a gold watch inscribed: 'Oil, youse a poil. Frankie.'

But there were still doubters who needed the Paramount booking of October 1944, the following year, to be persuaded. Coming in the Columbus Day period, this appearance brought on the mightiest demonstration of female hysteria that any entertainment star had until then been accorded. When Frank arrived the first day for a 6 a.m. rehearsal, almost 1,000 girls in bobbysox were on line. Police estimated that the queue had begun forming at 3 a.m., despite Mayor LaGuardia's 9 p.m. curfew for juveniles. The very first in line had been there since 4.30 p.m. of the preceding day. As Frank rehearsed sleepy-eyed in the empty theatre, going over songs without singing while the Raymond Paige orchestra ran over the arrangements for tempi and dynamics, the line outside continued to grow. By 7 a.m. it stretched halfway down the block to Eighth Avenue. When the 3,600 seat theatre opened its doors at 8.30 a.m., enough youngsters were admitted to fill it to capacity. The picture preceding the stage show, *Our Hearts Were Young and Gay*, was utterly ignored. The bobbysoxers chattered, joked, exchanged Sinatra stories and intermittently set up cries of: 'We Want Frankie! We Want Frankie!' And after he was on stage, excitement reached such proportions that he had to plead for quiet and threaten to leave if the audience did not settle down.

The following day, a school holiday, was the haymaker. News reports spoke of 'The Columbus Day Riot at the Paramount'. It was hardly less than that. Over 10,000 youngsters queued up in a line, six abreast, that ran west on 43rd Street, snaked along Eighth Avenue, and east on 44th Street. An additional 20,000, according to police estimates, clogged Times Square, making it impassable to pedestrians and automobiles. Prowl cars were summoned by radio from outlying precincts while almost two hundred policemen were called from guard duty at the Columbus Day Parade on Fifth Avenue. According to news reports, the final police complement included four hundred and twenty-one police reserves, twenty radio cars, two emergency trucks, four lieutenants, six sergeants, two captains, two assistant chief inspectors, two inspectors, seventy patrolmen, fifty traffic cops, twelve mounted police, twenty policewomen and two hundred detectives.

The additional forces, including fifty extra ushers in the theatre, could not cope with the frantic crowds. The ticket booth was destroyed in the crush. Shop windows were smashed. Passers-by were trampled and girls fainted. When the first show finished, only two hundred and fifty came out of the 3,600 seat house. The average youngster remained glued to her seat for two or three Sinatra appearances. A woman on line with her daughter told a reporter that the girl had threatened to kill herself unles she saw the show.

'Several outside swooned on schedule,' the *Daily News* reported. 'One sixteen-year-old, who came from Lynbrook, L.I., rallied sufficiently to insist upon being allowed inside to look at The Voice. Her success prompted a succession of fake faints thereafter, but none was successful.'

On the third day, a small riot broke out inside the theatre when a stocky eighteen-year-old youth threw an egg at Sinatra. Frank was in the final bars of *I Don't Know Why I Love You Like I Do* when he was struck. Startled, he glanced down at the light grey jacket he wore, then walked offstage. Pandemonium broke loose. Girls began screaming. Others broke into tears. Still others made a dash for the egg-thrower. As the ushers and police realised what was happening, they raced down the aisles, pursued by an angry pack of girls. By the time they reached the egger, he was cowering in abject fear, the centre of a wild, screaming mass of bobbysoxers. As the ushers peeled off girl after girl, the orchestra struck up *The Star Spangled Banner*. It was a desperate attempt to quiet the turbulent audience, which did not simmer down until the marksman, surrounded like a criminal by a dozen ushers and police, was led off to the manager's office. After questioning, the bewildered egg-thrower was released without having any charge placed against him. One report had it that a newsman had paid him to do the egging. Later that day, Frank showed reporters the stain on his jacket. 'I don't think it was an egg,' he said, displaying a surprising degree of ruffled pride. 'It was small and moist enough to have been a grape.' The following day's magazines printed pictures, taken in the small hours of the morning, of sailors hurling over-ripe tomatoes at cut-outs of Frank atop the Paramount marquee.

The unrestrained displays of the bobbysox brigade were not limited to NYC. In Boston Frank was greeted by three hundred kids. In Chicago the windows of his train were shattered and a priest was knocked down and trampled. In Pittsburgh, school authorities were so outraged by absenteeism that they threatened to expel anyone who missed school during Sinatra's engagement.

The slavish antics of his fans were beyond belief. Frank could not discard a cigarette butt without having girls make a scramble for it. A girl whom he accidentally touched in a crowd, covered the spot with a bandaid, which she did not removed for weeks. Girls hid in his dressing-rooms, in hotel rooms, in the trunk of his car. Cleaning maids were bribed for an opportunity to lie between his bedsheets before they were changed. After the girls discovered where he lived in New Jersey, they camped outside his house day and night, making human ladders to get a glimpse of him inside. Occasionally, a girl would ring the doorbell and plead to be allowed to use the toilet. When it snowed, girls fought over his footprints, which some took home and stored in refrigerators. Older women were not immune to the orgiastic hysteria. In the Waldorf one evening, a smartly dressed woman approached him as he waited for an elevator, opened the top of her dress and begged him to autograph her bra.

The idolatry was not limited to females. Baritone Alan Dale, who later subbed for an ailing Sinatra at the Paramount, tells of being 'among the first' in line for Frank's first date at the theatre. 'We brought our lunch,' Dale writes in his autobiography, 'and stayed to see him for three shows ... We had our hair cut the way he wore it ... We waited at the stage door of the CBS studio for a glimpse as he entered or exited ... We idolised him ... We envied him ...' And Sammy Davis, Jr., then an aspiring flash dancer, waited eagerly outside a Hollywood broadcasting studio in a mêlée of five hundred swooning girls. 'God, he looked like a star,' Davis recalls. 'He had the aura of a king as he sat signing autographs with a solid gold pen.'

Before long, interviewers were asking Sinatra how he could stand his fans. To a reporter who had to fight his way to his dressing-room, he replied: 'Now, wouldn't it be awful for me if there weren't people around that stage-door?' He added: 'I can't tell you much about how I handle them. It all depends on the individual case. Some of them follow me to restaurants in taxis. I don't mind that because it doesn't go too deep.

'There's one girl though who's always in the audience. When I look accidentally in her direction, she lets out an awful yell. And sometimes she gets hysterical. The other morning she got that way and they told her they'd let her come up and see me. When I saw her, she was still crying. After a while she promised she'd be a good girl if I'd give her my bow-tie—you know how girls have started to wear bow-ties. So I did and she promised to be quiet. The next day, I got out on the stage and there she was yelling worse than before.'

Some observers tried to dismiss the unprecedented bobbysox hysteria as a hoax and fabrication. But radio audiences were responding just like theatre audiences, and girls in Hollywood reacted just as hysterically as girls in New York. Reporters and critics were by turns amazed, baffled, incredulous or just cynical about Sinatra's appeal. Writing in *Life*, George Frazier snidely referred to Frank's bulging shirt-front, characterised his dinner coat as one that 'would horrify Lucius Beebe', noted that his talk was filled with 'youthful awe'—Harry James was *so* sensational, Dorsey *so* terrific, etc.—and described him as a chap whose neck was scarred, eyes sunken, cheeks hollow, hair a mop and ears too big. Frazier's verbal caricature was a reflection of a question being widely asked by querulous males: 'What's he got?' *Newsweek* echoed Frazier's bewilderment: 'As a visible male object of adulation, Sinatra is baffling. He is undersized and looks underfed—but the slightest suggestion of his smile brings squeals of agonised rapture from his adolescent adorers.'

Paul Bowles, novelist and then a music reviewer on the NY *Herald-Tribune*, admitted that he was both upset and bewildered by the reactions of Sinatra's fans. 'The hysteria which accompanies Sinatra's presence in public,' he wrote, 'is in no way an artistic manifestation. It is a slightly disturbing spectacle to witness the almost synchronised screams that come from his audience as he closes his eyes or moves his body slightly sideways, because the spontaneous reaction corresponds to no common understanding relating to tradition or technique of performance, not yet to the meaning of the sung text.'

Variety editor Abel Green, seeking to explain 'Why the Whole World's in a Sinatrance', concluded that Frankie possessed the ability to make the kids feel that he was *one of them* and that he was *genuinely* interested in their problems. (His press agents kept telling of his insatiable appetite for banana splits.) 'He's made us feel like we're something,' one youngster announced. Another wrote to *Down Beat*: 'Frankie has that certain something that makes every girl think he's singing just for her.' And she added less dispassionately that while she would forsake her beau for a jam session with Tommy Dorsey, Harry James or Benny Goodman, she would give her right arm 'for a smile from Frankie'. A sixteen-year-old girl who sat through thirty-one consecutive shows at the Paramount said: 'He looked into my eyes once.' She came from Stamford, Connecticut, supposedly the centre of Sinatrauma.

But many editors and writers felt that his ability to identify with the youngsters was a rather superficial explanation for the idolatry that enveloped him. Noting that the response to Sinatra was a generation response rather than the reaction of scattered individuals, they turned to the psychiatrists and psychoanalysis for an explanation.

'Purely mass psychology built up by his press agent,' a Brooklyn psychiatrist stated. 'They all *work* on each other. It's an emotional situation no different than the Holy Rollers.'

'Wartime degeneracy,' another analyst suggested. The absence of millions of young men from their communities deprived girls of dancing and courting partners. As a result, they made Frankie an image of their innermost desires, a person to whom they could address their pent-up drives.

Still another psychologist argued that Frankie's appeal was a product of the maternal urge 'to feed the hungry'. In the yearning, beseeching quality of his voice, 'almost like the plaintive cry of a hungry child', the doctor found an amazing auditory equivalent of Sinatra's famished appearance. This particular analyst felt that a noticeable increase of weight could destroy Sinatra's magical appeal. There is a story that Frankie once emerged from an overseas plane, his trench coat bulging with souvenirs; George Evans, his press agent who had come to meet him, took one look and exclaimed: 'My God, look at Frankie! He's put on so much weight, we're ruined!'

An English critic, Harold Hobson of the London *Sunday Times*, argued that it was not The Voice but 'The Smile' that worked the magic. 'The shy deprecating smile,' he wrote, 'with the quiver at the corner of the mouth makes the young ladies in the gallery swoon in ecstasy and the maturer patrons in the dress circle gurgle with delight.'

While there was some ribbing, some needling and some raillery in the attempts to explain the Sinatra charisma, there was also a great deal of concern. The unbuttoned display of feeling troubled the older generation. There was a sense of shocked embarrassment, as if mother or father had unintentionally come upon daughter in a moment of intimacy. The guardians of our heritage of Puritan restraint saw something unwholesome in the Sinatra hysteria.

In a long, intellectual article in the *New Republic*, Bruce Bliven averred that the bobbysox reaction, while it may have begun as a publicity stunt, was 'a genuine mass phenomenon ... a phenomenon of mass hysteria'. Such hysteria, he explained, occurred only two or three times in a century. The Sinatra euphoria was comparable to the Children's Crusade in the Middle Ages, or the dance madness that overwhelmed the young in certain medieval German villages. He reviewed different explanations for the baffling 'Dionysian ceremonial', including wartime female frustration, faddism, Sinatra as a father image or success symbol, as well as 'just plain sex'. To Bliven, the most significant consideration was that Sinatra aligned himself, not only with the younger generation, but against the adult world. He was thereby rejecting the things that teenagers allegedly hated in the crassly commercial cosmos of their elders and allowing them to express 'an unfulfilled hunger' for heroes and idealism. The Voice represented, in short, 'a selfless idolatry'.

Although there was something non-aesthetic in the reactions provoked by Sinatra, it is still strange that most commentators paid so little attention to his actual singing ability. 'There was this fantastic rage,' a historian was to write, 'for a nice, clean, skinny, practically *voiceless* [sic!] kid with jug-handle ears and golf-ball Adam's apple, who moved into a microphone and caused teenagers ... to go into spasmodic imitations of sex convulsions ...' Considering the hold which 'the voiceless kid' has maintained on the public's ears for more than two decades, there must have been something special about his singing and his showmanship.

'Elsa, what is there about that boy,' Loretta Young once asked Miss Maxwell, 'that makes you feel he is singing to you—and you, alone?' From the moment he trod upon the Paramount stage, women of all ages have had this feeling. There have been many explanations. At least one has never appeared in print before. It has to do with his eyes.

For me, their strange role and power were forcefully established at a Capitol recording session several years ago. Most singers prefer to work in an isolation booth or 'gobo' (spun glass enclosure), which provide contact with the conductor and control booth, eliminate all studio distractions and permit total concentration on the all-mighty microphone. By contrast, Sinatra demands an audience and likes to work close to the musicians. He makes a studied effort to reach both, singing not to the mike but to the people around him. Now, at this particular session, I was in the control booth. It was crowded, not only with the normal compliment of technicians, but with a very large entourage. The studio itself was mobbed. Large orchestra conducted by Nelson Riddle, a bubbling bevy of school-age youngsters, and in the area in front of the control booth, a group that included daughter Nancy, her fiancé Tommy Sands, orchestra leader Dick Stabile and actress Dorothy Provine, whom Frank had brought to the session.

Sinatra worked out in the open at the music stand, snap-brim on his head. He was about twenty feet from the double glass windows of the booth and at least fifty feet from me, with both the people in the booth and those outside between us. Yet every time he turned his head towards the booth, I had the feeling that he was addressing himself specifically to me. It was purely a matter of his eyes, which even now, after thirty years in the limelight, are still as piercingly a peacock blue and as clear in their outlines as if he were a young boy. If one can speak of hypnotic eyes, Sinatra has them. The 'you-and-me'

56

feeling, communicated by the eyes, is projected in their absence by a style whose keynote is intense intimacy.

Apart from a unique and identifiable sound that no one can miss recognising as Sinatra's, his singing represents communication of a rare order. It is so potent because it has been for him a vent for his own feelings. Like the blues singers of old, he sang to give expression to deeply felt needs and experiences. And in his early days, he was emotionally close enough to his youthful yearnings for affection so that the kids found an expression of their own unfulfilled longings.

It has been said that great actors are great for a double reason: one, they need applause, mass adulation, as other people need air; two, unlike other people, they are driven to 'undress' in public i.e. to make a public display of their feelings. In view of Sinatra's sustained fight for privacy it may appear that he did not want the public prying into his innermost feelings. But Sinatra's art, like that of most great actors, is a symbolical sharing, not of the specific experience, but of the emotions engendered by it. And this Sinatra always willingly and engagingly offered to his listeners.

Surprisingly, a facet of his early singing style that drew both humorous and scornful barbs was never properly evaluated for its contribution to the mass hysteria. I refer to the slow, the extremely slow tempo—*marche à la funebre* was one critic's derisive characterisation—at which Sinatra sang romantic ballads like *Fools Rush In, I'll Be Seeing You, Try a Little Tenderness, Dream* and *You'll Never Know*. Listening to early recordings of those songs, one can sense the tremendous tension, the mounting emotional anticipation, the demand for release that the delayed fondling of words and notes engendered. It required only a twist of the head, a glimmer of a smile to provoke a young audience, tried beyond endurance by the suspenseful sound. The shrieks and moans came in orgiastic relief.

Because of early references to Sinatra as The Crooner, his initial style has generally been called crooning. This is a misnomer. Since crooning is midway between humming and projecting with full voice, it is clear that Sinatra never really was a crooner. Not too long ago, he himself characterised his early style as *bel canto*, a mode of singing he allegedly developed in opposition to Crosby's casual, crooning delivery. Historically, *bel canto* is a vocal operatic style in which the emphasis is on beauty of tone rather than emotional expressiveness, on the inventive employment of ornament, and the smooth use of sustained tone rather than a declamatory or dramatic delivery. While Frank was less of a crooner and more a sustained singer than his early appreciators realised, he never subordinated feeling to form, thought to technique, or stress to style. His singing was never merely an entertainment but an experience to which audiences were compelled to respond, not only with applause, but with their hearts. From the start of his solo career, he was an involved singer who forced involvement upon his listeners.

This was a quality he shared with the great Negro songstress whose style deeply dyed his own, and whose influence, transmitted through Sinatra. made intensity of feeling a touchstone of pop singing. 'It is Billie Holiday,' Frank has said, 'whom I first heard in 52nd Street clubs in the early '30s, who was and still remains the greatest single musical influence on me.' And what was that influence? Depth of emotion was just one phase of it. There were others, like the use of contrasting textures, the feeling of intimacy, the intense personalisation of lyrics—and the glow of sheer sex.

The fact is that the pop singers before Sinatra, including Crosby, were sexless. Just as song-writing was then circumscribed by the euphemisms of Victorian nature imagery—the movies panned to the sea or sky to suggest intimacy—so most singers affected poses of nonchalance, ebullience, or gaiety to suggest, but also to shield audiences from, the realities of epidermis. Without thinking about it, Billie Holiday exuded sex both as a woman and as a singer. So did Francis Albert Sinatra. More than one fan succumbed to the spell of the flesh as well as the art of the voice.

v

THE PRICE OF SELF-POSSESSION

Despite the widespread manifestations of the Sinatra charisma, a suspicion persisted that it was a press agent's invention. 'Frankie originally vaulted into the big-name class,' Charles Hastings wrote in 1947, 'because of a phony publicity build-up.

Girls were hired by the score to scream and faint when he came on stage.' The man credited with this gargantuan hoax was a short, black-haired, black-eyed, black-bespectacled press agent whose office boasted after January 1944 a framed *Billboard* citation for 'The Most Effective Promotion of a Single Personality'.

George B. Evans, who went to work for Sinatra during his first solo year, always reacted furiously to the intimation that the Paramount panics were staged. At one point, to silence accusers, he offered to donate $5,000 to the favourite charity of anyone who could prove that he packed the house with ticket give-away's or paid girls to shriek and faint. It was true, however, that Evans, who had publicised Russ Colombo, Rudy Vallee and Glenn Miller, had a reputation for devising outsized gimmicks. Once he arranged for girls to wear extra-heavy lipstick so that their kisses left Sinatra looking like he was bleeding. On another occasion, he reportedly paid cab drivers to converge on a certain corner where Sinatra was to pass. The resultant traffic jam created much talk and column items.

Though Evans never acknowledged that he rounded up girls to swoon, Jack Keller, a West Coast associate, conceded that Evans stationed ambulances outside the box-office where bobbysoxers waiting to enter the shrine could see them and react. On the occasion of Frank's fiftieth birthday, Keller went further in admitting that they had primed the pump. 'We outfitted Frank,' he said, 'with breakaway suits and hired girls to scream when he sexily rolled a note. But we needn't have ... The girls we hired to scream swooned, and hundreds more we didn't hire swooned with them.'

Through the years, new singers have been introduced to a thundering accompaniment of hullabaloo, huzzahs and harangues. But no one has ever succeeded in making an H-bomb explosion with a firecracker. Neither Evans nor Sinatra could have manufactured what happened.

Before Evans, Sinatra had one other press agent, a gent named Milt Rubin. It was a short-lived relationship, some say because Rubin was called into the service, others because Rubin liked to be paid on time. In these early days of his solo career, Nancy Sinatra was taking care of Frank's finances. Although Rubin was pegged at only $50 a week, Sinatra fell many weeks behind in the payments. It was reportedly a calculated move, despite Sinatra's meagre earnings of the moment, in that Nancy felt that people worked harder when money was owing to them.

Later, when Frank was at the Riobamba, the club's p.a.s, Bayne and Zussman, supplemented Evans' efforts. Word-plays like Swoonatra, Sinatrance, Swoonatrance, etc., soon helped make Sinatra The Swooner, as Crosby had been The Crooner. *Newsweek* observed: 'The word "swoon" re-entered the nation's vocabulary when a girl in his audience (at the Riobamba) fainted because of the heat and columnists exaggerated it into a mass syncope over his voice.' That year (1943), The Swooner became The Voice (shortened from The Voice That Thrills Millions, his earliest solo handle), just as Marie McDonald became The Body, Lauren Bacall, The Look and Betty Grable, The Legs. When Grable married Sinatra's ex-boss, Harry James, a tabloid head read: 'Legs Bride of The Horn'.

Early in their association, George Evans moved into a level of intimacy and affection that led to his involvement in Frank's personal as well as his public affairs. Although extra-marital flings later seemed only to enhance the Sinatra charisma, Evans worried because Frank's fans had adopted his family along with him. They sent gifts, not only on his birthday, but on the birthdays of the two Nancys. Frank himself promoted the relationship by closing each broadcast, 'Goodnight, Nancy', and making such outsized comments in interviews as: 'Nobody comes before my wife Nancy. That goes for now and for all time...' (September 1943).

The effort to preserve the family image led Evans into difficult and dangerous manoeuvres. He could do little about Frank's appetites. (Humphrey Bogart told an interviewer: 'I don't think Frank's an adult emotionally. He can't settle down.') But Evans did try to reduce the contrast between the girls Frank met in show biz and the small-town girl he came home to. To improve Nancy's appearance, he had her teeth capped, took her to Helena Rubinstein for make-up consultation and led her on shopping tours through the chic Fifth Avenue stores. More than anyone else, perhaps, Evans tried to prevent the break-up of Frank's first marriage. His advice, pleading and manoeuvring were pivotal in killing highly publicised romances with both Lana Turner and Marilyn Maxwell.

A man of intelligence and culture, Evans was interested in

60

the larger social issues of the day and helped broaden Sinatra's perspectives and image. Inside press circles, he was frequently called 'Frank-enstein's Monster', later shortened to The Monster.

Sinatra was as intrepid and fearless as his p.a. was canny in assessing public relations. During the summer of 1943, just after the first pour of publicity, Frank sang with four of the nation's leading symphony Orchestras. These concerts were undertaken allegedly in response to pleas for help in reducing symphony seasonal deficits. George Evans never indicated in what form the pleas came from the Philharmonic Symphony, the National Symphony of Washington, the Cleveland Symphony and the Hollywood Bowl Orchestra. But it is not difficult to detect his deft hand, or to recognise it as an attempt to stir adult interest in Sinatra. Nor was it hard to predict the deprecating reactions of the long-hair critics.

The concert on August 3 at Lewisohn Stadium with the Philharmonic Symphony resulted in a unanimously negative verdict. *Newsweek* observed that despite 'squeals of girlish passion', only 7,500 attended whereas *Traviata* and *Carmen* with Metropolitan Opera casts had drawn 17,000. In the *Herald-Tribune*, Paul Bowles was amused by Sinatra's thank-you speech in which Frank referred to the Philharmonic virtuosi as 'the boys in the band'. He granted that his voice was 'pleasant', his personality projection 'satisfactory' and his diction 'excellent'. The NY *Sun* characterised his voice as 'rather nondescript' while Mark Schubert of *PM* found him 'embarrassingly out of place in the huge arena'. *Life* covered the concert in a series of pictures with derisive captions. Claiming that Sinatra was 'plenty upstage and obnoxious' at rehearsals, it contended that he got 'under the skin of the orchestra' even more at the concert. The caption under its final picture: 'No sell-out.'

Undaunted by the critical scallions thrown at him, Sinatra appeared on the coast in 'Symphony Under the Stars' two weeks after the Stadium concert. Although he filled the giant Hollywood Bowl to capacity, the *LA Times* thought it a disgrace that a symphony should be supported by 'lending its name to entertainers of this type'. The sponsoring So. California Symphony Association replied that it saw 'no great sacrifice of aesthetic principles to give people what they liked instead of catering to old ladies who pretend to like the three B's.'

'Mr. Swoon Bowl Debut Super,' *Daily Variety* reported. But the accompanying story took a lofty view of the proceedings. It contrasted the squealing of the girls with a rather unfriendly male reaction, and noted that the orchestra was outclassed in the competition with portable radios—Frank was on the air and arrived late from the Hit Parade broadcast. 'As he was whisked away by a flock of traffic cops,' *Variety* concluded, 'there was a final chorus of gurgles, mingled with masculine sounds redolent of nightblooming raspberry.'

Frank always remembered this concert as one at which he physically felt fan impact. 'They converged on our car,' he recalled, 'and practically picked it up. Musta been 5,000 kids jammed up behind the forty or fifty people mashed against the car. It was exciting. But it scares the wits out of you, too.'

Just before he left for the coast, Sinatra made the 52nd Street scene; it was then known as Swing Street because of its many jazz clubs. At the Onyx, Billie Holiday was appearing with Cozy Cole on drums, Hank D'Amico on clarinet and Johnny Guarnieri at the 88. As Frank and Hank Sanicola sat listening to Lady Day, two men parked themselves near the tiny bandstand for a better view of Billie. 'Would you mind,' Frank asked, as his temper began to rise, 'would you mind not standing in front of our table?' As the two turned and recognised Frank, one exclaimed 'Who the hell do you think we are? A couple of Sinatra fans?' Frank was instantly on his feet and the guy never saw the fist that rocked him. Before his friend could pitch in, Sanicola was in action. Other customers intervened to halt the fight.

As time went on, Frank's fast fists came in for their share of notoriety. The truth is that he had plenty of provocation, at least in his early days as a celebrity. Operating on the likelihood that entertainers cannot chance a public fracas, a certain number of club-goers enjoyed riding celebrities. In Sinatra's case the extensive publicity about his physique and his romantic appeal to females prompted belligerent drunks to have a go at him. What they did not reckon with was that Frank was a frustrated prize-fighter. Between shows at the Paramount, he frequently worked out backstage with gloves, or he dashed up to Sullivan's Gym, near Columbus Circle, to watch well-known boxers work out. At times, he boxed with Al Silvani, trainer of heavyweight contender Tami Mauriello, who became one of Frank's close friends and gave Frank his identification bracelet when he was drafted. Not to be discounted is the possibility that George Evans saw in an occasional punch, properly provoked and justified, a way of adding masculine appeal to The Voice's image.

Apart from his father's and uncle's association with boxing, Frank was following entertainment tradition by his display of interest in the sport. Walking in the footsteps of Crosby and other headliners of the period, he invested in several fighters, including Mauriello. Today, successful singers are little interested in sports as investment. Connie Francis, Johnny Mathis, Steve Lawrence *et al.* are much more concerned with real estate, an area that eventually became of interest to Frank. For a long while, however, fighters remained a vital part of his entourage.

As his income grew, Frank entered the music publishing field. Instead of payola, insured through open or covert affiliation with an established publisher, Frank wanted ownership. 'I submitted *If You Are But a Dream* for a plug,' Ben Barton, an ex-vaudevillian, has said, 'and wound up in business with Frank.' The association developed at the Astor Roof where WAAT disc jockey Paul Brenner introduced the owner of the struggling Barton Music Corporation to Frank. Before long, the corporation had three partners, each owning a third; Hank Sanicola left Embassy Music, a Dorsey firm, for an equal share of the three-way arrangement. Barton's daughter Eileen, later known for *If I Knew You Were Comin' I'd've Baked a Cake*, became Sinatra's protégé on his weekly Wednesday night broadcasts for Vimm's Vitamins.

Barton Music grew rapidly after Sinatra became associated with it. Soon it was the proud possessor of Frank's radio signature *Put Your Dreams Away* whose lyrics were the work of Ruth Lowe, responsible for *I'll Never Smile Again*. In 1943 it had *Close to You*, which became a Sinatra perennial and the title of a later album. The following year Barton had a Hit Parade song in the Cahn-Van Heusen ballad *Saturday Night (Is the Loneliest Night in the Week)*. In 1944 it also had *Nancy (With the Laughing Face)*, the song dedicated to Frank's daughter, with music by Jimmy Van Heusen, who reportedly dedicated his royalties to her. The words were credited to comedian Phil Silvers who, according to insiders, received uncredited assistance from both Sammy Cahn and Johnny Burke, Van Heusen's former writing partner. Barton Music, the first of a complex of publishing companies developed by Sinatra, flourished during Frank's big years, floundered and went bankrupt during his decline, and came back strong in 1955. By then, an all-powerful Sinatra was able to garner the publishing rights to the themes of films like *Not as a Stranger* and *The Tender Trap*, and to the score of the TV version of *Our Town*, in all of which he starred. The last-mentioned yielded *Love and Marriage*, one of the few song-hits to emerge from television.

Along with George Evans and Hank Sanicola, Frank's close friends and advisers of these early days included Manie Sachs, a large-eyed, hollow-voiced, mild-mannered Philadelphian with whom Sinatra became acquainted in the Harry James days. Starting as public relations director of his hometown station WCAU, Sachs was associated for seven years with MCA, first heading the Acts department and then, the Orchestra and Record division. Appointed Director of A & R at Columbia Records in September 1940, he was instrumental in shaping the careers of Dinah Shore, Charlie Spivak, Les Brown as well as Harry James. Although he underwent treatment for leukaemia for several years prior to his death in 1959—by then he was vice-president of RCA Victor—his illness was an amazingly well-kept secret. His premature death at fifty-three came as a sad shock to the entertainment industry. In a business where competition can be tough and mean, Manie was one of the few executives who was genuinely and universally liked.

During the autumn months of 1942, immediately after Frank left Dorsey—months made troubling for a new artist by the musicians' ban on recording—Manie proved a tower of strength. It was he who arranged for the CBS radio show that gave Sinatra continuing contact with an audience and kept his name before the public. It was Manie who brought him into contact with GAC, a contact that led to Sinatra's springboard-into-fame appearance at the Paramount. And it was Manie who unlocked the recording situation for Frank.

On his Dorsey exit, it had been assumed and was, in fact, rumoured that Sinatra would sign with Victor; he had cut his first solo sides the preceding spring for its Bluebird subsidiary. There was a hitch in that Sinatra had no intention of settling for the subsidiary again, and it appeared that his former boss, who had originally kept him off the parent label, had no intention of changing his attitude. While the Victor executives wanted Sinatra, they were apparently unwilling to offend the truculent and then-powerful Mr. Dorsey. Once the recording ban went into effect, all record companies ceased signing new talent—and so the situation remained at a standstill into the spring of 1943.

Long before then, the disc companies had begun ransacking their vaults for platters that could be re-issued. In the process, Manie Sachs uncovered the flop Harry James recording of *All Or Nothing At All* with vocal by Frank Sinatra. Whereas the James band had, on the initial release of the disc in 1939, been a new, floundering unit, it was now quite popular. And Sinatra was, of course, the vocal sensation of the day. On its reissue, the label copy underwent a significant change, commemorating in its own way the end of one era in popular music and the beginning of another. Instead of HARRY JAMES and his Orchestra/Vocal Chorus by Frank Sinatra, the label now read FRANK SINATRA/with Harry James and his Orchestra.

Spurred on by Lou Levy, the enterprising publisher of the song, Sachs re-released the disc in May 1943. Sinatra re-introduced it on a new variety show, *The Broadway Bandbox*, accompanied by the Raymond Scott orchestra. By July 10, *All Or Nothing At All* was No. 1 on the Hit Parade. In the period between the disc's re-release and its rise as a best-seller, the record companies began manoeuvring to break the nine-month-old musicians' strike. Since singers were not members of Local 802, they were presumably not bound by the Petrillo edict. During May, rumours spread that Decca, then the upstart of the record industry under the aggressive and imaginative leadership of Jack Kapp, was planning to record a new singer *a capella*—backed, that is, solely by a vocal group. The singer was Dick Haymes, Sinatra's successor with Dorsey, who was stepping out on his own. On June 3, 1943, Haymes was rushed into the Decca studios under a veil of secrecy, there to cut four sides with the sole backing of a well-known vocal group, the Song Spinners.

The rumours regarding Haymes and Decca spurred Manie

Sachs to action. Contract in hand, he dashed out to the Meadowbrook where Sinatra was appearing after his smash engagement at the Riobamba. The Columbia contract, which he proffered and Frank signed, antedated the Decca/Haymes session by two days. By June 7 Frank was in a Columbia studio recording *You'll Never Know*, the lovely Harry Warren–Mack Gordon ballad which Haymes had already cut. It is worthy of note, in view of Sinatra's veneration of Billie Holiday, that the vocal group backing him was led by Bobby Tucker, a Holiday accompanist. Though *You'll Never Know* was a hit for Sinatra, Haymes' record, which had a four-day advantage, actually outsold his.

Sinatra's initial Columbia contract, a two-year letter agreement dated June 1, 1943, was re-dated November 11, 1944, as of the eventual lifting of the protracted Petrillo ban. It provided for sixteen sides, subject to orders of the War Production Board, with Sinatra receiving an advance of $100 per side and Columbia paying the cost of the accompaniment. Before it expired in November 1946, it was renewed by Sachs for a two-year term. Before its expiration, it was extended for a five-year period, beginning January 1, 1948, with an advance of $360,000 to be paid in monthly instalments of $6,000. In the autumn of 1949, this arrangement was altered to assist Sinatra in his tax situation, but the terminal date was not altered. Dwindling sales and difficulties with Mitch Miller, who succeeded Manie Sachs when the latter moved to RCA Victor, brought the Columbia association to a terminus in December 1952. Between 1943 and 1952, Sinatra participated in a total of ninety-six recording sessions and cut two hundred and eighty-one songs. The peak recording year was 1947 when he cut almost every other week and registered a total of twenty-five dates.

Of the three songs he recorded on his first session in June 1943, two became big records: in addition to *You'll Never Know*, which won the Academy Award, *People Will Say We're in Love* from *Oklahoma*. A perfectionist even in those days when everything was happening for him, Frank re-recorded the Rodgers–Hammerstein ballad not once, but twice, before he permitted Columbia to release it. Of the nine songs he cut *a capella*, four climbed to No. 1 on the Hit Parade and one reached No. 2. Here are the interesting statistics:

	No. 1	Times on	Started
You'll Never Know	9×	24	8/5/43
People Will Say We're In Love	3×	30	19/6/43
Sunday, Monday or Always	6×	18	14/8/43
I Couldn't Sleep a Wink Last Night	1×	10	29/1/44

At the end of 1943, when Frank was embarking on a theatre tour, *Down Beat* ran a gag cover. It showed Frank in glasses playing the clarinet while Benny Goodman mugged at singing. It was a pictorial observation, perhaps unconscious, that the days of the big bands were numbered. The Top Ten records of the moment included five vocal discs where a year earlier there had been none.

Manie Sachs also played a pivotal role in Sinatra's buy-out of the Dorsey contract, which occurred two months after Frank affiliated with Columbia. Buy-outs of this type are not uncommon in the music business. When Everett Crosby assumed the management of his brother Bing in 1930, it took $35,000 to buy back pieces Crosby had sold of himself to different agents and managers. Not too long after Sinatra left Harry James, the trumpeter shelled out $25,000 to buy himself back from his ex-boss, Benny Goodman. Money had been advanced to both Crosby and James, but Dorsey owned $43\frac{1}{2}$ per cent (including his lawyer's share) of his former vocalist without having advanced a penny.

In a sympathetic editorial captioned 'Pieces Once Were Songs to Sing but Now He Knows', *Down Beat* estimated that Sinatra was paying out $93\frac{1}{3}$ per cent of his earnings. It broke the whopping figure down as follows: $33\frac{1}{3}$ per cent to Dorsey, 10 per cent to lawyer Leonard Vannerson, 10 per cent to new manager Bobby Burns, 20 per cent to booking agency GAC, and at least 20 per cent to Uncle Sam. Nor did this breakdown include the salaries of his accompanist, arranger Axel Stordahl and publicity man George Evans. There were unverified rumours that Sinatra had actually sold over 100 per cent of himself. 'Everybody owned a piece of him,' Walter Winchell wrote. 'Frank was allowed to keep the write-ups.'

In May, shortly after his smash debut at the Riobamba, Frank flew to Chicago in a fruitless attempt to settle with Dorsey. On his return, he sounded off against people who did nothing for their shares except be present when deals were being negotiated. While he was on the RKO lot later, Leonard Vannerson, against whom his remarks had been directed, brought a $17,000 attachment suit. At a press conference, Frank said : 'Sinatra can be quoted as saying loud and long that he believes it is wrong for anybody to own a piece of him and collect on it when that owner is doing nothing for Sinatra. I will fight this thing to the last ditch.'

Sinatra's efforts to free himself from Dorsey and Vannerson failed until Manie Sachs took him to his attorney, Henry Jaffee, and Jaffee took Frank to Jules Stein, the head of MCA At the time, Sinatra was under contract to GAC, one of MCA's smaller competitors, partly because MCA, which handled Dorsey, had not wanted to dare the Sentimental Gentleman's wrath by handling his ex-vocalist. As a result of several conferences, MCA offered to buy out Dorsey and Vannerson provided that Sinatra would sign with it on the expiration of his GAC pact. In effect, this meant that for the balance of his unexpired GAC contract, MCA would book Frank gratis, allowing GAC to continue collecting commissions. With Frank's assent, MCA shelled out $35,000 in cash. Frank added $25,000, advanced to him by Columbia Records on Sach's recommendation, giving Dorsey and Vannerson a total of $60,000.

Long-range and speculative though the deal appeared, there was an ace in the hole for MCA. In the movie contract negotiated by GAC with RKO, Sinatra was free to make one outside picture a year. In this provision, MCA had the mechanism through which it could recoup its advance. In fact, this was how Sinatra came to make *Anchors Aweigh* for MGM. But even this clause did not eliminate the speculative nature of MCA's move. 'The publicity build-up has been overdone,' one trade-paper observed. 'There is a good chance that the Sinatra bubble has been blown up to a point where it may disintegrate with a pop into thin air.'

When he arrived in Hollywood in August 1943 for the Bowl concert and work on his first RKO picture, Sinatra was treated to one of the most tumultuous receptions of his career. 'An estimated crowd of 5,000 to 6,000 (mostly teenage girls),' the NY *Herald-Tribune* reported, 'fought all over the station platform to get a close look at their idol.' Ostensibly to avoid this occurrence, Frank had left the Santa Fe Chief at Pasadena instead of

Los Angeles. But the West Coast Sinatra fan clubs, skilfully administered by Marjorie Divan of the Evans office, had somehow heard. In fact, as his train pulled into the station, a loudspeaker began blaring *All Or Nothing At All*. When Frank stepped off the train, the girls charged, pinning him in a crush on the station platform for almost twenty minutes. One reporter was bitten on the forearm by a girl trying to get close to Frank.

'Stupendous!' Vladimir Bakaleinikoff was reported as saying. 'Never have I seen anything like it!' Bakaleinikoff, who was to conduct the Bowl concert, had come to the station to welcome Frank officially. Song-writer Jimmy McHugh, who came as RKO's greeter and who wrote new tunes for *Higher and Higher*, also found himself trapped in the terrifying mêlée and waited for Frank for two hours in a garage where they took refuge until the panic subsided.

To a reporter who asked: 'Frankie, how about Crosby? Looks like you've taken away the play, eh?' Sinatra replied: 'Bing was my first singing idol—and he still is. He'll always be tops. For that matter, there's no comparison between us. We're entirely different in style.' That Crosby was far from a has-been was demonstrated at the end of the year when he nosed out Sinatra on sales of *People Will Say We're in Love* and racked up seven discs in *Down Beat*'s Top Ten. There was no real friction between the two, despite press attempts to fan the flames and the partisanship of fans.

The conservative *Los Angeles Times* devoted almost four full columns to Sinatra's arrival. In a front-page story with a two-column headline, 'Secret of Life Told by Crooner—It's Love', a gushing female reporter concluded: 'He is a romanticist and a dreamer and a careful dresser and he loves beautiful words, and music is his hobby. He makes no pretensions at all.'

Claiming that he had a library of five hundred symphonic albums and that he could be 'just as enthusiastic about classical music as those kids out there', Frank denied having any operatic aspirations. 'I can't read music,' he acknowledged. Of his singing style, he said informatively: 'I use all the colour changes I can get into my voice. The microphone catches the softest tone, a whisper.' He picked songs for their lyrics, he explained, and regarded music as a backdrop. 'I sing love songs and mean them,' he stated. 'They're for two girls named

Nancy.' In discussing his background, he could not resist repeating the press-agent fabrication that he had been 'a sports reporter on a little New Jersey paper'.

Sinatra sold himself well. The female reporter was convinced that he was naturally sensitive. Louella Parsons, who met Frank at this time, claims that he had, 'Noah Webster, forgive me, humility. He was warm, ingenuous, so anxious to please.' Snubbed by Frank in later years, she said in retrospect: 'Sinatra couldn't have been so boyishly unspoiled, so natural and considerate. But I have to admit he was. After I met him, I was enrolled in the Sinatra cheering squad. And I stayed in a long, long time.'

After the Bowl concert on August 14, Sinatra remained on the coast for two months, working on his first starring role in RKO's *Higher and Higher*. His co-stars in the Rodgers and Hart musical that had been a Broadway flop, were Michele Morgan and Jack Haley, and the cast included Leon Errol (with the trick ankles), Barbara Hale (later Perry Mason's secretary Della Street), Victor Borge, Mel Tormé and Dooley Wilson, the Negro pianist, remembered later for his *Casablanca* rendition of *As Time Goes By* ('Play it again, Tham').

In addition to singing three new songs interpolated into the R & H score by Jimmy McHugh and Harold Adamson—*I Couldn't Sleep a Wink Last Night* was a 1944 Academy Award nomination—Frank did a few dance steps under the tutelage of sad-faced Paul Hartman. When the film was released in January 1944, the reviewer of the Hollywood *Citizen-News* found his singing 'captivating' and commented: 'He portrays himself so naturally that you catch yourself thinking. "He can act too."' Favourably impressed, the NY *Herald Tribune* observed: 'His ugly, bony face photographs well: and he handles himself with hints of comic authority.'

Returning east late in September 1943, Frank carried with him the contract for a new film, scheduled to roll in December. Since the movie-makers were not waiting for the reaction to his first major vehicle, Broadway inferred that either the picture people were sold on him or that they were uneasy about how long the Sinatra craze would last. After a frenzied greeting by a crowd of devotees, Frank made a fast appearance at a Banshee luncheon at the Waldorf. Then, under doctor's orders, he went to his home in Hasbrouck Heights, NJ, to nurse a bad cold. The pace of his first tumultuous year in the limelight was beginning to tell.

The following month, Frank's draft status became of concern of his fans. On October 22 he passed a preliminary physical examination. When he was classified 1-A the following month, Frank announced that he 'was 'kinda restless' and that he wanted to serve although he was a pre-Pearl Harbor father. In the early days of December, as the nation's females trembled over the possibility that they might lose their new singing idol, Frank was called back for another physical check-up. Although efforts were ostensibly made to keep the scene of the examination secret, NY and NJ fans showed up in droves at the Newark centre. Through a long, cold winter day, they waited restlessly—warmed occasionally by hot coffee proffered by Sinatra's handlers. When he finally emerged, rejected for service as a 4-F, his followers broke out into spontaneous tears of joyous relief.

'I've got a hole in my left ear drum,' Frank explained, adding that the doctors had found several other things wrong, including 'a need for sleep and rest'. He confessed that he was 'unhappy at being rejected for military service because I've been bragging to friends that I'd get through'. Entertainment business, like the rest of the USA, had then been at war for two years. Frankie Laine was working in an aeroplane parts factory. Eddie Duchin was in the Navy. Glenn Miller was leading the Air Force band while Rudy Vallee conducted the Coast Guard band. Since petrol rationing and car shortages made travel difficult for dancers as well as musicians, radio had become a crucial form of entertainment. Moreover, the mood of the time was well-disposed towards the intimate communication afforded by a romantic voice buzzing out a set in one's own bedroom or den. Sinatra's style was thus a superlative expression of the times.

In *Down Beat*'s 1943 end of the year poll of the nation's most popular singers, Frank swamped Bob Eberly, Dick Haymes and Perry Como, and, nosing out Crosby who had been ahead for much of the voting, came in first. In December, too, Frank embarked on an eastern theatre tour, accompanied by Jan Savitt's orchestra. As he favoured Alec Wilder, an arranger who was a graduate of the Eastman school of music and whom he called 'the Professor', so he was partial to the none-too-successful Philadelphia orchestra leader because of his classical erudition. The tour smashed all existing box-office records, despite that fact, documented by *Newsweek*, that truant officers cut into theatre attendance by hounding swoon-crazy girls.

Curiously, Frank never broke box-office records at 'the shrine of disorder' or 'the house of swoon', as the Paramount was called in those days. While the management took extraordinary measures to flush the dedicated out of their seats, like forcing fans to leave their lunch boxes in the lobby, nothing helped. Fans stayed for more than one show. In fact, one girl claimed an attendance record of fifty-four stage and screen shows during a three-week Sinatra engagement. To Frank, the ardour of the dedicated brought an estimated first-year income of over a million dollars.

THE BATTLER

Sinatra's was a lone voice among popular singers when he embarked on his anti-discrimination activities. He had not forgotten the streets of Hoboken where epithets like 'Wop!' and 'Guinea!' made him reach for a loose brick, or the divisive impacts of words like 'Nigger', 'Mick' and 'Sheenie'. During his years as a roadhouse and band singer, acts of prejudice had triggered his all-too-ready fists. Now, he sensed that education, not violence or invective, was crucial. He made a documentary film short attacking racial prejudice and recorded *The House I Live In*: *'What is America to me ... a certain word "democracy" ... all races and religions ... the right to speak my mind out ...'*

His activities stirred controversy. But against the urging of his friends who feared for his career, he refused to back down. If he lost the support of influential columnists, he attracted the adulation of young people everywhere—and the respect of some adults. Like the followers of writer-singer Bob Dylan who gloried in his rebellion, Sinatra's audiences applauded his defiance. They felt that he was fighting the battle of the little guy and they loved him because he refused to play it safe.

Although his tolerance work was an outgrowth of his participation in FDR's fourth-term campaign, he never became a programmatic rebel. Rather, he was an unyielding individualist who insisted on 'the right to speak my mind out', the right to associate with whoever he chose (including pugs and hoods), and the right to lead his life as unconventionally as he pleased.

From the start, he had the underdog's hypersensitivity to humiliation or rejection. He would cockily dare injury rather than tolerate indignity or a slight of his pride. His approach to authority, even as a youngster, was defiant, and later to the press and public, provocative.

As a youth, he had 'betrayed' the men in his family by not becoming a boxer, a frustrated ambition of both his father and an uncle. The challenge to his masculinity, originating also in his mother's neglect or rejection of him in his childhood, freighted him with a cocky hostility. With his temper, he could not avoid being a brawler. The stubborn battler came later, as did the rebel and non-conformist. Eventually, his unconventional behaviour made his Law of Privacy, and his controversial efforts to enforce it, a powerful weapon in reverse for grabbing space.

The mid-'40s, when the bedroom balladeer became the argumentative libertarian, marked the beginning of Sinatra's bad-boy appeal.

VI

FROM NEW JERSEY SUBURBIA
TO HOLLYWOOD HIGH SOCIETY

At a January 1944 press conference, as Frank chatted with newsmen in CBS's Hollywood studio, his eyes kept darting to a corner where his cousin Ray Sinatra, musical conductor of the show, had gone to make a phone call. Suddenly, without offering an explanation, Frank cut out of the circle of reporters and dashed to the phone. The following day, a trade-paper reported that his abrupt exit had offended the fourth estate. 'First Signs of Trouble with Press', the headline read.

It was a tempest in a nursery. Concerned over the impeding birth of his second child, Frank had responded automatically to his cousin's signal that Nancy was on the phone. The reporters did not wait for an explanation. Trivial and inconsequential, the incident was a forecast of later developments in Sinatra's relationship with the press.

Franklin Wayne Sinatra, now known simply as Frank Sinatra, Jr., made his appearance in Jersey City on the afternoon of January 10, just about the time that radio listeners were beginning to hear a ditty that went 'mairzy doats and doesy doats and little lambsy divy'. Frank was then engaged in the shooting of his second RKO starring film *Step Lively*. As the child's godfather, Frank chose Manie Sachs. The priest who was to officiate at the christening did not approve. Noting that one of a godfather's major responsibilities was the religious education of a child, he suggested that the godfather of a Catholic child should preferably be Catholic. Manie Sachs was Jewish. Frank refused to make a substitution. It was not just a question of friendship but of tolerance. There was an argument and Frank took a walk. Instead of being an event, the christening became an incident.

Soon, the newspapers manufactured a Sinatra controversy. The peg was a statement by an Indiana University professor ascribing Frank's popularity to the rebellion of teenagers against classical music. From Artur Rodzinski, then conductor of the NY Philharmonic Symphony, the *Sun* elicited a statement which it spread like a major newsbreak across its front page. Rodzinski indulged in the absurd gambit of attributing juvenile delinquency to jazz—and, therefore, to Sinatra. Leopold Stokowski, conductor of the Philadelphia Orchestra, issued a statement supporting Sinatra. Singer Lily Pons seconded Rodzinski's charge. Frank sat this one out.

A month later, Frank was not an innocent bystander. The fracas involved AFTRA, the American Federation of Television and Radio Artists, and stemmed from Frank's desire to broadcast his radio show from studios on Sunset near Vine, instead of the CBS studio at Sunset and Beverly, which had been used up to then. To reporters, Frank denied that he had threatened a walkout. But AFTRA officials asserted that shortly before the broadcast, they had been compelled to order Frank to perform or face immediate suspension. Contending that there never was a question as to whether he would go on, but that he objected to being ordered around, Frank dismissed the fracas as 'another exaggerated yarn'.

On the set of *Manhattan Serenade*, based on the Broadway hit *Room Service*, and released as *Step Lively*, Frank referred to Gloria De Haven, his co-star, as The Comb—she was constantly brushing her blonde tresses. One day Frank refused to do a scene with her. When the director queried Frank, he motioned to a high hat Miss De Haven was wearing. The director hesitated. Frank did not. He walked off the set and waited until The Comb had changed to something 'more flattering' to him. A columnist who reported the incident found charm in Sinatra's directness and noted that Erroll Flynn and Mickey Rooney were also frequently concerned about their height.

One day the set of *Step Lively* was ordered closed. RKO executives were concerned over the number of secretaries who deserted their desks to watch Frank. According to a Hollywood columnist, Frank always obligingly came off the set between takes to sign autographs and chat with the girls, proving that he was still 'one of the nicest guys in the world'. Frank's entourage had other explanations of his considerate conduct toward attractive secs and stenogs.

'I like making movies,' Frank told a reporter who interviewed him on the set, 'though sometimes it nearly drives me crazy to wait. You see, for years I have been used to rapid work—radio and bands. Out here, I hate to sit and wait between scenes.' The inner tension and restlessness, which were to prove a trial to film makers through the years, were already in evidence.

Shortly before D-Day in Normandy, Nancy Sinatra was ensconced in the Beverly Hills Hotel, awaiting the arrival of furniture from their home in Hasbrouck Heights, New Jersey. Purchased at the start of Frank's rise, the two-storey, white-clapboard house sat in a nondescript suburbia not too far distant from the George Washington Bridge, where middle-income Italian families then moved. Now, in California, Frank was the possessor of a Mediterranean-style home in the select Toluca Lake area where, not surprisingly, Bing Crosby also had a large house. The Sinatra house was across the lake from the exclusive Lake Shore Country Club to which the Crosbys belonged, but which the Sinatras were not invited to join. After a time, a single-masted, rose-coloured sailing-boat, a gift from Axel Stordahl, lay moored at the private dock. Nancy dubbed the home, which had once belonged to actress Mary Astor, The House That Music Built. Frank's den bore a framed Schopenhauer aphorism: 'Music is the only form of Art which touches the Absolute.' More elegant and more attractive than the Hasbrouck Heights' *Warm Valley* home, as Frank called it, the new pink-stucco and terra-cotta house was hardly more satisfactory as far as the Sinatra's domestic relationship went.

Frank had a sense of order and tidiness which, with two growing youngsters about, did not make things easy for Nancy. Even when he dressed hurriedly, he never dropped clothes on the floor but laid them out neatly. Before he returned home, she had to follow a ritual of checking the house over. His sharp, blue eyes instantly detected an ash tray that was turned askew.

Moving into the posh milieu of the movie colony posed severe problems of adjustment for Nancy. One does not change overnight from a housewife in a small NJ suburb to the wife of a rich singing idol and movie star. 'Hollywood expected to get a look at Mrs. Sinatra,' a columnist wrote in August 1944, 'at a fashion show staged by Lilly Daché for the WACs. But her chair remained vacant all afternoon.' After a time, although her own inclination was to shop at small, inexpensive stores, Nancy began using the clothes designers and beauty experts who catered to the movie colony. She was elated, when at a luncheon, Joan Crawford complimented her on a new hat.

Frank had his own problems adjusting to Hollywood and his new status. 'It's terribly difficult to remain completely stable,' he said years afterwards, 'when you suddenly zoom from one place to where you're constantly surrounded by people pulling you in several directions. The money is always there ... although you really don't know how much is there. Soon you get confused and you don't care.... Every time I felt insecure, I used to go out and buy ten more suits.'

Outwardly, the Sinatra ménage could not have appeared happier. On the occasion of their first dinner in the new house, Nancy found a diamond wristwatch at her place. Soon after, Frank gave her a Cadillac convertible and, while she was learning to drive, insisted that she call him every afternoon to report that she was OK. After his broadcasts, she was the first person he phoned to learn how the show had gone. But beneath the surface, there were deep crevices. Charged with great nervous energy, Frank had to be constantly on the go, and particularly at night when Nancy preferred to remain at home. Although jealousy was not part of her make-up, she was not insensitive to the rumours about Frank's evening companions. 'Allan Curtis seems interested in Marilyn Maxwell,' a gossip columnist wrote, 'who formerly accompanied Frank Sinatra here and there.' Nancy preferred her own family to the people who hung around Frank and who were not infrequently surprise dinner guests.

Sinatra's entourage was at this time a curious mixture of the talented and the tough. It included Mark McIntyre, a would-be concert pianist who had become Frank's accompanist in August 1943 and remained with him for five years; songwriters Sammy Cahn and Jule Styne, whom he promoted for the song assignments in *Step Lively, Anchors Aweigh* and *It Happened in Brooklyn*; blond, balding, genial Axel Stordahl, his arranger-conductor; bull-chested Hank Sanicola; and sundry song pluggers and plug-uglies who laughed at Frank's funnies and functioned as 'go-fers'—'go for coffee, pick up song copies, etc.' It was a free-wheeling, hard-talking, easy-drinking men's group, and it got under Nancy's feet and skin.

Frank, on the other hand, found little kinship with the members of Nancy's family, some of whom had followed her to the West Coast, and tended to be less then friendly when they were around the house. In the July 1944 issue of *Photoplay*, an article appeared under Nancy's by-line. It was not too informative except for the title: *It Isn't All Roses*.

Just before he started work on *Anchors Aweigh*, the first film he made after settling on the coast, the British had their first look at Sinatra. They were not impressed by *Higher and Higher*. While one critic thought he would go far—'his voice has tenderness'—and another suggested that his singing had the quality 'of slightly worn velveteen', a third described him as 'a very ordinary young man ... his appeal eludes me'. And a fourth said quite superciliously: 'Pardon my yawn.'

Earlier in the year, the brilliant American film critic, James Agee, had been more eloquent, but no more flattering. '*Higher and Higher* is one for the museums,' he wrote, 'nor is that just a crack. Sinatra adds to his most famous advantage that of being, obviously, a decent enough sort; he also has weird, fleeting resemblances to Lincoln, which I think may help out in the audience sub-conscious. Through most of the film Sinatra is just a sort of male Mary Pickford, a mock-shy, poised young man huskily husking Occidental and very mortal corn. At the end, thanks to a stroke of simple genius on the part of director Tim Whelan, he stands without visible support among the clouds, in an effect which could be described only in the unassailable terms of an erotic dream and swells from a pinpoint to a giant. Higher and higher indeed . . .'

Young Sinatra's list of female admirers was, however, still growing. It then included even one of Broadway's most acidulous columnists, with whom he was later to feud viciously. In a 1944 fan magazine article, Dorothy Kilgallen listed *The Stars I'd Like to Be Married to (If I Weren't Already Mrs. Richard Kollmar)*. Frank's name not only figured in a list that included Crosby, Joel McCrae and Don Ameche; it led all the rest. Kilgallen gave two reasons for choosing Sinatra to head her heart-parade: he wouldn't swoon over anybody else and he would never lack for sweet words.

When Frank arrived on the MGM lot for the shooting of *Anchors Aweigh*, friends reported—and how fortunate that Miss Kilgallen did not know at the time—that he hung a list of desirable females in his dressing room. As the shooting proceeded, pencil lines were drawn through various names. One day Frank, in sailor uniform, visited another set to talk with Lana Turner in WAC uniform; she was starred in another wartime vehicle *Keep Your Powder Dry*. Then divorced, Lana was making the rounds with Turhan Bey, Robert Stack, Peter Lawford—and before long, with Frank Sinatra.

If Frank's nights off the set were not without complications, his days on the lot were not without controversy. One involved a certain radio and newspaper columnist who claimed that Frank told him: 'If you want to speak to me, get in touch with my agent.' The rumour spread. Frank tried to explain that this had nothing to do with other press people. On the air, the snubbed columnist blasted Sinatra for getting 'too bigheaded'. After a time, Frank's dressing-room door carried a sheet of paper tacked to it: 'We, the undersigned and those who know him well,' the statement read, 'know that Frank's head size is normal and that his hat will continue to fit.' Signed by his co-stars Gene Kelly and Kathryn Grayson as well as every member of the cast, it did not put a quietus on the charge.

'Frank was born to be a star,' publicist George Evans once said, 'but he was also born to be a controversial figure, and a star and controversial figure he will remain until the day he dies.'

By October 1944 he was in the middle of the earliest, and one of the hottest controversies of his career. Papers across the country carried a UP story in which he was quoted as saying: 'Pictures stink. Most of the people in them do, too. I don't want any more movie acting. Hollywood won't believe I'm through, but they'll find out I mean it.' Film stars came in for a stinging slap: 'It's a good thing not any of these jerks came up as rapidly as I did. If they had, you couldn't get near them without running interference through three secretaries.'

For two days there was no comment from Sinatra. But behind the scenes, there was much activity, involving his press agent and manager, attorneys, and outraged studio people. Finally, a statement of denial appeared in *Daily Variety*: 'Now, wouldn't I be a sucker,' it read, 'to shoot off like that? Hollywood and the picture people have been good to me. Sure, I'm going to stay in pictures. That is, as long as they want me. But for those things the paper quoted me as saying, I was downright amazed when they showed me the clipping. I couldn't believe that such a story could be made of some reporter's imagination.'

But the UP correspondent who wrote the story denied that the quotes were a figment of his imagination. Hal Swisher told *Daily Variety* that he had interviewed Frank on the evening of October 8 at the Hollywood Bowl and that Hank had been accurately quoted. Sinatra announced that he would demand a retraction and that legal redress was being considered. Swisher countered that Frank had said everything attributed to him 'and more'.

At this point Sinatra's personal manager stepped into the fray. Al Levy did not deny that Frank had made the statement. 'It was the hottest day of the year,' he told *Daily Variety*, 'and Frank was pouring sweat while attendants were helping him out of a heavy sailor suit. One of the grips twitted him, "What do you think of pictures now?" When his head finally came out of the sailor blouse, Frank grinned: "They stink." Naturally he was tired. But the crack was never intended for that fellow with the glasses (Hal Swisher), who was interviewing Jose Iturbi (he played a Hollywood Bowl concert in the film) a short distance away. That, I assure you, is as close to a UP man as Frank got that day.'

Levy's explanation sounded plausible. But MGM studio heads were not satisfied. Contacted by studio publicists, Swisher agreed to use a prepared statement. Sinatra's statement as it came from the MGM press department read: 'It's easy for a guy to get hot under the collar. Literally and figuratively, when he's dressed in a hot suit of navy blue and the temperature is 104° and he's getting over a cold to boot. I think I might have spoken too broadly about quitting pictures and about my feeling towards Hollywood. I'm still under a seven-year contract to RKO, which has six years to run. I have one more commitment at Metro following *Anchors Aweigh* and believe me I intend to live up to my contractual obligations.'

The following day *Daily Variety* reported that Frank had decided to forget his differences with UP. As threats of possible legal redress evaporated, he was put to bed by his doctor who found he was running a fever along with the cold he was nursing. ' "Pictures stink," ' *Daily Variety* observed, 'may go the way of all unsolved mysteries.' Not long afterwards, Frank told a music trade-paper 'I never made that statement ... My friends in Hollywood know me too well to believe that I'd ever be that kid of ingrate. I'm too fond of Hollywood and the people who live there.'

For much of the year, Sinatra and his advisers puzzled over the problem of controlling his youthful following, particularly during broadcasts when the shrieks irritated home listeners. Once when he was on the air from New York, he said sternly to balcony squealers 'You and I are going to have a serious talk about this.'

'With earnest shyness, the precise quality that brings on the shrieks,' according to a female reporter who was present, he proceeded to explain that the show was recorded and shipped overseas for re-broadcast. 'They don't like all that noise,' he said, 'and after listening to the records, I don't blame them ...' He paused. Then, grinning boyishly under a golden suntan and with new caps showing on his uppers, he added: 'After the show you can tear down the balcony if you want to.'

Shortly afterwards, Frank and his associates tried another approach. Youngsters entering the broadcasting theatre were greeted with prominently displayed signs that read: 'Only children under fifteen allowed to squeal.' Yet when Frank came to New York for his big Paramount date on Columbus Day 1944, the fans seemed beyond control. As the curtain rose for his first broadcast, he was greeted with a roar that overloaded the transmitting lines. 'It's always wonderful to come back to New York,' he grinned, 'because well—because this always happens.' Then he warned the bobbysoxers that police were stationed throughout the theatre to eject anyone who screamed. 'If you've heard our shows from California,' he added, 'you know how nicely our girls out there behave themselves.'

A major reason for the concern of Frank's advisers over uninhibited fan antics was their desire to broaden his following and attract adult listeners. By the end of 1944, both George Evans and Wick Crider, who handled press relations at the J. Walter Thompson advertising agency, felt that Frank had made real headway in coping with this problem. Observing that many more older people were attending his broadcasts, they traced this development in part to Frank's political activity.

The entry into politics came one afternoon in September 1944 when Sinatra and a bunch of the boys were having drinks at the Store (an inside designation for Toots Shor's restaurant in Manhattan). A long-distance phone call took the owner momentarily away from the prolonged cocktail hour. On his return, the shiny-faced, ruddy-complexioned Mr. Shor announced nonchalantly that he had just had a phone call from the White House. Democratic national chairman Robert E. Hannegan had invited him and his wife to attend a reception. 'I knew my missus couldn't go,' he said later, 'because she wasn't feeling well and I knew how much Frank admired FDR. So I asked if I could bring him and Rags Ragland with me. Hannegan called back and said it was okay.'

On September 28, the crooner, the comic and the ex-bouncer-turned-restaurateur, flew to Washington where a large complement of reporters met them at the White House east gate. Over tea, Sinatra was able to exchange a few words with President Roosevelt.

'Fainting, which once was so prevalent,' FDR reportedly kidded Frank, 'has become a lost art among the ladies. I'm glad that you have revived it.' Then, he asked Sinatra what song would be No. 1 on the Hit Parade the following Saturday. At the time, this information was a closely guarded secret; not even the musicians and technicians who rehearsed for the weekly show knew the exact order of numbers until the 'dress rehearsal' just before the programme went on the air.

'I felt as if I'd seen a-a-a vision', Frank later reported. Speaking at a Carnegie Hall rally of Young America for Roosevelt, he said: 'I thought here is the greatest guy alive today and here's a little guy from Hoboken shaking his hand. He knows about everything, even my racket.'

The hue and cry that went up in the press and among politicians is not easy to understand, despite the heat usually generated in an election campaign. In the Baltimore *Sun*, Frank R. Kent called the visit 'a cheap little publicity stunt'. Senator Wherry, a Nebraska Republican, announced: 'That crooner! Mr. Roosevelt could spend his time better conferring with members of the Senate who will have to pass upon his foreign policy.' Mocking him as the 'New Dealing crooner', Westbrook Pegler angrily denounced him for meddling in politics. The anti-Roosevelt brigade of columnists quickly joined the anti-Sinatra outcry.

If his critics thought that a concentrated attack would make him back off, they were not reckoning with Frank's contrary personality, the depth of his feeling for FDR, or the influence of his family background. As a youngster, he had been well indoctrinated by his mother's activities in the Democratic Party; he had marched in parades carrying posters for Al Smith and other Democratic candidates. As for FDR, 'he's the kind of man you'd want for your father', he kept telling friends. His son Franklin Wayne had been named after FDR.

Long before the White House visit, Frank had been considering active participation in the election fight between Dewey and Roosevelt. With the exception of George Evans, Frank's advisers warned against it. But Frank had no sympathy with the show business tradition of neutrality and non-participation. 'If I want to have my say as a citizen,' he argued, 'and doing it is going to hurt me in show business, then I say to hell with show business.' Later he wrote 'My first real criticism from the press came when I campaigned for President Roosevelt in 1944. A few columnists took me to task, insisting that entertainers should stick to entertaining. Most stars agree with this. They also realise it is bad public relations to indulge in politics because you may lose fans who don't agree with you. However, I feel it is the duty of every American citizen to help elect the candidates of his choice. Ginger Rogers, George Murphy and other stars supported Tom Dewey during this campaign, and I noted that *none of my critics lambasted them.*'

Joining the Independent Voters Committee of the Arts and Sciences for Roosevelt, he volunteered as a speaker to Democratic national headquarters and the Political Action Committee. 'I don't want these meetings ballyhooed like a show,' he stipulated. 'When I go some place to talk, I'm Frank Sinatra, citizen, not an entertainer.' Presenting himself as 'a little guy from Hoboken', he made a number of pro-Roosevelt talks over the radio. When he contributed $5,000 to the Democratic war chest, along with Sam Goldwyn and the Warner brothers, it was Sinatra who got the headline.

Among the columnists who joined the anti-Sinatra brigade over his politics was Lee Mortimer of the now-defunct Hearst tabloid, the NY *Mirror*. Two days after the announcement of Sinatra's contribution, Mortimer devoted much of a column to Frank. 'Even I grow humble,' he wrote, 'before the compelling force' of Sinatra's impact. 'It is inexplicable, irrational but it has made him the most potent entertainer of the day.' He added: 'I'll go further. I think Frank is a showman without peer, he has a unique and pleasing personality plus talent of the first lustre.' Now, Mortimer trained his verbal gun on Frank's fans, who had apparently been filling his mail-bag with accusatory missives: 'I love Sinatra but my stomach is revolted by squealing, shouting neurotic extremists who make a cult of the boy. As a friend, I call on the Hero of Hasbrouck to disown his fanatics. Neither they nor his projection on to the political scene can help his brilliant theatrical career....' This was the beginning of the Mortimer–Sinatra feud, a feud that eventually exploded into a fist fight in a Hollywood night club.

Frank's political activities also almost brought him to an impasse with his radio sponsor. The script for a guest appearance on the Jack Benny show called for a humorous reference to Frank's visit with FDR. Some time during the afternoon of his guest shot, the item was deleted. When Frank discovered the excision, he stormed out of a run-through. For a long, furious hour, he refused to return to the rehearsal set. When his advisers pointed out that a walkout would jeopardise his Hit Parade appearances, which were financed by the same sponsor, he relented and went on the show.

While he was still at the Paramount, announcement was made that he would appear at a Steel Workers' pro-Roosevelt rally at Trenton, New Jersey. The main speaker was Philip Murray, national president of the CIO United Steel Workers. On October 15 the capacity crowd at the State Fair grounds included more than a normal complement of girls below voting age. When Murray was introduced, he was greeted with a steady chant of 'We Want Frankie! We Want Frankie!' He waited patiently but the chanting continued. Then, the M.C. told the crowd that hazardous flying conditions prevented Sinatra from making plane connections in time to return for his theatrical appearances. The front rows of the stadium emptied in record time.

The climax of Frank's activities on behalf of FDR's fourth term came at a mammoth Madison Square Garden rally on October 31. Harry Truman, Fiorello La Guardia and all the big guns of the New Deal were present. When Frank stepped into the glare of the Garden spotlights to make his speech, his knees quivered and his tongue froze in a dry mouth. Completely self-assured as a singer, he was an awe-struck 'little guy from Hoboken' on the political platform. He managed to say that he was for Roosevelt 'because he is good for me'. He added: 'Since he is good for me and my kids and my country, he must be good for all the other ordinary (?) guys and their kids.' When he had completed his brief statement and left the Garden stage, he was like a shaken football player. 'Weak and dizzy and excited!' was the way he described it. 'But everybody was coming over to shake hands or pat my back. I'm not ashamed to say it—I felt proud.'

Editors of a current-events volume later evaluated his politicking as follows: 'Even the most rugged Sinatra-despiser had to admire the forthrightness with which he electioneered in the 1944 campaign. Except for Orson Welles, no radio performer was so effective a speaker for either candidate.'

On election night, Frank, Orson Welles and others awaited

returns in a suite at the Waldorf where he was to begin a singing engagement. Columnist Westbrook Pegler occupied another suite. When it appeared from radio returns that the fourth term was assured, someone in Sinatra's suit began kidding about how Roosevelt-hating Pegler would take the victory. 'Let's go down and see if he's as tough as he writes,' Frank supposedly suggested.

In a Blue Network broadcast, Drew Pearson claimed that, when Frank did not find Pegler in his suite, he mussed up the columnist's room. 'This was an absolute fake,' Pegler wrote in his own column. Asserting that Sinatra spent the evening at labour-leader Sidney Hillman's PAC headquarters, Pegler claimed that on his return to the Waldorf, Frank was tight and 'caused large disorder and was subdued by a house detective'. As for his room, Pegler stated flatly: 'He never did come near my quarters either in my absence or after my return about 1 o'clock in the morning.'

In a column he wrote at the time, Orson Welles stated that he and Sinatra had listened to election returns not at the Waldorf or Hillman's headquarters, but at Toots Shor's. Sinatra himself denied that he broke into Pegler's suite or mussed the room. He admitted, however, that he and his entourage had knocked at Pegler's door and had left quietly when there was no response.

Some years later, a Pegler aide presented still another version of the alleged incident. 'Peg was inside,' he stated, 'and he kept needling Sinatra through the door with things like "Are you that little Italian boy from Hoboken who sings on the radio?" Sinatra became so frustrated that he went back to his suite and busted up his own furniture, throwing a chair out of the window.'

Though this version appeared in Look in June 1957, almost thirteen years after the event, Pegler did not let it pass without comment. 'I was in my room at the Waldorf-Astoria continuously,' he wrote to the editors, 'from about 11 p.m. until rising time the next morning. No person knocked at my door during that time, and your statement that I was inside and the implication that I was afraid to open the door and confront a drunkard who had come to see how "tough" I might be is false, and no "aide" of mine ever made that statement to your reporter.' Look replied: 'There was no intention to impute cowardice to Pegler. Bill Davidson (the writer) obtained his information from a former Pegler aide.'

A more amusing episode of the 1944 campaign occurred one day in the street outside the Waldorf. While Thomas Dewey was greeting a crowd, Frank passed by. 'Two minutes later,' according to reports, 'Dewey was facing a handful of hard-core Republicans while nearby everybody else was trailing down Park Avenue after Frank Sinatra.'

In mid-November another columnist became critical of Sinatra. Harriet Van Horne, radio commentator of the defunct NY *World Telegram*, did not quarrel with Frank's politicking and even praised his courage in daring sponsor wrath. However, after a visit to a broadcast of the *Frank Sinatra Show*, she charged that 'an ingratiating boyishness' seemed to be changing to 'brashness'. The show was then experimenting with a new format, boy-and-girl routine plus a guest star, after Frank had met critical opposition for his efforts as a comedian. Although *Variety* found Frank's vocals superior to his Hit Parade warbling, Miss Horne soon followed her critical column with a second headed: 'Sponsor Drops Sinatra.' Observing that, perhaps, Frank's frail figure was not right for a vitamin sell—the sponsor was Vimm's Vitamins—she returned to the matter of Frank's patronising attitude towards his bobbysox adulators.

In a candid note to her, Frank conceded that some of his humorous remarks about his fans were, perhaps, in poor taste. 'Maybe I'm tired,' he wrote. But he admitted that he was also baffled. 'Did you know that dozens of kids have been hurt since I've been in NY this trip?' he asked. 'And did you know that the Police Dept. has specifically asked me not to stop on the street any more than I can help? I'm not playing the big hero part. I just like the kids and I'll be damned before I'll see any of them hurt because of me.'

Although Decca Records had settled with the Musicians' Union in October 1943, both Columbia and RCA Victor held out all through 1944. Shortly after the Election, at 6.15 of Armistice Day to be precise, both companies capitulated to Petrillo—and the rush to record was on. The following day, a Sunday, Victor hurried Vaughn Monroe into a studio. On Monday, Columbia cut Harry James. Frank recorded for the first time in a year on Tuesday the 14th. After the flurry of *a capella* recording the previous year, he and other singers had agreed to respect the picket lines of the Musicians' Union and he had not cut any sides after November 10, 1943. Before the year was out, Frank had participated in four sessions and recorded seventeen songs.

Saturday Night (Is the Loneliest Night in the Week), the Cahn–Styne wartime ballad cut on the first date, rode the Hit Parade for ten weeks up to the No. 2 position. *I Dream of You*, another Sinatra Hit Parader of 1945, remained for fourteen weeks in the Top Ten. Frank's choice of songs revealed a very selective taste that favoured show tunes, film songs and a small coterie of writers. (Sammy Cahn, with whom he had become friendly in the Dorsey days when he was writing special material for the band, and Jule Styne were his 'personal' writers, as Burke and Van Heusen were Crosby's and Cahn and, Van Heusen later became his.) Although Frank cut the well-known *Nancy* song on his third session in 1944, he held it back for a year until he made a version more to his satisfaction.

Today, most performers reject lyrics that exploit racial stereotypes and prejudices. In his December 3 recording of the *Show Boat* classic, *Ol' Man River*, Sinatra deleted the word 'niggers' and sang '*Here we* all work on the Mississippi', even before Oscar Hammerstein, 2nd, substituted the word 'darkies' in the printed version of the song.

VII

'THE HOUSE I LIVE IN'

In the eventful year that brought the death of FDR, the dropping of the first atomic bomb, the end of the war and the formation of the UN, Frank encountered movie director Mervyn LeRoy on a cross-country train. LeRoy, who was responsible for such favourite films of Frank's youth as *Little Caesar* and *I Am a Fugitive from a Chain Gang*, began asking Frank about his tolerance crusade, which was then garnering extensive coverage in the nation's press. As they talked, LeRoy became more and more impressed with Sinatra's sincerity. Quite spontaneously, he suggested: 'Why not put your ideas on the screen? Think of how many more youngsters you could reach.'

Frank had become a tolerance crusader as a natural out-growth of his espousal of Roosevelt liberalism. While his entry into politics brought criticism, his efforts to combat prejudice made him a hotly controversial figure. Everyone seemed to applaud when he slugged a Southern counter-man for refusing to serve a Negro musician. But when he spoke at a Carnegie Hall youth rally, some of the press threw scallions instead of orchids. All that Frank did was to urge youngsters 'to join with the youth of the United Nations so that we can live in peace with our neighbours across the sea as well as our neighbours down the street'.

In April 1945 he addressed a Philadelphia gathering of high school editors and Student Council presidents offering an analysis of the evil consequences of race prejudice. Whether they heeded the message or not, they came in droves to listen. In fact, two months later, close to 15,000 bobbysoxers tried to crash the Philadelphia Academy of Music when a rumour spread that Frank was attending a rally on juvenile delinquency. For two hours, police had difficulty in moving traffic and persuading a milling throng that Sinatra was not inside the Academy.

'This prejudice,' he told a reporter, 'it's nothing new to me. In Hoboken when I was a kid ... and somebody called me a "dirty little Guinea", there was only one thing to do—break his head. After I got older, I realised you've got to do it through education.'

Frank had taken steps to educate himself as soon as he sensed his power over the nation's youngsters. According to George Evans, he began asking about books he could read and avidly dug into Gustavus Myers' heavily documented *History of Bigotry in the United States*, Gunnar Myrdal's scholarly study of the Negro problem, *The American Dilemma*, Mary Fitch's *One God*, and other works dealing with prejudice, poverty and related problems. For a long while, he carried them with him, reading in planes, dressing rooms and through sleepless nights. Nevertheless, he told a reporter: 'I'm not the kind of guy who does a lot of brainwork about *why* or *how*. I get an idea—maybe I get sore about something. And when I get sore, I do something about it ... With grown-ups, it's not so easy—education. Kids are at a more receptive age.'

In an appearance before the House Un-American Activities

Committee, Gerald L. K. Smith, a home-grown admirer of Hitler and Mussolini, spent part of his time attacking Sinatra. Some columns seized the opportunity to suggest that even if Frank's eyes were blue, perhaps his ideas were a deepening shade of pink. Troubled or not by these unfounded allegations, Frank did not run scared. Sponsored by Lee Hats, he undertook a fifteen-minute coast-to-coast programme in which, instead of singing, he spoke on such matters as Veteran's rights, the Paris Peace Conference, and other public issues. 'I'm not a heavy thinker,' he kept saying.

At one point, after the Harlem riots of 1945, he addressed two integrated high school assemblies. 'Every race produces men with big, strong muscles,' he said, 'and guys like me ... There's no point in going around calling other kids names or indicating your racial prejudices.' In closing, he urged the students 'to act as neighbourhood emissaries of racial good will towards younger pupils and among friends'. Afterwards, he sang *Aren't You Glad You're You*, the Burke–Van Heusen ditty from Bing Crosby's film *The Bells of St. Mary's*.

About a week later, Frank flew out to Gary, Indiana, again to address a high school student assembly. White students were boycotting classes in protest against the admission of Negroes. When Sinatra arrived, the auditorium of 4,800 seats were completely filled. Students jammed the aisles and a crowd estimated at 1,000 stood in the street to hear him over amplifiers. At first, he was jeered and booed, according to a *Life* picture story. But before long, the students quietened down and listened attentively as he spoke and sang *The House I Live In*. 'A few people,' Sinatra said to an editor of *Ebony*, 'thought that I was way out of my depth in entering the explosive situation.'

The high point of Frank's tolerance campaign was, of course, the making of the movie short *The House I Live In*. Since Mervyn LeRoy and Frank were both on the RKO lot, studio boss Frank Ross was persuaded to donate film and facilities for the production of a non-profit short. LeRoy and Sinatra contributed their services while the screenplay was written without remuneration by Albert Maltz. The proceeds went to agencies involved in social work among adolescents.

The short has a slender story line. During a recording session Sinatra steps out of the studio for a cigarette. He encounters a group of kids hurling insults at a Jewish youngster.

Sinatra talks to the group about racial and religious prejudice, and climaxes his comments by singing the eloquent song that gave the short its title. (Written by Lewis Allen, writer of *Strange Fruit*, and Earl Robinson, responsible for *Ballad for Americans*, and presented originally in a Broadway revue in 1942 that folded overnight, the song became a world-famous copyright as a result of Sinatra.) In a discussion of the film, Frank told Louella Parsons: 'The children themselves are not to blame for religious and racial intolerance. It's the parents.... Kids hear their parents talking about the McGintys or the Ginsbergs and then think there must be something awfully wrong with being a Catholic or a Jew...' Adverting to juvenile delinquency, he said: 'No child is born bad. If parents were less selfish and took the time to teach their children that there is something else in the world besides greed and hate, we'd have a better world ...'

Columnist Harriet Van Horne, who had criticised Frank's attitude towards his fans, now wrote of an interview: 'I left with the feeling that here was a sincere, hard-working young man with a deep sense of his brother's wrong and a social conscience that hasn't been atrophied by money or fame.'

Before the year was over, Frank was the recipient, not only of brickbats, but of an impressive flock of citations. These included the Newspaper Guild's Page One Award, the Unity Award of the Philadelphia Masons and the first annual award of the Bureau for Inter-Cultural Education. Plaques were presented by the Hollywood Women's Press Club and the Amusement Division of the National Conference of Christians and Jews. At a Division luncheon attended by all the movie bigwigs, Frank said of the film short: 'You can't beat the kids on the head with eloquence and fancy words. You have to talk to them in their own language.'

Periodically subject to attacks in succeeding years for his anti-discrimination stand, Frank found himself being labelled 'red' as late as 1949. In July of that year, California Senator Jack B. Tenney released a list of celebrities whom he charged with various kinds of 'alleged fellow-travelling and Communist leanings'. Frank found himself in the distinguished company of John Garfield, Katherine Hepburn, Danny Kaye, Gregory Peck and Nobel Prize-winning novelist Thomas Mann. *Down Beat* headlined its story: *Clear the Decks—Sinatra Called Red*. Although Tenney used Frank's name, as the

House Un-American Activities Committee had previously done in statements to the press, Frank was never summoned to a hearing or given a formal opportunity to answer the unfair charges.

Regardless of the inner satisfaction he derived from his tolerance crusade, the greatest public recognition came in March 1946. On the 7th, the Academy of Motion Picture Arts and Sciences voted him and Mervyn LeRoy Special Oscars for their contribution to *The House I Live In*.

1945 began for Frank with a professional problem. On January 20, his Hit Parade salary was scheduled to rise from $2,800 an appearance to $4,000. However, on January 2, the public was informed that Frank had made his last appearance on the Parade and that his contract with American Tobacco Company, the sponsor, which had four years to run, had been amicably dissolved.

There had been beefs on both sides during his two-year tenure with the programme. From the start, Frank had not found the brisk tempo or the brassy, marching-styled arrangements to his liking. Nor was he too happy with some of the songs he had to sing. He had done whatever he could to reorientate the weekly review of popular song hits from a 'Happy Days Are Here Again' band programme to a singer's show. But he still had to adapt his own style to that of the programme. Once in the middle of a rendering of *Don't Fence Me In*, he had muttered over the microphone: 'This song has too many words.' A performer who liked to live with material before he presented it to the public, he did not enjoy learning several new songs a week.

George Washington Hill, president of the American Tobacco Company, had his own complaints. Prototype of the dictatorial advertising tycoon caricatured in the best-selling novel *The Hucksters*, he felt that Sinatra slowed the programme down and diluted the 'happy marching sound' he wanted the show to maintain. After Frank moved to California and his portion of the Parade was picked up from a studio theatre in Hollywood, Hill developed another beef. Sinatra entertained the live audience in the theatre during the periods when he was not on the air. But this, much to Mr. Hill's displeasure, prevented them from hearing the rest of the Parade and, in particular, the Lucky Strike commercials.

However, it was Frank's move to the coast that presumably led to the dissolution of his contract. To broadcast his portion of the Parade from Hollywood involved a $4,800 charge for use of musicians, studio KFWB and telephone lines. Since this extra charge had not been part of the original agreement, Frank was obliged to bear it. On a fee of $2,800 an appearance, he lost $2,000. When the January 20 option date approached, Frank's attorneys proposed that the American Tobacco Company either assume the burden of the Hollywood pick-up, or move the entire show to the coast. Mr. Hill vetoed both suggestions. Since Frank's salary was scheduled to rise to $4,000, the $4,800 charge would have raised the cost of the Hollywood portion of the show to $8,800. Furthermore, Hill wanted the show to originate from the east where it would be under his personal supervision. Frank's attorney offered a third alternative: that he be permitted to take a thirteen-week lay-off each year, which would allow for a reduction of the loss to him. When Hill vetoed his proposal, Saul Jaffee requested a contract release, and it was granted.

Sinatra immediately began a new radio series for Max Factor while the American Tobacco Company retained the vocal services of Lawrence Tibbett, Metropolitan Opera baritone. Mr. Tibbett also had difficulty in singing the lyrics to *Don't Fence Me In* at the George Washington Hill tempo.

In February, fourteen months after he had been classified 4-F because of the punctured eardrum, Frank's draft status once again became a highly publicised issue. Much to the consternation of the country's swooning females, he was ordered to report for induction on February 8. In a drizzle, which made slush of the snow that had fallen earlier, he appeared at Local Board 18 in Jersey City. With thirty-two other draftees, he was taken to an induction centre in Newark. He was accompanied by George Evans and Manie Sachs. As the group approached the 113th Infantry Armoury, a mob of 150 girls, who had been gathering since 7.30 a.m., spotted Sinatra and charged. He was pinned against a steel wire fence, his overcoat caught on the pointed, twisted strands at the top. George Evans tried to free him, but succeeded only in ripping his own forearm. Before Frank could escape from the mass of frantic girls, each of whom wanted a memento, not excluding a piece of his flesh, MPs had to be summoned.

At noon, the induction officer for the NJ district announced that Sinatra had passed all physical requirements, except for the condition of his eardrum. Later in the day, reporters were informed that Frank was to be taken to Governor's Island for further observation. When the news reached the girls, many of whom had waited in the slush and rain through the day, a wail went up and a number dashed across the street to St. Augustine's RC church, where they remained to pray and light candles.

By the time Frank came out of the Armoury, surrounded by MPs, only one girl was outside. In her arms, she clutched what had once been a heart-shaped Valentine's Day candy box, but was now nothing more than a sodden mass of red, rain-streaked paper and squashed chocolates. When the girl saw Frank, she charged. The MPs intercepted her and pushed her before them as they moved towards an army car that was taking Frank to Governor's Island. The girl refused to back away but continued pressing to reach Frank. Finally, the MPs got him into the car. As it rode off, the girl stood staring woefully after it, the crushed candy box still clutched in her arms, her tears mingling with the falling rain.

After the visit to Governor's Island, Sinatra's status was changed from 4-F to 2A-F, meaning that his work was 'essential to the national health, safety and interest'. But early in March, his draft board decided that his swoon-making activities were 'not essential'. He was thereupon re-classified as 4-F, and the likelihood of his being drafted disappeared.

On a Friday afternoon in March, Frank boarded a New Haven railway train with George Evans. He was scheduled to appear at an interfaith rally in Boston. Just before the train pulled into New Haven, he arose from his seat, telling Evans he wanted a drink. Some time after the train left the New Haven station, Evans decided that he, too, needed a drink and headed for the club car. He was surprised not to find Sinatra there, but assumed that Frank had returned to his seat. Frank was not in his seat, nor was he to be found on the train. Evans spent the remainder of an uneasy trip, trying to invent a plausible explanation for Sinatra's failure to appear at the rally.

On his arrival, Evans told the disappointed assembly that he and Frank had started for Boston together, but that a sore throat with which Frank had wakened, had become so bad that he had left the train to seek medical aid. Most of the fans accepted the explanation. The more cynical, however, manifested their disappointment vocally. As the shouts of displeasure began to mount into a demonstration of disapproval, a fan rushed to the microphone and cried: 'You ought to be ashamed of yourself doubting Mr. Sinatra. He is saving his throat for us.' After that, things quietened down and the rally proceeded as scheduled.

The only trouble with George Evans' explanation was that the following day a picture appeared in a NY tabloid showing Sinatra at the Tami Mauriello fight in the Garden. Frank was obviously shouting encouragement to the fighter in whom he reportedly had an interest.

In the spring of 1945, Sinatra took a trip up the Hudson River Valley that reflected the sadness of millions of people around the world. It was to attend memorial services for President Roosevelt. Frank made the sorrowful journey in the company of Jo Davidson, the bearded sculptor who was chairman of the Independent Citizens Committee of the Arts, Sciences and Professions. According to the columnist Cal York, no one in Hollywood felt the loss of FDR 'more keenly than Sinatra'. Noting that Frank had a large colour photograph of the wartime President on his bedroom wall and another next to his bed, York observed that Sinatra's 'devotion almost amounted to worship'.

By the middle of the summer, Frank was involved in a new controversy, this one generated by remarks he made after a six-week USO tour. Even before he departed, he took a beating in the press. 'Veteran of Okinawa "Bumped" by Sinatra' was the head on a May 21 AP dispatch. The NY *Times* was among the papers that printed the story of a signalman 3-C who had allegedly been delayed in Los Angeles, on his way home from the Pacific, because he was forced to yield his seat to Sinatra. The signalman from Mt. Vernon, Illinois, admitted that Frank had waited with him until he was assured of a seat on the next plane. 'Frank did not bump any one,' manager Al Levy said in a release: he had been given a priority so that he would be in New York for a USO rehearsal, before leaving to entertain the troops overseas. Since the *Times* was not anti-Sinatra, as much of the Hearst press was, its use of the incident suggested a growing alienation in the public's attitude towards Frank.

Unquestionably, his 4-F classification did not help his popularity with servicemen and their families, as his former manager, who was stationed at Camp Haan in Riverside, Calif., had already warned him. Frank had tried to increase his visits to army hospital and camps. One afternoon, in a recuperation centre in Van Nuys, he became acquainted with a group of sixteen soldiers awaiting discharge. When they returned to their homes, each found a $100 cheque with a friendly note from Frank.

As he embarked on his USO tour in a small company, which included comic Phil Silvers and song-writer Saul Chaplin as his accompanist, Frank was not unconcerned as to how he would be received. A GI who attended a show in Leghorn, Italy, later reported that crowds not only jammed the stadium but hung out of the trucks parked nearby. 'There were few nurses or WACs' the sergeant wrote. 'Most were GIs come to see what all the shouting was for ... Finally, the moment arrived. Silvers gave Frank a fine build-up. Sinatra was a little nervous ... A few jeers came from the boys. But after a few songs, his personality took its toll and the audience began to get the feeling that here was a helluva swell guy. Frank relaxed and began to joke and ridicule his affect on the soxers. Everyone began to have fun, including The Voice. They began applauding as they recognised some of the songs he sang ... It took guts to face those boys. If this is any criterion, his overseas jaunt should help Sinatra a great deal.'

It doubtless did. But it did not prevent the onset of a large-sized brouhaha on his return. Instead of tactfully remaining silent, Frank sounded off against USO camp shows for the poor quality of shows sent abroad, the arrogant handling of touring artists, and the lack of professional show-biz experience among Army Special Services men who assembled the shows. 'Shoemakers in Uniform', was one of the phrases attributed to him and given wide circulation.

He was immediately assailed by his usual detractors. 'This time it appears,' Lee Mortimer wrote, 'that Sinatra took on more than the juve delinqs can shriek off for him ... What angered the Rialto most of all was the thought that the 4-F from Hasbrouck Heights waited until hostilities were over in the Mediterranean to take his seven-week joy ride, while fragile dolls like Carole Landis and ageing, ailing men like Joe

E. Brown and Al Jolson subjected themselves to enemy action, jungle disease and the dangers of travel through hostile skies from the beginning of the war.'

If Frank could shrug off Mortimer, he was certainly not insensitive to the critical attitude of *Stars and Stripes* and a number of performers. 'Mice make women faint too,' the service newspaper sneered. And Marlene Dietrich, who had spent considerable time entertaining troops before V-E Day, remarked: 'You could hardly expect the European theatre to be like the Paramount.'

In his column, Ed Sullivan supported Frank's contention that USO shows were inferior and ran letters commending Sinatra for his forthright stand. Frank sent an appreciative wire: 'I am terribly grateful to you, Ed. If I hadn't said what I did, I would have felt like a traitor to those guys overseas. They were the ones who complained to me about conditions over there and you and I both feel that the GIs come first. I didn't mind taking a few raps if it will result in better things for those swell guys.'

As the controversy grew, Frank attended Joan Edwards' opening at the Waldorf. General Jonathan Wainwright, the hero of Bataan, was present at another table. Lee Mortimer commented: 'For once the surprised hero of the bobbysoxers was left severely alone by the autograph hounds who concentrated on the smiling hero of Corregidor. Maybe the world is returning to sanity after all.'

A few weeks later when Sinatra himself played the Waldorf to overwhelming kudos, Mortimer's review took this shape: 'Sinatra opened with *Paper Moon*, then alibied for not singing his best. Last year also at the Waldorf, Frank Sinatra pleaded the strain of the FDR campaign. This time, said strain of five-a-day at the Paramount took everything out of him. Then *Might As Well Be Spring* and *Laura* and another alibi. A patron called out *Chickery Chick* and FS said not his style. Sang *It's Been a Long, Long Time, How Deep Is the Ocean, Nancy With the Laughing Face*. FS said last number reminded him of someone in the nursery with an "infectious" smile. Mild applause and FS returned with no urging to *My Romance*. Again apologised saying: "I hope you'll excuse the rehearsal." Sang *These Foolish Things, Bess, Where Is My Bess, Embraceable You*. Customers coughing so FS did only one more, announcing in his cherce Joisey dialect—*Some-*

where Over the Rainbow from *The Wizard of Arz.*'

Most reviewers, however, discerned qualities in Sinatra's performance, which won him the *Metronome* Award as the Act of the Year (1945). 'Sinatra's act at the Waldorf,' the *Metronome* editors wrote, 'is typical of his actions before the public throughout the year. As in theatre appearances, as on radio, as in movies, he is sincere, straight-forward, completely unaffected, with no signs of temperament, no sign of the self-conscious artist, no indication whatever that he is conscious of how big he is or how much influence he wields...' In its citation, the jazz tradepaper praised his work for tolerance and his fearlessness in speaking his mind on the quality of USO shows. 'Ever since *Metronome* has known him, and especially during 1945, we have been impressed with the way he believes in himself, with his courage, with his direct approach to his fellow men...'

1945 was the first of Frank's three heaviest recording years on the Columbia label. Most of the tunes were ballads, sung at a so-called 'dream' tempo to lush, soft-rhythm, string-dominated backgrounds. Sid Skolsky's comment was: 'I like to hear Frank Sinatra, Dick Haymes or Andy Russell sing as much as the next guy, but they sing so slowly that I want to give them a shove and hurry them to the next word...' By comparison with his current sound, Frank's was smoother, more liquid and higher-pitched. His greatest, and most subtle, musical quality was his feeling for 'the colours' of sound. Shifting from deep chest tones to light head notes, from spoken words to extended vibrato, from softly whispered tones to hard-hit words, he was so skilful at varying texture that old melodies always sounded new. And the changing timbres gave the words an expressiveness in which no shade of feeling, however delicate, tender or painful, was lost.

1945 was the year of the wonderful ballads from *Carousel*: *If I Loved You* and *You'll Never Walk Alone*. It was a 'dream' year in popular music and Frank had *Put Your Dreams Away*, his closing radio signature, and *Dream*, a Johnny Mercer hit. Other strong Sinatra sides included *Oh! What It Seemed to Be*, one of his favourite songs, and two song-hits by Sammy Cahn, Axel Stordahl and Paul Weston, *I Should Care* and *Day by Day*, the latter the song that caused Doris Kapelhoff to change her name to Doris Day.

During 1945 Frank began to adventure as a recording artist. In May he did a session with the Charioteers, the well-known Negro group, cutting gospel songs like *I've Got a Home in the Rock* and *Jesus Is a Rock in the Weary Land*. And because the Latin sound was enjoying a revival with songs like *Tico Tico* and *Besame Mucho*, he cut two sides with Xavier Cugat, *Stars in Your Eyes* and *My Shawl*, Cugat's theme. In December Frank attempted the most ambitious of his experiments, an album in which he did no singing at all.

The novel project evolved when arranger-composer Alec Wilder brought to his Paramount dressing-room records of two compositions he had written for oboist Mitch Miller and the Columbia Symphony Orchestra. After listening to them, Frank inquired whether Wilder had enough similar material for an EP. When Wilder nodded, Sinatra said: 'Great! I think I can conduct. What's more, using my name might do you some good.' With that, Frank phoned Manie Sachs. 'I swear,' Alec recalls, 'I could hear Manie's chair going over backwards.'

'Conduct!' the Columbia recording chief exclaimed. 'Why, Frank, you can't even read music!' Nevertheless, Sinatra succeeded in persuading Sachs to let him do the album, *Frank Sinatra Conducts Alec Wilder*. On Frank's insistence, both names received equal billing.

When he arrived for the first session on December 5, Frank was unaware that a professional conductor was standing by, retained by Sachs to step in if he went to pieces. Wilder had prepared a chart showing at what measure various soloists entered. Later, a surprised and amused Sachs said: 'Here were all these symphony cats sitting around with their Stradivarius fiddles and goatees when Frank walks in, mounts the platform just like Stokowski, and raps for attention with the little stick. The musicians didn't know what to make of it. But Frank was smart. "I need your help," he said right off. "And I want to help this music." By the time he was through, they were applauding him and hugging him and patting him on the back.' Sleeve notes were written by Goddard Lieberson, then head of the Columbia Masterworks Division. (Frank calls him 'Valdimar', a corruption of Vladimir, ever since Lieberson took him to visit the great concert pianist, Vladimir Horowitz.)

In 1945 Sinatra also took giant steps in the film world. *Anchors Aweigh*, a big moneymaker for MGM, was rated No.

10 among the year's Best Pix by *Film Daily* while in Screen Guide's Anniversary Poll, it swept ahead in the balloting for Best Film and outdistanced *Lost Weekend* and *Bells of St. Mary's*. To Louella Parsons, it was the picture that 'moved Sinatra right up into the major star class'.

But despite his successes and the controversy and excitement Sinatra generated, 1945 was in many ways an even bigger year for Bing Crosby than for Frank. 'Bing's Bangup Box office in '45', *Variety* averred in a streamer head across the top of its front page and characterised The Groaner as 'the hottest guy in show biz today'. Its trade enthusiasm was quickly reflected in a *Newsweek* cover story that opened with a quote from Bob Hope: 'Don't worry about Bing. He's the man that made Sinatra's mother swoon and, in 1960, he'll be the man who'll make Sinatra's daughter swoon.' Earl Wilson told of how Crosby, in an LA hospital for a check-up, received 'the loveliest, the most adorable present' from his friend, Spike Jones. 'It was a picture of Frank Sinatra handsomely entwined with autumn flowers and framed in a bedpan.'

The end of the year brought Sinatra back to the Paramount and to the Waldorf where his now-relaxed approach to the swank set manifested itself in easy banter with the sometimes self-centred audiences. For the Waldorf date, Frank used Skitch Henderson on piano. 'I think I'd been out of the Air Force only two days,' Skitch later said, 'when he found me and brought me to New York. It was a terribly elegant engagement, just one show at midnight. That meant we had a lot of extra time, so he used to take me to the theatre almost every night ... He really rescued me.'

At the Paramount, Frank's conductor was Jan Savitt, another musician he had befriended. Although the engagement was without the street rioting that had marked previous engagements, the youngsters were a trial inside the theatre. A *Metronome* reviewer reported: 'Frank wore an alternative harried and bewildered expression as he tried his best to (1) introduce the acts, (2) sing himself, (3) keep the kids quiet, all to no avail. It's three years now that Frank has been doing this; it's a great testament to his showmanship and laryngeal talents.' Outside the theatre, the Inquiring Photographer of the *Daily News* asked passers by: 'Can You Describe Your Wife?' Frank replied: 'My wife is the most understanding and tolerant woman in the world. Just visualise what I have gone through in recent years and try to imagine how a wife can stand by, faithfully, continue encouragement, and raise a family. Believe me, sometimes I've sweated blood ...'

At about this time, Ed Sullivan devoted an impassioned column to a defence of Sinatra. Naming Rudy Vallee, Nick Lucas, Whispering Jack Smith, Cliff Edwards, Will Oakland, Van and Schenck, Morton Downey and Al Jolson as singers without social consciousness, Sullivan wrote: 'Then along came World War II to spawn a Frank Sinatra. From the unlikely springboard of crooning, Sinatra now has vaulted to the high and honourable position of the ancient minstrels, who became famous for bringing comfort to the underprivileged.' Sullivan added: 'Some performers will object that Sinatra is stupid to step out of character, suggest that singing and social significance shouldn't be coupled. But it seems to this observer that Sinatra instead has added something new and important to popular singing, a species of disinterested public service we should all render to the things in which we believe.' The column concluded: 'Sinatra strikes a graceful note in a national symphony that often seems too cynical and selfish.'

VIII

MINOR CHORDS AND MAJOR DISCORD

Late in 1946 a columnist of the Los Angeles *Daily News*, received a telegram from Frank Sinatra: 'Just continue to print lies about me and my temper—not my temperament. Will see that you get a belt in your stupid and vicious mouth.'

It was Frank's intemperate response, apparently without benefit of George Evans' counsel, to a column item that read: 'Where there is temperament I guess there's always a beef. First it was wife trouble. Then an argument with MGM over the singing of a song on the radio before its release in a movie. Before leaving for New York, Frank was mad at the LA press. And now it's a battle with a recording company.

While most citizens were suffering from shortages in the first year after the war, Frank's difficulties seemed to arise from over-abundance—too many bookings, too many meetings, and, as was apparent to the Hollywood community, too much night life. The many strains under which he had been living—exciting but nerve-wracking bobbysox adulation, domestic tensions, the fatigue of running all day and swinging all night, the strain of being constantly in the limelight—all began to take their toll. He was to quarrel publicly with his studios, the press, concert producers, the Screen Actors Guild, friends like Toots Shor, his wife and even his fans. And the year was to end with a landslide vote of the Hollywood Women's Press Club naming him 'the least co-operative star of 1946'.

There were good developments, too. At the beginning, a *Down Beat* Award, the third in a row, as the country's Favourite Male Singer. Various citations for his crusade against bigotry. And in April, just after he received the special Oscar for *The House I Live In*, a five-year contract with MGM. Providing a guarantee of $1,500,000, the MGM deal allowed him one outside film a year, sixteen radio guest shots, and the publishing rights to the music of alternate films. His weekly Old Gold show was renewed at $12,000 a programme. And there were record-smashing appearances at various theatres: in Chicago, for example, he set a new city record of $93,000 for a week's engagement. To better the previous high of $77,000, established when busty Jane Russell appeared on stage and on the screen in the sensationally publicised film *The Outlaw*, Frank had to push himself to do forty-five shows a week, singing eighty to a hundred songs a day.

Frank was not entirely responsible for his taxing schedule. On doctor's orders, he had tried to cancel out of the Chicago Theatre booking as well as the preceding week's appearance at the Downtown Theatre in Detroit. Brushing aside the medical warnings he had received, the managers of both theatres ran to *Variety* and announced that they were 'burned up' because Frank was being given greater guarantees than any previous performer. In Detroit his deal called for $25,000 a week against a fifty-fifty split while in Chicago, it was $25,000 against fifty-fifty of everything over $60,000. The adverse publicity, which appeared on page one of *Variety*, did its work. Disregarding his doctor's advice, Frank played the Downtown during the week of May 9 and the Chicago a week later.

In the midst of this professional tussle, Sinatra found time to step, as *Billboard* reported, 'into the middle of the Spanish question with an anti-Franco blast'. The Catholic *Standard and Times* of Philadelphia countered with an anti-Sinatra editorial, labelling him a publicity seeker and a 'pawn of fellow-travellers', and suggesting that Bing Crosby was a better equipped spokesman for American youth. 'Crosby, of course,' *Billboard* noted, 'has on more than one occasion gone all out for causes in which he believed, the most recent being his infantile paralysis chairmanship.'

A crisis of a different order developed at the time of the Louis–Conn championship fight in June. Frank and Toots Shor had planned to sit together. But Toots did not know that Frank was planning to bring actress Marilyn Maxwell. Since Toots was taking his wife, he was rather upset when he learned of Frank's intention. Though Sinatra was apparently talked out of bringing Maxwell, he sat, not with Toots, but with Marlene Dietrich and Joe DiMaggio.

Obviously, the relationship with Marilyn Maxwell had broader ramifications than just sitting together at a prize fight. Some friends believed that Frank was then edging towards an open break with Nancy. They did separate, albeit briefly, in October. Marilyn allegedly confided to friends that she was planning to divorce John Conte, her bridegroom of little more than a year. Both George Evans and Manie Sachs were vigorously opposed to the relationship, partly because of the possible harm to Frank's career but also because they questioned its depth. And Frank himself, despite the entanglement, did not take lightly to the idea of leaving his children. 'Hard work and extended play, I mean after hours, never hurt Frank,' George Evans once said. 'But emotional tension absolutely destroyed him. You could always tell when he was troubled. He came down with a bad throat. Germs were never the cause unless there are guilt germs.'

In August, as MGM was preparing to film his biography, Jerome Kern, composer of *Show Boat* and other hit musicals, collapsed while visiting New York and died on a Park Avenue sidewalk. A memorial concert was arranged. Long regarded as one of Kern's finest interpreters, Sinatra became the star attraction. At a rehearsal the evening preceding the concert, Frank became aware that Negro baritone William Gillespie was to sing *Ol' Man River* as the final number before the intermission. Frank was himself to perform the *Show Boat* perennial as the Grand Finale. Suddenly, the producers of the memorial show found themselves facing an unpleasant choice: Frank did not think the song should be done twice. Gillespie was paid but did not appear.

The aggressive career man could also be an unabashed sentimentalist and dedicated friend. On August 20, while he was still working on *It Happened in Brooklyn*, Frank received a frantic call from Phil Silvers. On the eve of the Copa opening of Silvers and Ragland, comic Rags Ragland had suddenly died. (One of Sinatra's companions on the famous visit to FDR, Ragland carried a $150 gold cigarette case inscribed: 'From Riches to Rags.') Frank did not hesitate. He flew to New York to sub for the dead comic. *Variety* headlined its story: 'Sinatra's Stoogery for Phil Silvers NY Nitery Preem an Inspired Event,' and commented: 'That appreciative gesture by Sinatra understandably sets him in a niche all his own in the big sentimental heart of show business.'

October brought two new pressures to bear on Sinatra. One came as a result of a ruling of the Musicians' Union raising recording fees. Like other companies, Columbia requested that its artists make as many records as possible before the new rates went into effect. Frank tried to crowd three sessions into October. It was a mistake. Of five songs cut on the first of the three dates, he later remade four: *Poinciana, Strange Music, The Music Stopped* and *None But the Lonely Heart*.

The other pressure developed as a consequence of a strike called by several craft unions against the major movie studios. Sinatra immediately announced that he would not cross their picket lines. But just before a meeting of the Screen Actors Guild called to discuss the situation, some strikers threatened to throw acid in the face of any actor who violated their lines. Sinatra arose at the meeting and informed a packed hall that nobody was going to tell him what to do; and that if anybody got tough with him—why, he knew some tough guys too. As Sinatra talked, members of the liberal bloc of the Actors Guild listened in consternation. Before anyone could reply to him, Frank left the meeting. Gene Kelly took the floor and, though he was a friend, condemned Frank's attitude and urged Guild members to support the strike. Tempers flared as another actor rebuked Kelly for criticising Sinatra in his absence. When tidings of the controversy reached Frank, he derived no satisfaction either from his impulsive comment or from Kelly's criticism.

On the Sunday night news broadcast following the Guild meeting, Sinatra fans were startled to hear that Frank had moved out of his Toluca Lake home into a bachelor apartment. He and Nancy had been married for more than seven years and this was the first open break. Although no reasons were given for the split, the columns had been buzzing for weeks with blind items. Louella Parsons observed: 'The items, even the innuendo, had some basis in fact. Frank was on a tear and he was tearing about publicly.' For a time, gossip had fixed on actress Marilyn Maxwell. But the name that kept coming up just before the separation was Lana Turner.

Immediately after it became public, Miss Turner tearfully told Louella Parsons: 'I am not in love with Frank and he is not in love with me. I have never in my life broken up a home. I just can't take these accusations.' To Hedda Hopper, Nancy 'confided' that Frank wanted freedom without a divorce. George Evans commented 'You know Frank has had a lot of career for one man and he hasn't had much time for home life. I think they'll get it straightened out.'

In the midst of the rift, a curiously prophetic encounter occurred in a Palm Springs night club. On a week-end evening Howard Hughes, millionaire industrialist and film producer, was in the Chi Chi with Ava Gardner, whom he was then reportedly dating. Sinatra and Lana Turner were likewise dining in the club. In the course of the evening, as they danced, the couples changed partners. For Ava and Frank, contact, but not the beginning of the relationship that actually terminated his marriage to Nancy.

Steps to bring the Sinatras together were immediately initiated by Frank's advisers. Manie Sachs flew to the coast. The Hollywood columnists, particularly the female contingent, all cheered for a reconciliation. 'Nancy refuses to attend any party,' Hedda Hopper reported, 'until she's sure Frank isn't going for fear it might embarrass him. Yes, she still loves him.' And Florabel Muir wrote: 'The betting is heavy for a quick patch-up.'

The estrangement ended dramatically, and publicly, little more than two weeks after the split. Frank came alone to Slapsie Maxie's, where Phil Silvers opened on the night of October 23. Somehow, Nancy came, too, in a party headed by Jule Styne. In the course of the evening, Phil invited Frank to do a song. Frank's choice was *Goin' Home*. As he finished singing, Silvers took his arm and led him to the Styne table. Frank sat down, embraced Nancy whose eyes flooded with tears, and they kissed. Chuckling, Phil Silvers put his arms around them to boisterous applause by the opening night audience. Leaving the table a few minutes later, Frank and Nancy spent the night at his bachelor apartment. The following evening, he moved back to the Toluca Lake home.

By coincidence, the issue of the NY *Daily News* that reported the reconciliation, 'Girl He Married/Frankie's Again', carried a story in an adjacent column headed 'Art's Note Flat/ Ava Goes Free'. It dealt with the divorce of Ava Gardner from Artie Shaw, married October 17, 1945 and separated July 8, 1946.

When Frank came east for his November 29 opening at the Waldorf's Wedgwood Room, he was accompanied by Nancy. Recently recovered from an attack of sinus and a chest cold, he looked so drawn that columnists commented on his need for rest and expressed the fear that he was pushing himself to the edge of a nervous breakdown. In a press conference, Frank announced that Nancy and he were definitely reconciled, but 'despite that California radio oracle', presumably Jimmy Fidler, they were not going to have a baby. He predicted that he would spend more time in the east, something that Nancy desired very much, and that he would build a house in Connecticut.

But Frank's predictions went awry. He did not spend more time in the east and he did not build a Connecticut house. But they did have a baby.

In October, just after the temporary separation from Nancy, five hundred film folk attended a dinner-dance at Ciro's to celebrate Frank's being voted 'the most popular screen star of the year' by the readers of *Modern Screen*. He had beaten Van Johnson and Cornel Wilde, who came second and third in a ballot of 180,000 readers. The dinner followed an air ceremony in which Louis B. Mayer, head of MGM, presented Frank with a bronze bust of himself. Commissioned by the publisher of *Modern Screen* at a cost of $10,000, the bust was the work of the eminent sculptor, Jo Davidson. Louella Parsons, on whose radio programme Frank had been a guest, reported that she had never seen Frank, 'who sometimes acts a little blasé and bored, as touched and pleased by anything as he was by the

Davidson bust'.

Frank and the bearded artist had been friends for almost two years when he sat for the bust. It was a strange friendship, considering the thirty-five year gap in ages and the contrast Davidson made in appearance, interests and cultural outlook with the men who composed Frank's entourage. From the days of the 1944 election campaign, they attended meetings of the Independent Citizens Committee of the Professions, Arts and Sciences of which Davidson was chairman and Sinatra, a vice-chairman, later of the newly formed UN Security Council and National Conference of Christians and Jews. The sculpting of the bust took the better part of a week. Only the lively discussions that took place between the two men, who had a genuine regard for each other, made it possible for Sinatra to sit still during the long sittings. 'His face has a curious structure,' Davidson said later. 'Those cheekbones! Those bulges around the cheeks! That heavy lower lip! He's like a young Lincoln.'

Neither honours nor the continued growth of his career prevented Frank from increasing manifestations of ill temper. Not too long before he left the coast for his Waldorf engagement, the Hollywood columns buzzed with rumours of a squabble with MGM. The studio contended that Sinatra had walked off the set for a rehearsal of his radio show before his day's work was completed. With Frank vehemently denying the charge, some columnists claimed that the studio was fed up with his presumptuous conduct and was ready to call it quits. Other columnists suggested that Frank was not overbearing but just overworked and tired. One reported that he had fainted a few minutes before his weekly broadcast.

He began his Waldorf act with a timely touch. Sipping a cup of coffee—the country was then suffering a shortage of java beans—he sang *The Coffee Song*, a novelty tune he had recorded late in July. Although he was well received, he was not relaxed. Whereas during earlier engagements he had been playful and charming in his handling of hecklers, now he turned on them with ill-humoured ferocity. One evening he shouted at a heckler—'You must be glad the war is over. Now you can get parts for your head!' Although the crack garnered applause, he later walked off the floor in the middle of a song.

While he was still at the Waldorf, he became embroiled in a

squabble that jeopardised even his carefully nurtured relationship with those responsible for his phenomenal rise—his fans. The faithful were still capable of such unrestrained displays that at the Boston Theatre while singing *Embraceable You,* for the lyrics 'Come to papa, come to papa, do' he urged, 'Please be quiet, please be quiet, do!' Late in November, concerned that adult listeners were losing patience with noisy studio displays, he suddenly eliminated live audiences from his broadcasts. After experimenting with this unsatisfactory set-up for two weeks—Sinatra needs a live audience even when he records—he made what turned out to be an even more dangerous decision. On December 10, CBS announced that all persons under twenty-one years of age would thereafter be barred from Sinatra broadcasts.

The howl of rage and resentment that rose from the ranks of Frank's followers caused CBS to request special police protection. They feared a riot at Playhouse No. 3, the shrine on Broadway and 53rd from which Frank broadcast. The riot did not materialise, but a sharp squabble in the nation's press did. Performers joined avidly in the controversy. Perry Como announced: 'Regardless of what happens elsewhere, bobbysoxers will never be barred by me ... If they want to let out a shriek now and then, well let them!' Van Johnson, whom Frank had nosed out in *Modern Screen*'s popularity poll, sided with him: 'Those kids in New York make life miserable for you.'

Precisely what part Sinatra's sponsors played in Frank's action is not clear. That Chesterfield was not entirely happy with him was widely known in advertising circles. The cigarette people were apparently not pleased with his desire to take a month's rest cure beginning the middle of January and were upset by a Sinatra guest shot on a Sunday show that competed with the *Parkyakarkus Show*, also sponsored by them. 'Apparently the crooning brigade can make everybody swoon,' wrote columnist Sid Shalitt, 'except the sponsors. Maybe all this explains why Frankie recently brushed off bobbysox followers in favour of adult fans. He wants listeners who are old enough to smoke!'

The controversy and speculation continued until December 19. On that day, just nine days and two broadcasts after the original announcement, Frank relented. He informed the press that when he resumed his broadcasts from the coast, bobbysoxers would once again be welcome in the studio.

During 1946 *The Coffee Song* was one of Frank's best-selling records, perhaps not as big as the Cahn–Styne rhythm ballad *Five Minutes More*, which Sammy Davis remembers hearing on the turntable of every Hollywood disc jockey he tuned in during a three-minute interval. Frank's other big discs of the year were the Styne nostalgic ballad *The Things We Did Last Summer* and the heart-rending *Full Moon and Empty Arms*, adapted from a theme of Rachmaninoff's *Second Piano Concerto*, and published by his own music company. Although he cut three of the top songs from Irving Berlin's smash score for *Annie Get Your Gun*, other artists had the hit discs on *They Say It's Wonderful, Doin' What Comes Naturally* and *The Girl That I Marry*.

Despite his onerous radio schedule, movie work and personal appearances, Frank crowded fifteen sessions into the year to cut fifty-one songs. October proved the busiest recording month, but not the most successful, for he discarded all the sides except one. During the year, he remade at least half a dozen other sides, including the famous *Soliloquy* from *Carousel*, a potent number in personal appearances but less successful on wax. Overwork was apparently affecting his voice as well as his nerves.

Doubtless the recording date that gave him the greatest satisfaction was a non-paying session, the last of the year, in which he recorded *Sweet Lorraine* under Sy Oliver with a group of the country's leading jazz musicians. The session originated in Frank's designation as Best Singer of the Year by *Metronome*. It was his fourth consecutive win. The supporting all-star band was composed of poll winners on each instrument: saxists Johnny Hodges, Coleman Hawkins and Harry Carney, trumpeter Charlie Shavers, trombonist Lawrence Brown and pianist Nat 'King' Cole. The session was an early indication, not only of Sinatra's feeling for improvisational music, but of the respect in which he was held by jazzmen themselves.

In 1946 Sinatra also enjoyed a distinction rarely visited upon popular singers even up to the present. He was the subject of a sympathetic, three-part profile in the *New Yorker*. The series by E. J. Kahn, Jr., appeared under the title *Phenomenon*, which became *The Story of an American Phenomenon* when it served as the sub-title of a slender volume *The Voice*.

IX

THE COST AND COMFORT OF VIOLENCE

In the early months of 1947 readers of *Modern Screen* became aware of a controversy that had been raging between Frank and Louella Parsons. In her monthly magazine column, Lolly printed a telegram from Sinatra, which read: 'I'll begin by saying that if you care to make a bet, I'll be glad to take your money that MGM and Frank Sinatra do not part company, permanently or otherwise. Secondly, Frankie has not been a very difficult boy on the lot. Frankie has only been heard from when it concerns the improvement of the picture, which you will find happens in most pictures where you use human beings. Your article claims my pout was caused by something about a song. (Lolly had rumoured in a November 14 article that Frank was being difficult because he was refused the publishing rights to a song in *It Happened in Brooklyn*.) Regardless of where you got this information, from some gossipmonger or otherwise, you can rest assured that if I pouted at all, it would have been for a much bigger reason than a broken-down song. As an added thought, I have always been one of the most stalwart defenders of the phrase "nobody is indispensable", so apparently your line about my being irreplaceable was all wet. Last but not least, in the future I'll appreciate your not wasting your breath in any lectures because when I feel I need one I'll seek such advice from someone who either writes or tells the truth. You have my permission to print this if you desire and clear up a great injustice. Frank Sinatra.'

The following month Lolly wrote that she was willing to call it quits even though Frank was allegedly still taking sideswipes at her. 'He isn't a well boy,' she announced, 'and when I heard he was really ill, he had my deepest sympathy. I was ill for a long, long time last year myself and I know that when you are sick, you just aren't yourself. What I am trying to say is that I can understand Frank's short temper and the way he feels. And I bet that when he's feeling shipshape again, we'll hear no more about his "temperament".'

A feud of more serious consequence erupted about the same

time between Frank and the late Robert Ruark of the Scripps –Howard papers. In the last week of February, Ruark ran three columns, datelined Havana, whose heads were: 'Shame, Sinatra!', '"Lovable" Luciano' and 'The Luciano Myth'. Ruark's target was the one-time head of the Mafia in the USA and his objective was ostensibly to expose the claim that Lucky Luciano had been freed from Sing Sing, after serving part of a fifty-year conviction, because he had helped in the Allied invasion of Sicily. As Ruark developed his exposé, he kept referring to the vice lord as 'Sinatra's boyfriend' and 'Sinatra's buddy'.

In his February 20 column, Ruark wrote: 'Sinatra was here (in Havana) for four days last week and during that time his companion in public and in private was Luciano, Luciano's bodyguards and a rich collection of gamblers and highbinders. The friendship was beautiful. They were seen together at the race track, the gambling casino and at special parties.' At one such party, given the day before Frank returned to Miami, according to Ruark, 'In addition to Mr. Luciano, I am told that Ralph Capone was present ... and so was a rather large and well-matched assortment of the goons who find the south salubrious in the winter, or grand-jury time ... Mr. Sinatra, the self-confessed saviour of the country's small fry ... seems to be setting a most peculiar example for his hordes of pimply, shrieking slaves. . . .'

Ruark's charge and innuendoes were quickly picked up by other newspapers. The NY *World-Telegram* itself dragged Sinatra's name into two front page stories about Luciano on succeeding days. Later, the list of Sinatra's alleged gangster acquaintances was amplified by others to include the Fischettis of Brooklyn, Miami and Chicago. It was claimed that Frank had been entertained in Florida by the three Fischetti brothers and that they had planned the Cuban junket on which Frank met Luciano. In an April column, Earl Wilson of the NY *Post* wrote that he 'got violently ill, but not in print as others did' when he learned that Joe Fischetti was to be Frank's host in Miami.

At the height of the press's attack, Frank informed one of the newspapers: 'I was brought up to shake a man's hand when I am introduced to him without first investigating his past. Any report that I fraternised with goons or racketeers is a vicious lie.' A much more detailed explanation was made by

Frank five years later in the *American Weekly*: 'What actually happened is that in 1947 I had some time off and decided to vacation in Havana and Mexico City. On the way, I stopped off at Miami to play a benefit for the Damon Runyon Cancer Fund. I ran into Joe Fischetti there and when he found I was headed for Havana, he told me he and his brothers were going, too. He changed his reservation to be on my plane...

'That night, I was having a drink at the bar with Connie Immerman, a New York restaurateur, and met a large group of men and women. As so often happens in big groups, the introductions were perfunctory. I was invited to have dinner with them and while dining, I realised that one of the men in the party was Lucky Luciano. It suddenly struck me that I was laying myself open to criticism by remaining at the table, but I could think of no way to leave in the middle of dinner without creating a scene.

'After dinner I went to the jai alai games and then, with an acquaintance, toured the night spots. We finally wound up at the Havana Casino where we passed a table at which were Luciano and several other men. They insisted that we sit down for a drink. Again, rather than cause a disturbance, I had a quick drink and excused myself. These were the only times I've ever seen Luciano in my life.'

This explanation was apparently prompted by a charge made in 1951 by Lee Mortimer of the NY *Mirror*, who accused Frank of going to Havana to deliver $2,000,000 in small bills to Luciano. Mortimer supported his claim by noting that, when Sinatra came off the Miami–Havana plane in the company of the Fischettis, he was carrying a valise. A photograph that appeared in *American Weekly* to illustrate Frank's 1952 by-line article did, in fact, show him carrying a small, overnight bag. Mortimer contended that stars like Sinatra did not generally carry their own hand-luggage off planes and that it was strange that the Fischettis neither carried hand-luggage nor offered to help Sinatra.

Frank's response was: 'Picture me, skinny Frankie, lifting $2,000,000 in small bills. For the record, $1,000 in dollar bills weighs three pounds, which makes the load I am supposed to have carried 6,000 pounds. Even assuming that the bills were $20s—the bag would still have required a couple of stevedores to carry it. This is probably the most ridiculous charge that has ever been levelled at me ... I stepped off the plane in

Havana with a small bag in which I carried my oils, sketching material and personal jewellery, which I never send with my regular luggage.'

(In passing, it should be noted that Ruark's exposé of Luciano's contribution to the Sicilian invasion was apparently in error. In a *New Yorker* profile (1964) of *The Honored Society*, Norman Lewis indicates that Italian resistance to the Allies collapsed when the head of the Sicilian Mafia began accompanying American invasion troops. The aid of the Italian mafioso was secured, according to Lewis, through the use of yellow flags and handkerchiefs bearing the black initial 'L', which stood for Luciano.

It should be added that in 1963 Ruark admitted that he had gone too far in his allegations against Sinatra. 'I am afraid I was unduly severe with Francis Albert for the company he kept ... Mr. Sinatra was a pigeon at the time because he was serving as a model for the nation's youth and the lads with whom he was cavorting at the Hotel Nacional did not seem fit associates for a model for the nation's youth.')

The verbal conflicts with Ruark and Lolly were a prelude to a more physical encounter with a columnist. On April 8, 1947, Frank dined with a group of music-biz friends at Ciro's on Hollywood's Sunset Strip. Lee Mortimer also dined at Ciro's that night. Before the evening was over Mortimer found himself lying on the heavily carpeted floor. Frank had indulged in what was to prove a costly form of self-expression.

The following afternoon, as he was rehearsing in a radio studio, Frank was arrested. At the Beverly Hills District Court, he pleaded not guilty to a charge of battery and requested a jury trial. The judge set bail at $500 and scheduled the trial for May 28. 'A thin, embarrassed smile sneaked across the skinny singer's face,' Florabel Muir wrote, 'as his hands went through his pockets and came up with nothing. Frankie couldn't cough it up. Spectators, lawyers and obliging reporters quickly pooled enough to let Frankie go free.'

In succeeding days, while investigators from the District Attorney's office interviewed witnesses, the LA papers fought the fracas over and over. One paper reported that Mortimer was nursing a bruised cheek, another that he was suffering from wrist bruises and a pain in the neck while a third stated that he was treated for a blow behind the left ear. 'What hurts most,' Mortimer reportedly said, 'is having to go through life admitting Sinatra knocked me down.'

According to the columnist, the attack on him was unprovoked; he claimed that Sinatra jumped him in the foyer of Ciro's as he was leaving, that he was struck from behind, and that, when he fell to the floor, he was worked over by three members of Sinatra's retinue. Frank asserted that he was goaded to the attack by verbal insults. 'For two years, he's been riding me,' he said. 'He called me a dago and I saw red.'

'How could I call him names,' Mortimer countered, 'when I didn't even know he was there? If I had known, I could have thought of lots worse things to call him than he claims. But as they pulled him off me, he said: "The next time I'm going to kill you, you degenerate"—degenerate, I guess, because I don't like his singing.'

Mortimer asserted that he had taken a Chinese singer, Kay Kino, to dinner to discuss her role in a show he was writing for the China Doll café in NY. The surprise attack, he claimed, occurred as they were leaving at 11.35 p.m. 'Sure, I've made a couple of cracks about Sinatra palling with Lucky Luciano,' he said, 'but I was privileged to do so and I don't retract a word of it.'

Sinatra stated that he had come to the club alone and joined some friends. After a time, he spotted the columnist and nodded a greeting across the room. 'He gave me a look,' Sinatra said, 'I can't describe it. It was one of those "Who do you amount to?" looks. I followed him out. I hit him. I'm all mixed up.'

Sinatra's attorney, Albert Pearson, insisted that the fracas was started by Mortimer who called Frank 'a dago' and lunged at him when the singer told him to mind his business. And Pearson denied that Sinatra had been assisted by anyone in the fracas. However, a photographer, who had been at the Ciro bar, came forward to lend support to the columnist's version of the affair. He claimed that he found Mortimer on the floor being pummelled by three or four guys. Four days after the encounter, Mortimer's NY outlet the *Mirror* announced that investigators from the DA's office had concluded that the attack was unprovoked and that at least one of Sinatra's friends, two hundred pound music publisher Saw Weiss, had participated in it. Weiss has always maintained that he did not participate but merely tried to separate the participants.

Daily Variety contended that more than the normal creakings of justice were behind Sinatra's arrest. At first, it noted, neither the DA's office nor deputy sheriffs were too interested in Mortimer's complaint. But the situation changed when the city editor and attorneys for the LA *Examiner* moved into the picture. 'It looks as though Frankie Boy has taken on the whole Hearst organisation,' *Daily Variety* observed. Apparently Frank had. There were headlines and stories in Hearst papers for five days running. In *Time*'s view, the space devoted to the incident was 'almost fit for an attempted political assassination'.

The divergent opinions of three NY columnists were typical of the split among the nation's newsmen. Ed Sullivan of the *Daily News* rejected the charge of gangster association as silly —'Some of the most reputable citizens of NY and Chicago met Lucky in Havana'—and argued that Mortimer had given Frank plenty of provocation for the attack. Jack Lait of the *Mirror*, Mortimer's superior and later his collaborator on *New York Confidential*, wanted to know 'who qualified Sinatra to clean up juvenile delinquency, plead for the underprivileged and assail discrimination?' and claimed that Frank hit his associate because he was 'the smallest'. Earl Wilson of the *Post* kidded that 'Frankie Shouldn'ta Done It,' but contended that Sinatra had struck a blow for his fans, whom Mortimer had characterised as 'imbecilic, moronic, screaming-meemie autograph kids'.

For his slugging of Mortimer, Frank faced a possible jail term of six months. The head of MGM, Louis B. Mayer, advised him to make a settlement. On June 4, 1947 at 6 p.m. Mortimer and Sinatra faced each other in the District Court at Beverly Hills. Frank arose and stated that the incident had occurred when an acquaintance, who stopped at his table, claimed to have overheard Mortimer make a remark which had aroused his anger. However, upon further inquiry, Sinatra had ascertained that Mortimer had made no such remark and that no provocation had really existed for the subsequent fisticuffs. Sinatra expressed keen regret over the whole affair. Mortimer arose and read from a typewritten yellow sheet edited in pencil. He had received satisfaction for the injury suffered; also, Sinatra had publicly acknowledged that he had not been called the vile names he had attributed to Mortimer.

Therefore, the DA requested a withdrawal of the charges against Sinatra. Mortimer consented. Instructing Sinatra to pay court costs of $50, the Judge dismissed the case. The proceedings took six minutes.

The out-of-court payment to Mortimer was known to be $9,000. But this represented only a portion of the total cost to Sinatra, estimated as follows by close friends:

		$
Court costs		50
Lee Mortimer		9,000
Sinatra's attorneys		7,500
Mortimer's attorneys		5,000
Detectives		2,000
Publicity representatives		2,000
	TOTAL	$25,550

'Was the Mortimer brawl,' a reporter asked Frank, 'part of your fight against intolerance?'

Frank replied: 'We all have our human weaknesses.'

While Mortimer and Ruark generated major problems, Frank was also plagued by a series of minor headaches. In January, tensions between him and his sponsor over a guest appearance on a competing show led to the cancellation of his Wednesday night CBS show. In March, after he had agreed to appear on the Academy Award show, he bowed out when he learned that he had presumably been called in to sub for Crosby. In April, the Hearst papers headlined a story: 'Sinatra Faces Probe on Red Ties.' Most of the article was actually devoted to composer Hans Eisler. But it was stated that the House Committee on Un-American Activities wanted to query Sinatra about his association with Communist front organisations 'as well as his written contributions to Communist periodicals'. No evidence was cited, none really existed, and Sinatra was never queried by the committee.

June brought Frank an estimated loss of $50,000. It came as a result of his first, and last, attempt to compete with the Twentieth Century Sporting Club. Frank sponsored the Jersey Joe Walcott–Joey Maxim heavyweight bout, which drew so small a crowd that Hollywood's Gilmore Stadium looked empty. Two weeks before the event, Frank had presumably tried to pull out of the deal. According to sports writer Dan Parker, he was 'told by the boys he'd have to go through with it or else...'

In September, the Hearst papers made a new move to smear Sinatra, this time by dredging up a seduction charge that Frank had faced during his Rustic Cabin days. 'The attempted smear of Sinatra on 1938 charges,' Ed Sullivan wrote, 'is rather stupid. The woman was thirty years old, mother of an eight-year-old child, not unmarried as alleged! The Grand Jury twice threw out her charges of "seduction" ... The stage-struck woman, and there are hundreds of them, still later was found guilty on disorderly conduct charges, preferred by Sinatra's mother, and sentence suspended by Recorder Romano in Hoboken Police Court. The date was December 29, 1938...'

Adverting to an article that Paul Gallico, sportswriter-turned-freelancer, had written a year earlier for *Liberty* magazine, Sullivan observed 'Paul really must have been looking into a crystal ball when he warned what the hate merchants would attempt to do to Sinatra. The public, however, isn't easily fooled ...' Gallico had written: 'My boy Frankie was doing all right for himself just mooing his songs and nobody had the rap out for him. He went and picked this magnificent fight all by himself...' By tackling the dark forces of prejudice, Gallico had warned, Frank was 'laying his career and popularity on the line and courting disaster...'

Despite the winds of controversy constantly raging around him and the unabating antagonism of an influential sector of the press, Frank's popularity seemed secure in 1947. When Jimmy Fidler conducted a poll of his ABC listeners on the 'Most Popular Living Person', Frank's name appeared in a group that included Dwight Eisenhower, General MacArthur, Eleanor Roosevelt and Bob Hope. 271,000 voters gave the No. 1 spot to Bing Crosby, the No. 3 position to Pope Pius XII while Sinatra scored as No. 2. In March Leonard Feather, the noted jazz critic, went to the Waldorf to investigate the rumour that Frank was on the verge of a nervous breakdown. 'I swear,' Feather wrote, 'he gets more sensational all the time...' Writing in *Motion Picture* magazine, Charles Hasting, a well-known journalist, contended that except for Rudolph Valentino, show business had not had a popular idol like Sinatra for half a century. After probing the sources of Frank's appeal, Hastings concluded that while Frank had started as a 'thrill salesman', 'he is ending up as the most important human being in all show business'.

Mid-March, *It Happened in Brooklyn* made its bow at the Capitol in New York. 'Great!' *Box Office* magazine wrote. 'One of the exceptional pictures that bulge theatre walls on week-ends.' Bosley Crowther of the *Times*, who had reservations about the story, as other critics had about the songs, observed that 'Mr. Sinatra turns in a performance of considerable charm. He acts with some ease and dexterity . . .'

Lee Mortimer agreed with his colleagues on everything except Sinatra. 'You'll giggle and laugh plenty,' he wrote, 'but only when Jimmy Durante is on the screen . . . Otherwise this excellent and well-produced picture . . . bogs down under the miscast Frank (Lucky) Sinatra, smirking and trying to play a leading man . . .' Referring to Frank as 'the apparition' Mortimer wrote: 'In uniform, he looks like a Western Union boy.' The review was dated March 14, less than a month before the punch that surprised Mortimer in the foyer at Ciro's.

Two days after the brawl, Frank appeared at a rally at Times Square to help raise money for the research fund of the American Cancer Society. Thousands hung from windows of office buildings, and more than 100,000 people jammed the streets, giving the Square on an April afternoon the appearance of New Year's Eve.

In June, Robert W. Dana compiled a list of the season's ten best night club performances. In reverse order, his top five were: Hildegarde at the Persian Room, Mitzi Green at the Copa, Carl Brisson at the Versailles, Jane Pickens at the Wedgwood Room, and, leading all the rest, Frank Sinatra at the Wedgwood.

Nevertheless, before the year was out, storm clouds were gathering on the horizon of Frank's popularity.

From November 13 to December 3 he appeared on stage at the Capitol Theatre in New York. In retrospect, this booking takes on special significance as the portrait of a new audience attitude. Walter Winchell reported that Sinatra's name was displayed in letters five times as large as those of Lucille Ball and Franchot Tone, stars of *Her Husband's Affair*. Seeking to capitalise on Frank's hectic receptions at the nearby Paramount, the Capitol advertised: 'First Aid Station for Swooners.' Not only was there no swooning, the overall attendance proved disappointing. Naturally, the *Mirror*'s columnist derived much satisfaction from this initial defection. 'Broadway whispers this will be Sinatra's last appearance here,' Lee Mortimer chortled, 'and that didn't kill my appetite for the family turkey dinner.'

The *Billboard* review was a rave. 'Sinatra is showmanship personified,' Bill Smith wrote. 'Sinatra is box-office today.' But despite *Billboard*'s enthusiasm, Frank was not box-office and Mortimer's joy was based on fact. At the end of the second week, Mortimer could gleefully cackle: 'Another big reverse is Frank Sinatra at the Capitol ... The crooner, expected to pile up new highs, almost hit a new low. His second week (in which he missed no performances) was a sickly $71,000, half of the advance estimate...' A more neutral newsman, Harold Conrad, also concluded: 'The Hoboken Hummingbird's popularity is on the wane.'

What caused this slip in attendance in person, the first for Frank? Doubtless, the headlines about his alleged fraternisation with hoods and so-called left-wing leanings, had had their effect, despite Ed Sullivan's hope that the public would not be fooled. That Sinatra and his advisers were aware of the potentially dangerous impact of these press raps is indicated by two meetings in which Frank participated. One was with Col. McCormick, owner of the ultra-conservative Chicago *Tribune*. According to Hedda Hopper, who was present, Frank 'talked with such animation that his bow tie flapped like gull's wings'. The other was with William Randolph Hearst, owner of the newspaper chain that included the *Mirror*, the *Journal-American* and the LA *Herald Examiner*, all papers that had been sniping at Sinatra.

1947 was the year of what has been called 'the witch-hunt in Lotus Land', the investigation of the movie industry by the House Un-American Activities Committee. Although Frank was not part of the Committee for the First Amendment, a protest group of Hollywood luminaries headed by Humphrey Bogart, that flew to Washington on October 28, Frank sided with those who were critical of the investigation. 'Once they get the movies throttled,' he said in a press statement, 'how long will it be before the Committee gets to work on freedom of the air ... If you made a pitch on a nation-wide network for a square deal for the underdog, will they call you a commie?'

Analytical stories by Hollywood correspondents may also have helped alienate fans. 'What's Wrong with Frankie?' Hedda Hopper asked, enumerating his ban on bobbysoxers at broadcasts, his conflict with a radio sponsor and his walk-out on Nancy. Arguing that Frank had married prematurely, Miss Hopper felt that he was suffering from accumulated nerves and too much success. 'Frank's tired,' she wrote. 'Let's don't hoist him on a pedestal with one hand and reach for a tomato to heave the moment he wobbles.' Even if he had been willing to slow down, which he tried to do at critical junctures, those who profited from his talents were unconcerned about the ill health that had begun to plague him so long as the public demanded him. In August, only five days after he finished the filming of *The Kissing Bandit*, he began work on *Miracle of the Bells*. And before the year ended, due to an impending musicians' strike, he was involved in a rash of recording dates that would have taxed even a less tired man. During the year Frank participated in twenty-five separate sessions, cutting a total of seventy-two songs; in December alone, he appeared in the Columbia studios for eight exhausting dates.

Not only was he in danger of 'over-recording', evidence was accumulating of a shift in pop music taste.

A signpost to the future appeared in the form of a stocky singer named Frankie Laine, who revived 1931's *That My Desire*. Employing a strenuous, foot-stomping, muscular delivery, Laine became the first of a new school of pop singers, 'belters' not crooners. Hillbilly or country music was also entering the mainstream of popular music, a development reflected in hits that Tony Bennett (*Cold, Cold Heart*), Rosemary Clooney (*Half As Much*), Joni James (*Your Cheatin' Heart*) and other pop singers derived from country songs. In the six years between 1947, when the hugely talented Nashville writer-performer, Hank Williams, was signed to an MGM recording contract, and 1953, when he died accidentally, country music enjoyed a great flowering—and, conversely, Sinatra's star drifted steadily downward.

That Frank was cognisant of the emergence of a new taste pattern is apparent from one of his December recordings. On the 8th, he spent most of a session cutting *A Little Learnin'* (*Is a Dangerous Thing*) with Pearl Bailey. Instead of Axel Stordahl, he used Sy Oliver, who had helped develop the driving style of the famous Jimmy Lunceford band. Whether he was motivated by the overnight success of the other Frankie, troubled by his weak box-office at the Capitol, or simply tired of the lush ballad style on which he had risen to fame, Frank clearly was beginning to seek a new mode of expression. *A Little Learnin'* foreshadows the swinging style Frank later developed on his Capitol discs.

Despite problems with his health, nerves and schedule, Frank went back on the Saturday night Hit Parade in the autumn of 1947. His dissatisfaction with the show's format led him to insist on using his own arranger–conductor, Stordahl. With Doris Day as his singing *vis-à-vis*, the portents were good. The results were not. 'The show is alternately dull, pompous and raucous,' *Metronome* wrote. 'Frank sings without relaxation and often at tempos that don't suit him or the song. Axel plays murderous, rag-timey junk that he, with his impeccable taste, must abhor. And poor Doris Day, making her first real start in commercial radio, is saddled with arrangements which sound as though they were written long before anybody ever thought of having a stylist like her on the show ... Frank sounds worse these Saturday nightmares than he ever has since he first became famous...'

If the Capitol Theatre appearance marked the onset of a downward trend for Frank, it cemented an important personal relationship. Appearing on the bill which included another Sinatra protégé, Skitch Henderson, was the Will Mastin Trio. It was their first major Broadway booking and represented a jump in pay from $300 a week to $1,000 plus transportation. Sammy Davis, Jr., then an unbilled member of the group, had known Frank since the Dorsey days. They had met at the Michigan Theatre in Detroit where the Trio once substituted for Tip, Tap and Toe, Tommy's regular opening act. On his release from the Army four years later, Sammy had attended a Hit Parade broadcast and was amazed to find that Frank remembered him and asked to see him backstage.

In his autobiography *Yes I Can*, Sammy tells of the lengths to which Frank went in order to bring the Trio to the Capitol. 'Just fantastic!' Sammy comments. 'He button-holed the Capitol manager and said: "There's a kid—Sam something. Don't know his last name but I want him on the bill!"' Locating the little-known Will Mastin Trio was not that simple; but apparently by systematically checking bookers and ultimately AGVA, the group was found. When Frank saw the theatre marquee, he came to their dressing room and shook his head: 'No,' he said, according to Davis, 'It's gotta read the Will Mastin Trio—starring Sammy Davis, Jr.!' Davis adds: 'It was the first time I ever got billing. It was the most. And the build-up that he gave us when he brought us on stage. For me, it was really the beginning. All the great things happened after that. Now, can you help loving a guy like that. And is it hard to understand why I idolise him?'

IMAGE 3

THE BLEEDER

At first this was an image of a man passionately in love but at war with himself. Unable to reconcile his drives as a lover with the guilt of a father leaving his children, he vented his frustration on newsmen. The public hardly approved of his intemperate outbursts and abusive conduct, or of his public wooing of Ava Gardner while he was still married to Nancy. But it sensed something of his torment from acts of self-pity in which he indulged and self-destructive tendencies which he manifested. The divorce he bought at considerable cost to his health, voice and career, brought little inner peace. The consuming romance turned quickly into a tempestuous marriage.

After the separation from Ava, his capacity for self-dramatisation asserted itself in maudlin scenes for which he used members of his entourage as his mirror. As the idyll of the great love faded into the image of the heartsick lover, he recorded songs like *No One Cares, It's a Blue World, There Will Never Be Another You*. He called his albums *In the Wee Small Hours* and *Point of No Return*. The lush, romantic backgrounds of arranger Axel Stordahl were replaced by brooding, Tchaikovsky-stepped scores by Gordon Jenkins. The songbird of yearning was now the bittersweet balladeer of heartbreak.

Clowns had long been his favourite subject as an amateur painter. By the time he chose a Volpe painting of himself as a clown for the cover of an LP, he was fabulously successful and wealthy again. But the ambivalence of the Pagliacci image had already been imprinted on the public's consciousness, and its torsional contribution to the Sinatra mystique persisted.

x

DOWNDRAFT

Late in 1948, Sammy Davis, Jr., was cantering through Manhattan's theatre district. Spotting Sinatra at a distance, he began to call to him but immediately suppressed his cry—for 'Frank was slowly walking down Broadway with no hat on and his collar up and not a soul was paying attention to him. This was the man who only a few years ago had tied up traffic all over Times Square ... Now the same man was walking down the same street and nobody gave a damn!'

The year that Harry Truman was able to grin at a headline prematurely giving the presidency to Thomas E. Dewey, Hollywood's bigwigs were holding their heads over TV's inroads into film grosses. And Sinatra was in an aspirin mood over a bevy of bad press notices. It started with *Miracle of the Bells,* released by RKO in March.

Frank had actively sought the role of the Catholic priest, desiring a more challenging part than the song-and-dance man and shy singing sailor he had been playing. Riding west on the Chief, he had read the novel by Russell Janey, and remembering, perhaps, what a priest role had done for Bing Crosby, he wired Lew Wasserman of MCA. It took some string-pulling, for several columnists threw red mud to keep him from getting the role of Father Paul. It was only after producer Jesse Lasky had consulted the Catholic hierarchy and found that there was no objection to Sinatra, that the role was his.

Miracle had a $3,000,000 budget. A complete church was erected on the Culver City lot. Frank was so excited over the prospect of a new kind of movie career that, on receipt of a tolerance award voted by five hundred newspaper editors, he announced that he would turn his salary over to the Church. To preserve the character of the humble priest, he sang only one song *Ever Homeward*, and this, *a capella.*

Then in March 1948 came the reviews. Despite a script by Ben Hecht and Quentin Reynolds, the reviews were salted with adjectives like 'pompous', 'unreal', 'over-stated', 'murky', 'sentimental' and 'overlong'. The most favourable comment on Sinatra was that he was 'thoughtful' and 'appealing'. Most critics described his performance as *lifeless* while *Time* was typically acidulous: 'Frank Sinatra, looking rather flea-bitten as the priest, acts properly humble or perhaps ashamed.' Not even a moderately good box-office, which prompted *Time* to remark that the picture was 'a measure of the depth of US pseudo-religious depravity', could make up for comments like: 'Sinatra plays the priest with the grace and animation of a wooden Indian.'

'It was a blow to his ego,' Louella Parsons observed, 'and his reaction was to get tougher, meaner and harder to get along with...' Frank's contract called for his presence at the film's première, a charity affair at a San Francisco theatre. Unwilling to go but unable to persuade producer Jesse Lasky to let him off the hook, he took petulant revenge. With the trip's expenses being borne by the studio, he spent lavishly, charging quantities of men's wear purchased for his entourage at a swank shop and the cost of having a piano delivered to his suite one morning at 4 a.m. For the trip back to Palm Springs, where he had just built a new home, he rented a chauffeur-driven limousine at studio expense.

The adverse press on *Miracle of the Bells* was not the only blow to his ego. About the same time, *Life* came out with a wrap-up review of the preceding year's films. As 'the worst single moment' in any film, it selected a scene in *Till the Clouds Roll By*: 'MGM struck a high point in bad taste when Frank Sinatra stood on a fluted pillar and crooned *Ol' Man River*, including the line "You and me, we sweat and strain...", wearing an immaculate white suit.' *The Kissing Bandit*, released by MGM late in the year, fared no better than RKO's *Miracle*. The picture was dismissed as 'a grand technicolor vacuum' and 'a costume piece ... with a little vaudeville thrown in'. Of Sinatra's performance, Bosely Crowther wrote in the *Times*: 'Except for appearing gawky, which seems not very hard for him to do, and singing the Nacio Herb Brown songs rather nicely, he contributes little...' Justin Gilbert of the *Mirror* went further: 'While his songs aren't bad,' he wrote, 'his acting is.'

While Earl Wilson interviewed him one day at the Toluca Lake house, a store delivered a book on the *Technique of Oil Painting*. Frank worked at the new hobby with the kind of concentrated intensity he gave to any new undertaking. He particularly liked painting clowns for the bright colours they required; also, perhaps, because he had begun to see in them a reflection of his own tragic-comic situation. Through sleepless nights, he avidly read new novels, searching for dramatic roles. When the part of Nick Romano, the young killer of *Knock on Any Door*, went to John Derek, he felt frustrated. Restive, he occupied himself with forays into various grandoise business schemes. One involved a $2,000,000 development at Salton Sea, Calif., to rival Palm Springs. Considering the teeming community that has since sprung up there, it was obviously a sound idea. But like other schemes, specifically a West Coast Madison Square Garden, it never got beyond the talking stage.

Frank was hardly in a frame of mind to repair his splintered marriage. But he was trying. In June of 1948 came the birth of Christina, his third child. It was the only birth at which he was present, pacing the waiting room of the Cedars of Lebanon Hospital on the 20th. His flagging spirits were given a lift, doubtless, by the purchase of a new $250,000 home in the swank Holmby Hills section of Beverly Hills. Situated near Humphrey Bogart's house, it boasted fifteen rooms, a pool and a walled-and-cobbled courtyard. It is still occupied by the first Mrs. Sinatra.

There is no indication, however, that any of these developments really helped to bolster the sagging home foundation. Hedda Hopper, among other visitors to the new home, came away feeling that the union was finished. Through dinner and a festive evening, Frank was restless and bored, according to Miss Hopper, and Nancy, openly petulant, 'as if she sensed that she had lost the battle'.

During the filming of *Take Me Out to the Ball Game* in which Frank played a dancing ball player, L. B. Mayer asked him to sing at a meeting of the National Conference of State Governors at Sacramento. The request for Sinatra had come from the California Governor Earl Warren, who had offered to fly him there and back in his private plane. Since Mayer and Warren were Republicans, and Frank was to be the only entertainer, the invitation was a feather in Sinatra's cap as well as Mayer's. A tyrant about working hours, L. B. agreed that Frank could leave the set at 2 p.m. One hour later when Jack Keller, his press agent, and Dick Jones, his accompanist, arrived to escort him to the waiting plane, Frank was not to be found. Reluctantly, they notified Mayer's office. A further check of the studio lot revealed that Frank's car was still parked in the spot reserved for it; but there was no sign of Sinatra. After a time, an irritated and furious Mayer wired Warren that Frank had been taken ill. Why Frank changed his mind remains unexplained, unless it was just his way of mocking authority. Those who were curious about his whereabouts that afternoon learned that he had ridden past the studio gate, hidden in the back of a pick-up truck, and gone home.

Figures released by the Securities and Exchange Commission for 1948 indicate that, despite his waning popularity, Sinatra received $325,833 from MGM. This was just $39,000 less than Warner Bros. paid Bette Davis, then the most highly paid star on the screen. But rumour had it, as Sheilah Graham reported, that Sinatra 'not only can't save anything but that he is behind with his income tax'. In her end of the year *Photoplay* article, Miss Graham suggested that it would be a grand New Year in Hollywood if Sinatra could 'actually accumulate some of the millions he earns annually'; also, parenthetically, if Ava Gardner would say 'yes' to Howard Duff, who had been wooing her for more than a year.

Frank's easy way with a buck was something of a novelty in Hollywood. 'Movie stars are among the most penurious souls in creation,' according to magazine-writer Bill Davidson, who claims that in twenty years of cocktails and meals with luminaries, only two ever picked up his check—Spencer Tracy and Clark Gable. With Sinatra, conspicuous spending was natural, if not compulsive. Sheilah Graham estimated that he had earned $11,000,000 in six years but had a struggle paying his taxes, and that a dream cottage in Palm Springs slated to cost $30,000 wound up being a $150,000 nightmare. In this period, Frank joked with Sid Skolsky about a book he was planning to write. It was to be called : *All That I Am, I Owe . . .*

What made this period even more trying than criticism of his acting was that for the first time, Sinatra had to swallow adverse reactions to his singing. 'The Swoon Is Real Gone (and not in jive talk),' Lee Mortimer gloated, noting that there were no Sinatra discs among the Best-Selling Records and Most Played on Juke Boxes, and that the only Sinatra disc in a list of the fifty Most Requested of Disc Jockeys, was No. 49. In Mortimer's view, Sinatra's slide had started with the Luciano incident; but he was not unwilling to consider two other possibilities (a) that the bobbysoxers had 'merely grown up and grown out of Sinatra', and (b) that the swooning hysteria had just been 'an unhealthy wartime phenomenon'. If Frank could dismiss Mortimer's animadversions, it was not so easy to disregard the accumulating negatives in other columns. 'To Frank Sinatra, I award a new crop of bobbysoxers,' Sheilah Graham wrote. 'The old screamers are now in their sedate 'twenties. And without hullabaloo, Frank's voice doesn't seem quite so potent. Am I right?'

Judged in terms of sales and hits, Miss Graham was right. During the year, Frank's recording schedule was very much like that of 1944, the year of another musicians' strike; but the records did not register the same success. He had a record of *Nature Boy* a capella with the Jeff Alexander Chorus, but Nat 'King' Cole had the hit (arranged incidentally, though not publicised at the time, by Nelson Riddle). He had a record of *Once in Love with Amy*, key song of Frank Loesser's hit musical *Where's Charley* but the song was Ray Bolger's triumph. With the Phil Moore Four, Frank recorded *Why Can't You Behave* from Cole Porter's smash show *Kiss Me Kate*, again to no avail. Nor did the songs by hit-writer Nacio Herb Brown for *The Kissing Bandit* yield a best-seller.

'Right now certain conditions in the music business really have Sinatra down,' George Simon observed in *Metronome*. 'Chances are that he can't stand "Your Hit Parade" any more than most of us can. He hates almost all the agents savagely, so much so that he's planning to start his own agency ... But his biggest gripe is the terrible trash turned out by Tin Pan Alley ...'

'About the popular songs of the day,' Frank told Simon, 'they've become so decadent, they're bloodless ... All you get is a couple of songs like *Apple Blossom Wedding* and *Near You* ... The song-writer in most cases finds he has to prostitute his talents if he wants to make a buck. That's because not enough publishers are buying the better kind of music ... And the recording companies are helping those guys by recording such songs...'

Another Frankie had no complaints about songs, perhaps because Frankie Laine then had smash records in *Mule Train* and *Cry of the Wild Goose*. Neither did Vaughn Monroe, who was riding best-seller charts with *Ghost Riders in the Sky*. But just as Monroe faced Gene Autry's competition on *Ghost Riders*, so Laine had to out-run country artist Tennessee Ernie on *The Wild Goose*, emphasising the interplay of pop-and-country that was increasingly characteristic of the time.

In 1949 Frank recorded *Some Enchanted Evening* and *Bali Ha'i* from *South Pacific*; *The Hucklebuck*; *Let's Take an Old-Fashioned Walk*, the Irving Berlin show-stopper from *Miss Liberty*—a duet with Doris Day; also, such song-hits as *That Lucky Old Sun*, *The Old Master Painter* and *Don't Cry Joe*. Perceptive as was his choice of material, these songs, too, were smashes for other artists. Frank's sensitivity to the changing taste of the public and his own problems as a vocalist were manifest in an increasing use of new arrangers, different instrumentation and varied vocal backing. Nevertheless, in March 1949, *Downbeat* said of a group of sides recorded with Phil Moore: 'They don't quite get the intimate between-you-and-me feel that was attempted and Frankie hits a few off-pitch ones to boot.' The following month, Frank derived little satisfaction from a more favourable notice, which read: '*Comme Ci* is delicately sung without the indecision of phrasing and tone that has plagued him off and on during the last year. He is a shade less sure on *Angelus* with that Lucky Strike tendency to sing sharp. No wonder he wants off the show.' Frank did part company with *Your Hit Parade* in May and accompanied his departure with a sharp statement that he did not like the material he was compelled to sing or the style of singing he was forced to adopt.

Sinatra's awareness of his loss of popularity was reflected in many developments. In March 1949 he attended a week-end party in Palm Springs. A retired businessman named Jack Wintermeyer was acting as bartender. The drink that Wintermeyer mixed was not to Frank's liking and he said so. Precisely what Wintermeyer said at this point is not clear, nor could Police Chief Kettman determine whether he was affable (as he claimed) or truculent (as Sinatra maintained). One fact is indisputable: Wintermeyer was treated at the Palm Springs Community Hospital for a slight gash on the forehead. Since

127

he did not fall, it seems indisputable that the gash was made by a fast fist swung by a bony man in an ugly and explosive frame of mind that had little, if anything, to do with the drink. The following day, a peace meeting arranged by Sinatra's friend, Charles Morrison, owner of the Mocambo, took place in the presence of the PS chief of police. 'It was just one of those things,' Frank said, employing the words of a song he sings rather well. 'We're all friends.' And he and Wintermeyer shook hands to close the incident.

Years later, Vincent X. Flaherty of the LA *Examiner* offered another version of how Frank successfully avoided a lawsuit. Flaherty claimed that he secured a promise from the victim to drop the matter if Sinatra would apologise. Frank refused. After a second approach by Flaherty, Frank agreed and the columnist drove him to the Wintermeyer home. However, after they arrived, Frank could not bring himself to make the apology; he blurted out a gruff hello and then, after an awkward moment, extended his hand. 'He just can't bear to apologise,' Flaherty wrote, 'no matter what the cost—career, money, anything.'

Sinatra's concern over his dwindling audience soon reflected itself in his dealings with his associates. In succession, 'the trouble' spread to Mark McIntyre, his accompanist; Bill Richards, Columbia's West Coast recording director; and even Axel Stordahl, his arranger-conductor. From 1943 on, Frank had used Stordahl almost exclusively on his record dates; but from 1949 on, he began to cut sessions with an increasing number of new arranger–conductors. In the use of Phil Moore and Sy Oliver, there were intimations of motion towards a jazz-oriented style.

Like Stordahl, McIntyre had been with Frank from 1943 on. A sensitive man who had studied to be a concert pianist but given up the dream because he lacked instantaneous recall, McIntyre had found the first five years with Frank, as he put it, 'a ball'. He was 'a doll. There were record dates when he purposely coughed on a last take to give the boys half an hour of overtime at double pay. Of course, you had to laugh at his funnies.' In 1948, after five years of accompanying Sinatra, McIntyre found himself without a job.

Bill Richards' dismissal from his Columbia post grew out of a tussle involving a tune that both Harry James and Sinatra wanted to record. 'It did not seem to matter to Frank,'

Richards said, 'that the tune was in a picture starring Mrs. Harry James (Betty Grable). Frank's manager warned me that my head was on the chopping block, even though the final decision was not mine really, but New York's. But Frank never learned how to back down gracefully, or admit a mistake. He wouldn't give in, even though Nancy and Hank Sanicola went to bat for me. Later, when my wife was in the hospital giving birth, he was very considerate.'

Although he was slipping, Frank was still hot newspaper copy. In August 1949 the Philadelphia papers gave him a working over. Scheduled to appear at a Variety Club benefit for Handicapped Children, he met a barrage of stories claiming that he had threatened to pull out if a certain local singer also appeared on the programme. The singer was Jack Leonard whom he had succeeded in the Dorsey band. After several days of unfavourable headlines, the Philadelphia *Daily News* conceded that Frank had not really known of Leonard's inclusion in the programme, and that Leonard had been dropped by the sponsors, once they knew they could get Sinatra.

Despite his experiments and personnel shifts, the reviews of his discs did not improve. The August *Down Beat* wrote of a new album *Frankly Sentimental*: 'Expertly done but Sinatra could never have become a name on this ... For all his talent, it very seldom comes to life.' The reviewer added: 'Commercially, it should be a highly successful album since even lack-lustre Sinatra is infinitely better than most singers.' In December, there was not even a grudging pat on the back: '*Lost in the Stars* seems pitched too low for Sinatra—he has trouble making the notes of "dim" and "him" nor is he able to make the rather complex lyric hang together. On the simple *Old Master Painter*, he fares better. A hit song ... though Sinatra's is not the best record.'

Down Beat's end of the year poll confirmed the omens. Whereas Frank had for years held the No. 1 spot, and usually by a wide margin, Billy Eckstine came in first. Frankie Laine placed second, indicating the growing appeal of a more muscular and sensual style of singing. Bing Crosby and Mel Tormé were tied for third. Sinatra was in fifth place, with a vote that was a quarter of Mr. B's. More upsetting, perhaps, than this chart was a list of the Best Discs of the Year compiled by an editor partial to Frank. Among the fifteen discs were two by Eckstine, two by Doris Day and one each by Laine,

Como, Damone, Nat 'King' Cole, Sarah Vaughan and Ella Fitzgerald. Even Dorothy Kirsten appeared with a recording of *You Go to My Head*. Frank was conspicuous by his absence. Although this was just one critic's list, it was further evidence of a trend that the next four years failed to reverse.

And yet 1949 was not without its professionally heartening moments. At odds with the American Tobacco Company when he 'fired' the Hit Parade in May, by autumn Frank had the spot vacated by the Chesterfield Supper Club and an increase of $2,500 a week over his Hit Parade salary. The new deal with the American Tobacco Company for *Light Up Time*—fifteen minutes every weekday night in prime time—was for three years.

'Despite all the trade talk that Frankie is "slipping",' a review of his first programme read, 'the chances are that he'll not only hold his own following in this series, but gain new adherents...' The idea of 'new adherents' was cued by Frank's *vis-à-vis*, Metropolitan Opera star Dorothy Kirsten. It was frank recognition by Sinatra and Lucky Strike that his appeal was now to a more musically mature audience. Instead of Stordahl, Frank's conductor was Jeff Alexander, who was later replaced by Skitch Henderson.

Less than a month after the première of his new NBC show, Frank began another series on Mutual. In these taped fifteen-minute shows, he did not sing but acted as a record commentator (disc jockey). Mutual merchandised it on an 'open-end' basis, meaning that the programme was sold to sponsors who could insert their own commercials. Referring to him as 'the sometimes unruly crooner whose exuberance over rapid fame has left him in staggering financial debt', *Newsweek* estimated that his total weekly take from the two shows was over $10,000.

During November, Frank headed eastward, combining appearances on behalf of Lucky Strike with advance promotion on his new film *On the Town*. At Richmond, Va., Frank paused for three days to be crowned king of the annual Tobacco Festival, a regency promoted by Lucky Strike. A cover of *Billboard* shows him singing to a vast audience of 6,500 that jammed every inch of available space on the roof of a local department store. The king was not yet dead.

The Radio City Music Hall première of *On the Town* took place on December 9. Unlike his two other recent picture releases, *The Kissing Bandit* and *Take Me Out to the Ball Game*, the screen adaption of the Comden–Green–Bernstein tale of three sailors on a Manhattan spree met with almost universal acclaim. Frank Quinn's thumbs-up review was typical: 'A most exhilarating holiday treat. It has the tempo of the subway, the merriment of Coney Island and the glamour of Broadway.' The noise at the box-office was equally exhilarating. Of the fourth week when *On the Town* set an all-time record for a week's take at the Music Hall, *Motion Picture Daily* wrote: 'Never before has any motion picture grossed as much on any one day in any theatre anywhere.'

Although the warm reception accorded *On The Town* sweetened the end of a trying year, Frank's stay in New York was made noteworthy by another opening. On the evening of December 8, a hit show called *Gentlemen Prefer Blondes*, with a score by Sammy Cahn and Jule Styne, made its bow. It became the more significant of the two premières, for this was the occasion on which Frank first 'encountered' what a Hollywood correspondent later described as Hurricane Ava.

Returning to Hollywood for the holidays, Frank signed a contract for a two-week appearance at the Shamrock Hotel in Houston. He was the first of many stars to play the new location and, despite the talk of his slump, his salary was rumoured to be $5,000 a week. The Shamrock booking, scheduled for January 28, was marked by two extremely significant occurrences. Important as each was in itself, the simultaneity of the two events was crucial in shaping the years from 1950 to 1954 for Frank. On his way to Houston, Frank received the shocking news of the sudden death of his press agent, George Evans. And during his stay at the Shamrock, word trickled through of a new relationship that Frank developed—a relationship so explosive that it was to make copy across several continents for several years.

XI

PANDORA AND THE FLYING AMERICAN

In the early hours of a cold morning in January 1950, George B. Evans sat drinking coffee with two of his clients, Frank Sinatra and Lena Horne, in the quarters of a third, the Copa. Because they wanted to talk, the group chose the quieter reaches of the Copa lounge upstairs rather than the brassy club below. Their meeting was partly in the nature of a reconciliation. Sinatra and his press agent had been at loggerheads for a long while; it was the only period of rupture in a warm, seven-year relationship. Neither ever talked about the cause of the rift, but it was believed to relate to Evans' activities on Sinatra's domestic, not professional front. When the trio broke up, it was nearly dawn. Frank was about to leave for the engagements at the Shamrock.

Little more than seventy-two hours elapsed before the upsetting news of Evans' death came crackling over a long-distance phone. Jimmy Van Heusen, accompanying Sinatra on the flight to Houston, said: 'For Frank the sudden death of George Evans was an emotional shock that defies words. He forgot about the Shamrock and immediately grabbed a plane for New York.' At the Park West Chapel on Manhattan's west side, Frank learned what little was known of Evans' untimely death—he was forty-eight. He had just stepped out of a shower on the morning of the 28th when the fatal heart seizure came. He was dead in a matter of minutes, another victim, as Earl Wilson put it, 'of Broadway's killing pace.'

The loss to Frank was incalculable. Whether or not he had planted swooning teenagers in the Paramount and squealing bobbysoxers in radio studios, as *Variety* credited him with doing, he had been an imaginative drumbeater and a reliable friend. He had guided Frank skilfully through periods of controversy and helped him achieve a dimension that Sinatra could not have had as a mere warbler. His passing could not have come at a more critical juncture in Frank's personal and professional affairs. The same issue of *Billboard* that reported his death, announced the resignation of Manie Sachs from Columbia Records, removing another moderating influence from Sinatra's immediate circle. Obviously, Evans could not have prevented what developed between Frank and Ava Gardner. But it is highly unlikely that he would have permitted the deterioration in Sinatra's relationship with the press that occurred during his courtship of her.

The Shamrock engagement became memorable less for what happened on stage than off. 'A major mistake,' Frank later admitted, 'was inviting Ava to Houston. I hadn't been divorced yet and it did look bad having her there. But I was so in love I didn't care.' And the Hollywood air was charged with the electricity of another unconventional love affair.

Frank's state of mind just before he met Ava was not unlike Ingrid Bergman's before Italian film director Roberto Rossellini entered her life. On Ingrid's susceptibility, director Lewis Milestone has said: 'The truth is that she was plain bored—emotionally and artistically. And she was scared. Suddenly, everything was going wrong for her. She was a set-up for any guy ...' And Ingrid has said: 'I was exploding inside.' Considering the depressed state of Frank's career and marriage—he was separated at the time although no public announcement had been made—he, too, was triggered for an explosion.

Frank's difficulties with the press began practically the first night of the Shamrock engagement. He and Ava dined at a small out-of-the-way Italian restaurant. 'A photographer asked to take a picture,' Frank reported later. 'I refused very graciously and he left. The next day the story broke (in the *Houston Post*) that I not only refused to allow the picture to be made but threatened to punch the photographer in the nose.' Their romance had become a public matter almost before it was an affair.

On February 15 Hedda Hopper and others reported that the Sinatras had separated on the preceding day (Valentine's Day) and that Henry Jaffee, Frank's attorney, was coming from the east to confer with Nancy's attorney about a property settlement. Nancy had told Hedda that life with Frank had become 'unhappy and almost unbearable. But I do not see a divorce in the foreseeable future.' Indicating that it was their third separation, she said: 'He's done it before and I suppose he'll do it again. But I'm not calling this a marital break-up.' Nevertheless, the decision to separate this time had been Nancy's.

Towards the middle of March, Frank arrived in New York

for his first Copa date in several years. He took a luxurious suite at the Hampshire House overlooking Central Park. 'Stars Staying at Same Hotel', read a headline in the *Journal–American*. The story advised that Miss Gardner, voted the 'sexiest female in the world' by Hollywood extras, occupied an equally luxurious suite on another floor. Central Park South became a camp-out for newsmen intent on gathering crumbs to feed the pigeons of gossip.

On the evening of March 15, Sinatra and Faye Emerson were to be crowned king and queen of the Mid-Century Bock Beer Festival at a benefit ball for the American Red Cross. The preceding afternoon, twenty-five society women gathered at a fund-raising luncheon in a Park Avenue restaurant where pictures were to be shot of Frank and Faye as advance publicity for the ball. At 1.30 p.m., Faye was straining to leave for a TV rehearsal and Frank had not yet put in an appearance. Reluctantly, press photographers began shooting her alone. As she was about to leave, Frank walked in. The following day's newspapers, reporting a salty verbal exchange, overflowed with innuendoes as to the cause for Frank's delayed arrival. The following evening, Frank failed to appear at the ball. Columnists reported that he had instead gone night-clubbing with Ava. Queried if there was a romance between them, Ava remained silent while Frank allegedly snapped: 'I'm still married.'

On the 25th, Earl Wilson reported that Ava was leaving for England. She said that she had to get away from the torrent of insulting and abusive letters, 'vilifying her for her relationship with Sinatra'. It was only the first of a series of geographic withdrawals by Ava. Nancy, who was to indulge in a counter-series of tactical delays, had a birthday on the 26th, and friends reported that she appeared at a Palm Springs party in her honour, sporting a new mink coat sent by Frank.

Frank was so keyed-up for his Copa opening on the 29th that he had to be treated by a doctor before he went on. A throat condition, which had bothered him through the year, was much worse than he realised, or was ready to admit. (While the condition might have been psychosomatic in origin, as George Evans always believed, the 'guilt germs' were potent enough to produce blood-specks on his morning toothbrush.) Ava was in the first-night audience and a good luck wire from Nancy was in his dressing room. 'Am I speaking too loud for you, ladies?' Frank demanded of a crowd that was unusually noisy. Later, he pleaded: 'This is my opening night. Give me a break.' He tried comedy bits, including a dance number from *Take Me Out to the Ball Game*—'Could Pinza do this?' he joked. At one point, he put on a coonskin hat, swung a whip and blew duck-calls in a take-off of his new Columbia mentor's record hits, *Mule Train* and *Cry of the Wild Goose*. (Mitch Miller, Sachs' successor, was reputed himself to have produced the sound effects on the Frankie Laine hit recordings.)

Business at the Copa was good. But the critical reaction was typified by a review in the *Herald Tribune*: 'Whether temporarily or otherwise, the music that used to hypnotise the bobbysoxers—whatever happened to them anyway, thank goodness?—is gone from the throat. Vocally, there isn't quite the same old black magic there used to be when Mr. Sinatra wrenched *Night and Day* from his sapling frame and thousands swooned.' Noting that Frank substituted showmanship for great singing, the reviewer added: 'He relies on what vocal tones are operating effectively ... He uses carefully made musical arrangements during which the orchestra does the heavy work at crucial points.'

To those who worked with him on three recording sessions held during the Copa engagement, it was quite apparent that Sinatra was having serious problems with his throat. Not even Ava's presence in Columbia's reconverted church studio on East 30th Street seemed to help. Percy Faith, who conducted the sessions, was compelled to recast several of the arrangements. But the recordings of *Peachtree Street* and *There's Something Missing*—a curiously apropos title—still reveal an amazing deterioration of vocal quality.

Sinatra's vocal chords were more seriously strained than he realised or was ready to accept. But he was also suffering from great emotional strain, as a bizarre incident revealed. One evening, Ava left the Copa ostensibly to wait for Frank at the hotel where both were staying. Instead, she went night-clubbing with a writer friend, Richard Condon, later author of *The Manchurian Candidate*, and a girl-friend, Ruth Cosgrove, later Mrs. Milton Berle. At Bop City, a club where Ava's ex-husband Artie Shaw, was making a comeback, they were seated at Shaw's own table. Ostensibly to allay Frank's uneasiness about her whereabouts, she phoned him from the club. 'When Frank learned on the phone that Ava had gone to see Artie Shaw,' a friend later reported, 'he went to pieces. You never saw such a frantic display of jealousy. He shouted that he was going to kill himself. When Ava pooh-poohed the threat, he pulled out a gun—he had a permit—and fired two shots so that she could hear them. The occupant of an adjoining suite heard them, too, and phoned the police. On their arrival, Frank acted as though nothing had happened. After a thorough search, during which they could find neither bullets not bullet holes, they left. The reason they could find nothing was that Frank had fired them into a mattress, and the mattress had been hurriedly exchanged for another before the police arrived.'

On April 26, Nancy filed for separate maintenance in Santa Monica. But Frank was a miserable and destructive year-and-a-half away from a divorce. Estimating their property at over $750,000 and his previous year's earnings at $934,700, she requested alimony, division of community property and custody of the three children. No divorce was contemplated, she told reporters because they were both Catholics and 'neither of us wants one', a statement that did nothing to ease Frank's distraught state of mind.

The following day, rumours of a split between MGM and Sinatra were confirmed. In a joint announcement, MGM and MCA, representing Frank, stated that he had asked for a release from his contract, and received it. The alleged reason he wanted to be free to accept TV offers which required him to live in New York. Although neither Frank nor the studio made any statement beyond the formal announcement of an amicable parting, it was known that he was tired of playing singing sailor roles and that the studio was displeased over his affair with Ava.

By then Ava was abroad, working on *Pandora and the Flying Dutchman* in a role that MGM had conveniently found for her. Since the picture was to be made wholly in Spain, it was an obvious studio attempt to break up the romance, or at least to separate the lovers and reduce the barrage of adverse publicity aimed at Ava. While Frank was still at the Copa, reports began coming out of Spain that Ava was constantly in the company of Mario Cabre, a professional bullfighter in the film. Some of the papers printed love poems that Cabre wrote to her. It was good publicity for the picture. It was good for Ava since it exerted pressure on Frank to settle his domestic affairs. But it could not have been worse for Frank, who,

136

according to friends, resentfully began entertaining Copa cuties.

Among those who bore the brunt of Frank's tangled emotions was Skitch Henderson, who was serving as his Copa accompanist and conductor. 'The understatement of the year,' said Henderson later, 'would be to say that he was difficult. Frank, you know, has always respected sidemen, so when the band played badly (as house bands generally do), he'd get hacked at me instead of them. He was bugged, too, because he couldn't get a hit record while a harmonica group had a million copy seller in *Peg O' My Heart*. One night when the band was especially horrible, it all boiled over and he turned to me and uttered very sarcastically, "If I'd tried a little harder, maybe I could have gotten the Harmonicats to back me." It cut me deeper than anything that has ever been said to me ...'

On a Monday night, during the dinner show, while he was singing *Bali Ha'i*, his voice seemed to break painfully. But he managed to finish the show. Later, it was learned that he had gone on against the express orders of the physician who had been treating his throat. 'He crawled out of bed,' Jack Entratter, who ran the Copa, told reporters, 'only because he heard that a columnist he hated bet me $100 that he would never complete the engagement.'

The columnist won his bet. During the third show that night, Frank suffered a sub-mucosal throat haemorrhage, and was forced abruptly to leave the floor. 'It was tragic and terrifying,' Skitch Henderson recalls. 'He opened his mouth to sing after the band introduction and nothing came out. Not a sound. I thought for a fleeting moment that the unexpected pantomime was a joke. But then he caught my eye. I guess the colour drained out of my face as I saw the panic in his. It became so quiet, so intensely quiet in the club—they were like watching a man walk off a cliff. His face chalk white, Frank gasped something that sounded like "Good night" into the mike and raced off the floor, leaving the audience stunned.'

Frank was ordered to take a complete rest for two weeks and to avoid using his voice, even for speaking. At his request, Billy Eckstine, who was then appearing at the Paramount and had twice been No. 1 in popularity polls, went on in his place. At the end of that week, Mr. B. collapsed from nervous exhaustion.

Brushing aside his doctor's warnings, Frank took off for Barcelona on May 10, only eight restless, agonising days after the throat haemorrhage that forced him out of the Copa. Reporters who saw him off at the airport and needled him about Ava, wrote that he looked ill. Instead of waiting for a scheduled flight from London, he chartered a private plane for the flight to Barcelona. Reporters who met him and his friend, song-writer Jimmy Van Heusen, at the airport, observed that he carried a small object wrapped in tissue paper off the plane. Bombarded with questions, he said that he was under doctor's orders and could do little talking. While he tried to evade the press, Van Heusen rented a car. Followed by reporters, who noted that the tissue-wrapped parcel had remained at customs, they headed for the Sea Gull Inn in a neighbouring beach resort town, where Ava awaited them. After meeting in private, as the press put it, Frank and Ava went off for a night drive along the Midi Coastal Highway.

The next day, the Mediterranean was swept by a spring downpour, which delayed shooting on *The Dutchman*. Still suffering from a sore throat, Frank drove to Ava's rented villa where he spent the afternoon while reporters maintained a steady vigil in the rain. Bullfighter Mario Cabre was reportedly thirty-five miles away in Gerona, where ostensibly he spent the day writing a new ode to Ava. Some Spanish newspapers carried stories of a possible duel between Sinatra and Cabre.

It rained the second day of Frank's stay in Spain, forcing the lovers to remain indoors. Again reporters maintained an all-day vigil outside. Word was flashed to the world that the tissue-paper parcel impounded by customs had been delivered to Frank. It reportedly contained an emerald necklace, which Ava was required to take out of Spain on her departure.

On the third day, Tossa del Mar was hot and sunny. Frank strolled through the village, happy to warm himself in the sunshine. Ava was quoted as saying: 'I adore Mario. We all adore Mario. He is a wonderful guy but there is no question of love. The whole story was absurd.' And of her future with Sinatra: 'Frank is a wonderful guy. The press and everybody is talking about marriage but Frankie and me. It's too soon. Frank hasn't even got a divorce.' Interviewed at his villa, Frank was quoted as saying: 'Ava is a terrific girl. All I can say is there is no change in the matrimonial situation.' And Cabre reportedly said: 'Ava Gardner is the woman I love with all the strength in my soul. I believe this love and sympathy are both reciprocal and mutual. Twice I have been gored by bulls, both times in the thigh. But Ava, she has hit me harder than any bull, in the heart.' And Cabre offered the press a new testimonial of his devotion in the form of a love poem, which many American papers reprinted.

In the United States, the papers noted that Nancy had spent Mother's Day alone with the three Sinatra children, enjoying gifts from them but not from Frank, who, it was emphasised, had just given Ava a $10,000 necklace. The following day when Frank discovered how American papers had been handling his visit, he was visibly shaken by the possible effect on his children. 'They can't make this one of those things,' he claimed. 'We have been chaperoned every minute we have been together.' Glumly, he added: 'We know now that because of this publicity, it was a mistake for me to come here.' Frank now announced that he was leaving Spain twenty-four hours ahead of schedule. From Cabre came the comment: 'After Sinatra's visit is over, and Ava and I are alone again, I think you will see that our love has survived.'

The day before his departure, Frank had lunch and dinner with Ava at her villa, again besieged by reporters and photographers. Cabre remained in Gerona where sunshine permitted a resumption of work on the film. Reached by phone from Tossa del Mar, after some of his bullfighting sequences had been shot, Cabre said: 'The rain has been terrible. It has kept me from my beloved. But perhaps by tomorrow I will be able to see her.' Cabre allegedly added: 'Whether Sinatra stays or goes tomorrow is of no difference.'

Frank left Spain on May 17. The next day, the *Los Angeles Times* ran a story, which required unusually careful reading to distinguish between real actions and action for the camera reel:

'Tossa del Mar. Ten minutes after Frank Sinatra left for Paris Ava Gardner ran into the street, blowing kisses to Mario Cabre. Frank Sinatra left thirty seconds before Cabre rode down main street in a horse-drawn carriage to an ovation by flower-throwing villagers and peasants, all staged for *Pandora and the Flying Dutchman* in which Ava Gardner co-stars with James Mason.

'Miss Gardner ran to the village from her villa a few

minutes after bidding good-bye to Frank Sinatra. She elbowed her way to front ranks. When the carriage passed, Ava shouted: "Mario mio, Mario mio" and blew kisses, but stayed out of camera range. Cabre beamed.

'After the scene, Cabre walked over and gave Miss Gardner a bouquet. The crowd in the square applauded as he kissed her on each cheek and hugged her saying: "Hello, baby. Okay, baby."

'Cabre bared his chest, showing where bull's horns penetreated [sic] yesterday. Cabre (in Spanish): "I was thinking of Ava even when the bull had me up against the rail. I think of her all the time. She is sublime."

'Ava dined with Frank Sinatra last night, breakfasted with Frank Sinatra this morning. Tonight, Miss Gardner dines with Cabre.'

On the 21st, Frank paused in New York on his way to LA. Stating that he was returning to work and to see Nancy, he denied that Cabre had chased him from Ava's side. Calling her 'only a dear friend', he denied that he had brought her a $10,000 necklace. 'The only present I gave Ava,' he was quoted as saying, 'was six bottles of Coke. Ask the Barcelona customs people.' At the LA airport where he was met by a large cordon of reporters, he said: 'When I got to Spain, I figured somebody would say something about romance. But I hadn't counted on that bullfighter. He was an added starter they ran in at the last minute. I never did meet him. I assume that what he said was just a publicity stunt.'

Loaded with gifts, Frank drove out to his Holmby Hills home early on the evening of his arrival. Only the two older children were up to receive their presents. To Nancy, Sr., Frank brought a gold charm bracelet from Paris inscribed: 'Eiffel Tower and stuff.' Of his visit, he told reporters: 'Nancy and I had a long talk. We've never had anything but kind words. We're always friendly. But there's no reconciliation.'

Frank returned to his home the following morning to see his youngest child. As night fell, he was on a plane bound for New York in the company of Bob Hope. Years later, when he was on top again, Frank used Hope to kick-off a new TV series for Chesterfield. 'I couldn't get a job until Bob came along with his first TV spec.' Sinatra later said. 'In 1950 there weren't many people around like him. People were frightened of

me ... But Hope! He and his writers wrote his entire spec
around me. I didn't get a lot of money but the show was of
tremendous psychological help to me.'

XII

MAN ON A HIGH WIRE

With Ava impatie... ...ed the London Palladium in July 1950.
the coast, Frank playe... ...en, and still is today, the European
The Palladium was th... ... of the 1920s, a vaudeville shrine. In
equivalent of our Palac... ...eviews his records had been receiving
contrast to the lukewarm r... ...s about his career, the comments
and the funereal prediction... ...d mass hysteria. Was it wonder-
were heartwarming: 'I watche... ...Sinatra is a superb performer
ful? Decidedly so, for this man ... ...nce spellbound ...' (Musi-
and a great artiste. He had his aud... ...e is as satisfying a one-
cal Express). 'Bless me, he's GOOD! H... ...ever seen.' (Sunday
man performance as the Palladium ha... ...watching from a
Chronicle). At one performance, with Ava ...e lights in order
front row, the management had to turn out th... ...ritish bobby-
to save him from an over-enthusiastic mob of B... ...sang at a
soxers. Princess Margaret sat at his feet, as he ...
crowded party at the home of a British peer.

Just as the American press had indulged in psychological
speculation regarding his magical effect on audiences, th...
British papers tried to probe the secret of SRO houses that
'mobbed, ogled, idolised him'. The Daily Express called him
the Ambassador of Miserabilism (the cult of loving misery):
'He is thin-faced, tired-looking, carries that world-weary look
which comes of being so long a totem of the tearful.' Another
critic wrote in the conservative London Times: 'Here is an
artist who, hailing from the most rowdy and self-confident
community the world has ever known, has elected to express
the timidity that can never be wholly driven out of the boast-
fullest heart. To a people whose idea of manhood is husky, full-
blooded and self-reliant, he has dared to suggest that under
the ... crashing self-assertion, man is still a child, frightened
and whimpering in the dark.'

141

Unlike the Spanish press, which had hounded them constantly and reported their every movement, British newsmen were friendly, considerate and discreet. Frank and Ava were treated as guests whose personal affairs were their own concern.

On his return to the United States, Frank was greeted with a *Collier's* article entitled *That Lucky Old Laine*, an unple[asant] reminder of the changes that had occurred in pop m[usic] ...sant in his own standing. Referring to Frankie Laine a[s] ...usic and derella Boy' of the record industry of 1947–50, [...] as the 'Cinderella Boy' of the record industry of 1947–50 [...] Dean Jennings described him as 'the crooner with steel ton[...] Dean Jennings air with his arms and stomps out the bea[...] ...sils', who flails the doesn't bend notes but 'cripples' them [...] t with his feet, who fans into buying 8,000,000 of his platt[...]..., and who 'fractured' sparse hair, an eagle beak and the [...] ...ers. 'Thirty-seven, with thrower,' Jennings concluded, 'he ha[s] [...] dimensions of a discus ful qualities of Frank Sinatra, Vic [...] s none of the fragile, wistful qualities of Frank Sinatra, Vic [...] Damone or Mel Tormé.'

By 1950 teenagers were wea[ring] ...ring hair ribbons lettered with Frankie Laine's name and da[...]...bing his initials in purple polish on their finger nails. They [...] were also buying other 'belters' like Eddie Fisher, Teresa B[...] ...rewer and Georgia Gibbs. In its emotional intensity and [...] hard, driving metrics, the new school of female as well as [...]male singers approached Rhythm and Blues, ghetto music of [...]the urban Negro. Their discs spun to a 'Roxy ending', a fi[n]al, fortissimo set of notes that could rattle the rafters of a movie palace. They exploited sound gimmicks. The major and most successful proponent of the new style was Frank's own A & R man at Columbia Records—he was also Frankie Laine's. Between Mitch Miller, whom Frank called the Beard, and Sinatra, to whom Miller referred derisively as Old Iron Rod, there was little empathy.

Frank's efforts to cope with the new tide were apparent in a Miller-inspired album then about to be released. Titled *Sing and Dance with Frank Sinatra*, it contained eight rhythm standards scored in bright, dance tempi by George Siravo, an arranger who had worked with Frank on his Light Up Time radio show. The sides with Siravo had been 'tracked' before Frank's departure for London. (Tracking, outlawed shortly thereafter by the Musicians Union, is a procedure whereby the orchestra is recorded first and the singer's voice is added later; it saves musician costs since the singer can do as many takes and take as much time as he pleases.) On the release of the new

LP, Mitch Miller reminded reviewers that Sinatra's best-sellers had not been merely lush ballads but jump tunes like *The Coffee Song* and *Five Minutes More*.

During 1950 Frank cut records with arranger-conductor Percy Faith, with jazz trumpeter Billy Butterfield, with actress Jane Russell (to promote a misadventure *Double Dynamite* in which he sang two songs), with singer Helen Carroll, and with Rosemary Clooney, who made it that year with *Come On-A My House*. He even recorded three sides with Mitch Miller and covered a country hit *Chattanooga Shoe Shine Boy*. Critic George Simon contends that Frank produced 'some of his most emotional recordings during this period. Perhaps, they weren't his best technically. But some tremendously warm phrasing, sometimes combined with a feeling of great loneliness and desperation, sometimes with deep passion and tenderness filled the grooves of such sides as *Nevertheless* (which had the beautiful Billy Butterfield trumpet passage), *You're the One* (theme of his TV show) and *Love Me* (Victor Young and Ned Washington's beautiful song).' Nevertheless, the experiments did not arrest the downcurve of Frank's record sales.

On September 28, Nancy appeared in the Superior Court at Santa Monica. After a ten-minute hearing punctuated by her crying, she won by default her suit for separate maintenance. Frank and Ava were then in New York attending the Joe Louis–Ezzard Charles heavyweight fight at Yankee Stadium. The property settlement signed by Frank a week earlier gave Nancy, who had been receiving temporary alimony of $2,750 a month, one-third of his gross earnings on the first $150,000, 10 per cent of the next $150,000 and a decreasing percentage thereafter, but in no case less than $1,000 a month till death or remarriage. In addition, Nancy got the Holmby Hills house, thirty-four shares of the stock of Sinatra Music Corporation, their 1950 grey Cadillac, furs, jewellery and the custody of the children. Frank kept the Palm Springs house, a jeep, 1949 convertible Cadillac, bank accounts, oil interests in Texas, and all musical compositions, records and transcriptions. 'It doesn't look now,' said Greg Bautzer, who represented Nancy, 'like they will ever get a divorce.' To photographers who met her outside the courthouse and requested that she pose for pictures, she said simply: 'I don't feel like smiling.'

About this time, Nancy enrolled at the University of California and Los Angeles as a special student. It was reported that one of her courses was music appreciation.

Sinatra made his debut on TV on October 7. To those who had been conducting obsequies over his career, it came as something of a shock that CBS would sign a five-year contract guaranteeing $250,000 a year. The opening show was a standard musical revue, the high point of which was a take-off on *The Kid*, with Ben Blue playing Charlie Chaplin and Sinatra playing Jackie Coogan. Although Frank's opening song was *When You're Smiling*, there were no smiles when the reviews appeared the following day. Jack Gould of the NY *Times* called the hour-long programme 'a drab mixture of radio, routine vaudeville and pallid pantomime'. Arguing that Frank required a more intimate setting, Gould cracked: 'Sinatra walked off the TV high dive but unfortunately fell into the shallow end of the pool.' The *Herald Tribune*'s John Crosby saw in Frank a 'surprisingly good actor but a rather bad emcee'. Granting that Sinatra was a performer 'with considerable charm, ease and the ability to sell a song'. *Variety* found the pacing bad, the scripting inferior and the camera work poor.

Frank's popularity among entertainers, if not with TV critics, was displayed by a party held at Toots Shor's after the show. Although invitations were sent to a hundred and fifty people by his new press agent, Nat Shapiro, over three hundred show-biz friends came. *Look* was so impressed by the number and importance of the celebrities who attended that it covered the proceedings in a picture story.

1951 saw an unpleasant continuation of the preceding year's downward trend in Sinatra's record popularity. During the early months, the two top discs in the country were Patti Page's *Tennessee Waltz* and Guy Mitchell's *My Heart Cries for You*. Both were produced by Mitch Miller. The latter tune had been offered to Frank who had passed it up. 'I was mixed up,' Frank later admitted. 'My singing was affected and I knew it...' Moreover, moving about as he did in pursuit of the elusive Ava, he did fewer recording sessions than in any year, except those of the musicians' strikes.

Of the six dates he kept in 1951, one proved particularly memorable. Frank's choice of songs, especially at critical moments of his life, has been dictated by prevalent emotional states. This is what has given some of his records their overpowering poignance and sense of immediacy. At the March 27 session, he recorded *I'm a Fool to Want You*, a song of which he was in fact co-author. 'Frank was really worked up,' Ben Barton, the head of his music company, recalls. 'So worked up he couldn't do more than one take. But that take was so tremendous, it didn't need more than one.' Critic George Simon regards the side as 'the most moving Sinatra has ever recorded'.

In May, Mitch Miller signed Dagmar, a busty blonde, to a Columbia record contract. To jack up Sinatra's sagging record sales, Mitch suggested that Frank cut a duet with her. Hurting from his mistakes in rejecting *My Heart Cries for You*, Frank was ready to try almost anything. One of the songs selected for the session was a novelty called *Mama Will Bark*. 'I growled and I barked on the record,' Frank said later, 'but the only good it did me was with the dogs.' The dogs did not help, even though 1951 was Miller's *annus mirabilis*.

Four of his other artists accounted for some of the year's biggest smashes. Rosemary Clooney had *Beautiful Brown Eyes* in addition to *Come On-A My House*. Guy Mitchell, cum braying French Horns, had *The Roving Kind* and *My Truly, Truly Fair* as well as *My Heart Cries for You*. Tony Bennett, singing slightly flat, had *Because of You* and *Cold, Cold Heart*. And Johnnie Ray had a two-sided, million copy disc in *Cry* and *The Little White Cloud That Cried*. Statistically, Frank was a record 'has-been' who did not place a single disc in *Billboard*'s recap of 1951's Top Tunes, Records and Artists, and whose average sales sank below 10,000 copies a release.

Frank was also losing out on radio and TV. Sponsors cancelled out of his Sunday night open-end disc jockey show on Mutual as well as his TV series on CBS. Nor were the film studios rushing him with offers of attractive roles. With no great enthusiasm, he accepted the lead in Universal International's *Meet Danny Wilson*, a potboiler by Harold Robbins. Louella Parsons, then still a Sinatra rooter, tried to make the assignment seem important. 'Those crepehangers,' she commented, 'who said Sinatra was through in pix may now cheerfully choke on their words. It's true he left Hollywood under a cloud of troubles with Nancy and his front-page romancing with Ava. But those dark times seem past.' Miss Parsons' forecast proved overly optimistic and premature.

Late in April of 1951, Ava left Frank in New York with the ultimatum that she would not see him again until he could come to her a free man. While Frank remained east for appearances at the Paramount and Latin Quarter, she began cultivating former husbands and boyfriends, among them Mickey Rooney and Howard Duff, with whom she had had a well-publicised romance. On May 18 and again on May 25, Frank flew to the coast for confrontations he deeply dreaded. It was difficult to face the woman who had been his help-mate from the Hoboken beginnings of his career; the proximity of the children added to his torment. But the fear of losing Ava overshadowed all other emotions. There were a number of meetings, during which he manifested a kind of desperation that frightened Nancy. 'If I cannot get a divorce,' he reportedly pleaded, 'where is there for me to go and what is there for me to do?'

On May 29 Earl Wilson reported 'Nancy and Frank Sinatra reached the decision in a series of quiet, friendly, dignified talks in Nancy's Hollywood home. "This is what Frank wants," Nancy stated, "and I've said yes. I have told the attorneys to work out the details." ' Louella Parsons quoted Nancy: 'I refused him a divorce for a long time because I thought he would come back to his home ... I am now convinced that a divorce is the only way for my happiness as well as Frank's. I think it is better for the children, too ...' Hedda Hopper later added a perceptive footnote: that Nancy wanted to be out of the headlines, not only because of the children but because the tide of public opinion had turned against her. If Frank thought that Nancy's announcement meant the end of controversy and tension, he was doomed to disappointment. Five months were to be consumed in legal manoeuvring, months as frustrating and headline-filled as the preceding fifteen.

During June Frank was occupied with the filming of *Meet Danny Wilson*, a film that contributed nothing to his career as an actor or singer. Towards the end of July, in their first public appearance after Nancy's announcement, Frank accompanied Ava to the première of *Show Boat*, a film that did much to elevate her standing as an actress. *Photoplay* observed that within a year Ava, whose career was supposedly finished because she wouldn't give up Sinatra, had become Hollywood's hottest star. A few days after the première, Ava and Frank left for a week's vacation in Mexico.

Trouble started at the LA airport when Frank and Ava arrived with so much luggage that their trip hardly looked like a brief, holiday jaunt. Rumours were immediately touched off that a quickie Mexican divorce was in the making—and possibly an elopement and honeymoon. The plane's departure was delayed as Frank refused to board until the movable ramp was cleared of photographers—Ava had sneaked aboard earlier. Word was flashed along the plane's route of the couple's presence. At El Paso, where the flight paused for a forty-five minute stop-over, the press was waiting *en masse*. At Mexico City, the terminal was swarming with newsmen. 'Why can't you leave us alone?' Frank demanded. Shaking his fist, according to a Hollywood paper, he shouted: 'You can tell stateside for me what we do is our own business. It's a fine thing when we can't go on a vacation without being chased.' In a cover story on Ava, *Newsweek* alleged that Frank greeted reporters with: 'You miserable crumbs! You s.o.b.s!' The LA *Times* observed: 'The attempt to slip quietly [*sic*] into Mexico by air last night became the most publicised romantic goings-on since the Rita Hayworth–Aly Khan trip before their marriage.'

Jorge Pasquel, at whose home they were to stay, had coincidentally been the subject of a 1947 exposé by Robert Ruark—as a 'gunner'—immediately after the columnist's attack on Sinatra. Frank and Ava arrived at Pasquel's palatial house in Acapulco amidst rumours that he had obtained a quickie divorce and that they had been secretly wed in Cuernavaca. The rumours persisted even though officials in Cuernavaca denied them.

During their stay in Acapulco, they spent one evening at the Mirador's famous La Perla, a club situated in the face of a rocky cliff. Several levels of tables offer an unobstructed view of the Pacific, with only the sky and the stars as a canopy, and the bar is a stone cave looking out on the sea. La Perla was being managed by Teddy Stauffer, then married to Hedy Lamarr. Claiming that Frank and Ava were snubbed by Hedy, the LA *Times* elicited from one snoopy patron the information that the couple slipped on to a balcony for 'a passionate

147

embrace ... They thought nobody could see them in the dark. But they were wearing white clothes and it was better than a floor show.' The floor show was then, as it still is, a diving act that Acapulco natives stage after sundown, swan-diving from La Quebrada cliff, opposite the club, into a narrow channel 136 feet below.

Later that evening, Ava, Frank and entourage went to the exclusive Beachcomber Club. As they were about to enter, an American photographer asked them to pose for a picture. Frank refused, but the photographer did not wait. The moment his light-bulb flashed, a Mexican bodyguard went for the camera. When police appeared, the photographer handed his camera over to them and Frank was permitted to yank the exposed film from it. With Ava on the verge of tears, an infuriated Sinatra cursed the newsman so loudly that patrons came spilling out of the club to listen to the unprintable epithets. It was at moments like these that the man she loved—attentive and affectionate as Mickey Rooney had not been, outgoing and tender as Artie Shaw had not been—reminded her of all the roughnecks she had known, from the vulgar, tobacco workers and poor white trash of the North Carolina hamlet where she had been born to all the sharpies and wise guys of the Hollywood Hills.

Although Ava was unhappy about Frank's handling of the press, the remaining three days of their Mexican holiday passed without incident. Just about the time when they were leaving Acapulco in Pasquel's private plane, the motion picture editor of the Hollywood *Citizen News* wrote: 'It takes a big man to fill the shoes of a big position. It takes a man of depth to keep his balance when constantly in the public spotlight. On both counts, Sinatra doesn't measure up ...'

Their return to Hollywood brought new embarrassments. Somehow they avoided the horde of photographers and newsmen at the airport until they reached Frank's car. As the car began to move, a newsreel cameraman turned his floodlights on it. 'Kill that light—kill that light!' Frank yelled through an open window. Accelerating the motor, he headed for an exit, 'scattering newsmen like dogs', as one paper put it. 'The car's bumper grazed the leg of one newsman,' the LA evening *Express* reported.

William Eccles, an airport photographer, later described the incident as follows: 'Sinatra turned the car into me to scare me away. I figured he'd swerve from me so I shot the picture and didn't move. He slammed on the brakes, and at the last minute I jumped. I went up over the fender and rolled off on my stomach, dropping my camera.' Jim Bacon of the AP commented: 'I don't think Frank deliberately tried to run anyone down. I think he was just confused as to how to get out of the airport.'

Eccles did file a criminal complaint against Frank—but withdrew it after Frank wrote a letter of apology. Years later, at a party, Frank told Jim Bacon: 'I admit I was mad. I figured the crippled photographer was planted there just to get me to take a swing at him. I slammed my foot on the gas without realising the wheels were turned. The car swerved before I could straighten it. I'm sorry.'

While the return from Mexico yielded unpleasant newspaper headlines, it also brought good tidings. The same news stories dealing with his alleged attempt to run down newsmen, announced that Nancy had agreed to permit him to file for a Nevada divorce. Since Frank was scheduled to begin a singing engagement at the Riverside Casino in Reno on August 11, it meant that he could start his residence almost immediately.

The road to the divorce court, clearly marked though it seemed to be, was to develop some unforeseen turns. But on his arrival at Reno, Frank was a charmer to reporters. 'I hope I'm going to get along with you fellows,' he said, with a smile. Shaking hands with each newsman, he invited them to his hotel suite for questions. He laughed at stories, repeated by newsmen, that he was too broke to seek a Nevada decree. Two weeks at Reno would bring $25,000 and with the opening of the autumn TV season, he was beginning a new show in New York. As for Mexico, the reports of his conduct were 'grossly exaggerated' and untrue. 'I got sore because I got some pretty rough handling from a couple of guys,' he said pleasantly. 'They were the exception to the rule, though, for the press has done a lot for me.'

As Ava arrived in Reno ten days later, new rumours had it that Nancy might fight a Nevada divorce. Sitting side by side and holding hands, Frank and Ava permitted themselves to be interviewed. 'I honestly don't know what she'll do,' Frank said in response to a question about Nancy. 'But I think you can safely say that Miss Gardner and I will be married.' Frank was sporting a newly grown moustache.

Just about two weeks after the pleasant interviews, the country's papers headlined a new Sinatra scandal. 'Report Sinatra Felled by Sleeping Pills,' the NY *Mirror* said on September 1. And the Hollywood papers carried long stories out of Crystal Bay, Lake Tahoe, in which Frank denied that he had tried to commit suicide after a spat with Ava.

'I've never heard anything so damn wild and ridiculous,' he said. 'This would be a hell of a time to do away with myself. I've been trying to lick this thing for two years and I've practically got it licked now. I did not try to commit suicide. I just had a bellyache. What will you guys think of next to write about me?' With Ava sitting at his side, Frank gave the following account of what had happened: 'Tuesday night, Miss Gardner, my manager Hank Sanicola and Mrs. Sanicola dined at the Christmas Tree Inn on Lake Tahoe. Ava was returning to Hollywood that night. We came back to the Lake and I didn't feel so good. So I took two sleeping pills. Miss Gardner left by auto for Reno and the plane trip back to Hollywood. By now it was early Wednesday morning. I guess I wasn't thinking because I am very allergic to sleeping pills. Also, I had drunk two or three brandies. I broke out in a rash. The pills felt kind of stuck in my chest. I got worried and called a friend who runs the steak house here. He sent a doctor who gave me a glass of warm water with salt in it. It made me throw up and I was all right. That's all there was to it—honest.'

Frank completed the six weeks' residence necessary to file for a Nevada divorce on September 19. But when it appeared that he could win his freedom at any moment, new complications arose. On the advice of her counsel, Nancy was planning to secure a prior California divorce, better to protect the Sinatra children. On the first day that Nancy could legally sign a notice of appearance and waiver, thereby making the Nevada divorce uncontested, Frank's attorney informed him that Nancy would not co-operate. According to her attorney, the property settlement agreed upon for separate maintenance was no longer acceptable, and Nancy claimed an alimony arrearage of $40,000

With Frank, nevertheless, filing for a Nevada divorce on the 20th, Nancy hurried into a California court and obtained a levy for back alimony against a Sinatra-owned building at 177 S. Robertson Boulevard. Her attorney maintained that for the first six months of 1951, Frank's income had totalled $328,000 and that he had paid only $27,000 and still owed $40,805.

Six days later, while he was in New York conferring with CBS on his new TV series, the law firm that represented him in his negotiations with Nancy, added new problems to his woes. It sued Frank for $12,250 in legal fees and secured a lien on the property at 177 S. Robertson as well as on his Palm Springs home.

According to friends, the impasse with Nancy hinged, not only on the amount of money claimed for arrearage, but on the mechanics of the payment. Frank declined to hand over the money until he had his freedom. Nancy ostensibly refused to give him his freedom until she had the money. Then, on October 13, Nancy's attorney revealed that Frank had signed a new property settlement, increasing the money for separate maintenance. Two days later, Nancy filed for her California divorce.

On October 30, while Ava and Frank were in New York, Nancy appeared in the Santa Monica courthouse where she had won a separate maintenance agreement thirteen months earlier. Remaining composed and dry-eyed, Nancy walked out of the courthouse fifteen minutes later with an interlocutory decree of divorce. She was to receive one-third of Frank's gross income up to $150,000 a year and 10 per cent of earnings above that.

Although the interlocutory decree would not become final for a year, Frank and Ava were now—after twenty months of public harassment, private manoeuvring and personal travail —in a position to wed, as soon as he picked up his uncontested Nevada divorce. This he did on November 1, in a five-minute closed session of a Las Vegas court. Now, he was legally free. Emotionally, however, the tie to the mother of his children was long to remain an unbreakable silver cord.

XIII

AND SO TO WED

Within twenty-four hours after Frank picked up his Nevada divorce, he and Ava were in Philadelphia applying for a marriage licence. They were accompanied to the judge's chambers by two Philadelphians, Manie Sachs, who was to give the bride away, and Isaac Levy, a CBS board member. The papers described the Friday trip from New York as 'nearly secret'. Frank was 'highly nervous' as he filled out the required form while Ava was said to be 'highly calm'. Pennsylvania law requires a seventy-two hour waiting period before the issuance of a marriage licence. Since Frank did not request a waiver, newsmen surmised that Monday the 5th would be the time, and the home of Isaac Levy, the place. The plans were actually for a quiet ceremony at Levy's home on Wednesday. Then, suddenly, it appeared that there might be no wedding at all.

Returning to New York on Saturday, Frank and Ava took the James Masons to the Colony for a pre-wedding celebration. Afterwards, the quartet went to the Sugar Hill night club. Precisely what provoked Ava during the evening's festivities is not clear. But after they had parted from the Masons and returned to Hampshire House, Ava tore her engagement ring from her finger and, hurling it out of a window, angrily cancelled the wedding. A six-carat emerald set in platinum with pear-shaped diamonds along each sloping side, the ring was never recovered.

'I was so jealous,' Ava later admitted, 'every minute he was away from me. When I couldn't get him on the telephone right away at Las Vegas or wherever he was, I wanted to kill myself. It was stupid, I suppose. But I did it.'

All through Sunday, they remained in their respective suites, nursing resentments and waiting for the other to ask forgiveness for slights, real and imagined. Frank had given up home, children and one-third of his income for life. Ava's sacrifice had been less formidable, but she had braved studio wrath and public calumny for Frank's love. Now, after two difficult years, it appeared that it might all be for naught. On Monday afternoon, however, mutual friends succeeded in mending the situation, and the ceremony was on again.

On Wednesday, November 7, reporters outside Hampshire House spotted the Sinatra wedding party leaving the hotel. Ava came first, escorted by Axel Stordahl, who was to be best man. Frank followed with June Hutton (Mrs. Stordahl), the matron of honour. All refused to answer questions, and Frank 'put his hand over the lens of a Movietone TV camera when the cameraman tried to film the scene'. The wedding party, which rode to Philadelphia in a rented, chauffeured Cadillac, included Ben Barton, Frank's music-publishing partner, and Dick Jones, an ex-Dorsey arranger who had served as producer of the Hit Parade and was then a Capitol Records executive.

It was raining as the party drove up to the West German-town home of Lester Sachs, a cousin of Manie Sachs. When Frank saw the crowd of people surrounding the entrance, he was surprised, irritated and upset. All the attempts at secrecy, including a last-minute switch of location, had been futile. 'How did these creeps know where we were?' Frank allegedly demanded. 'I don't want no circus here! I'll knock the first guy who attempts to get inside on his can—and I mean it!' Later, in a by-line piece in *American Weekly*, Frank explained that he had used the word 'creeps', not with reference to the assembled newsmen, as the press reported, but to the rest of the crowd.

The list of wedding guests was rather small, being limited to close friends and a few relatives, like Ava's sister Beatrice and Frank's father and mother. When all were assembled, Dick Jones played the Wedding March on the piano, and, after a moment, *Here Comes the Bride*. 'I was so excited and ner-vous,' Ava later said, 'when Manie and I started down the stairs ... that I slipped and we slid down three steps. I had a quick vision of the bride in a heap at the foot of the stairs. But we regained our footing and made it down the rest of the way. As soon as I saw Frank standing there, I wasn't nervous any more. He looked so composed. But he told me he had a lump in his throat.' It was a twin-ring ceremony, with Ava and Frank exchanging thin platinum bands. Frank's wedding pre-sent to Ava was a sapphire blue mink cape stole while her gift to him was a large, heavy gold locket with a St. Christopher medal on one side and a St. Francis medal on the other; it contained an inscribed photograph of her. At the end of the brief ceremony, the guests ringed around them and toasted them with champagne. Ava cut slices of a seven-tiered wedding cake. Axel Stordahl filmed the proceedings on a home movie camera and later presented the Sinatra's with a colour print.

Before the ceremony, Frank had stepped outside to inform news photographers that his own private photographer would take numerous pictures, which would quickly and freely be made available to all papers. One lensman objected. 'My editor wants *my* pictures,' he said, and according to Sinatra, added belligerently, 'and I'll get them!' Frank said: 'I'll bet you $50 you don't get a picture and another $50 that if you even point that camera at me, I'll knock you on your ear.'

It was a quiet wedding. But one large circulation publication reported that the proceedings were 'a shambles, thanks to Sinatra's edict that it would not be covered'. Shortly after the ceremony, they drove to the Philadelphia airport, where they boarded a privately chartered plane. They planned, after an overnight stop in Miami, to hop to Cuba for a three-day honeymoon, after which Frank had to be back in New York for rehearsals of his weekly TV show. The three days narrowed to two, as they were compelled to wait at a Miami hotel for Ava's clothes, which had accidentally been left behind.

Their day at the Green Heron, a beach-front hotel in the northerly Sunny Isles district, was quiet and relaxed. Reporters trying to locate them concentrated their search on the posh, centrally situated hotels of Miami Beach. It was a chilly day for the beach resort and a brisk wind dotted the ocean with whitecaps. As they strolled along the deserted beach in the afternoon, a lone photographer shot one of the most appealing pictures ever made of them. Their backs to the camera, they walk barefoot, hand-in-hand. Frank's trousers are rolled up above his thin ankles. And Ava is wearing Frank's jacket over an old blouse and sports skirt.

Ava's clothes reached them late in the day, giving them a two-day stay at the swank Hotel Nacional in Cuba. (After the marriage broke up, it became known that Ava had footed the bills for the honeymoon as well as the wedding. 'High taxes, high living, lavish generosity and the price of a huge settlement with Nancy,' a friend said, 'left Frank with little in reserve.') On their return to New York they were met by a noisy crowd of reporters. Asked where they were going to stay, Frank reportedly shouted: 'None of your damn business.'

When newsmen pursued them to a private limousine, Frank allegedly slammed the door in their faces. 'Snarling Frank, Giggling Ava Back', was a tabloid's descriptive headline. Two days earlier, another tabloid had headlined a story, 'What a bore is Frankie'. Conjecturing that he still had some nuisance value, it asked editorially: 'But does anyone really care a low-grade damn about the doings and misdoings of Frank Sinatra?'

The evening of their New York return, they dined at a small, Italian restaurant on West 56th Street. Like Patsy d'Amore's original restaurant in Hollywood, which Frank had helped popularise despite the lack of a liquor licence, Patsy's in New York was a favourite eating spot of Frank's early career. Papa showed you to a table, the sons served excellent Italian cooking and mama collected the cash. The only booth, on the street floor in the rear, was constructed to give Frank privacy. Two nights later, they crossed the Hudson for a courtesy call on Frank's parents in Weehawken. Dolly Sinatra, who liked Ava as much as she disliked Nancy, cooked a big Italian dinner.

After the Tuesday telecast of his show, the last from the east, they flew to Hollywood, where the resignation of L. B. Mayer as head of MGM signalised the end of big-studio domination of the screen and Big Brother rule of the Hollywood scene. Suffering from TV jitters, the film capital was immersed in a troubled search for survival that brought three-D, Cinerama, Cinemascope and Todd A-O.

'We're going to redecorate Frank's home,' Ava told friends. She was referring to the Palm Springs house, which had a pool shaped like the top of a grand piano and a $7,000 motor to draw the curtains of the tall picture windows facing it. Sheltered by seven-foot oleander bushes, the luxurious home at 1147 Alejo was in a sparsely settled section, with the awesome quiet of the desert around it. Long after they broke up, Ava thought of the house as the site of 'their happiest memories'. Indicating that they planned to spend much time at the Springs, Ava said: 'I'm going to learn to make all of Frank's favourite dishes. Mama Sinatra has promised to send the recipes. Oh, it's all so thrilling and wonderful! And Mrs. Sinatra—you know, I'm not used to my new name and it takes a second before it clicks—Mrs. Frank Sinatra is the happiest girl in the world!'

'New Name for Happiness' was the title of an article in a fan magazine. Four months later, a story in the same publication was titled: 'The Battling Sinatras'.

Frank's new TV show had had its première telecast on October 9, a month before his marriage. The budget for talent was $40,000, which was high for the period. Max Gordon, the well-known theatrical impresario who had been chosen as Sinatra's producer, said he was shooting for 'high comedy—not rough, low comedy without any ideas behind it'. This was an indirect slap at Milton Berle, against whom Sinatra was being pitted. Frank commented: 'It's like backing into the pennant. Berle's a big man to knock down.' Then known as Mr. Television, Uncle Miltie had the highest-rated show on the TV screen.

Newsweek called the evening of Frank's first telecast 'a battle of the budgets' and 'a singer's scrap'. Frank used $41,500 to present the Andrews Sisters, Frankie Laine and Perry Como while Berle spent $50,000 for Rosemary Clooney, Tony Bennett and the Mills Brothers. Although Frank managed to shave nine points from Berle's rating, critical reaction to his programme was mixed. To *Variety*, the show was 'fast-paced and bright with some dull spots'. Sinatra had demonstrated that he was 'a hep showman on all counts'. Neither the *Herald Tribune* nor the *Times* was as favourably impressed. 'Mr Sinatra wandered about casually,' John Crosby wrote, 'and sang a few songs in what (it's now clear) is just a remnant of the celebrated Voice.' Jack Gould felt that the evening's honours were captured 'effortlessly and smoothly by another gentleman, Perry Como'. Arguing that Frank was not 'the ideal, dominant personality needed to sustain a sixty-minute show', Gould also felt that 'the passing of the years has taken away much of his distinctive styling and phrasing, and there is not the same lyric quality to his voice.'

The mixed critical reception was the start of a gentle, downward spin that the show developed and was never able to correct. 'The smooth, easy and infectious personality', which *Variety* felt should build in succeeding weeks, never built, or came across the TV channel.

Early in December, Frank and Ava made a flying trip to London where he sang at an Anglo-American charity sponsored by the Duke of Edinburgh. Just before they left Hollywood, Frank phoned Fern Marja of the NY *Post*, who was then writing a six-part article on him. Offering to assist her in any way he could, he proceeded to answer questions for almost an hour—it was long distance at his expense. This was apparently the result of a post-honeymoon conference in which Ava had supported Mack Miller, Frank's new press agent, who wanted him to take positive steps to mend his relations with the press.

In the course of his conversation with Miss Marja, Frank maintained that 80 per cent of the time he was unjustly misquoted and badly treated. The rest of the time, he admitted, 'I lost control of my temper and said things. They were said under great stress and pressure. I'm honestly sorry.' He was feeling better, he told the *Post* writer, his voice was improving, and he and Ava were 'extremely happy'. In her not unfriendly articles, Miss Marja conceded that Frank had succeeded in ingratiating himself with her. Nevertheless, she called her series *The Angry Voice*, a reflection of Sinatra's then current public image. Frank's approach to Miss Marja represented the beginning of a woo-the-press campaign that continued into 1952 and reached its climax, perhaps, in the two-part confession of his mistakes *Frankly Speaking*, which he wrote for the Hearst press in July 1952.

Frank and Ava's stay in London was disturbed, not only by a lukewarm reaction to his singing, but by the theft of $16,000 worth of jewellery from their hotel suite. Among the items removed by a thief who climbed thirty feet from the street to their hotel window was the diamond-and-emerald necklace, which Frank had once denied giving Ava. The robbery occurred while Frank and Ava were at the Coliseum Theatre for a rehearsal of the benefit show—during which, according to the British press, Frank 'tangled with the orchestra' and had a tantrum because the brass section was drowning out his soft notes.

Over a hundred American and British stars, including Tony Curtis, Janet Leigh, Rhonda Fleming and Orson Welles, appeared at the performance, which raised over $50,000 for the Duke of Edinburgh's charity. Ava had originally agreed to sing a duet with Frank. (Despite what the public may have believed, her singing of songs in *Show Boat* and in other films had been done by other singers—against her wishes, let it be said.) But at the last moment, she lost her nerve and sat in the stalls instead. In contrast to his Palladium appearance a year earlier, Frank received only perfunctory applause. 'The Voice Falls Flat at British Yawn Party', was the headline in NYs *Daily News*.

Returning to the USA, Frank found New Yorkers reading the Marja series in the NY *Post* and 'knock' reviews of his new records. 'By every ordinary standard, *London By Night* and *April in Paris* are poorly sung,' *Down Beat* wrote. 'Frank sounds tired, bored and in poor voice, to boot.' In later years, Frank confessed that he could not listen to the records of this period without wanting to destroy the masters. Musically, 1951 had been a year of significant change: a revival of folk music was in the making with the phenomenal success of the Weavers and Harry Belafonte's turn from pop to folk; the click of cider-jug ditties', as *Variety* called them, indicated the continuing breakdown of barriers between country and pop music; jazz seemed to be turning cool, intellectual and intro-spective, with the Dave Brubeck Quartet scoring a hit on the West Coast. The results of *Down Beat*'s end of the year popu-larity poll, then on the stands, were almost as disappointing as the previous year's canvas. Billy Eckstine still came first and though Frank had moved up to the No. 2 spot, he registered a meagre 276 votes to Mr. B's 1,354. The same issue of *Down Beat* carried a story of how humble Johnnie Ray felt about his spectacular rise.

XIV

THE HUMBLE BIT

'April is the cruellest month/Mixing memory and desire...' T. S. Eliot wrote. April 1952 was a cruel month for Frank Sinatra. At the scene of some of his most triumphal moments, the NY Paramount, he was on the screen as well as on stage. The film was *Meet Danny Wilson*, in which, playing a singer, he co-starred with Shelley Winters.

Spurred on by Manie Sachs and Bob Weitman, Paramount Theatre executive, Frank arrived in New York ten days before the opening to try to rebuild relationships he had disrupted during his tumultuous wooing of Ava. Coming off the plane from Los Angeles, he ingratiatingly offered to pose for pictures. But, to his dismay, most of the photographers passed him by. As supine in his remorse as he had been uncontrolled in his belligerence, he dispatched a note to the Press Photographers Association: 'I'll always be made up and ready in case you ever want to shoot any pictures of me.' For the first time in years, he went visiting disc jockeys at radio stations—it was then an accepted aspect of record promotion—and tried to charm them into playing his new record, *I Hear a Rhapsody* backed with *I Could Write a Book*.

'In the last year,' George Frazier wrote, after interviewing him backstage at the Paramount, 'Frank Sinatra has found a new humility.' Informed by Frazier that his piece in *Cosmopolitan* might turn out to be unflattering, Frank winced, and for a moment stared at him in sullen silence. 'Then, nodding, he became amiable again,' Frazier wrote. ' "Look," he said, "I won't mind if it pans me just as long as it helps me correct the things I've been doing wrong" ... It was the first time I ever heard him concede,' Frazier observed, 'that Sinatra is only human.' And the magazine writer added: 'For the first time, he seems sceptical of his own infallibility ... He no longer takes the view that he is a law unto himself. His sullenness has given way to an authentic eagerness to be pleasant and co-operative ...'

Frank's new demeanour had its impact in certain areas. *Variety* headed a front-page story 'Sinatra Croons Sweetly to Press: "So Sorry Now"'. *Billboard*'s headline was: 'Eager, Friendly Frankie Gets Smash/Reception Heading Click Paramount Bill'. But the general press was not altogether ready to forget years of ill-tempered outbursts and embittered clashes. Typical of the antagonism which persisted was a mocking feature article in the *World-Telegram* on Sinatra's appearance at the Paramount. Written in the form of a letter to Frankie, the article alternated between lamenting and snickering over the audience's utter lack of interest in his singing. The three-column headline made its point neatly: 'Gone on Frankie in '42; Gone in '52' and a subheading sprayed the cut with acid: 'What a Difference a Decade Makes—Empty Balcony.' Reporter Muriel Fischer told of how she heard three girls at the stage door murmuring 'Frankie' 'soft and swan-like' 'I asked, "How do you like Frankie?" They said: "Frankie Laine, he's wonderful." I heard a girl sighing, "I'm mad about him," so I asked her who. "Johnnie Ray," she cried.'

The *World-Telegram* feature merely served to emphasise what *Down Beat* headlined on its front page: 'Johnnie's Golden Rays/Dazzle Music Business.' Noting that Ray had been virtually unknown in December 1951, *Down Beat* asserted that he had 'most certainly established himself as the phenom of the music-record business of the second half of the century.' On stage at the Paramount, Frank acknowledged Ray's fabulous rise with a parody of *Cry*, then approaching a sales mark of 2,000,000 discs, which ended: 'When I think of Ava, then I no longer cry.' In *Billboard*'s Honour Roll of Hits, Ray's tortured tonsilling accounted for no fewer than four numbers in the Top Ten.

During 1952 one structure after another of his professional life toppled over. The lukewarm reception at the Paramount was followed by an even cooler shoulder in Chicago where Ava flew to be with him. The Chez Paree night club, which could comfortably seat 1,200, drew as few as a hundred and fifty patrons. Things were equally disastrous on the record front. Frank recorded only twelve songs in four sessions, the fewest he cut in any one year of the ten he had been with Columbia. By September, it seemed clear that the company would not renew his contract, which terminated at year-end, or even move to cut the additional twelve sides provided for in the contract.

While he was still at the Paramount, a tussle developed between Frank and the talent agency that had represented him after the buy-out of his Dorsey contract. Claiming that it had to wait in line for its money, MCA complained that Frank owed $40,000 in back commissions. Frank contended that he owed no more than $26,000. To trade-paper reporters, he scoffed at rumours that the agency would drop a client who had earned $693,000 the previous year and whose TV package alone had yielded $65,000 in commissions. But MCA did drop Sinatra. It was, as a friendly reporter put it, 'the final indignity, the kiss-off of a fallen idol.' Frank admitted: 'The hurt was deep and lasting.' For years afterwards, he would ask in pained disbelief: 'Can you imagine being fired by an agency that never had to sell you?'

Even before MCA had written Sinatra off, CBS had torn up

its contract with him. On one of his programmes, Milton Berle had introduced several performers: 'These people have never been seen on TV before. They were on the Sinatra show last week.' Not only were the notices disappointing, but the network had failed to find a sponsor for more than a brief quarter hour. Industry wise-acres claimed that the Sinatra show had cost CBS a million dollars.

To bring Frank's career to an even lower ebb, Universal International failed to follow through on reports that it would sign Sinatra for a new film. UI executives felt that *Meet Danny Wilson* was a better film than its notices suggested and attributed the adverse reactions to Frank's difficulties with newsmen. But the film company, like the record company, like the talent agency, like the TV network, like his once-slavish public—all treated him as though he was an untouchable.

In July his new humility became evident to the public at large. For *American Weekly*, the Hearst syndicated magazine, he by-lined two articles in which he apologised for his mistakes ('I'm a high-strung, emotional person who does things on the spur of the moment'); acknowledged the contribution of the press ('Without their help, I never could have become famous or earned so much money'); and took the blame for altercations with newsmen ('Most of my troubles with the press were my own fault'). Apart from eating humble pie, Frank tried to cope with harmful gossip and charges in three areas: his domestic life; his politics ('I am no communist'); and his alleged association with gangsters.

Figuring prominently in his methodical rebuttal of the gangster charge, though unmentioned by title, were two publications. *U.S.A. Confidential*, a sensational tome then in book stores, called Frank 'a mob property'. Its co-authors were two old *Mirror* 'friends', columnists Jack Lait and Lee Mortimer. The latter was also the author of an inflammatory article in the *American Mercury* entitled *Frank Sinatra Confidential/ Gangsters in the Night Clubs*, in which Mortimer traced Mafia domination of show business to Sinatra and which the *Hollywood Reporter* described as 'the most vicious attack ever printed on an entertainer ... the filthiest piece of gutter journalism ever composed'.

Of his domestic situation, Sinatra wrote that a year after his marriage to Nancy, he realised that he had mistaken friendship for love; but that, being family-minded, he had tried for years to make the marriage work. He conceded that his public wooing of Ava and their trips together had been mistakes—but, he pleaded, they were too much in love to evaluate public reaction.

If Frank found a way of being conciliatory with the press and public, conciliation was not as simple when it came to his new bride. Ava was emotionally as complex, insecure and full of contradictions as Frank. The powerful physical attraction between them allayed incompatibilities of temperament only for limited periods. Friends said that Ava was still taking revenge for hurts inflicted by ex-husband Artie Shaw and that Frank was still following the emotional pattern of the mother-rejected boy—now he wanted to be petted; now to dictate; now he was full of self-pity; now he was arrogantly domineering. While Frank demanded a machine-like precision in the order of things around him, Ava seemed to glory in disorder. The moment she arrived home, she kicked off her shoes. She mixed martinis with her fingers. When she went on a trip, she always carried small parcels—things that she had forgotten to pack and had snatched up at the last moment. Inescapably self-centred, each expected unremitting attention, and absolute understanding from the other, and every slight, however trivial, became personal rejection.

Explosions were frequent. 'He has a fine old Sicilian temper,' Ava said, 'that explodes as often as mine, and he has an irritating habit of walking out of the room in the middle of an argument, leaving me burning inside.' It did not seem to matter who was around, even Frank's children, with whom Ava did not get on very well. Frank's efforts to fulfil his responsibilities as a father created strife; Ava was resentful of the time he spent at ex-wife Nancy's home and of the attention he lavished on the children.

What producer Stanley Kramer once said of her as an actress seemed to have pertinence to her role as a wife. 'She is unwilling,' Kramer observed, 'to admit she cares about what she is doing. She regards such an admission as weakness of some kind, with the result that she will not give of herself as fully or as effectively as she can.' Yet she proudly signed her autographs *Ava Sinatra*, and permitted the studio to suspend her, rather than leave Frank to make a film in Mexico. When Frank played the Cocoanut Grove late in May, she insisted on attending the opening even though she had been ailing for weeks. Within ten days, she was rushed to the Cedars of Lebanon Hospital for emergency surgery. The trouble was never made public, but friends believe she suffered a miscarriage.

In September Frank played the Riviera at Fort Lee, NJ. He was well-received, even as he had been at the Grove and the Desert Inn in preceding months. 'Whatever Sinatra ever had for the bobbysoxers,' *Variety* opined, 'he now has for the café mob. It adds up to showmanship rather than any basic singing appeal.' Appearing on the same bill was Joey Bishop, who had been booked at Sinatra's request. It was the beginning of the big-time for Bishop, who later acknowledged his debt in a letter advertisement that read: 'In 1954 my career really started when you first had me on the bill with you at the Copacabana. You then took me into the Sands Hotel in Las Vegas with you and further enhanced my career. And you put me into two motion pictures *Ocean's Eleven* and *Sergeants Three*, establishing me as an actor. From that I got my own television series which lasted four years. Thanks to you I now owe the government $87,000 in back taxes. Go to hell, Frank! Love, Joey Bishop.'

In his Riviera appearance, Frank also joked about back taxes: 'I owe the government a lot of money,' he said. 'And Uncle Sam doesn't know whether to put me in jail or recognise me as a foreign power.' Frank sang mostly standards, apologising for the lack of good, new songs. His performance was notable, *Variety* concluded 'for self-assurance and a knowing way with a crowd, whatever the misadventures of his personal life and career'.

A major misadventure was, however, in the making. On September 12, Ava flew in for the première of *The Snows of Kilimanjaro*, the Hemingway story in which she co-starred with Gregory Peck. Because of the Riviera's schedule, Frank could not attend the première with her. But during a break, he hopped in a car, tore across the nearby George Washington Bridge, zipped down the West Side Highway—and brought Ava back to the Riviera for the last show.

The spacious, elegant club was packed. But Ava instantly spotted a face that made her own turn green. Sitting at one of the tables up front was an old Sinatra flame, actress Marilyn Maxwell. When Frank sang one of the love ballads that was a regular part of his act, Ava decided that Frank was addressing the song to Marilyn. While he was still performing, and in full view of the audience, Ava rose from her chair and flounced out of the club. Before Frank knew what was happening, she was on a plane bound for Hollywood. A few days later, Frank received her wedding ring through the post with a bitter note.

Although Frank wanted desperately to follow Ava to the coast, he was booked to play the Chase Hotel in St. Louis after closing at the Riviera—and his handlers would not let him cancel out. After all the reverses his career had suffered, they felt it would be suicidal for him not to fulfil the date. The success of the Chase booking did not allay Frank's troubled state of mind. 'I've got problems, baby,' he told Sammy Davis, Jr. 'That's what happens when you get hung on a chick!' In public, he announced that the disagreement was trivial. 'We have a career problem,' he said. 'I'm going to see my wife in about ten days in Hollywood. I think everything will work out all right. It's anything that might happen between a man and his wife—just a mild rift.'

But as the days wore on and he read in Hollywood columns that Ava was making the party rounds while he was still tied down at the Chase, he became increasingly upset. 'I'm nuts about her,' he told Earl Wilson, 'and I don't think it's dead. But it certainly is all up in the air.' Scheduled to accompany Ava to Africa where she was to star in *Mogambo* with Clark Gable, Frank had begun taking shots. Now, he stopped and seemingly cancelled his plans to accompany her. But having lost the wedding ring that Ava had returned to him, he had a duplicate made, apparently in the troubled hope that she would accept it on his return to Hollywood. Friends felt he was on the verge of a crack-up and were uneasy when he talked about the futility of life.

On his return to Hollywood, there was a reconciliation, including a well-publicised, hand-holding visit to the bullfights in Tiajuana. But the tender period of togetherness was short-lived. The following week-end, there was a new explosion, this time at Palm Springs. Probably because of undue press exposure, it assumed an exaggerated significance.

There are at least two versions of the incident of October 18. A petty quarrel in Hollywood had provoked Frank and Ava to drive separately to the Palm Springs house. According to one version, when he arrived around midnight, Frank was startled to find Lana Turner and her agent Benton Cole week-ending at his home. Angered that Ava had apparently lent the house without telling him, he invited them to leave. As words were being exchanged, Ava appeared. Frank turned on her and suggested that she leave with her guests. According to a variant version, Frank arrived at the Springs after Ava, not before. On entering the house, he was surprised to hear voices. Ava and another female were lamenting their unhappy experiences with sundry husbands and lovers. Intemperate and bitter words were climaxed by Frank's requesting Ava and Lana to get the hell out.

In any event, Frank and Ava both stormed out of the house, each returning separately to Hollywood. By the following day, Ava was sulking in their Hollywood residence while Frank was dejectedly ensconced with a duffle-bag full of clothes in Jimmy Van Heusen's home. Coming up on the agenda was a rally for Democratic presidential candidate Adlai Stevenson at which Ava was scheduled to introduce Frank. They had also planned a trip to Ava's family in Smithfield, North Carolina, before departing together for Africa.

Frank spent the week-end before the Stevenson rally in Las Vegas. On Monday, Earl Wilson flashed the news: 'Frankie Ready to Surrender; Wants Ava Back, Any Terms.' Wilson went on to report that, after painful days of unhappiness, Frank had come to realise that, more than anything else, he loved and wanted Ava. Wilson's column was Frank's way of trying to reach Ava, who had had her unlisted phone number changed.

All through the day, officials of the Stevenson rally were on tenterhooks worrying whether Ava and/or Frank would appear. But that evening, they arrived together. After a backstage embrace, Ava appeared on the platform first and told a Palladium crowd of 4,000: 'I can't do anything myself. But I can introduce a wonderful, wonderful man. I'm a great fan of his myself. Ladies and gentlemen, my husband, Frank Sinatra.' Although the newspapers had been ablaze for days with stories of the Palm Springs brawl, the audience warmed to the overtones of the reconciliation.

A few days later, Frank and Ava, accompanied by Ava's sister Bea, arrived at Idlewild in New york, *en route* to North Carolina. After a brief visit with Ava's family, they returned to New York and flew to Africa.

Frank made two trips back to the States before the year was out. The first was to fill an engagement at the French Casino in New York. 'A funny thing happened to me on the way to Africa,' Frank later said. 'I met Abe Lastfogel.' That was the name of the William Morris agency executive who booked him into the Casino and brought him into the talent agency. Observers of the engagement in the early weeks of December, confirmed what had been evident at earlier personal appearances. 'The solution of the domestic problems,' a reviewer wrote in the *Mirror*, 'makes him amiable and gracious ... Without the mental and emotional stress, he is completely relaxed and sings as of yore. Frankie is at ease, quips about his personal life and handles himself with comfortable dignity...'

But another reporter with whom he talked for almost an hour, after asserting that he 'just didn't have the time to sit down and talk', probed deeper and found Frank 'a restless unhappy man in his middle thirties who wants very much to re-establish himself and who wants to be an actor, not just a singer playing himself'.

The second trip from Africa took him out to Hollywood. Frank made this one in connection with a film called *From Here to Eternity*.

xv

PRIVATE MAGGIO AND THE BAREFOOT
CONTESSA

In *Act I* Moss Hart discusses the sense of timing in an actor's life, the critical urgency of recognising the right role and 'seizing the *moment* without wavering or playing it safe'. The moment in Frank Sinatra's career came when he read James Jones' mighty novel of World War II. 'For the first time in my life,' Frank has said, 'I was reading something I really had to do. I just felt it—I just knew I could do it, and I just couldn't get it out of my head.' Later, at filming time, he said: 'I knew that if a picture was ever made, I was the only actor to play Private Maggio, the funny and sour Italo-American. I knew Maggio. I went to high school with him in Hoboken. I was beaten up with him. I might have been Maggio.'

But Frank was Maggio. The late head of Columbia Pictures (King) Harry Cohn, who ultimately requested that Sinatra be tested for the role, told Buddy Adler, his reluctant producer: 'Did you ever see that guy without a shirt on? This is a thin, little guy with a caved-in chest but with a great heart...' Certainly, it was not difficult for Frank to identify with Maggio in the dark days of 1952 when both his career and marriage were tottering. To top his pile of woes, Internal Revenue had presented him with a bill for back taxes going back to 1946; the staggering total was $109,996. 'Frank is in a very destructive frame of mind,' friends said with concern. 'Half the time, he just can't see any reason for living.'

The rest of the time, Frank was intent on one thing. He had previously campaigned for other movie roles: the William Prince part in *John Loves Mary*, which had eluded him in 1947, and the role of Father Paul, which he had landed in *Miracle of the Bells*. No project had been marked by the desperation of his drive to play Private Maggio. As soon as Columbia had purchased the screen rights to *From Here to Eternity*, he had begun badgering studio executives.

'But it's an acting part, Frankie,' Buddy Adler told him.

'It's me,' Frank said. 'Buddy, I've never asked you for anything before. But I'm ready to beg. Give me the part and you'll never be sorry.'

Adler, who was dubious, said: 'We have a number of actors under consideration and we're testing five of them. I'll have to think about it.'

Anxiously, he watched the news releases coming from Columbia. Montgomery Clift was signed as Prewitt. Fred Zinnemann won the directorial assignment. Succeeding releases named Burt Lancaster as Sgt. Warden, Deborah Kerr as Capt. Holmes' wife, Karen, and Donna Reed as the prostitute Lorene. As long as there was no Maggio, he had a chance and he kept hounding the studio. He talked with Zinnemann, who was unreceptive. He had Ava contact Harry Cohn. Finally, he himself went to see Cohn.

'Look, Frank,' Cohn, who relished his reputation as a bastard, said, 'Maggio's an actor's part. You're a singer.'

Disregarding the rejection, Frank talked on and on, making every argument he could think of. He was aware that Cohn was not listening half the time. After a while, he knew that he had lost. Always the shrewd businessman, he decided to try a dangerous gambit. He knew that people who sold themselves cheap were seldom bought, and he was aware that buyers like Cohn tended to judge the value of anything by the price tag. Yet a buyer like Cohn could, perhaps, be attracted by a bargain, even on a picture with a three million dollar budget.

'About the money——' Frank said.

'Who's talking money?' Cohn countered. 'But what about the money?'

'I've been getting $150,000 a film——'

'You *used* to get $150,000,' Cohn interrupted.

'All right,' Frank granted, 'I *used* to get it. But do you know what I'll play Maggio for?'

'I'm not buying, Frank,' Cohn said. 'But just for the record, what's the fancy price?'

Frank skilfully delayed his response to build it up. He would have played the part for nothing. 'I'm not kidding, Harry,' he said finally. 'But you can get your Maggio for—a thousand a week.'

Cohn studied Frank's face. 'That's how bad you want it?'

'I've got to have it,' Frank replied. 'It was written for me—for *me* and nobody else.'

All that Cohn would say was: 'We'll see, Frank. We'll see. Meanwhile, we've got some other actors—regular actors—to test.'

As he was about to leave, Frank might have considered reminding Cohn of a favour he had once done for the Columbia picture chief. It involved a mild comedy *Miss Grant Takes Richmond* for which Cohn wanted a Broadway première. He had called Frank, who was about to make a personal appearance at the Capitol, and asked him to request the film on the bill. Frank had done so and Cohn had his Broadway première. Before the engagement was completed, Frank became ill and was compelled to remain in bed in a NY hotel room for several days. Cohn had flown into New York and kept Sinatra company until he was recovered. Uneasy that his well-known reputation as a bastard might be hurt by this considerate conduct, Cohn had warned Frank: 'You tell anyone—and I'll kill you.'

Frank left King Cohn without mentioning the incident. He was not hopeful about the outcome of his visit. A few days later, however, Cohn did phone and promise that he would be screen-tested for the role. He was elated. But then, as the days passed, he kept hearing of regular actors being tested—men with fat acting backgrounds and big names. And then it was time for them to fly to Africa for Ava's work on the film *Mogambo*. In an abject mood, he made the trip to Nairobi.

Things did not go too well between him and Ava on the *Mogambo* set. The location itself kept reminding him that his wife was the star of one of the year's big budget films while he could not land a part as a supporting player. The inevitable bickering was building to a crisis when a cable came from Buddy Adler. Cohn had kept his promise. An invitation to appear for a screen test, it did not include an offer to share or reimburse him for the cost of the 27,000 mile round-trip. However, Frank did not hesitate.

'I caught the next plane to Hollywood,' he said later. 'For the test, I played the saloon scene where Maggio shakes dice with the olives and the scene where he's found drunk outside the Royal Hawaiian Hotel. I was scared to death. The next day, I flew back to Africa, probably the longest route an actor ever travelled for a fifteen-minute screen test.'

Buddy Adler later said: 'He surprised us by appearing in Hollywood within thirty-six hours after my cable to Nairobi. I was a little startled when I gave him the script of the drunk scene and he handed it back. 'I don't need this,' he said. 'I've read it many times.' I didn't think he had a chance, anyway, so I said, 'Well, okay.' Since his was the last test of the day, I didn't intend going down on the stage. But I got a call from Fred Zinnemann, 'You'd better come down here. You'll see something unbelievable. I already have it in the camera. I'm not using film this time. But I want you to see it.'

'Frank thought he was making another take—and he was terrific. I thought to myself, if he's like that in the movie, it's a sure Academy Award. But we had to have Harry Cohn's okay on casting and he was out of town. So Frank went back to Africa.'

Bearing Christmas gifts bought with money borrowed from friends—some friends say that Ava lent the money for the trip and the gifts—Frank returned to Nairobi in an exultant frame of mind. His hopefulness continued through Christmas Eve when he led a group of natives in the singing of carols. But as the days wore on and he began despairing of getting the Maggio role, he once again became testy and defensive—and the delicately maintained balance of feelings between him and

Ava began to tilt to the unpleasant side. Then suddenly, the cable arrived. His six-month campaign was over. He had what was to prove the turning point of his career and, as his friends and Ava believed, of his marriage to her.

'Now, I'll show all those wise guys!' he exclaimed, as he paced back and forth before their African tent, waving the precious rectangle of cable. 'I'll show all those mothers!'

Early in her stay in Nairobi, Ava became ill, so ill that she had to be flown from Kenya to London. Some papers reported that she had a severe case of anaemia. *Look* called it dysentery. Interviewed at the Savoy Hotel, twelve pounds slimmer and still feeling shaky, she gave the impression that all was not well in the Sinatra *ménage*. 'Ava needs a nice, normal guy she can lean on,' a friend told writer William Attwood. 'She'd love to have a conventional home life with a big, strong, conventional guy and a Hollywood career on the side, like a pastime.' Neither friend nor reporter surmised what had really brought Ava to a London hospital. It was not until later, after the marriage to Frank was nothing but a document in a safety deposit box, that she confessed to a newsman: 'It was actually a miscarriage and we lost the baby we both wanted so much.' This was possibly the second infant they lost, for Ava had reportedly had an earlier miscarriage in May 1952.

Between the time of his selection as Maggio and the March–April filming of *From Here to Eternity*, Frank took another step that was almost as crucial as his campaign for the Maggio role.

Although his contract with Columbia Records did not expire until the end of 1952, Frank did no recording after September 17 of that year, at which time he cut a single song *Why Try to Change Me Now* with Percy Faith. It was not a 'knuckler', as Frank called it in baseball jargon, any more than the three other dates of the year had been. And yet those who would like to believe that Frank was not singing well at this time have his recording of *The Birth of the Blues*, cut on June 3, to reckon with. The voice has vigour and fine sustaining power. The band rocks and he swings. Nevertheless, Frank finished his ten-year career at Columbia owing the surprising sum of $110,000 in unearned advances. (Since then, his LPs have not only amortised the advances but have brought him royalties of over $50,000 a year—and Columbia continues to repackage the available sides.)

During the month following the expiration of his Columbia contract, no record company moved to sign him. Manie Sachs, then a top executive at RCA Victor and, as ever, a faithful friend, tried hard to sell Sinatra to his colleagues. The William Morris office, which began handling him in December 1952, approached other record companies. There was little receptivity, no enthusiasm, and no willingness to put up any front money. Capitol Records, based in Hollywood, finally proffered a contract: there was no advance, arranging, copying and musicians' costs were to be borne by Sinatra, and the deal was for just a year. In addition to agency pressure, it took the combined urging of three friends inside Capitol to close the deal. Axel Stordahl, whose wife June Hutton was a Capitol artist, talked with Glenn Wallichs, then president of the company. Dick Jones, who had played the piano at the Gardner–Sinatra nuptials and who was then a Capitol producer, added his affirmation, as did Dave Dexter, Capitol's jazz producer, who was Sinatra's biggest booster.

Out of the association with Capitol, which lasted for more then seven years, came the mature singing stylist, the 'swinging' Sinatra. A feeling for jazz apparent through the years flowered into a 'ballad-with-a-beat' style that made him the pop singer most popular with jazzmen. Two Capitol recording men were pivotal in this development.

One was Voyle Gilmore, a drawling ex-drummer, who became Sinatra's record producer. Frank rejected Dave Dexter, despite his key role in bringing him to the label, ostensibly because Dexter had written adverse reviews of Sinatra discs while he was a *Down Beat* critic. Gilmore, who admits that he was not a Sinatra fan at that time, was certain of one thing: they had to move away from the 'out-of-tempo, rustle-of-spring approach' of the Columbia era. The other man responsible for the Capitol Sinatra was, of course, arranger-conductor Nelson Riddle, whom Frank once called 'a tranquilliser—calm, slightly aloof. Nothing ever ruffles him.'

On Frank's first Capitol session early in April 1953, Axel Stordahl handled the baton. They cut two tunes: *I'm Walking Behind You* and *Lean Baby*, the latter a Billy May instrumental to which Roy Alfred had written a lyric, taking May's title to mean a thin chick instead of a request to bend.

171

Although Capitol was not displeased with the sale of the disc, Gilmore felt that the soft-rhythm approach was wrong for a market receptive to the hard-driving, belting, rhythm singers of the day. Eddie Fisher, not Sinatra, had the hit record on the English importation, *I'm Walking Behind You*. Before Gilmore could discuss a new approach with Sinatra—the use of a new arranger was involved—Stordahl accepted an offer to conduct the new Eddie Fisher–Coca Cola TV show. Since the show came from New York, the door was open to the employment of a new arranger.

For his second Capitol session, on April 30, Sinatra selected Billy May, former Charlie Barnett, Glenn Miller arranger-trumpeter. May was to score *I Love You* and *South of the Border*. To arrange the other tunes, *I've Got the World on a String* and *Don' Worry About Me*, Gilmore chose Nelson Riddle who had scored Ella Mae Morse's big Capitol hit *Blacksmith Blues*. ('Billy is driving, Nelson has depth,' Sinatra later said, 'while Gordon Jenkins'—another arranger he came to use—'is great for creating a mood.') A day or two before the session, May, who was on tour with his band, phoned from Florida to bow out of the assignment. Although he received label credit, all the arrangements used on the April 30 date were the work of Riddle. Frank has continued to use Billy May through the years. The driving bite of his arrangements and his inventive use of shrill, slurping saxes are heard in albums like *Come Fly With Me, Come Dance With Me, Come Swing With Me,* and more recently, in *Sinatra Swings* on Reprise.

But beginning with the session of May 2 when he recorded the ageless *My One and Only Love*, Frank developed a musical relationship that carried him to the top of the record world for the second time and that made Nelson Riddle, former trombonist with Jerry Wald, Charlie Spivak and Tommy Dorsey, one of the most sought-after arranger-conductor-composers on the Hollywood scene. As Axel Stordahl had created the lush, light-rhythmed, string-woodwind sound of the Columbia Sinatra, Riddle was the major architect of the swinging Capitol Sinatra.

'There's no one like him,' Riddle has said. 'Frank not only encourages you to adventure, but he has such a keen appreciation of achievement that you are impelled to knock yourself out for him. It's not only that his intuitions as to tempi, phras-

172

ing and even figuration are amazingly right, but that his taste is so impeccable. This is because his interest in music has never been hemmed in. He was the one who got me all excited about the work of the contemporary Engish composer Vaughan Williams.'

Sinatra–Riddle recordings possess a quality which is rare even today on popular discs. Most record-makers press for the sound that will grab the listener and, through the use of contrast, hold his interest. Sinatra and Riddle were vitally concerned with an additional factor: form or architecture. 'In working out an arrangement,' Riddle has said, 'I look for the peak of a song and build to it. We're telling a story. It has to have a beginning, a middle, a *climax* and an ending.' Guided by Frank, whose concern with lyrics is legendary, Riddle constructed his scores to document the words. The graph of the arrangement pursued the trajectory of the story.

'Working with him was always a challenge,' Riddle admitted. 'And there were times when the going got rough. Never a relaxed man, as Nat Cole was, for example, he was a perfectionist who drove himself and everybody around him relentlessly. You always approached him with a feeling of uneasiness, not only because he was demanding and unpredictable, but because his reactions were so violent. But all of these tensions disappeared if you came through for him. I can't help thinking of him with a certain sadness. This man is a giant. Not that there aren't other good singers around. But he has imagination and scope of the rarest. After all these years, there is still no one who can approach him.'

Not long ago, Sinatra said: 'It was a happy marriage. Nelson had a fresh approach to orchestration and I made myself fit into what he was doing.'

Together, the two wrought a major change in the sound of ballad records, for they added the brassy drive of swing to the lovely swirl of strings.

'He dreamt, slept and ate his part,' producer Buddy Adler said of Sinatra in *From Here to Eternity*.

'He played Maggio so spontaneously,' director Fred Zinnemann said, 'we almost never had to reshoot a scene.' So great was his identification, in fact, that crew members stopped calling him 'Frank' and unconsciously began addressing him as 'Maggio'.

'I was working,' Frank said later, 'with the finest pros. I felt like I was playing with the Yankees and I knew it was going well. I learned from all of them. But Montgomery Clift was particularly helpful ... The way he pitched, I couldn't help shining as a catcher.' Nor could Frank help imitating in later films some of Clift's mannerisms, like his crouch and shoulder-hunching.

'Sinatra has the most amazing sense of timing,' Buddy Adler said, 'and occasionally he'll drop in a word or two that makes the line actually bounce. It's just right. He never made a fluff. And this from a fellow who really never had any training. I must admit that I kept thinking of him as a singer before the test, and couldn't visualise him in the role. But once the test was made, it was a case of a natural performer up against some great actors. The natural performer was better.'

The natural performer was also available. The role came to Sinatra after Eli Wallach had chosen the Tennessee Williams play *Camino Real* in preference to the James Jones' film. The play was a flop.

The $1,000 a week, which Frank received for his acting, was a pittance, not only by comparison to what he had once commanded at MGM, but compared to the $25,000 he was paid by the Riviera or the $10,000 a week he received from the French Casino in the darkest days of 1952. But he came out of the eight weeks of shooting, looking like what Louella Parsons and others were soon calling 'the New Sinatra'. Interviewing him on May 5, just before he left for Europe, Miss Parsons wrote: 'The nervous unhappy Frank Sinatra, who declared war on newspaper people and let his hot Italian temper get him into trouble, is a character of the past. The new Frankie has put on weight. His eyes are clear and untroubled and better still, he's happy. This *is* a new Frankie.'

But apparently the improvement did not show on the domestic scene. 'When he was down and out,' Ava said in August, 'he was so sweet. But now that he's got successful again, he's become his old arrogant self. We were happy when he was on the skids.' Doubtless, what Ava meant was that *she* had been happy.

Early in May, having completed shooting on *From Here to Eternity*, Frank began a three-month tour of Europe, making personal appearances in major cities. Ava accompanied him and it could have been a gay holiday, a second honeymoon. It was not. After a time, word began to trickle around about Frank's fantastic performance in *Eternity* and the high expectations Columbia had for the picture and Frank's part in it. As the revival of his career gained momentum, the race of his marriage to destruction also seemed to pick up speed.

Arriving at London airport just after the plane's doors had been sealed, Frank and Ava got into a fracas with BEA personnel because they were not permitted to board. At the airport in Rome, there were unpleasant brushes with the papparazzi (free-lance photographers). In Naples, Frank twice walked off-stage, provoking audience outbursts that required police intervention, 'Frank Sinatra Booed as Ava Skips Town', was the headline in a Neapolitan paper. In Stockholm, where Frank left an audience crying for more, lest he miss a connection to Denmark, the customers were so upset that a NY magazine reported : 'Swedes Boo Our Frankie.' Frank's short temper in public was apparently a reflection of mounting tension between him and Ava. The press did not help. It tried to pry, not only into their disagreements, but into their most intimate moments. 'One photographer,' Ava reported, 'tried his damnedest to get a picture of us in bed.'

Frank returned to London feeling, in the words of British bandleader Cyril Stapleton, 'as cheerful as a drunk in a milk bar'. When he was well received on the BBC, his spirits rose. On his second broadcast, he broke up Stapleton and the British musicians when he showed up carrying a rolled umbrella and, in true Bond Street style, wearing a bowler hat and wash-leather gloves. The British reaction to the concert tour that followed was pithily summarised by *Musical Express* : 'Sinatra is still the greatest male singer in pop music. His range and power seem greater than ever.'

Meanwhile, with tender interludes, the bickering between Frank and Ava continued. Ava always talked with sadness of their apartment in London. 'You see,' she would say, 'we wanted a home rather than a hotel suite. Places in London were still hard to find. But this one was big—and did the trick.' They had it throughout the period when Ava was filming *Knights of the Round Table*. According to Ava, when Frank was there, they were so happy that 'we just stayed home. We didn't do much gadding about, just kind of sat around and let ourselves be ourselves.' But this also was the apartment in which so violent a quarrel occurred that they were reportedly threatened with eviction.

The shooting on *Knights of the Round Table* was complete except for some small scenes and Ava had a few days off. Due to open at the 500 Club in Atlantic City, Frank wanted Ava to accompany him. She preferred to go to Madrid to rest. The argument was so boisterous that other tenants called the building management. Having stormed out of the apartment, Frank returned to find himself locked out. Later, he learned that Ava had gone to a Piccadilly club where Walter Chiari, who was to become a post-Sinatra swain, did a take-off of Frank. Friends reported that Ava sat ringside laughing uproariously and egging the Italian comic on with loud cries: 'That's exactly the way he does it! It's so funny! More! More!'

Frank arrived in New York on August 12 to find show business agog over his performance in *From Here to Eternity*. *Look* magazine had already predicted that his portrayal of Maggio would win an Academy Award nomination. *Variety* announced 'Since *Eternity* Everybody Wants Sinatra for TV.' Signed to help kick off the new Milton Berle show, Sinatra received a guest fee of $6,000, almost as much money for one evening's work as he had earned in eight weeks before the *Eternity* cameras. NBC-TV also reopened negotiations regarding an exclusive contract, negotiations that had come to a halt a year earlier when CBS had dropped him.

Reviews of Sinatra's performance in *Eternity* abounded in superlatives. 'For the first time,' Richard Watts wrote in the NY *Post*, 'I find myself in the ranks of his ardent admirers. Instead of exploiting a personality, he proves he is an actor by playing the luckless Maggio with a kind of doomed gaiety that is both real and immensely touching.' Watts' unreserved admiration was shared by reviewers from coast to coast.

Her chores in *Knights of the Round Table* completed, Ava returned from Europe on September 2. Still piqued over their last quarrel, she did not cable Frank about her arrival nor was he at the airport to welcome her. Moving into Hampshire House, she waited for Frank to phone while Frank ostensibly remained at the Waldorf, waiting for her to apprise him of her arrival. Two days later, when he opened at the Riviera, Ava went to the première of a Broadway show. Frank was crestfallen. Not even the ovation he received made up for the snub.

Between shows and between greeting friends, he sank into a low-keyed moodiness that escaped nobody's notice. The following day, as columnists made an episode of Ava's absence, his aggravation settled into deep resentment.

A TV commentator who was friendly with both sought to effect a reconciliation. His idea was to interview Frank about *Eternity* with Ava present. Frank agreed. But Ava balked: 'This is a personal matter. It's my marriage, my life, and it has no place on your show. I won't come.' Another friend tried a slightly more obvious manoeuvre. He phoned Ava from Frank's apartment and then told Frank that Ava was on the phone and wanted to talk to him. According to Earl Wilson, each thought that the other was making the apology—'so each was aloof, haughty and disdainful'—and the whole thing blew up, as receivers were slammed down in a childish display of pride.

It was Dolly Sinatra who effected a brief reconciliation. Either because Ava confided her unhappiness to her mother-in-law, or because Dolly realised how despondent her son was, she arranged a small dinner party. Ava arrived first since Frank was still playing the Riviera. The moment his first show was over, he zoomed down the Jersey shore road to his parents' new home in Weehawken. The second show was an exciting one: Ava returned with him after they had made up over his mother's dinner.

'With Ava in the audience,' Earl Wilson reported, 'Frank changed one of the gestures in his act that had been getting a good laugh during the battling. Singing *I Get a Kick Out of You*, Frankie had illustrated it—as though he were getting booted in the *derrière* by love, represented by Ava. He dropped that . . .'

The following day, Frank moved to Ava's apartment in Hampshire House. Several nights later, instead of returning to their apartment after the second show, Frank sat around Lindy's with the boys into the small hours of the morning. When he finally returned to the hotel and Ava remonstrated with him, Frank allegedly played it cool. On the urging of friends, instead of placating, he was trying a new technique.

On October 2 Ava and Frank attended the première of *Mogambo* at the Radio City Music Hall. The following day, they walked arm in arm from the plane that had brought them to Hollywood. An MGM official said: 'They're together—and that's the main thing.' Ava left almost immediately for Palm Springs 'to rest up', as the papers put it, while Frank flew to Las Vegas to fulfil a personal appearance.

Frank's inner distress expressed itself in many ways, including his treatment of the musicians backing him at his opening at the Sands on October 19. *Billboard* observed several days later 'Frank Sinatra, the spindly crooner who is not noted for his warmth towards an audience, this week tried hard to change his ways in the Copa Room, and succeeded, after drawing severe raps from local papers, for his rough treatment of musicians behind him on opening night.'

Just three weeks later, MGM handed out a release that shook up the movie colony and show business. It stated simply that Ava and Frank could find no mutual basis on which to continue their marriage, that their separation was final, and that Ava would seek a divorce. The marriage had lasted twenty-three months and twenty days. (Four weeks after the announcement of October 27, movie fans were reading a *Photoplay* article whose closing sentence read: 'Ava and Frank are happier than anyone has seen them for a long time.')

That the announcement was not a joint statement became apparent when Frank phoned Earl Wilson and said: 'If it took seventy-five years to get a divorce, there wouldn't be any other woman.' But Ava complained: 'Frank doesn't love me. He would rather go out with some other girl, almost any other girl.' And she told Wilson that when she had tried to get together with Frank in their Palm Springs home to patch things up, he had invited some of his buddies along. 'It is rather amazing,' Wilson wrote 'that Ava, long ago adjudged one of the greatest sex-appeal women in Hollywood, should ever feel that Frank cared more for somebody else. Yet she felt this way keenly and not infrequently.' In retrospect, Ava later said: 'Maybe if I had been willing to share Frank with other women, we could have been happier.'

Florabel Muir and Hedda Hopper blamed the bust-up on Frank's failure to meet Ava on her return from Europe, but also reported that while Ava had sulked at Palm Springs, Frank was 'less than sulky with an unidentified girl in Vegas'. To Louella Parsons, it was a clash of careers. When Frank admitted that he was so upset he could not eat or sleep, and

Louella asked why he didn't phone her, Frank replied that the first move had to come from Ava. Earl Wilson suggested two reasons for a possible divorce: Ava, on the verge of a nervous breakdown, tended to exaggerate Frank's faults and their differences; and, she was too proud to tolerate Frank's domineering ways.

Two days after the MGM announcement, Frank flew to Carson City where he appeared before the Nevada Tax Commision. His application for the purchase of a 2 per cent interest in the Sands Hotel had been pending for three months. One of the commissioners had blocked a purchase licence on the ground that the $54,000 should be used by Frank to pay taxes he owed the Federal government. The same commissioner still opposed Frank's petition even though he explained that he was paying off his debt to Uncle Sam at the rate of $1,000 an engagement and that he had already repaid $70,000 of the $160,000 levy. The Commission voted 6 to 1 in Frank's favour.

Queried by reporters about his marriage, he admitted unhappily that it was 'on the rocks'. He reportedly said: 'I guess it's over if that's what Ava says. It's very sad ... It's tragic. I feel very badly about it.'

The following day, New York papers carried an AP photo of Frank and two Vegas chorus girls. It had been snapped at a Halloween costume party thrown by Frank, who was dressed as a clown, at the Sands. The same day Hedda Hopper announced that, although Ava had talked with Frank on the phone, there had been no reconciliation. 'The break-up is a pity,' Miss Hopper write, 'as Ava is still evidently in love with Frank.' When Hedda wondered whether a third party was involved, Ava replied: 'As far as I know, there isn't.' That day, newspapers quoted Nancy Sinatra as saying: 'There is positively no chance of a reconciliation between us. All the rumours about Mr. Sinatra and me are false.'

Ava and Frank were playing a curious and costly kind of game with each other. It was almost as if Ava had made the announcement of her divorce intentions to test how Frank felt and how far she could push him. By his initial cool demeanour, it appeared that he was prepared to play out the game. But Frank's feelings ran much deeper than he was ready to admit publicly, or perhaps even to himself.

For recording sessions in November 1953, instead of the brassy swinging type of band he had used on earlier dates, Frank's backing consisted of a chamber-music group, violins, viola and 'cello, two saxes and no brass, that emitted a soft, tender, almost mournful type of sound. On November 5, his songs included *My Funny Valentine*, *They Can't Take That Away from Me*, and *A Foggy Day in London Town*, one of his great vehicles and a song that must have evoked memories of days with Ava in the British capital. The wee-small-hours recording session on the following evening, which employed the same moody backing, included the introspective *Little Girl Blue* and another Ava-oriented tune, *I Get a Kick Out of You*.

Twelve days later, he flew to New York to tape a new twice-weekly radio series for NBC. Dinah Shore had taken over a spot vacated by Eddie Fisher, and Sinatra had been signed for the Tuesday/Friday slot at 8.15 p.m. Apart from lucrative club and theatre proffers, he now had a choice of several attractive movie roles. Twentieth Century-Fox wanted him for *Pink Tights* and offered a salary that made Marilyn Monroe, who was to receive top billing, angry and sullen. Columbia was dangling the title role in *Pal Joey*. But all of this did not mitigate the tension and hurt caused by the break-up of his marriage. About friends who said that Ava was mixed-up and too complex for him, he would say: 'Sure, it's easy for them to say give her up . . . when they're not in love with her . . .'

Learning that Ava was planning to leave for Europe on an extended stay, he began taping as many advance segments of his NBC show as he could squeeze into working days. The day before he was to return to Hollywood, he felt so spent that, after taping two full shows, he went to see a physician. His weight was then down to 118 pounds from 132, and he looked so run-down that the doctor insisted that he enter a hospital for observation.

On his admission to the private pavilion of Mt. Sinai Hospital, it was found that he had superficial cuts on several fingers, the result presumably of a broken glass. He had himself covered the cuts with bandaids. The examining doctor noted that he was suffering from 'complete physical exhaustion, severe loss of weight and a tremendous amount of emotional strain'. Aware of his capacity for dramatic acts of self-pity, friends were, nevertheless, so worried that they tried to persuade Ava to come to see him. They were unsuccessful.

After two days, Frank fled the hospital, despite strenuous objections by his physician. 'He told me it was impossible to stay here,' the doctor reported, 'because he *had* to get to the coast.' He added: 'There's nothing seriously the matter with him except nervous exhaustion. He's even put back several pounds of the fourteen he lost in the last few weeks.' Before he left for Hollywood, he told Earl Wilson of several phone conversations he had had with Ava: 'During our last phone call,' he said wanly and hopefully, 'we didn't have one fight—it was wonderful.' Although he managed to avoid the press at La Guardia by boarding the plane in the hangar, he was met by a large press group in Hollywood. Taciturn but not bellicose, he permitted the photographers to take pictures.

That night he dined with Ava at the home of her sister Bea. After dinner Ava left for Palm Springs but Frank remained in Hollywood. MGM issued an official bulletin: 'Ava and Frankie met Friday evening. She is leaving next week for Rome on a loan-out picture. She still plans a divorce but no time has been set.' The following Thursday, Ava departed for Italy to make *The Barefoot Contessa*.

At the airport in Rome, Ava gave serene 'No comment' replies to each question concerning Frank and their marriage. Later she admitted that she had left Hollywood because of the break-up. 'I was frantic,' she said, 'when the split came. I went to everybody at the studio, Dore Schary, Eddie Mannix, Harry Rapf and even Bennie Thau. He always liked me. I raised the roof. I told him I'd always been the good girl of the company, doing every lousy part in every lousy damned picture. I told him I just had to get out of Hollywood now—right now—or I'd blow my top. I guess that scared him.'

Joseph Mankiewicz, writer-director-producer of *Contessa*, nodded sympathetically. 'I guess it did,' he said. 'But do you know the deal I finally agreed to? ... MGM is getting $200,000 to lend you to us plus 10 per cent of the gross after the first million.'

'That's Metro,' Ava chortled. 'And I'm getting a lousy $60,000 plus six months expenses of $1,000 a week! And I though they let me go because they understood how badly I had to get away. What a laugh!'

Morose and self-contained, Frank did two recording sessions in December, both difficult dates. Of the two songs he cut on December 8—union regulations permitted the recording of four—one was suggestively titled *Why Should I Cry Over You*. The session on December 9 ran ninety minutes overtime, and with an orchestra numbering twenty-seven men, the cost to Sinatra rose from a planned $1,072.50 to $2,145. In the four and a half hours, which finished at 1 a.m., only three songs were cut. Two of the tunes were *Rain* and *I Could Have Told You*. The third was *Young at Heart*, one of the few songs in his career that, as Frank put it, 'came in over the transom'.

Originally an instrumental by Johnny Richards, *Young at Heart* with lyrics by Carolyn Leigh, had been turned down by Nat Cole and several other singers. It was song-writer Jimmy Van Heusen who persuaded Sinatra to cut the tune that proved a second launching pad for his fabulous record career. By March 1954, *Young at Heart* was on the Hit Parade where it eventually climbed to No. 1.

As Christmas approached, Frank phoned Ava in the Italian capital and told her he would like to come to Rome for the holidays.

'It'll be a mess,' Ava told her press agent. 'Why the hell does he do it—and this of all times. I was so looking forward to Madrid.'

David Hanna, her press agent, agreed. 'If he comes here, the press will murder both of you.'

'But what can I do?' Ava said. 'I can't tell him not to come.'

Ava did not tell Frank not to come. But on Christmas Eve, after an impromptu champagne party, she took off for Madrid. It was not until he arrived in London, loaded down with gifts, that Frank learned of her departure from Rome. With all Madrid flights booked solid for the holidays, Frank chartered a private twin-engined plane. On Christmas night, which was also Ava's birthday, she and Frank sang carols together at the Madrid home of film executive Frank Grant, where she was staying. Frank spent the following day in bed in an attempt to knock out a bad cold from which he was suffering.

When they arrived in Rome on the 29th, Ava also had a cold. Although the Italian press kept a round-the-clock stake-out of their apartment in the Corso d'Itallo, there were no incidents. Frank tried hard to postpone his departure and telephoned officials at Twentieth Century-Fox. They were unmoved by his plea that he and Ava were 'trying to work things out', and insisted that he return for the start of production.

At the Rome airport, reporters noted that Ava did not come to see Frank off. 'She still has the 'flu. She's running a temperature,' he said. Smiling, he added: 'I have a cold, too.' However, friends claimed that Ava was busy posing for sculptor Assen Peikov, who was making the statue of her used in *The Barefoot Contessa*. Ava later told her press agent that there had been no reconciliation. When Hanna inquired what they had done for the three days before Frank's departure, Ava replied that they had just stayed put in the apartment. 'Hell, sweetie,' Ava said, 'we couldn't have gone out if we wanted to. I had the measles, the German measles.'

From 1955 to 1964 Frank lived in a bachelor house he built at the summit of Coldwater Canyon in Beverly Hills. In the garden stood a memento of his reconciliation trip to Rome. It was the life-size statue of Ava sculpted by Peikov.

XVI

THE PHOENIX CARRIES A TORCH

Frank returned from Rome to stage a professional comeback that electrified show business. There were other comebacks in 1954—Judy Garland in *A Star is Born*, Lillian Roth from the wasteland of alcoholism and even Vaughn Monroe, who latched on to a new dance craze with his hit record of *They Were Doing the Mambo*. But the tale of Frank's re-emergence as a star soon acquired the same fascination for writers and readers that the saga of his hypnotic hold on audiences had had in 1944. It became a legend almost before it was a fact. 'It's the greatest comeback in theatre history,' wrote editor Abel Green in *Variety*. 'One good picture is all it takes. Now, it's coming down in showers for Sinatra and everybody in show business is rooting for him. They never stopped!' And columnist Sid Skolsky commented: 'He proved you could flop and make a comeback. And he did what every performer wants to do:

become a success in other fields.'

The crux of Frank's comeback was, of course, the Academy Award for the Best Supporting Performance (Male) of 1953. 'The greatest change in my life,' he said afterwards, 'began the night they gave me the Oscar. It's funny about that statue. You walk up on the stage like you are in a dream and they hand you that little man before twenty or thirty million people and you have to fight to keep the tears back. It's a moment. Like your first girl or your first kiss. Like the first time you hit a guy and he went down. I've heard actors kid about the Academy Awards. Don't believe them. It was a big moment in their lives.'

The evening before the Awards were presented, Frank had dinner with Nancy and their three children at her home. Although on the preceding day, he had received the *Look* award for the Best Supporting Performance of the year, what really mattered was the little gold man—and Frank's children knew it. When dinner was over, Frank discovered a small box near his coffee cup; it was their Oscar award to him. On one side of the gold medal was an image of St. Genesius, patron saint of actors, and on the other, a tiny Oscar in bas-relief with the inscription, 'Dad, we'll love you—from here to eternity.' As he studied the medal, Frank was most aware of the eyes of their mother—for he knew that the medal was an expression of her feeling as well as theirs. It was one of the most tender, one of the toughest moments in Frank's life.

The following evening, March 25, as he rode to the theatre where the Oscars were to be awarded, Frank, Jr., and Nancy, Jr., sat beside him, their goodluck charm was around his neck. It was just 3,000 miles from the Pantages Theatre in Hollywood to the Paramount Theatre in New York where he had scored his initial success as a singer; but it seemed like 3,000 years instead of ten for the singer now seeking an award as a dramatic actor. 'A peculiar thing happened and I can't explain it,' Louella Parsons wrote afterwards. 'I ran into person after person who said, "He's a so-and-so but I hope he gets it. He was great!" No one had to name the antecedent of "he".'

The award for the Best Supporting Performance (Male) came towards the end of the proceedings. Presentor Mercedes McCambridge read the names of the five nominees Eddie Albert in *Roman Holiday*, Brandon DeWilde in *Shane*, Jack Palance in *Shane*, Frank Sinatra in *From Here to Eternity* and

Robert Strauss in *Stalag Seventeen*. Frank and his kids were sitting far back in the theatre when his name was announced. Tears streamed uncontrollably from Nancy, Jr.'s, eyes, as applause rocked the theatre. Frank leaned over and kissed her. As he trotted down the aisle to the stage, the applause rose like thunder. It was the loudest and the longest ovation of the evening. It was one of the emotion-wracked Academy Awards, not unlike Joan Crawford's comeback role in *Mildred Pierce*, Ingrid Bergman's triumph in *Anastasia* after Rosselini had walked out on her, and Elizabeth Taylor's award for *Butterfield Eight* after her near-fatal bout of pneumonia.

'Nobody cheered out of rosy affection for the guy,' a recent brochure published by Frank's own record company asserts. 'He got no sympathy votes. He just plain won the gold all by himself.' A cocky Sinatra himself told Tom Pryor of the NY *Times*, as he later told Joe Hyams in *Cue* and, again, a reporter for the London *Globe and Mail*: 'People often remark that I'm pretty lucky ... Luck is only important in so far as getting the chance to sell yourself at the right moment. After that, you've got to have talent and know how to use it.' Hyams reported that Frank refused to regard his new popularity as a comeback. 'It would be more accurate,' he said, 'to call what happened to my career "the rise and fall and rise again".'

At a party after the Academy Award presentations, Frank phoned his mother in Weehawken. Friends who could not help overhearing his end of the conversation, report that it consisted largely of phrases like 'Yes, mama,' and 'No, mama.' A few minutes earlier, he had been the great showman who had twice shaken the entertainment world by storm. Now, he was suddenly a lonely, love-hungry, small boy seeking his mother's affection and approval by parading his fantastic accomplishment before her.

Once off the phone, he was again the jaunty, wise-cracking man aglow with a sense of triumph. But afterwards, in the bachelor maisonette he shared with composer Jule Styne, the night was a sleepless one. Styne, who lived with Frank for almost a year after the break with Ava, has reported that he would generally find the maisonette in near-darkness when he returned at night. 'I enter the living room,' Styne said, 'and it's like a funeral parlour. The lights are dim and they just about light up several pictures of Ava. Frank sits in front of them with a bottle of brandy. After I get into bed, I can hear him pacing back and forth. It goes on for hours. At 4 a.m., I awake to hear him dialling someone on the phone. It's his first wife, Nancy. I hear him say, 'You're the only one who understands me.' After he hangs up, he starts pacing again. He seldom falls asleep until the sun is high in the sky. He can have almost any girl he wants by wagging a little finger. And he has lots of them. But he gets no satisfaction. And he suffers as much as the guy who never had one.'

'Loneliness is very wretched for an actor,' Jackie Gleason has said, 'because there's no one around to witness his misery.' But what if there is someone around? One evening, Frank refused to join his cronies in a game of poker and instead, closeted himself in his den. After a while, lyricist Sammy Cahn went to see if Sinatra's depression had lifted. Frank was drinking a toast to a picture of Ava 'with a tear running down his face'. A few moments later, the card players heard a crash. They rushed to the den to find that Frank had smashed Ava's framed photograph. As they entered, he was in the process of ripping the picture into small pieces. 'I'm through with her,' he cried. 'I never want to see her again.' The game resumed, still without Frank. After a time, Sammy Davis went to the den, only to find Sinatra on his hands and knees gathering up the torn pieces of the photograph and trying to reassemble them. When Frank became frantic because he could not find Ava's nose, all his friends joined the search. As they were about to give up, the doorbell rang. It was an errand boy bringing liquor. When the door was opened, the missing piece suddenly fluttered into sight. Frank was so delighted that he tore his gold watch from his wrist and handed it to the overwhelmed delivery boy.

Not too long after this, Dorothy Kilgallen claimed that agent George Wood of the William Morris office was assigned to stay close to Frank to 'try to keep him from slashing his wrists'. A more friendly source, Earl Wilson, portrayed Frank as a man who became unhappy when he was too happy. (As if to confirm Wilson's hypothesis, Frank recorded the Rodgers and Hart ballad *Glad to Be Unhappy*.) Reviewing affairs with Marilyn Maxwell, Lana Turner and Ava, Wilson contended that Frank seemed deliberately to court disaster at moments of greatest triumph. Soon, Frank starred in a number of films that provided an artistic equivalent of his self-destructive tendency. But in the meantime, the appealing image of the romantic pursuing a fatal destiny, à la John Garfield, was being projected on the screen of public consciousness by foe as well as friend.

1954 was the year in which the fulcrum of Frank's professional life swung from records to films. Suddenly, there were more movie roles than he could play in a dozen years.

During April, Frank went before the cameras in *Suddenly*, playing a psychopathic killer hired to assassinate the President of the United States. He was still on the payroll of Twentieth Century-Fox for *Pink Tights*, shelved when Marilyn Monroe objected to the script and delayed shooting by her marriage to Joe DiMaggio. Fox paid out the cash so that it could maintain a first-call hold on Sinatra's screen services. While it searched for a script for him, Warner Bros. offered the lead in *Young at Heart*, a remake of *Four Daughters* in which he was to play the John Garfield role. And MGM, which had let him go during the years of his decline, now wanted him to do *St. Louis Woman* with Ava, or a new picture with Gene Kelly.

At one point during the shooting of *Suddenly*, Frank went to producer Robert Bassler to propose some changes. 'I steeled myself,' Bassler later admitted, 'for there is nothing more disturbing than the cerebration of an actor. But Frank wasn't making demands to exploit himself at the expense of the picture. The suggestions he offered made sense for the picture.' To a reporter who interviewed him about his 'going dramatic', Frank stated: 'Actors who can't sing can't switch to our side. But there's no reason why a singer can't go dramatic. A singer is essentially an actor.' Before shooting on *Suddenly* was finished, Frank signed a contract for a starring role in *Not as a Stranger*, with filming scheduled for August.

Towards the end of May, Ava returned from Europe. For some time, there had been stories of an involvement with a handsome bullfighter. Luis Dominguin became quite widely known in America after Ernest Hemingway, in *Life*, described a series of *mano-a-mano* corridas between him and his brother-in-law Antonio Ordonez, Spain's other most celebrated matador. Ava spent her last hours in Spain in the company of Dominguin, and newspapers reported that they held hands and kissed warmly before she left. Asked during a stop-over in London and later in New York whether she was still planning to divorce Sinatra, she replied: 'I was never more certain of anything.' Apprised of her statement in Palm Springs where he was holding hands with actress Mona Freeman beside his piano-shaped swimming pool, Frank replied that he was flipped over Mona.

In June Ava drove from LA to Lake Tahoe and rented a plush cottage on the lake's eastern slope, ostensibly to establish Nevada residence for a divorce. Almost at the same moment, Frank opened an engagement at the Sands in Las Vegas. In the parlance of the film capital's gossip columnists, 'Hollywood held its breath', over the realisation that Ava could now see Frank without interrupting her residence. But there were no fireworks during the six weeks of Ava's stay—although there was much speculation as to whether a reconciliation was in the making. On the day Ava was due in court, a large cordon of reporters appeared. But the day passed without Ava's showing. For several days afterwards, the press maintained its stake-out. Then, quite suddenly, Ava was gone from Nevada, the divorce action left uncompleted.

Afterwards, Ava said that 'matters of a financial settlement' had prevented her from picking up the divorce papers. Although it was known that Ava had lent or given Frank money during his dark days, friends doubted that money played any role in the divorce proceedings; they pointed out that she had asked nothing of Mickey Rooney or Artie Shaw. Ava's press agent later wrote: 'She didn't have the courage to face the heavy battery of newsmen waiting for her at the courthouse.' Still another explanation is suggested by the pattern of Ava's conduct: just as she had announced her original decision to divorce in the hope of bringing Frank to his knees, she had now gone through all the motions of setting up residence, hoping, perhaps, to force his penitent return.

Just before the coast première of *The Barefoot Contessa*, p.a. David Hanna was Ava's house guest at their Palm Springs home. Late one night, at her request, they drove by the house in which she had lived with Frank. 'I was happier there,' Ava said, 'than any place I've ever been.' Sidney Skolsky, who interviewed Frank for a Tin Type on the set of *Young at Heart*, reported that he kept a picture of Ava pinned to his dressing-room mirror. Kendis Rocklin, who used the item in the LA *Mirror-News*, received a telegram: 'It's too bad you're such a lying, low, dishonest reporter.'

In the weeks before the NY première of the *Contessa* (September 29, 1954), Ava took a trip to South America where Dominguin was fighting the bulls. On her return to New York. according to friends, Ava turned down a proposal of marriage. While Dominguin was in New York, he and Ava ran into Sammy Davis at Danny's Hideaway. On Davis' invitation, Ava went up to the Apollo Theatre in Harlem, where Davis was appearing, accompanied by a UA press agent and disc jockey William B. Williams of WNEW. Since the Apollo was packed, the three watched the show from backstage. At one point, Sammy brought Ava on stage for a bow—it was an easy plug for *The Barefoot Contessa*, then in its première run—and 'she gassed everybody', as Sammy put it.

Sammy added: 'I would have cut off my dancing feet to prevent what was to happen. The next day a column carried an item about Ava's appearance. In parentheses was planted the snide question: "Wonder what went on backstage?" I was real upset about the innuendo. Not only because of the injustice to Ava but because of what Frank might think.'

Still to come was a story in a trashy exposé magazine. Sammy was in Hollywood several months later when he received a frantic call from his press agent, who came over looking 'as though the roof had collapsed on him'. Jesse Rand had been tipped that Sammy was to be the main story in the next issue of *Confidential*. 'It's on you and Ava. I hear they got a cover picture, too.' Suddenly, Sammy recalled that after Ava's visit at the Apollo, *Our World*, a Negro magazine, had run a Christmas cover of the two of them. The picture had been shot in Ava's suite at the Drake. The Negro photographer had also shot some less formal pictures—Sammy sitting on the arm of a chair, a coke in his hand, and Ava in the chair, with her shoes off, a habit dating back to her childhood in North Carolina.

Davis' concern that the fabricated *Confidential* story might hurt his friendship with Frank was put to rest shortly afterwards. Driving late one night from Las Vegas to LA—to record the theme song of a Jeff Chandler film after he had completed his shows at the New Frontier—Sammy was in the car crash that almost took his life and that did cost him an eye. Sinatra was an almost daily visitor at the San Bernardino hospital during the weeks of his recovery.

'He was the first one,' Sammy said later, 'to talk to me seriously after they removed my eye. All the others—Dad, Uncle Will Mastin, Jeff Chandler, Tony Curtis, Janet Leigh, Jesse Rand, Charlie Head—they were being gay, as if it never happened. Not Frank. He knew that I was sick with worry about how it would affect my career—and he was the first to try to help me face it. "This isn't going to make a bit of difference to you, Sam,' he said. I was always Sam to him, never Sammy. "You'll come through this better than ever. You'll see, Sam." He was right.'

When Davis left the hospital, Frank said, 'Rest, don't rush,' and offered his Palm Springs home for the recuperative period. Later, when Davis tried to rent a home in Hollywood, prejudice forced him into a hotel. After Sinatra learned of the discrimination, Davis encountered no difficulty in finding a lovely home in a quiet section of Beverly Hills. 'Frank would never let anyone pull the colour line,' Sammy has said. 'To him, there's only one race—the human race.'

Shortly before the première of *Suddenly*, Ralph Edwards presented a TV bio of 'The Pied Piper of Hoboken' on *This Is Your Life*. Repeating many of the myths which had been widely circulated, Edwards gave Frank's birth year as 1917, claimed he was a star forward on his high school basketball team and had won swimming trophies, stated that he was a cub reporter in the sports department of the *Jersey Observer*, and asserted that young Sinatra had won a Major Bowes amateur contest singing *Night and Day*. However, there was no mention of Frank's alleged adolescent poverty, his fighting cops, or his youthful mingling with hoods, all part of his early tough-guy mythology. In this respect, the show marked a beginning in the reconstruction of Sinatra's biography.

The release of *Suddenly* in October brought Sinatra new kudos. Typifying the majority, Alton Cook wrote in the NY *World-Telegram*: 'Sinatra carries a one-man show on his once lifeless acting shoulders for almost the entire length of the picture. He dominates even such forceful stars as Sterling Hayden and James Gleason. Every gesture is economical and right ... If he keeps it up, only the long memories will hark back to the days when Frankie had to make his living as a singer.'

Not as a Stranger, completed in November, was to bring

even more favourable comments on his acting. 'When the film was lying on the floor dead,' a member of the production staff said, 'along came Sinatra as Dr. Boone and revived it by the force of his personality. It was a beautiful thing to watch.' During the filming, Frank, Robert Mitchum and Broderick Crawford occasionally pursued their on-screen medical roles off-screen, performing mock operations on defenceless dummies. They also rode other members of the cast, particularly Olivia De Havilland, whose lady-like demeanour became the special butt of their shenanigans. 'Clowning,' according to Stanley Kramer, who produced the film, 'was a saving grace for Frank's emotional outbursts.' Mitchum later said of Sinatra : 'Frank is a tiger—afraid of nothing, ready for anything. He'll fight anybody and about anything. He's really an amazing guy —frail, undersized, with a scarred-up face who's ready to take on the whole world. It's easier when you've got as much talent as he has.' More recently, Mitchum said : 'The only man in town I'd be afraid to fight is Sinatra. I might knock him down but he'd keep getting up until one of us was dead.'

During 1954 recognition returned to Frank for his power as a singer. In *Billboard*'s annual poll of disc jockeys, he swept the board, scoring as No. 1 male vocalist and having *Young at Heart* picked as the year's No. 1 disc and his *Swing Easy* album as the No. 1 LP of the year. The record business was then undergoing a change that was to prove highly favourable to Sinatra's singing style and choice of repertoire. The year saw the opening of a new market for albums, a market that today accounts for over 70 per cent of all record sales. The LP of those days was a ten-inch, eight-song package. Frank was suddenly freed from the constricting demands of what he has called 'the three hard-thrill minutes of commercial music.'

Songs for Young Lovers, his first release in the new genre, was a compilation of songs from his night-club programme. Although Nelson Riddle wrote special introductions for some of the tunes, *My Funny Valentine, Violets for Your Furs* and the other numbers were recorded to the accompaniment of a small combo of four strings, two reeds and rhythm section. *Swing Easy*, cut in April 1954, was also a small combo LP, but with the emphasis on brass and reeds. Employing five saxes and a four-man trumpet-trombone section, and adhering to what Riddle described as the 'tempo of the heartbeat', Frank sought to capture the rocking-chair/swing quality of the Red Norvo combo with which he had made satisfying personal appearances. Frank's choice of songs, *Just One of Those Things, Wrap Your Troubles in Dreams, I'm Gonna Sit Right Down and Write Myself a Letter, All of Me* seemed to be pertinent to his thoughts about Ava.

These same overtones are apparent, too, in *The Girl That Got Away*, the great Harold Arlen torcher, *When I Stop Loving You*, and the tortured *You, My Love*, all grooved in the course of the year's seven record sessions.

Metronome's end of the year issue named Sinatra Singer of the Year while in *Down Beat*'s annual reader poll, for the first time since 1947, he was designated No. 1 of the Most Popular Male Vocalists. He had outdistanced Nat 'King' Cole, Billy Eckstine, Eddie Fisher and Perry Como. At the end of the year, Frank took out a full-page ad in *Billboard*. Enumerating the various awards he had received and the films in release, shooting and starting, he signed the ad with a cocky—'Busy, busy, busy—Frank.'

Despite his new 'mature, dignified outlook' as one columnist described it, Frank made headlines in December as the result of a café brawl. On the night of the 9th, after attending a housewarming party at the Sammy Davis's, Frank, Judy Garland, oilman Bob Neal and model Cindy Hayes went to the Crescendo on the Sunset Strip to hear Mel Tormé. They were leaving the club at about 2 a.m. when Frank got into a fight with the Crescendo's p.a., Jim Byron.

As with a number of other brawls, there was no agreement as to how it happened. Byron claimed that the four walked out of the club carrying their drinks hidden under their coats. In the course of explaining that this was illegal, he asked Bob Neal who his date was. 'What business is it of yours?' Frank allegedly demanded 'You're either a cop or a reporter. And I hate cops and newspapermen!' Sinatra went on 'ranting and raving and calling me unprintable names', Byron told newsmen. After warning him to take off his glasses, Frank then allegedly struck him on the side of the face. In the exchange that followed, Byron seemingly landed several blows on Frank's nose.

As Sinatra described the incident, Byron wanted to know who *his* 'broad' was, not Neal's. Frank objected to Judy Garland being called a broad. 'Then, suddenly, two guys held my arms,' Frank told reporters, 'and Byron tried to knee me. He succeeded in denting my shinbone and clawing my hand. I couldn't do anything because I was held by the two men. I broke loose. It ended when I gave him a left hook and dumped him on his fanny.'

'Nobody dumped anybody,' Byron asserted. 'People, led by the parking lot attendant, pulled us apart.'

Several years later, Sinatra said of the fracas: 'Sure I hit him. If I hadn't hit him, he'd have had in the columns that I was dating Judy while Sid—her husband—was out of town. For cripe's sake! I wasn't with Judy. We were both in the same crowd, that's all.'

The 'I hate cops' line became the subject of widespread press comment. Barry Gray, a radio commentator then writing a column in the NY *Post*, sided with Frank: 'I've always been a Sinatra fan,' he wrote. 'Mark it up to my respect for his independence—his moxie ... The fact is Sinatra has studiously been a humanitarian and a liberal in every way except his attitude towards reporters.' Gray noted that while newspapers had given wide coverage to the Crescendo brawl, they had not found space for Sinatra's considerate conduct when Sammy Davis had lost an eye. Acknowledging the press' part in provoking Frank, Gray concluded: 'I just wish those golden days when George Evans lived could be recreated—when Frank was taught to walk off his resentment, his anger at men who pried professionally in order to do their jobs. Too-personal questions were turned aside with an Evans smile, a joke and the boys understood ...'

Before the year ended, the press twice more invaded Frank's personal life. Among those present at his December opening at the Copa, described as 'one of the most exciting and crowded in the café's fifteen-year history', was actress Anita Ekberg, who told a columnist that Frank had paid for her round-trip ticket from Hollywood to New York. There was just one atonal note. Columnists emitted a loud horse-laugh because Miss Ekberg sat holding hands, as Sinatra sang, with a young, tall, wealthy real-estate man who accompanied her to the Copa.

After completing his act, Frank joined Joan Blondell and one of his favourite newsmen, sportswriter Jimmy Cannon. Seated with them was a striking, raven-haired young woman with large, sparkling black eyes. She was heiress Gloria Vanderbilt, who was about to announce that she was leaving conductor Leopold Stokowski after nine years of marriage. By the time she made the announcement on December 30, she and Frank had been seen together at El Morocco and the Embers. When Frank took her to the opening of the Harold Arlen–Truman Capote musical *House of Flowers*, the press broke the story. The world learned that Frank brought her to the theatre fifteen minutes before showtime; that he then dashed over to the Copa; that he returned to her side at the beginning of the second act; and that, after his late show at the Copa, they went to El Morocco. To columnist Louis Sobol, who interviewed them in the club's Champagne Room, Miss Vanderbilt said: 'There's no romance whatsoever. It's not like that and I hope that impression doesn't get around.' Earl Wilson explained that Frank was not at all involved in the break-up of the Vanderbilt–Stokowski marriage. 'I didn't meet Miss Vanderbilt until less than two weeks ago,' Frank told him. 'It's pretty silly for anybody to consider this a romance.'

But the press found Sinatra good copy whether he was buoyant, blue, brawling, or just dating a brunette.

IMAGE 4

THE TALENTED BASTARD

Beyond the appeal of other Sinatra images, minted or mirror, was the magic of his comeback. From the beginning, his career possessed legendary properties. He was not merely a singer or entertainer, but a kind of modern Pied Piper, able to cast an almost hypnotic spell over the young. Now, the legend was itself to undergo a legendary rebirth, rising phoenix-like from the pyre of celluloid and vinylite ash to which his career had been reduced.

The press was mesmerized by his re-entry from the outer space of the has-been. Reporters and free-lance writers fell all over themselves to glorify the underdog who had beaten the tough odds against climbing back. Over and over, they repeated the tale of 'the rise and fall and rise again', the phrase that Sinatra preferred. Only he had not just risen. He had miraculously propelled himself into a new career as a character actor. The superstar and multimillionaire were in the making.

His buoyancy reflected itself in a new record style and one that accorded with a shift in popular musical taste. The finger-snapping charts of Nelson Riddle and Billy May replaced Axel Stordahl's lovely romanticism, as Capitol Records superseded Columbia. To pool-like woodwinds and murmuring strings was added a large complement of swinging brass and rhythm. Bounce and verve and drive became the earmarks of a kick-ballad style, as he chirped *Young at Heart*, his first Top Ten record in years, *I'm Gonna Live Till I Die*, and *Come Fly With Me*.

But since his role in *From Here to Eternity* was a project he alone had conceived, he alone had fought for despite the cynicism of producers, directors, studio heads and even his own staff, and he alone had won with his business acumen and talent, he soon became cocky and overbearing as well as buoyant. Offscreen, Maggio had hauteur as well as heart; he could be mean as well as magnificent.

During the years of his courtship of Ava Gardner, he had worried himself sick over press prying into his private life. He was to continue enforcing Sinatra's Law on Privacy. But after a time, his career and public appeal suffered no real setbacks from the harshest revelations about his affairs. He was to demonstrate that one could be a bastard as long as one was really talented and did not dissemble with the public. A variant of Humphrey Bogart's appeal (tough and no bullshit), this image became a new canon in superstar publicity.

XVII

BUOYANT, BUSY AND BUSINESS
BROUHAHAS, UNLTD.

'Man, I feel eight feet tall,' Frank said late in 1955. 'Everything is ahead of me. I'm on top of the world. I'm buoyant.' Some felt that the more appropriate word was 'arrogant' or 'cantankerous'. 'The Phoenix of the Films,' as Don Ross dubbed him in the NY *Herald-Tribune*, had every reason to feel good, for the 'Cool Crooner Had Become a Hot Actor'. With several hit records, a new TV deal and club offers of $50,000 a week, 'Sinatra is just about the biggest thing in the entertainment industry today,' Ross concluded.

But despite all the buoyant talk, Ross felt that Frank still had a chip on his shoulder and was not happy. Friends agreed that too many of his dates were with girls who could have served as stand-ins for Ava. 'Man, if I could only get her out of my plasma!' His entourage, which had lost much of its significance in the Ava period, once again became a tightly knit group. Frank went nowhere without a crowd that generally included Hank Sanicola, his dedicated manager; Bill Miller, his accompanist, who was known as Sun-Tan Charlie because of a sallow complexion; 'Beans' Pondedell, his make-up man; Don McGuire, a writer; Jimmy Van Heusen, the song-writer; and sundry 'hunkers' who looked like alumni of Stillman's Gym. On movie sets, cast and crew learned to use the entourage as a gauge of Frank's mood if the mob was buoyant, they knew that the Man was swinging, but if it was not, then Frank was touchy—and watch out!

Whatever the emotional cost of the break with Ava, it gave him the opportunity he eagerly sought to be close with his children. With Nancy, Sr., allowing him the run of her home, he spent so much time with his youngsters that Nancy, Jr., could later say: 'My father may have left my mother, but he never left home ...' Nancy, Jr., then fifteen, became his frequent date at premières, and in October, despite a frantic work schedule, he kept a promise to appear at her high school. To help celebrate a successful PTA membership drive, he sang *Side by Side* with her at two assemblies. He also took her on a twelve-day tour of Australia, which netted him $40,000 for four days of singing. Nancy, Sr., met the plane that brought him and Nancy, Jr., back to Hollywood. So did a crowd of reporters who aggravated him with questions about a romance between Nancy, Jr., and Bing Crosby's son, Lindsay. Rumour had it that the Australian jaunt had been used to separate them. 'It's ridiculous,' Frank said. 'They're only kids. There isn't anything to this romance jazz.'

Guys and Dolls began filming in March, with Frank in the role of the tinhorn gambler, Nathan Detroit, played by Sam Levene on the Broadway stage. Frank, who later asserted that he was 'badly miscast', had wanted the role of Sky Masterson, played by Marlon Brando. Sky was not only the romantic lead; he sang all the love ballads. Detroit was a comedy character whose only big song was *Sue Me*. Apart from feeling that Brando was no singer, Frank had as little sympathy with 'method' acting as Humphrey Bogart. 'There's too much scratching,' Bogie used to say. For Frank, there was too much rehearsing and too many retakes. 'I don't buy this take and retake jazz,' Sinatra explained. 'The key to good acting on the screen is spontaneity—and that's something you lose a little with each take.' To writer-director Joe Mankiewicz, he said : 'Don't put me in the game, coach, until Mumbles is through rehearsing.'

Shortly before the cameras began rolling on *Guys and Dolls*, Frank became the third Hollywood actor whom United Artists agreed to finance in independent productions; the others were Robert Mitchum and Joan Crawford. Frank's deal called for six pictures in five years and included one directing chore.

During the filming of *Guys and Dolls*, Ava and Frank appeared together in public on a number of occasions. But no real speculation was stirred up about a reconciliation. David Hanna, Ava's press agent, claims that at this time he began to sense a new attitude on her part and a difference in Frank's approach to her. 'Having him so close at hand,' Hanna wrote, 'evidently convinced her that she was no longer in love with him and could finally blow out the torch she had carried for over a year. Instead of calling him Sinatra, she referred to him as "Francis" or "My old man". Being in Hollywood reminded her of things about him she wanted to remember affectionately ... She played his records constantly and proclaimed to all and sundry that he was the greatest of the great.' According to Hanna, Frank had come to represent, despite the split, 'the one dependable person in her life'. Frank seemed to enjoy their free-wheeling relationship and occasional displays of her dependence on him; he was known to instruct operators to get 'Mrs. Sinatra' on the phone.

During February Frank kept three recording dates, cutting standards like *Can't We Be Friends, What Is This Thing Called Love, O Get Along Without You Very Well*—songs that seemed a commentary on his new relationship with Ava. Using a soft, after-hours sound, with strings and reeds dominant, he enjoyed a best-seller in the bitter-sweet album *In the Wee*

Small Hours. Metronome commented: 'In the midst of great many remarkably untalented men and women, suddenly Sinatra has made singing something to hear with pleasure again.' And jazz critic Barry Ulanov wrote: 'Sinatra has always had a taste and an intuition for jazz nuances, for improvisational ornaments, for swinging beats, far beyond the call of popular singing duty.'

In March Frank tried a change of style. By then a new sound was rocking popular music. It was raucous and over-stated—hammering triplets in the treble, boogie-woogie figures in the base and a thundering afterbeat throughout. Small guitar-dominated combos replaced big orchestras. Spontaneous 'head arrangements' superseded tasteful, written-out scores. The Rock 'n' Roll generation had arrived. Concerned about the new developing trend, Frank cut a rhythm-and-blues record with a new A and R producer. He chose Dave Cavanaugh, who was responsible for the Peggy Lee hit *Fever*, a pop cover of the R and B disc by Little Willie John, its writer. 'Even ole Frankie has gone r and b,' *Metronome* observed, 'and the master can do no wrong even out of his natural habitat ... He gets a real rocking background out of the Nuggets. We give *Two Hearts, Two Kisses* five stars (top rating) but with reservations; we'd rather Frankie stuck to his own idiom. No doubt this release is an overture to win a following from the new teenage generation which still hasn't dug him.' Sinatra later admitted his effort was half-hearted.

He returned to his own idiom in his second March recording session, using a typical swing combo of eight brass, five reeds and five rhythm, and devoting two hours to one tune. They were well spent; Frank came through with a hit on *Learnin' the Blues*, a song he himself published. At the moment when Bill Haley and his Comets were riding the top of the *Billboard* charts with *Rock Around the Clock*, an opus that scored all over the world as the theme of *The Blackboard Jungle*, Frank was just two notches below with *Learnin' the Blues*. Before 1955 ended, Frank had another hit disc in *Love and Marriage*, a Van Heusen–Cahn tune he sang originally in the TV version of *Our Town*. In *The Tender Trap*, cut in September and theme of the movie in which he co-starred with Debbie Reynolds, he also had a brisk seller. By then, Elvis Presley, his swinging pelvis and rocking knees, had been introduced to the teenage world via the Tommy Dorsey TV show, evoking the same wild reaction Sinatra had himself once stirred. Presley's success on records did not come until the following year when his first hits, *Heartbreak Hotel* and *Love Me Tender*, racked up phenomenal sales in the millions.

During 1955 Sinatra more than maintained his position as record king. At the end of the year the *Down Beat* and *Metronome* All Star polls both showed him at the top of the Male Singer list. Reproducing the telegram that advised him of the latter award, Frank added two postscripts in a full-page *Metronome* ad. The first read: 'Thanks a lot.' The second: 'P.P.S. Mitch Miller???'

'Little Frankie Sinatra's all boiled up at the world again,' wrote Whitney Bolton in the *Morning Telegraph*, 'and threatening people, sending them notes, yelling over telephones, taking paid ads to send bitter notes to people he hates ... If he's unhappy, he should remember every man has carried a big torch at some time.' Describing him as 'the little man with broken dreams', Bolton observed: 'But instead of nursing them in private like a man, he stands on a corner and scratches everything that passes by.'

In the spring, Frank brought a libel suit against an English columnist, a chain of British newspapers and the owner of Les Ambassadeurs, a fashionable London club. Frank's membership had apparently been cancelled. Frank also sued Sam Spiegel and Horizon-American Pictures for $500,000 for going back on an agreement giving him the starring role in *On the Waterfront*. By then, the film had won an Academy Award, as had its star Marlon Brando, hardly one of Frank's favourite people. Frank contended that the producers had made an oral agreement on October 22, 1953, promising him $55,000 plus 1 per cent of the net profits. (The suit was not resolved until five years later when Frank settled for the installation of a hi-fi system in his home.)

The biggest tussle of the spring was a fracas with an old friend, Ed Sullivan, over a proposed appearance on his *Toast of the Town* show to promote *Guys and Dolls*. In a public statement, Frank said: 'It is not fair to do a show for Sullivan with no pay and then in the same breath ask others to pay me ... I turned down Sullivan for a similar free shot with *Not as a Stranger*. They can use film clips. But when you make a special appearance, you're entitled to compensation.' Sinatra elaborated on his position: 'If it's a TV trailer for Goldwyn who bought the airtime, I'd do it. I told Goldwyn if my schedule allows, I'll be glad to do personal appearances to help promote the picture when it's released. I told Goldwyn I'd work on the Sullivan Show if Sullivan paid and gave the money to charity...'

In a public statement, Sullivan indicated that he had planned to use Marlon Brando and Jean Simmons, who played the Salvation Army lassie Sarah Brown, and that he had offered to pay $32,000 to cover technical costs. When Frank called upon the Screen Actors Guild to clamp down on free TV appearances, Sullivan countered with a full-page ad in *Daily Variety*. Addressing it to Walter Pidgeon as president of the SAG, he wrote 'To date *Toast of the Town* has paid over $5,000,000 in salaries and has incidentally rendered substantial benefits to motion pictures...' Then, adverting to what might have been the provocation to Frank, he denied that he had asked Sinatra to appear at all. 'I haven't talked to Sinatra for some years,' he asserted. 'The fact that Sinatra, regularly trounced by us whenever he becomes part of the rival network's "spectacular", hardly qualifies as an important or disinterested witness.' Sullivan concluded his open letter with a postscript in which he harked back to enthusiastic columns he had written about Sinatra: 'Aside to Frankie Boy. Never mind that tremulous 1947 offer: Ed, you can have my last drop of blood.'

Frank replied in full-page ads in Hollywood's trade papers 'Dear Ed, You are sick. "Frankie". P.S.—sick, sick, sick.'

From *Guys and Dolls*, Frank went into the filming of *The Tender Trap* for MGM, playing the part of a hip bachelor manoeuvred into marriage by Debbie Reynolds. While he was before the cameras, Lee J. Cobb had a heart attack. One day Cobb answered the phone in his hospital room and was amazed to hear Sinatra asking whether he could come and visit. Although Cobb had worked with Frank in *The Miracle of the Bells*, he knew him only slightly. But for the time he remained in the hospital, Cobb had an almost daily visitor in Sinatra. 'In his typical unsentimental fashion,' Cobb said later, 'Frank moved into my life. I was in a low mental state then. I was divorced and pretty much alone in the world. I was sure my career had come to an end. Frank flooded me with books, flowers, delicacies. He kept telling me what fine acting I still had ahead of me and discussed plans for me to direct one of his future films. He built an insulating wall around me that shielded me from worry, tension and strain.' Because of the heavy medical bills, Cobb was in financial straits. Frank not only installed him in his Palm Springs home for the recuperative period, but when the summer desert heat became too much for Cobb, he moved him into a Hollywood apartment and paid the bills. 'After I recovered, our relationship tapered off,' Cobb said, 'until I hardly see him at all. He seemed to disappear as my need for him was over.'

After *The Tender Trap* was completed in August, Frank had three film commitments. In Otto Preminger's *Man with the Golden Arm*, he was to play the demanding role of a card-dealer who has to lick drug addiction in order to become a jazz drummer. In December, he was to shoot his first independent production, then called *The Loud Law* but eventually released as *Johnny Concho*. Between the two, he was to play Billy Bigelow in *Carousel*, the Rodgers–Hammerstein musical adaptation of Molnar's *Liliom*.

When he arrived at Booth Bay, Maine, on August 20 and discovered that *Carousel* was to be shot in Cinemascope as well as Todd A-O, Frank refused to go before the cameras. Apart from the extra time consumed in changing cameras, this meant that he would have to do each take at least twice. 'I have only one good take in me,' he insisted, in arguments with producer Henry Ephron and director Henry King. While he fought with reps of Twentieth Century-Fox on location, he was on the long distance phone fighting with his own agent, then Bert Allenberg of the William Morris office, whom he had originally sent after the role.

The impasse continued for two days, idling the company of a hundred and twenty-five. Even though the *Hollywood Reporter* sided with the movie company and called Frank's position on 'one take' silly, Sinatra refused to budge. On the morning of the 24th, 'just like in a gangster movie', according to the man who drove, three of Frank's buddies, 'looking furtively about', preceded him to a car. The driver took the vehicle to a point beyond the airport, where all studied the surrounding scene. Then they sprinted to a waiting plane. 'The guy has to live under pressure,' a writer commented. 'If there isn't any, then he invents some.'

On the 29th, while he was in New York, Twentieth Century-Fox brought a million dollar breach of contract suit against Frank. Spokesmen for the company asserted that the use of varying types of camera was not unprecedented, that only some scenes would have to be shot twice, and that a large cast and crew had been left stranded by Frank's walkout. By the time Sinatra reached California on the 31st, Gordon MacRae had been hired to replace him in a role that would have brought Frank $150,000 for ten weeks of work. 'Gordon's a good man,' Frank commented, 'and should do fine.' In later years, whenever Frank ran into MacRae at parties, he would quip 'Gordon does all my outside work.'

On September 19, Twentieth Century-Fox announced that *Carousel* would be filmed only in 55 mm. Although Frank was out of it, he had won his point. 'When musicians play on a sound stage for a movie,' he told a friend, 'you can't use their work on records without paying them again. Why should an actor make two films for the price of one? I'm not talking about the use of two cameras. They can shoot any scene with as many cameras as they want—and they do. I'm talking about *playing* the same scene twice.'

In the midst of the controversy with Twentieth Century-Fox, *Time* magazine appeared with its first cover story on Sinatra. Although it repeated many of the myths of Sinatra's youth, it did establish that he was 'a well-fixed boy in a poor neighbourhood'. The concluding sentences, presented as a direct quote from Frank, read: 'I'm going to do as I please. I don't need anybody in the world. I did it all myself.'

Many who knew the cocky Sinatra of this period were quite ready to accept these as Frank's words. But Frank insisted that he had never said them and certainly not to Ezra Goodman, who had interviewed him. His claim might have remained unresolved, except that Goodman later published a book about his Hollywood sojourn. In *The Fifty Year Decline and Fall of Hollywood*, the *Time* reporter stated that Frank was late for appointments or broke them, that he would not be photographed without his hat, and that he refused to answer questions about his private life. About the disputed remark, however, Goodman wrote: 'To tell the truth, he was right. Some creative writer or editor in *Time*'s New York office had helpfully put the words into Sinatra's mouth.'

On the crest of the *Time* cover tale, also a *Look* cover story, the movie editor of the LA *Mirror-News*, wrote a column demonstrating that while Frank could be 'nasty, rude, inconsiderate, uncooperative and ungrateful', he could also be 'quietly generous and considerate without even expecting thanks'. Kendis Rocklin revealed that, when Bela Lugosi, creator of *Dracula*, committed himself to a hospital as a narcotics addict, Sinatra was the only member of the movie colony who reached out an encouraging hand. 'It gave me such a boost,' Lugosi told Rocklin. 'I've never met Sinatra but I hope to soon. He was the only star I heard from.' The columnist indicated that, were it not for Lugosi, no one would have known of Frank's considerate gesture. 'He rarely speaks of the generous things he does,' Rocklin commented. 'He's too busy alienating reporters, hating cops and sneering his way to a cover on *Time*.'

The TV production of *Our Town*, in which Frank co-starred with Eva Marie Saint and Paul Newman, came off as scheduled on September 19, but not, however, without difficulties. The trouble developed apparently as a result of discussions between Frank and NBC-TV concerning a long-term pact. By August 23, when the talks broke down in an atmosphere of 'great bitterness', Frank was allegedly hinting at a walk-out while NBC was making *sotto voce* threats of legal action to force Sinatra to keep his commitment. Rumour had it that NBC had offered a five-year three-million dollar deal for seven shows a year, but 'that firm believer in men as islands unto themselves', as *Time* described him, rejected the offer.

On the day before *Our Town* was scheduled to be telecast, Frank reportedly skipped two important dress rehearsals. But despite the complications, rumours and threats, the musical was aired as scheduled and turned out to be one of the best ever presented on TV as well as one of the few TV shows that helped launch a song hit. The NY *Times* called it 'magnificent entertainment'. Contending that 'his unconcealed Hoboken-ese' betrayed Frank as an outsider in New England, the reviewer nevertheless felt that he was 'effectively unobtrusive and his songs were an important contribution to the success of the presentation. He was particularly winning when he sang the bright number *Love and Marriage*.'

One of the most absorbing roles in Frank's film career was that of the dope addict/drummer/card-dealer in *Man with the Golden Arm*. Frank grabbed the part after reading only sixty pages of the screenplay of the Nelson Algren best-seller. (It had once been purchased as a vehicle for John Garfield.) Filmed during late September and October, it elicited one of Sinatra's most dedicated acting jobs. Reporting to the studio at 8 a.m. in the morning, he seldom left before the day's rushes were screened almost twelve hours later. 'I was too tired to do anything except go home,' he later said, 'think about the day's shooting for a while and drop off to sleep. I had no time to party or be social.'

At the climax of the film, Sinatra, aided by Kim Novak, goes into withdrawal agonies. Aware of the extreme demands of the scene, producer-director Otto Preminger indicated a willingness to permit extensive rehearsals and as many retakes as were needed. Frank rejected the offer. He knew exactly how he wanted to play the scene: 'Just keep those cameras grinding,' he urged. With no rehearsals, the challenging scene was shot in one take. Preminger discovered what Stanley Kramer had already learned: 'Sinatra is the master of naturalness in acting.' (Next to the scene of Maggio dying in *From Here to Eternity*, Frankie Machine's withdrawal scene is, perhaps, Sinatra's finest bit of acting.) As the filming proceeded, Preminger became convinced that he had an Oscar contender and determined to rush the release to put it in line for the 1955 Academy Awards.

Since Sinatra played the role of a would-be drummer, much emphasis was placed on the musical sequences. A Stan Kenton-type band, led by jazz trumpeter Shorty Rogers, played an exciting score by Elmer Bernstein. Out of it came a pop-jazz instrumental with a throbbing kettle-drum figure that became widely known as the Theme of TMWTGA. 'It is a picture,' *Down Beat* commented, 'in which jazz references have been used effectively to document a character and, for once, jazz-minded movie goers won't have to cringe at the references.'

Film publicists worked at developing the usual gossip of a romance between the stars. Frank played along, taking Kim Novak to a party at Gary Cooper's, to two premières and to several of his recording dates. 'I respect him more than any actor I've met,' Kim told interviewers. 'He's real. He's honest. That's why he gets into trouble constantly.'

November and December saw the première of three major Sinatra films. Frank fared worst in *Guys and Dolls*. He was well received in *The Tender Trap* where reviewers commended his comedy and the warmth and 'jaunty insouciance' with which he played a man-about-town. Although *The Man with the Golden Arm* was denied a Production Code Seal of Approval and was described as 'immoral' by *Daily Variety*, most reviewers went with the LA *Times* whose headline read SINATRA'S ACTING REDEEMS SORDID FILM ON DRUG HABIT. Arthur Knight may have voiced an ingroup reaction in the *Saturday Review* when he applauded the film as 'definitely worth talking about, even cheering about'. But he sounded a majority attitude when he described Frank's performance as 'truly virtuoso' and observed that he had established himself as an 'actor of rare ability'. 'The thin unhandsome one-time crooner,' he wrote, 'has an incredible instinct for the look, the gesture, the shading of the voice that suggests tenderness, uncertainty, weakness, fatigue, despair. Indeed, he brings to the character much that has not been written into the script, a shade of sweetness and a sense of edgy indestructibility...' *The Man with the Golden Arm* may have been a controversial film. But Frank's fellow craftsmen nominated him for an Oscar, and early the following year, he received an award from the British Kinematograph Council of London.

In an end of the year assessment of his movie roles, the movie critic of the NY *Times* observed that no other star performer could equal Sinatra's record of five new films. Noting that he delivered an interesting performance in each, Bosley Crowther reserved his strongest accolade for *The Tender Trap*, 'a well-nigh perfect demonstration of the sort of flippant, frantic thing Sinatra can do best', and attributed the swinging pace of the film to 'Frankie's hepped-up, high-voltage person.' To Crowther, Sinatra had become one of the screen's most promising performers.

December found Frank starting work on *Johnny Concho*, an independent production which had to be completed so that he could report to MGM in January for *High Society*. He was due in Madrid in April for the shooting of *The Pride and the*

Passion. 'I like to keep working this way,' Frank told an interviewer. 'It's good therapy.' Talking between scenes of *Johnny Concho*—it was December 12, his fortieth birthday—Frank became expansive on a project that sounded like another of his pipe dreams. To promote international goodwill, he wanted 'to put on a show in each of the world's capitals for the benefit of children in that country'. His idea was to travel with two American stars, 'a name they all recognise like Gary Cooper or Marilyn Monroe. The tour could be set up through variety clubs, which have branches in foreign countries. I understand Nehru is a member. If it could be arranged, I'd like to do it in Moscow, too.' Six years later, the pipe dream became a reality.

Gloria Vanderbilt, signed to play the sole femme role in *Johnny Concho*, welcomed 1956 with Frank, as she had helped him celebrate the arrival of 1955.

Just a few days before the end of 1955, the Holmby Hills Rat Pack held its first annual meeting. It was also actually its last since it evolved spontaneously after several hours of drinking from a chance crack made by Lauren Bacall, then Mrs. Humphrey Bogart. As a group of Bogie's cronies assembled for dinner one evening in Mike Romanoff's posh upstairs room, Betty remarked : 'I see the rat pack is all here.' Several hours later, they had formed an organisation 'with a platform of iconoclasm—they were against everything and everyone, including themselves'.

'Remember, it was all a joke,' Bogie told Joe Hyams, who first broke the story in his column in the NY *Herald-Tribune*. As spokesman for the group, Bogart explained that the organisation had no function other than 'the relief of boredom and the perpetuation of independence'. Membership was open to 'free-minded, successful individuals who don't care what anyone thinks about them'. Since the Rat Pack led to Sinatra's Clan, it is interesting to note that Judy Garland was chosen First V-P; Lauren Bacall, Den Mother; Sid Luft, Cage Master; I. P. 'Swifty' Lazar, Recording Secretary and Treasurer; Nathaniel Benchley, Historian; and Sinatra, Pack Master or Chairman. Bogie was the Rat-In-Charge of Public Relations.

While Hollywood did not approve of Bogie's Rat Pack, the group never stirred the animosity or elicited the adverse press of Frankie's Clan. The groups overlapped and were similar in flouting convention, thumbing noses at stuffiness and creating their own concepts of 'in-ness'. But there were also contrasts arising from the different personalities of the two men. As Frank was more self-conscious, more domineering and more a power-seeker, so The Clan was more Leader-orientated and more of a talent combine than merely a group of carefree swingers. Incapable of the kind of amused self-depreciation in which Bogart constantly and slyly indulged, Frank seemed to require the hyperbolic admiration implicit in out-sized references to himself as The King, The Leader and The Pope.

Novelist-free-lancer Richard Gehman tells of an afternoon when, as he sat chatting with Bogart, two Helen Hopkinson-type women were ushered into Bogie's living room. They had come to do an interview for a small-town newspaper.

'What were you talking about?' one woman asked, as she saw that they had interrupted a conversation.

'We were just discussing fucking,' Bogie said matter-of-factly.

Neither Frank nor the members of The Clan were ever that cool. But in Bogie, Frank did find a no-bullshit friend of rare perceptiveness, honesty and empathy.

XVIII

THE AVANTE GARDNER OR
THE PRIDE AND THE PASSION

'Who? Mr. Sinada?'

'Sinada' was a concoction in which the last two syllables of his name were replaced by the Spanish word for 'nothing'. It was devised by Ava Gardner, who used it in the latter months of 1956, imitating perhaps another Spanish *aficionado*, Ernest Hemingway, whose loss of faith had once been expressed in a famous parody: 'Our nada who art in nada/Nada be thy name . . .'

One of Ava's close associates believes that her long European residence widened the gap between her and Frank because it made her more sensitive to certain limitations. Whereas she had always disliked his brashness and arrogance, and, in the words of David Hanna, criticised 'the sycophants who surrounded him and disported themselves more like bodyguards

207

than professional associates', she now was conscious of a lack of polish and savoir-faire. She felt that his clothes were too sharp and his hip language suggestive of immaturity. Instead of a man of the world, she saw in him the ineradicable marks of Hoboken, Broadway and Hollywood—places from which she fled physically and mentally.

And yet when Frank was heading for Spain in the late spring of 1956 to work on *The Pride and the Passion*, the rumours were that Ava was preparing her house to receive him. Ten miles north of Madrid, it was a ten-room, ranch-style villa called La Bruja (The Witch), so dubbed by its builder. When friends mentioned the possibility of reconciliation, Ava chortled as if it were the last thing in the world. And yet her mood became one of excited anticipation and she spoke with admiration of Frank's acting in *The Man with the Golden Arm*, which she had persuaded UA to screen privately for her. She did not put too much stock in the car he had sent her as a Christmas-birthday gift. Gestures of this kind, as she knew, were almost compulsive and revealed little about his feelings.

It was Frank who destroyed all hope of a reconciliation. Instead of coming to Spain by himself, he brought along a pretty starlet, Peggy Connolly, whom he had taken to the Academy Award presentations in April. Asked by a reporter whether he intended to marry again, Frank chuckled 'Are you kidding?' But if he thought he could provoke Ava's competitive instincts, Frank was unsuccessful. Privately, she blew her top at the public slap, and sulked. Publicly, she acted as though Frank was not there. And so, although neither had apparently found anyone to supersede the other, neither would give an inch.

Johnny Concho was one of two films that occupied Frank before his departure for Spain. The corny tale of a cowboy coward who eventually recovers his courage, it was ultimately criticised for slow pacing, a weak script and inadequate direction. Frank, whose loyalties are tenaciously long-lived, had given an entourage friend, Don McGuire, his first crack at directing a feature-length film, and had turned to him for the script, despite the limitations of his scripting on the film *Meet Danny Wilson*. *Johnny Concho* also gave Nelson Riddle his first opportunity to compose for the screen.

To learn the business of walking, talking and drawing

Western style, Frank went to Gary Cooper. Considering how fast Frank drew in the film, one might conclude that he was a very apt pupil or Coop, a great instructor. Actually, the effect was achieved through the use of a trick holster, which sprang open and hurled the gun up. With it anyone could outdraw the fastest gun in the West.

Frank's conduct on the set, a model of executive decorum, was apparently not relaxed. A reporter who visited the set one day, watched him drop into a camp chair. 'He squirmed, with his blue eyes roving as though they should be focused on something of which he should be aware. He sipped coffee in the manner of a sparrow at a bird bath and he treated questions respectfully as if they were coral snakes.' Although he handled his crew and staff with consideration, he was having problems with the only femme in the cast. The shooting had hardly begun when it became evident that Gloria Vanderbilt was too inexperienced for the role. Frank's handling of the situation eventually provoked Miss Vanderbilt to take a walk: 'I don't have to take this kind of treatment from anyone!' she told friends. *Sic transit Gloria ... Vanderbilt*, someone cracked, as Phyllis Kirk was substituted. The change did not help *Johnny Concho* as much as cast and crew had hoped.

During most of February, Frank was busy on the set of *High Society*, which he found 'a ball, a regular romp, the greatest!' A re-make of the Philip Barry stage hit *Philadelphia Story*, the MGM musical included songs by Cole Porter, easy performances by Bing Crosby, Celeste Holm and Grace Kelly, and hot jazz by Louis 'Satchmo' Armstrong. Out of the film came the hit ballad *True Love*, a duet between Crosby and Kelly, and the mid-August première brought favourable reviews for Frank's vocals as well as his portrayal of the snooping writer.

Celeste Holm, who sang *Who Wants to Be a Millionaire* with Frank, told a reporter: 'A woman doesn't have to be in love with Sinatra to enjoy his company. I wasn't and I did. He's a stimulating talker on any subject: books, music, cooking, his children whom he quotes oftener than most fathers, and sports.' (Sam Shaw, the photographer, who recommended books on acoustics, meteorology and naval warfare to help put Sinatra to sleep, soon afterwards found that Frank had become an amateur expert on these subjects.) Grace Kelly, to whom he crooned *You're Sensational* and *Mind If I Make Love to You*, reported: 'Frank has an endearing sweetness and charm as a person and an actor.'

Johnny Green, musical director of the film, had a more complex report to make. On a sound stage one day, he and Frank disagreed about a print. Green felt that Frank's rendering was not top Sinatra. Frank, who seemed to be in a hurry to go somewhere, said he was satisfied. One word led to another until Frank lost his temper and spewed forth his rage in a stream of four-letter words. Crosby, who was on the set, later said: 'Frank is a great guy to have on your side. But God help you if he's against you.' Green, however, stood his ground. 'You're not leaving,' he told Sinatra, 'until the producer hears this take and decides if he wants another.' Later, Green said: 'You don't evaluate a guy whom you've admired, a guy with whom you've had a fine professional and social relationship over a fifteen-year period, in terms of one afternoon. It was just a question of two artists looking for the best and finding their way through the brambles.'

Most people found Sinatra in a rare mood of exuberance during the *High Society* period. While the crew referred to Bing as 'Nembutal', they called him 'Dexedrine'. Even the appearance in the comic strip *Li'l Abner* of a character named Danny Tempest did not bother him. Whereas Liberace had threatened Al Capp with a lawsuit for a similar interpolation, Frank 'thanked me for putting him in'. To a new publicity girl in the MGM lot who was patently petrified by him, he said pleasantly: 'Never be scared of anything or anyone.' To reporter Joe Hyams, he said: 'The career is going ahead wonderfully. People are wonderful to me and I'm a happy, happy man.'

Yet, according to friends, he never wanted to be alone. Someone had to stay with him until he fell into an exhausted sleep—and he could not get more than five restless hours of forgetfulness. The rest of the time he was happy only if he was performing, recording, acting, wheeling and dealing; 'So long as I keep busy,' he told a reporter, 'I feel great.' So long as he's frantic, he's relaxed, friends said; when he begins to relax, he gets frantic.

'I've been recording my brains out,' Frank chirped in an April interview. 'Right now I wouldn't care if I never saw another disc.' In a four-week period, he had cut two complete albums and eight single discs. Before the busy year was over, he would keep twenty-two recording dates, a number exceeded only in 1947 when he participated in twenty-seven sessions. Perhaps the most interesting, though not the most successful, were three February sessions when he repeated an experiment he had tried at Columbia Records. This time, however, he *conducted* a large orchestra of fifty pieces. The compositions were by eight arranger-composers, each of whom attempted to convey his musical impression of a colour. Another display of musical breadth came in April when he used a thirteen-piece woodwind-string group to accompany him. Although the combo was manned by the virtuoso members of the Hollywood String Quartet and the arrangements were by Nelson Riddle, *Close to You* suffered as an LP from monotony of sound, tempo and mood—and most of all, perhaps, from an introspective quality that seemed out of joint with Sinatra's outgoing frame of mind.

His upbeat mood found more congruous expression in *Hey, Jealous Lover* and *Wait For Me*, two rocking singles that scored in an increasingly tough market—tough especially for middle-generation singers. The finger-snapping jauntiness spiced other records that increased his appeal to jazz fans. *Metronome* named *Swinging Lovers* one of the best jazz albums of the year and praised his vocals as a 'be-hatted, tie-loosened almost impeccable set of performances'. *Jazz Today* raved about *This Is Sinatra*, which it found 'alternately swinging and swaying, sensitive and searing, with at least half a dozen pure jazz performances'.

When *Metronome* asked a hundred and nine jazz artists to name *The Musician's Musician*, the vote polled by his nearest contender (Nat Cole) was less than a quarter of Frank's vote. Sinatra's was greater than the total number of votes received by all other nominees.

From mid-April until almost mid-August, Frank was occupied on and off with the filming of *The Pride and the Passion*, the Stanley Kramer production based on C. S. Forester's novel *The Gun*. According to David Hanna, the film's p.a., Kramer had sworn on the completion of *Not As a Stranger* that he would not use Sinatra again 'even if he had to go begging with a tin cup'. Yet Kramer felt that Sinatra could add so much that he overcame his fear of Frank's stormy disposition and his unpredictable moods. For a time, Kramer considered using Ava as his female star and Ava told Hanna she was willing to appear with Sinatra. But Kramer eventually fixed on Sophia Loren.

On the evening of April 4, Frank dined with his children and Nancy, Sr., at her home. Dinner over, he drove to Hedda Hopper's home for a last-minute interview. Early that morning he had driven to the top of Coldwater Canyon where he was building a new home. Digging of the foundation, he told Hopper, had just started, and he hated to be away while it was going up. This was to be home until April 1964 when the opposition of neighbours to a heliport in his backyard provoked him to sell. Affording a panoramic view of the world around the movie capital, the mountain-top house stressed oriental motifs even in the lettering of a truculent sign over a bell: 'If you haven't been invited, you better have a damn good reason for ringing this bell.'

After visiting his new house site, he had gone to a meeting with Harry Cohn of Columbia Pictures to discuss his starring role in *Pal Joey*. 'We talked things out,' Frank told Hedda, 'and then I saw an uneasy look coming into the faces of the Cohn braintrust and Harry himself. I don't like frightened people and I don't like being frightened myself. So I asked, "What's the trouble?" All were afraid to talk up. "If it's billing," I said, "it's okay to make it Hayworth/Sinatra/Novak. I don't mind being in the middle of that sandwich." Man, were they relieved!'

Hedda asked cautiously about his seeing Ava in Spain. 'If I do,' he said, as he fixed his probing blue eyes on Miss Hopper's, 'it will be in some public place. It will be a casual matter.' He did not mention that he was flying to Madrid with Peggy Connolly, who remained for two weeks, returned to the USA to promote her first record album, and then flew back in response to overseas calls from Frank. Adverting to his role as a Spanish guerilla fighter, he told Hedda of the special way he had studied his part: 'I engaged a guitarist Vicente Gomez. I gave him the script of *The Pride*, put him into a recording studio and had him read all my lines. I want to play this role like a Spaniard trying to speak English—not like an American trying to talk like a Spaniard trying to speak English.'

Before he set out for Spain, Frank called producer Stanley

Kramer and warned him that if a single newsman showed at the Madrid airport, he would take the next plane back to the States. David Hanna closed the publicity office the day of Sinatra's arrival. At the airport, however, as Miss Connolly slipped out of camera range, Frank agreed to pictures by the company photographer. The following morning, the Madrid papers carried front-page pictures of Frank and Peggy at a big movie ball, part of the Spanish Fiesta then in progress. 'It was an odd event,' Hanna said, 'for someone to attend on his first night in Madrid after insisting he wanted to see no press.'

When the shooting of *The Pride and The Passion* was completed, producer Stanley Kramer said: 'Sinatra didn't appear to be happy, but he worked hard and he insisted on doing a lot of things you'd normally expect a star to leave to a double. He ran through explosions and fires. I had him trudging up and down mountains, wading in rivers, crawling in mud from one end of Spain to the other, and he never complained once ... We were shooting in a desolate country about three and a half-hour drive over dusty roads from Madrid. We all slept together in tents at the location, or in accommodations available in the closest town. But Frank made the drive to Madrid every night, even though he had to start back some mornings at 4 o'clock to be on location.' Kramer added that he couldn't understand 'how Frank could go with little or no sleep for days at a time and still be sharp and bright. Occasionally, he would start a scene as if he didn't know what was going on. It looked like a palpable case of unpreparedness. But after a couple of minutes, he was going like some high-precision machine.'

Although Frank began work in *The Pride* in high spirits and was at first both relaxed and friendly, it was not long before he became restless. 'This is something I can't help,' he once told director Vicente Minelli. 'I have to go. No one seems able to help me—doctors, no one. I have to move.' (As early as *Step Lively*, filmed in 1944, he had told a reporter: 'I like making movies, though sometimes it nearly drives me crazy ... to sit and wait in between scenes.')

'Sixteen weeks!' he exclaimed to Kramer one day. 'I can't stay in one place sixteen weeks. I'll kill myself.' Shortly after this, the Hearst press ran a story that Sinatra was threatening to walk off the set. After several days, David Hanna persuaded columnist Louis Sobol to print a denial. In the meantime, Frank had reportedly gone to Kramer and demanded Hanna's head. The producer refused to fire his press agent. 'He planted that story himself,' Kramer told Hanna. 'He's been beefing about the schedule to anyone who would listen ... I'm afraid I'm going to have to change it.'

Since most of the scenes of *The Pride and The Passion* were exteriors, it was difficult to bunch all of Sinatra's scenes, as he demanded. There were also large mob scenes that took added time and had to be fitted in. But Frank, who had reached a stage of brooding when he was not before the cameras, or racing across Spanish roads, served an ultimatum: he expected to be finished on a given date, or else ...

Kramer said later 'When Sinatra walks in a room, tension walks in beside him. You don't always know why, but if he's tense, he spreads it.' He added: 'Frank is a tremendously talented man, intuitive and fast, which is good for him but not always good for the other actors. During the filming of *The Pride and The Passion*, he didn't want to rehearse. He didn't want to wait around while crowd scenes were being set up. Eventually, for the sake of harmony, we shot all his scenes together and he left early. The rest of the cast acquiesced because of the tension.'

While Kramer and Hanna may have had their problems with Frank, Sophia Loren, his co-star, said: 'Before he came to Spain, I hear all sorts of things. He is moody, he is difficult, he is a tiger, he fights. Here he is kindly, friendly. He has even helped me with my English, has teached me how people really speak in Hollywood. He is a regular gasser. I dig him.' Nor did Frank apparently forget friends back in the States. Jack E. Leonard, the comedian of the insult, who was in hospital with a number of ailments, reported that Frank's 'cheerful call came from Madrid every week'. And Nat 'King' Cole, who was attacked by a group of white supremacists while performing in a Birmingham, Ala., theatre, reported that Frank had called from Spain to express his concern and to condemn those who assaulted Cole.

During his stay in Spain, the Spanish press left both Frank and Ava alone, although their paths crossed. Once or twice, Frank, dining with his entourage, encountered Ava in a restaurant. He just nodded and seated himself at a remote table. On one occasion, when she was dining with her friends, Ricardo and Georgiana Montalban, and Frank was eating at a distant table, she pleaded a headache and left before the meal was finished. Patently, she could not stand being publicly ignored by the man who was still her husband.

When Frank left, there were no newspapermen at the airport, nor was there anyone from *The Pride and The Passion* company. According to David Hanna, 'Sinatra's leaving lifted a weight from the company. Tension eased and the production sped through its final weeks.' Ava, too, must have heaved a sigh of relief, for soon she began appearing freely around Madrid.

As Frank's plane was setting down at Idlewild on July 31, Ava announced from Rome that they had agreed on the last preliminaries necessary for an agreed-upon divorce. The papers had actually been signed in London prior to Ava's departure for Rome and Frank's return to the States. Since she had completed Nevada residence requirements, the divorce was hers whenever she wanted to pick it up.

When Frank played the NY Paramount in mid-August, it was his first appearance at the theatre since his dismal reception there in the dark days of 1952. Now, not even the mediocrity of *Johnny Concho*, the film on the screen, could dim the audience's new-found enthusiasm. Having sung the national anthem at the opening of the Democratic National Convention in Chicago on August 13, he arrived in New York for opening-day rehearsals to find fans queueing at the box-office. Two dozen kids had been gathering since 4 a.m. At about 8 a.m. married women, some with toddling youngsters, began arriving; they were bobbysoxers of the '40s returned to do homage thirteen years later. On stage with Frank were old friends: comic Joey Bishop and the orchestra of Jimmy and Tommy Dorsey, who were reunited at that point. Despite the favourable attitude of audiences and reviewers, Frank's psychosomatic bugaboo returned to plague him. On the fifth day, an attack of laryngitis prevented his appearance at three shows. Sammy Davis, Jr., subbed in the first, Alan Dale and Red Skelton in the second and Steve Allen and Julius LaRosa in the third. Frank managed to appear for the last two shows, which must have pleased his children who arrived from Hollywood the following day. They were able to see their father not only on the screen and stage of the Paramount but on the screen of the Radio City Music Hall where *High Society* was running.

Just as Frank was opening at the Paramount, it was announced that he would appear on Steve Allen's NBC show. Because of budgetary limitations, he would do no singing. 'We'll just chat,' Allen said. 'It'll be an ad lib session.' The *Herald-Tribune*'s radio editor commented: 'Perish the thought that Sinatra is merely plugging *Johnny Concho* or trying to help Allen's rating opposite old foe Ed Sullivan.' Said Allen: 'This Sullivan thing has nothing to do with Sinatra's coming on our show. Sinatra is an old friend of Skitch Henderson's and it was Skitch who first asked him to appear with me. He's really doing it out of friendship.'

Two days later, word was flashed that Sinatra was appearing on the Sullivan Show on the same night as Allen's and that he would sing. It was just fifteen months since the feud in which the two had blasted each other in trade-paper ads. Marlo Lewis, Sullivan's co-producer, gave this explanation: 'When Sinatra returned from Spain and heard that Ed was almost killed in an auto crash, he figured it was about time to cut out all this nonsense.' Sullivan was then bedridden at his Connecticut home, recuperating from chest injuries he had suffered in a collision while returning from a Fort Dix telecast. 'I want the guy to know how I really feel,' Frank said. 'I love Ed and I know he loves me. The feud? It was just a misunderstanding.' And Sullivan said: 'It is during such a time as this that a man can really tell who his friends are. And what better gesture could any friend make than Frankie has right now?' Marlo Lewis added: 'It's worth $10,000 if Sinatra does it. But he's doing it for nothing—just for Ed.'

And so came the evening of August 19. Frank was visible not only on the Sullivan and Allen shows, but on a third as well. 'Omnipresent', was the word used by the NY *Times*, which observed that he had somehow made three channels between 8 and 9 p.m. With Steve Allen on Channel 4, Frank just drank a cup of tea for his laryngitis. 'His appearance at the opening just standing there,' wrote Harriet Van Horne, 'evoked the wildest gusts of applause.' On Channel 2, while Red Skelton read a tribute to him penned by the ailing Sullivan, Frank also just stood and listened. And on Channel 7, he appeared during ABC's Famous Film Festival in a direct plug for *Johnny*

Concho.

With all the protestations of friendship, Sinatra had succeeded in 'hoodwinking three channels', as the NY *Times* put it, 'for free publicity for his picture'.

Having healed his breach with Ed Sullivan in August, came September and Frank vented his wrath on a pet hate: the man who had supervised his recordings at Columbia after the departure of Manie Sachs. Sinatra's weapon: a telegram to a House Judiciary Committee investigating the television industry. 'Before Mitch Miller's arrival at Columbia,' Sinatra wired Rep. Emmanuel Celler, 'I found myself enjoying a freedom of selection of material, a freedom which I may modestly say resulted in a modicum of success for me. Suddenly, Mr. Miller, by design or coincidence, began to present many inferior songs, all curiously bearing the BMI label (Broadcast Music, Inc.). Before Mr. Miller's advent on the scene, I had a successful recording career which quickly went into decline. Rather than continue a frustrating battle, I chose to take my talents elsewhere. It is now a matter of record that since I have associated myself with Capitol Records, a company free of broadcasting affiliations, my career is again financially, creatively and artistically healthy.' Sinatra called upon the antitrust committee to end practices 'which take from the artist those creative freedoms necessary to his talent'.

Mitch Miller had no inkling of the Sinatra attack until newsmen confronted him with the telegram to Celler. 'It's a hell of a way to run a hearing,' he said, 'when they accept a telegram as evidence. If they want to examine the record, they would find that under my aegis at Columbia, Sinatra recorded 95 per cent or more ASCAP songs and 5 per cent or less of BMI. It is a matter of "record". As far as Frank's career is concerned, he always was and is still a great artist. For the lapse in his career, he would do well to look into his own personal and emotional affairs at the time, and not try to blame it on the music.'

But Sinatra continued to associate Miller with his decline, and the following year, fired another telegram at the Chairman of a Senate Committee. This time he made a more serious charge, claiming that Miller had received money from writers whose songs he recorded. Sinatra quoted Miller as admitting under oath: 'Bob Merrill would bring all the songs to me first.

After the songs were a hit I got a cheque from his royalties ... It amounted to $5,000 or $6,000 ... The recent songs I received compensation on were *Mambo Italiano* and *Make Yourself Comfortable*. I would say about $4,000 ... There is a song called *A Guy's a Guy*. From that I received $1,200 ...' In a statement released by Columbia Records, Miller explained that his testimony had been given in a lawsuit—another facet of the battle between ASCAP writers and BMI—in which he was neither plaintiff nor defendant; he accused Sinatra of taking 'isolated portions of my testimony and putting them together in a manner which distorts completely the nature of my testimony'.

Sinatra's wire was sent to Sen. George A. Smathers, who had introduced an Amendment to the Communications Act requiring radio and TV stations to quit the music publishing and recording business, or give up their broadcast licences. In his wire, Sinatra asserted: 'The fact that Columbia and Victor recording companies are owned by networks has led to a great deal of skulduggery.' He contended that until the tie-ups were eliminated, payola would continue and American audiences would have to put up with 'broadcasters burying the songs they don't own' and plugging the songs they do own, '... masterpieces like *Hound Dog, Bebop-a-Lua* and *All Shook Up*'.

Some years after these exchanges, Frank came face to face with Miller in a Las Vegas hotel. 'Let bygones be bygones,' Miller urged, his eyelids fluttering.

Frank stared at Mitch out of hard, blue eyes. Disregarding the outstretched hand, he walked away, muttering an unprintable epithet.

By the end of October, Frank was at work on the Joe E. Lewis biopic. One of his first acts was to summon the picture's publicity chief and hand him a list of reporter's names. 'I don't want any of these crumbs on the set,' he announced, 'when I'm around.' The script of *The Joker Is Wild* was based on a book by the late Art Cohn, who was killed in the plane accident that took the life of Mike Todd, on whose bio he was then working. After reading *The Joker* galleys, Frank requested his agency to pick up the movie rights. Since William Morris handled Lewis as well as Sinatra, a deal was quickly negotiated. Shortly thereafter, Frank received a case of Scotch from the comic. 'Start rehearsing!' Lewis wrote.

The empathy between Frank and his subject was apparent to everyone who watched him on *The Joker* set. 'Joe was a helluva singer,' Frank told a reporter, 'before the punks heeled on him.' Frank was referring to the knifing that almost cost Lewis his life and that rendered him speechless for a time. 'Everybody who knew him then (when a Chicago café owner ordered him killed rather than let him go to a competitor), said he really had a voice. I wouldn't play just a singer in a movie—like a Russ Columbo or a Rudy Vallee. Joe's is a powerful story.'

Despite his feeling for the role and his dedicated acting, Frank continued to oversee many enterprises from *The Joker* set. *Daily Variety* was so impressed that it ran a front-page story headed SINATRA SAGA: FROM 'BOX-OFFICE POISON' TO 3-CORPORATION STAR IN 4 YEARS. Recalling that after *Meet Danny Wilson* in 1952, no studio wanted him at any price, the Hollywood trade paper reported Frank's salary for *High Society* and *The Pride and The Passion* as $250,000 each. *Pal Joey*, a Columbia Pictures property, was to be mounted by Essex Productions, a Sinatra company that had produced the Capitol soundtrack of *High Society*. For his role in *Pal Joey*, Frank was to receive $125,000, with Essex owning 25 per cent of the film for eventual sale on a capital gains basis. Another Sinatra company, Bristol Productions, owned 25 per cent of *The Joker Is Wild* and paid Frank $125,000 for his services.

Some years later, Hedda Hopper claimed that it was in *The Joker* dressing room that 'the Ava era finally ended for him'. As she described it: 'A Hollywood reporter had taken Ava driving in the desert around Palm Springs and had a microphone hidden in her car. Frank sat with a copy of the resulting magazine story in his hand, cringing like a whipped dog. Ava was quoted as complaining: 'Frank doublecrossed me ... made me the heavy ... I paid many of the bills." Even the ashes were cold after that.'

During December Frank played the Copa in New York and the Sands in Las Vegas. Both dates confirmed how his stock had risen. The Sands date, however, began badly. Arriving with two girls and Joe Fischetti, the 'clean young man' of the Chicago Fischettis, he was advised that, due to late check-outs, accommodations would not be ready until later. Miffed at the slight in the presence of friends, he created a scene in the lobby, which almost led to fisticuffs with Jack Entratter, the manager and an old friend. Thereafter, Frank reportedly refused to rehearse for the show. At showtime, it took the combined entreaties of Entratter and the comic talents of Jerry Lewis and Danny Thomas to bring him out of a sulk that delayed proceedings for a restless, capacity-filled crowd of two thousand diners. Although he was part-owner of the hotel, he later would not participate in ceremonies celebrating its fourth anniversary.

On Christmas Day, the management came to believe that he had walked out entirely. Although there were indications that he had slept in his room, he was not seen on the grounds all through the day. As show-time approached, Entratter began scanning the guest lists and bills of neighbouring hotels for possible substitute performers. But shortly before the show was to begin, an attendant found Frank in his dressing room quietly preparing for his appearance. Queried as to his whereabouts during the day, he indicated that he had chartered a private plane early in the morning, had flown to Beverly Hills and spent the holiday with his children.

XIX

WRONG DOORS—EXCEPT PROFESSIONALLY

At 2.10 on the morning of January 14, 1957, Humphrey Bogart died of throat cancer. The night of Bogie's death, Frank phoned the William Morris agency just before showtime at the Copa and told Abe Lastfogel: 'I can't go on. I'm afraid I won't be coherent.' The Copa management was fortunate: Jerry Lewis, who had a reservation for the dinner show, and Sammy Davis, Jr., who was attending the midnight show, both agreed to sub for Frank. Two months later, on his return to the coast, Frank began taking out Lauren Bacall in much the same way that Eddie Fisher had sought to cheer up the distraught widow of his friend, Mike Todd. While the Bacall–Sinatra relationship did not ripen as quickly as the Taylor–Fisher romance, it seemed for part of 1957 to be altar-bound, at least in the minds of some reporters.

In New York City, where Frank was moored at the time of

Bogart's death, January was an extremely cold month, frequently of below-freezing weather. It did not hurt business at the Copa where advance reservations taxed the club's capacity for every night of Frank's stay. Opening night, Joey Bishop, the comic on the bill, ad libbed: 'I don't know what all the excitement's about. It's the same act I've been doing for years ... You think this is a crowd? Wait till Sinatra's following shows up.' Sammy Davis, who had a ringside reservation for every midnight show, later wrote of Frank's impact: 'It was more than just his performance that was causing a sort of mass hysteria. The women were gazing at him with greater adoration than ever and now even the men were giving him a beyond-envy kind of respect ... nodding like *Yeah*: because Frank ... was the guy who'd fought odds and won, the man who stands on his beliefs "Like me or not" ... who professes to be no god ... but a man and like a man, all the mixtures are there: the good guy, the bad guy ... every known facet of his off-stage personality fusing with his performance, and his atmosphere lifting everyone to that peak of nearly hysterical excitement which surrounds a performer as he stands on the ultimate plateau.'

Before the performance, Sammy had trotted up to Sinatra's dressing room in the connecting Hotel 14, only to find that Frank had gone out for a walk by himself. 'It's great to be the absolutely hottest thing in the business,' Sammy mused, 'but how do you live up to being a legend?' And Davis had gone downstairs to the club not envying Sinatra that hour and feeling that it was right for him to be alone. 'The strength to face that audience,' he thought, 'could only come from the same place that he's drawn the power to attract them.' And then, as Davis later observed him on the floor: 'Within three songs, Frank had more than lived up to that legend; he had surpassed it.'

In rare form, Frank could not resist bantering with the audience—banter that displayed the smart showman's spontaneous sense of humour, but even at the moment of triumph, his unrelieved feeling of hostility. 'Dot Kilgallen isn't here,' he remarked. 'She's out shopping for a new chin.' Frank was repaying Miss Kilgallen for a needling series of articles she had written about him the previous year. The following day, Louis Sobol, and later Walter Winchell, took Frank to task on the ground that the crack was in poor taste. A *Look* reader wanted to know why columnists were more immune to satire than stars.

On February 7 Frank was scheduled to play the Stadium in Sydney, Australia. On the evening of February 4, before Frank and his party went to the airport in Honolulu, they visited the Hawaiian Village on the invitation of Henry Kaiser. When Frank found that the dinner table reserved for them seated only six instead of eight, he stomped out, refusing to wait until the table was re-set or a new one found. At the airport, a new complication developed. Their baggage was already on the plane when Frank discovered that only two berths were available for the flight. Angrily, he threw the eight plane tickets on the counter and demanded a refund. While the necessary papers were being prepared, attendants struggled to remove their baggage, delaying the plane's departure. Frank's last-minute display of *hauter* left a Sydney promoter with a heavy, advance, ticket sale to refund to disappointed customers.

At LA the next day, Frank told newsmen: 'Somebody goofed.' The Honolulu manager of Quantas countered: 'The Sinatra party had requested three berths—for Sinatra, Sanicola and Van Heusen. Two were confirmed. One was left on a "we'll try" basis. But there were no cancellations.'

A friend offered another explanation for Sinatra's conduct. 'Maybe Frank made the airline the heavy. But the real heavy is Frank's tight schedule. If he stops to tie a shoelace, he's keeping someone someplace waiting. He was due back in Hollywood to start work on *Pal Joey*. The picture was more important than the Australian tour.'

A few days later, the Australian promoter announced that a settlement had been reached 'in excess of $75,000'. The five musicians who were to accompany Frank were paid by him for the allotted time.

Before he began work on *Pal Joey*, Sinatra became enmeshed in a bizarre but troubling situation that dragged on for five months and that became known in the papers as 'The Case of the Wrong Door Raid'.

On February 16, as Frank lay asleep in his Palm Springs home, two men and a woman, armed with a subpoena from a Calif. State Senate Comm., approached his house. Sinatra was of interest to the Committee because he had been mentioned in a *Confidential* magazine story that purported to tell 'The Real Reason for M.M.'s Divorce'. It was 4 a.m. when the policemen opened the door to his house—they claimed that the key was in the lock—sneaked into his bedroom, flashed a light in his face, and, as he awoke, shoved the subpoena into his hand.

In the following day's papers, the State Committee revealed the strange set of circumstances they wished to investigate. The Beverly Hills police blotter of November 5, 1954—more than two years earlier—included information on a so-called burglary attempt at the home of one, Mrs. Florence Katz Ross of Waring Avenue. According to the *Confidential* article of September 1956, the purpose of the raid on Mrs. Ross' apartment had not been burglary, but to secure divorce evidence for Joe DiMaggio against Marilyn Monroe. The police had questioned Hank Sanicola and restaurateur Patsy D'Amore following the appearance of the article and now wanted to quiz Sinatra about his alleged participation in the raid.

WITNESS SAYS SINATRA LIED was the headline that reported Frank's appearance before the Kraft Committee. The witness was Philip W. Irwin, former LA policeman and an employee, at the time of the raid, of the Barney Ruditsky Detective Agency. According to Irwin, he, Ruditsky, and five other men, namely, DiMaggio, Sinatra, Sanicola, Patsy D'Amore, and a photographer, had, on the evening in question, gone to a house on Waring Avenue in front of which Marilyn Monroe's Cadillac was parked. They had crashed through an apartment door, had been amazed to find that they had raided the wrong apartment, and had fled in panic. According to Irwin, Frank had broken in with the others, and had, in fact, caused the panic by switching on the light that revealed their error. Instead of Marilyn, who had been dining with a woman friend in an apartment just above the raided one, they had found a strange woman shocked out of a deep sleep.

Sinatra clashed with Irwin on two major points. It was his contention that he had remained outside in a car and had not participated in the 'wrong door' raid. He also maintained the restaurateur D'Amore had not been on the scene at all. D'Amore's name figured only because the call from DiMaggio for the raid had come to Frank at the Villa Capri, D'Amore's restaurant, and because the raiding party had repaired there for coffee after committing its ridiculous, if not risible, error.

At the hearing testimony indicated that, when DiMaggio had refused to pay Ruditsky for the comedy of errors, the detective had threatened to give the story to *Confidential*. Even though a payment of $800 had been made, the story of the misadventure had been passed to the spicy exposé magazine. On the stand, Frank was affable and occasionally witty. But Irwin stated that he feared Sinatra and was apprehensive of being beaten up. Before the hearing was over, Frank was handed a new subpoena requiring his appearance before the LA County Grand Jury, which was conducting an independent probe into the wrong-door raid. The DA indicated that the conflicting stories told by Irwin and Sinatra formed the basis for a possible perjury charge. An indictment was also to be considered for 'felonious conspiracy to violate forcible trespass laws'.

It was not until March 12 that the DA, having studied a 1,200-page transcript of the Committee hearing, announced that the testimony did not produce conclusive evidence supporting a perjury indictment. However, the matter still did not seem a closed issue for the DA's office had a new chief investigator, who announced that he was gathering corroborating evidence to place before the Grand Jury.

On the 19th when the Grand Jury convened, Barney Ruditsky, who had planned the raid and was responsible for the *Confidential* story, was in Florida recuperating from a heart attack. Both Joe DiMaggio and Marilyn Monroe were in New York. Frank thus became the principal witness. Apparently the Grand Jury was satisfied by his forty-five minutes of testimony for it handed down no indictment. But Frank was not completely out of the mess until the middle of July.

On June 1, the woman into whose apartment the raiders had mistakenly broken, brought a $200,000 suit against DiMaggio, Ruditsky, Irwin, D'Amore, 'Seminola', three John Does, and, of course, Sinatra. Charging that she had suffered acute hysteria on the night of the raid, she claimed that she had since been so nervous that she could not continue in her $300 a month job. The suit was settled out of court for an undisclosed sum.

When Barney Ruditsky appeared before a second Grand Jury sitting in July, he took full responsibility for the raid. He corroborated Frank's testimony that he had remained in a car parked a block away. He testified that DiMaggio had gone into the building but had not set foot in the raided apartment. And he asserted that only he and his employee Philip Irwin had broken down the door on the night of November 5, 1954.

So, what had begun as an act of friendship and may have been a bit of spirited high jinks, turned out to be a costly comedy of errors. To at least one Sinatra fan club, that in Biloxi, Mississippi, the incident had a special significance: 'As a Sinatra fan there is one thing you should know,' the president of the club wrote in its bulletin, 'and that is Frank's definition of a friend—a friend is a person for whom you will fight and help regardless of what it may do to you. DiMaggio is Frank's friend and what Frank did was to help a friend.'

In March Frank began work in 'the only role I've dreamed of doing for many years outside of Private Maggio'. It was the title role in the John O'Hara–Rodgers and Hart musical *Pal Joey*. Asked whether he had seen Frank's film enactment of his character, author John O'Hara said: 'No, I didn't have to see Sinatra. I invented him.' Joey Evans was a heel, Frank well understood. But inevitably he emerged not the second-rate hoofer and heel-cum-appeal that O'Hara had created but a first-rate singer, fast with the chicks, flip with the con but tender of heart underneath. The soundtrack was a scintillating pot-pourri of great Rodgers and Hart tunes, including ballads like *There's A Small Hotel* and *My Funny Valentine*, which came from other Rodgers and Hart shows.

While Frank was in good spirits during the filming of *Pal Joey*, he did not forget a certain newsman who, he thought, had crossed him. When Ezra Goodman, who was doing a story on co-star Kim Novak for *Time*, appeared on the set one day, Frank walked away from the camera and informed director George Sidney that either Goodman or Sinatra was leaving the set. Goodman was compelled to leave. 'What can I do?' studio boss Harry Cohn asked Goodman. 'If Sinatra walks, we'll be out a day's shooting.' According to Goodman in *The Fifty Year Decline and Fall of Hollywood*, where he indicates that a *Time* editor had invented a Sinatra quote, Frank did take a walk that day.

On May 7 while he was still before the *Pal Joey* cameras, his attorney was in LA Federal Court filing a $2,300,000 libel suit against the publishers of *Look* magazine, and the author of a three-part profile. The first instalment of the Bill Davidson series, titled *Talent, Tantrums and Torment*, was then on the news-stands. The second, dated May 28, was called *Why Sinatra Hates the Press*, and the last, *Blondes, Brunettes and the Blues*. Describing the first article as 'lewd, lascivious and scurrilous' and marked by 'innuendoes and references of the same nature and type as are contained in ... "scandal" magazines', the complaint denied that Sinatra was 'a neurotic, depressed and tormented person with suicidal tendencies and a libertine'. ('Don't those jokers know I have kids!' Frank said to a reporter.)

Among the many items rejected by Sinatra as untrue was an incident involving Speaker of the House of Representatives Sam Rayburn. Davidson had reported that at the previous year's Democratic Convention, where Frank had sung the national anthem, an elderly gentleman had put a hand on Sinatra's arm as he was leaving the platform and inquired: 'Aren't you going to sing *The Yellow Rose of Texas*, Frank?' According to *Look*, Sinatra had replied: 'Take the hand off the suit, creep.' The old man was Speaker Rayburn. Attached to Sinatra's complaint was an April 30 telegram from Speaker Rayburn denying the incident.

In his second *Look* article, Davidson sought to explain 'Why Sinatra Hates the Press'. Davidson's thesis was this: because of emotional scars left by his childhood, specifically, his mother's neglect, Sinatra must perpetuate certain compensating fantasies and illusions; since the press can expose these myths, Sinatra fears and fights reporters. And Davidson proceeded to expose all the myths regarding his so-called underprivileged and delinquent youth. In actuality, this had first been done in *Photoplay* magazine (September 1956) when the testimony of Hoboken neighbours and adolescent friends had been presented to debunk press agent ballyhoo.

In his very title, Davidson was 'begging the question'. Westbrook Pegler, Dorothy Kilgallen, Lee Mortimer and Robert Ruark hardly constituted *the press*. Nor did Frank *hate* them because they exposed his past. Several disliked his politics, two hammered at his alleged gangster associations, and others focused on his romances. None bothered with his Hoboken youth. Moreover, all through the period when Frank was snarling at certain reporters, he remained on undeniably good terms with Earl Wilson, Walter Winchell, Joe Hyams, Tom

Pryor, Bob Thomas and other newsmen. In truth, few entertainers have been as publicity-conscious as Sinatra.

During the controversy with *Look*, it became known that, to protect his privacy, Frank had been willing to jeopardise a long-standing friendship with a reporter he greatly admired. Before the appearance of the Davidson series, he had accepted a sizeable advance to collaborate on an autobiography with sportswriter Jimmy Cannon. The collaboration ended before it began because Cannon had submitted a list of questions he wanted to ask, and Frank had ruled out all personal queries.

The suit against *Look* never came to trial. In December 1957, Frank altered the grounds from libel to invasion of privacy. 'I have always maintained,' he said, in announcing the new suit, 'that any writer or publication has a right to discuss or criticise my professional activities as a singer or actor. But I feel than an entertainer's right to privacy should be just as inviolate as any other person's right of privacy.' The general counsel for *Look* welcomed Frank's new action. But even this suit never came to trial, for on February 8, 1963, Sinatra's attorney filed to have it dismissed.

At the conclusion of work on *Pal Joey*, Frank chartered a 102-ft. yacht for a cruise from San Pedro to Coronado on the Baja California peninsula. Among those aboard the July 4 sailing was Lauren Bacall, whom Sinatra had been taking to premières, his own recording sessions, etc. While the *Celeste* sailed along the sun-drenched California coast, the final bill of divorcement between Frank and Ava was issued. On June 14, a few days after Ava had completed work in *The Sun Also Rises* in Mexico, where Walter Chiari had been her house guest, divorce papers had been filed in a Mexico City court. Frank had received formal notification some days later and had not contested the charges of desertion and absence for more than six months. When the divorce decree was issued on July 5, it was just less than four years since MGM's announcement of October 1953 that Frank and Ava had come to a final parting of the ways.

During the *Celeste*'s journey southward, Frank occupied himself by reading, among other things, a hit Broadway play *A Hole in the Head*. As soon as he was back in Hollywood, he was on the long-distance phone, purchasing the film rights from author Arnold Schuman for $200,000.

Frank now directed his energies to his new TV series, scheduled for an October 18 debut. For $3,000,000 proffered by ABC, he was to provide thirteen half-hour musicals, thirteen half-hour dramatic shows, and two live hour-long spectaculars. Twenty-four hours after ABC announced that it had signed Sinatra, a cigarette company bought the show. 'If I fall on my face, I want to be the cause,' Frank told a reporter. 'In my new series, no one has script approval except me. Neither the sponsor nor the network can dictate. They put their money in and that's all.'

Frank's ambitious plans called for the shooting of the thirteen musicals within a period of thirteen to twenty days. 'It can be done,' he said. 'Our theory is it's like a live TV show. We will rehearse fully and then shoot.' By the time Frank entered a set, numbers were to be fully rehearsed and ready for the camera. Until then, David White, an old song-and-dance man, functioned as Frank's stand-in. Once on stage Frank's quick recall, the teleprompter and the able direction of Frank Donahue (whom Frank called Mother), would enable them to get the scene in one take. On July 9, the day after Frank began filming the series on a sound stage of Goldwyn studios, Leonard Goldenson, head of ABC, flew to Hollywood and presented Frank with a cheque for $3,000,000.

On October 13 Sinatra joined Bing Crosby in an hour-long TV special to introduce the Ford Company's new car, Edsel. Although the car 'bombed', the hour was well received. Jack Gould of the NY *Times* reflected the enthusiasm of most reviewers when he wrote: 'The leisurely warmth and spontaneity of their talents and personalities enveloped the home screen. And the astonishing Mr. Sinatra was not only right in there, but often a step or two ahead . . .'

Five days later, Frank offered what was then described as 'the most expensive half-hour programme in TV history'. But Mr. Gould, who had praised the Edsel special, came down hard on Sinatra's own show. 'Rather banal', was his comment. Ben Gross of the *Daily News*, who was likewise unenthusiastic, felt that the script 'didn't catch fire with its heavy, soggy attempts at humour'. To John Lardner in the *New Yorker*, 'everything seemed under-organised and a little desperate'. Hearst columnist Jack O'Brian singled out Frank's interpolations of *Wise Guyisms* into song lyrics for condemnation. Citing the use of 'cotton-pickin' broads' for girls, O'Brian contended that these lyrical switches 'often changed a lovely romantic lyric into dirty double meanings'. (Some years later, he objected to Sinatra's insertion of the phrase 'you grab me' in Cole Porter's *I've Got You Under My Skin*.)

There were also yea-sayers. John Crosby of the NY *Herald-Tribune* praised the opening production number, which began with a close-up of Frank's fingers snapping rhythmically for *Lonesome Road*. His overall reaction: 'Frank was one hell of a performer and his first TV show a triumph in almost all departments.'

Although the first show's Trendex yielded a favourable rating, there were rumours ten days later of huddles between Sinatra, the ad agency, ABC and the William Morris office. By mid-November, the reports were that ABC-TV was disturbed over the show's ratings. Jack O'Brian headlined a column, 'Hottest Talent Cooling Off?' and noted that Frank's rating had dropped to a 'pitiful low', which made his 'the least looked-at network show in his time period'. Touted initially in *Variety* as ABC-TV's 'first big hit in adult programming', the Sinatra show had within a matter of weeks turned into 'a flop, rating and otherwise'.

Retreating from a position he had once taken, Frank announced that he was putting a new accent of *live*, rather than filmed shows. But even the use of a new writing team on a live programme featuring Dean Martin, did not turn the tide. After the November 29 telecast, there was no ducking the fact that the show was in serious trouble. With much of ABC's money buried in filmed segments, the question was how to save the programme? Out of December talks between sponsors, ad agency and talent agency, came a rather momentous announcement. After the 21st of the month, when he would be through acting in the film *Kings Go Forth*, he would devote his entire time to the ABC series, except, perhaps, for dates at the Copa and Fontainebleau.

But if the Christmas show was any indication of what the future held, the portents were not good. The guest was Bing Crosby, who, when he discovered that Frank was directing, allegedly said: 'Where are my things? I'm leaving.' Joke or not, Bing stayed and did fifteen Yule favourites with Frank. *Variety* found the show 'static, studied, pretentious and awkward'. It added: 'Even discounting the often sloppy production (of the entire series), the absence of a central theme or point of view, the fact is that Sinatra never seemed at his best or at his easiest, and the attitude infects his guests.' In *Variety*'s view, the shows would not improve either as a result of being live or using bigger guest stars—'until Sinatra starts being himself'.

It was to take time for Frank fully to assess the difference between the ear of the recording microphone and the probing eye of the TV camera. On wax, he came through as the uninhibited romantic, intense and spontaneous. On the TV screen, he displayed a kind of studied unconcern, which may really have been uneasiness, but which struck reviewers as smugness or arrogance. Missing, too, from the TV Sinatra was his 'tough' side, the controversial, the 'like me or not' truculence. In short, Frank's TV image was out of focus. Viewers were confused, unconvinced and, inevitably, uninterested.

Of the three films released during 1957, *The Pride and the Passion*, a summer release, received the least favourable comment. Frank fared much better both with *The Joker Is Wild* and *Pal Joey*. The former brought widespread acknowledgment of 'Sinatra's status as one of the screen's most accomplished actors'. Reviews rang with phrases like—'Sinatra creates a real man, not a cardboard statue' and 'Best film biography of a show-business personality since *Love Me or Leave Me*.' Joe E. Lewis quipped: 'Frankie enjoyed playing my life more than I enjoyed living it.'

Pal Joey also drew rave notices. 'Almost a one-man show', wrote the *Hollywood Citizen-News*. In *Down Beat*'s opinion, the film was the best wedding of song and comedy. 'Chiefly it has Sinatra,' Rose Pelswick noted in the *Journal-American*, 'who's nothing short of terrific. He does as exciting a job of acting as of singing. He brings vividly alive the glib, egotistical, raffish opportunism of John O'Hara's well-known story, and invests the part with such tremendous charm that he simply wraps up the picture.'

Speaking for the minority, Archer Winsten of the NY *Post* described the film as 'disappointing to admirers of the classic John O'Hara musical but full of clever trinkets for the current Sinatra mob'. Winsten noted unhappily that at a preview, Frank achieved 'the big boffola with an internal reference to Wheaties'. Why the *Post* critic considered this an *inside* reference it is difficult to surmise since *Confidential* had carried a cover story of Frank's alleged use of the cereal as a virility energiser. That Frank could joke about this matter is curious, too, since Hedda Hopper later reported that a thoughtless reference to Wheaties by her shattered her friendship with Sinatra.

Some remember the première of *The Joker Is Wild* because of what appeared to be a thoughtless display of the unpredictable Sinatra temperament. Las Vegas was the setting, and the proceedings began on a hilarious note when a horse ridden by Frank and comic Joe E. Lewis balked at entering the theatre. Unnerved by the attempt to manoeuvre it past the box-office, the animal defecated. 'Everybody's a critic these days,' Lewis murmured. After the screening, there was a big, public party at El Rancho Vegas where Lewis was then appearing. Lewis introduced Frank to thunderous applause. Then, instead of continuing with his own comedy routine, the comic invited Frank to do a song. The audience liked the idea. Frank remained seated. Lewis waited, and repeated the invitation. Then, in plain view of the large audience, Frank rose from his chair, helped his date (Lauren Bacall) from hers and walked rapidly out of the room.

It was a resounding rebuff to Lewis, even though, as became later apparent, Frank had reason to feel provoked. The audience could not have known that Frank had exacted a promise that Joe would not ask him to sing. Joe had agreed, knowing that it was Sinatra's policy not to perform in any Las Vegas hotel other than the Sands. 'If Joe wasn't really flying,' a friend of the two said, 'he would have remembered not to ask Frank to sing. I think Frank was wrong, but I also think it took real guts for him to take a walk.'

The Joker Is Wild not only added to Frank's stature as an actor; it yielded the beautiful Cahn–Van Heusen ballad *All the Way*, which won the Academy Award. In *Witchcraft*, Frank also had one of the big discs of the year, a record that was characteristic of the more hip singing style presaged in Sinatra's early Capitol discs. Apparent in *Learnin' the Blues* and *The Tender Trap* of 1955, the style took shape in *Hey, Jealous Lover* and the 1956 album of *Songs for Swingin' Lovers*, and flowered in the finger-snapping *Witchcraft* and the *Come Fly with Me* album of 1957. Characterised by flowing counter-melodies as well as driving rhythm figures, it was a combination of 'swinging/ballad', 'string-inflected/big-band' style.

In 1957, as the swing-and-string approach matured—Billy May added a barrelling, bartender quality to Riddle's ear-catching lyricism—Frank began using a third arranger. Composer-lyricist of the romantic *Manhattan Towers* cantata, Gordon Jenkins had a feeling for brooding, Tchaikovsky-like backgrounds. Frank did six sessions with Jenkins, actually one more than with Riddle in 1957. These resulted in two albums, one a Christmas anthology that included *Mistletoe and Holly*, a song credited to Sinatra, Sanicola and a Mr. Sanford, and *Have Yourself a Merry Little Christmas*, one of the few tunes Frank recorded three times. The other Jenkins LP was a compilation of introspective ballads like *Laura, Lonely Town* and the title song *Where Are You? Down Beat* regretted the lack of 'the sustained buoyancy of his swinging sets', but praised the collection as 'an education in setting a mood and in ballad singing of about the highest calibre there is today'. Jenkin's setting for *Autumn Leaves*, with its *Liebestod* overtones, evoked from Sinatra one of the most emotional performances of his entire record career.

During the year Sinatra again indulged his talents as an amateur conductor, this time to help promote the jazz-oriented but sometimes over-subtle singing of his Bowmont Drive neighbour Peggy Lee. The three sessions occurred in April while he was still on the *Pal Joey* set. A key musician on the dates said: 'I've worked before with stars who wanted to conduct, either for publicity or a lark. But Sinatra is a musician's musician.'

As the year wore on, Frank came out more and more strongly against the younger generation's taste in music and against ASCAP's competitor, BMI, for promoting teenage, rock material. 'Rock 'n' roll,' he was quoted as saying in *Western World*, a magazine published in Paris, 'fosters almost totally negative and destructive reactions in young people.' Dismissing the bulk of it as material 'sung, played and written for the most part by cretinous goons', he said: 'My only deep sorrow is the unrelenting insistence of recording and motion picture companies upon purveying this most brutal, ugly, degenerate, vicious form of expression.' Strangely enough, in attacking R 'n' R, Sinatra was in the same camp as Mitch Miller, the man whom he had attacked for working with BMI to promote inferior songs and who was the only outspoken critic of R 'n' R among A & R executives of major record companies.

The end of the year array of awards confirmed Sinatra's still-growing popularity. In *Down Beat*'s Readers Poll, he outpointed his nearest contender for the top Male Singer crown by a margin of 10 to 1 and in *Metronome*, he ran so far ahead of the field that the editors observed: 'Sinatra literally devoured this one; there was no chance for anyone else.' *Metronome* featured him on its cover as Mr. Personality while *Jazz* 1957 named him, along with Billie Holiday, as Singers of the Year. *Playboy*, launching its annual reader selection of an All-Star Jazz Band, gave him the nod as top Male Vocalist, a post he was steadily to maintain through the years. In a NY *Times* Sunday feature, Tom Pryor noted that he has 'no rival in the newly developed field of popular song albums' while Walter Winchell saluted him in *American Weekly* as 'The All-Around Entertainer of the Year'.

There was reason, thus, for the cockiness and sense of self-importance exposed by the revealing eye of the TV camera. In this period, in conversations with various reporters, Frank began rationalising even his break with MGM: if he had not 'cancelled out' of his contract, he would not have been free to do *From Here to Eternity* for Columbia and rebuild his film career. And yet even in these moments of 'supreme self-confidence', to use Jack Tracy's *Down Beat* phrase, reporters felt that he was not happy unless he had something to fight about or to make him miserable. *Metronome* found this ambivalence in Mr. Personality appealing. To editor Bill Cross, he was 'the most complete, the most fantastic symbol of American maleness yet discovered'; but in that virile personality, there was 'little comfort. There is much challenge in it, more than a share of danger.' In Frank's singing, as well as in Billie Holiday's, Cross discerned 'the loneliness of one who wants not to be alone but has no ability to share loneliness so as to find comfort'.

Frank's arrival in Nice for location shooting on *Kings Go Forth* was a tumultuous affair, with hordes of women breaking through police lines, boosting the 'boudoir Tarzan', as the French press called him, on their shoulders, and carrying him through the airport. Linda Christian, who had come to the terminal to meet him, could not get through the crowds, and was compelled to follow his rented limousine in her own car on the drive to Cannes.

Before he left for France, Frank and Lauren Bacall had dated frequently and dined regularly at the Villa Capri, occupying Frank's special booth—not the alcove where Mario Volpe's painting of Frank as a weeping clown hangs, but the lone, remote alcove in the bar area. Since Frank was seen on occasion with Marlene Dietrich, Gloria Vanderbilt and eighteen-year-old Joan Blackman, Hollywood speculated rather than gossiped about the relationship. Frank was suspected of still carrying a torch for Ava while Lauren was obviously trying to adjust to an existence without Bogart.

By the time he arrived in France, Frank was legally free to marry again. An English reporter, trying to smoke out the relationship, concocted a story of planned nuptials 'within six months'. His article in the London *Evening Standard* was picked up by the Hollywood papers and columnists, who reported that while Frank was abroad, Lauren never left her Bellagio Road home until she had received a daily overseas call from him.

Frank was back in Palm Springs when the pick-up of the London story appeared. Sunning himself at the former home of Al Jolson, which he had purchased for $90,000, he parried questions about marriage with a 'no comment' shrug. Newsmen who tried to query Bacall found that she 'was unavailable'. (That she was aware of Frank's sensitivity about marriage was indicated during a visit to the Hollywood set of *Kings Go Forth*; watching a scene in which Sinatra counselled Tony Curtis to marry the girl (Natalie Wood), Bacall let out a huge horse-laugh.) And so, with comparatively little tension, the flurry of phony publicity was weathered and they continued dating into March 1958 when another newspaper story, this one by Louella Parsons, brought on a major crisis.

As filming on *Kings Go Forth* proceeded in Hollywood and Monterey, Frank proved a delightful host to cast and crew. Each Friday night before they broke for the week-end, he had the Villa Capri cater an informal spread spread on the studio lot. Cast and crew reciprocated by throwing a surprise birthday party for him on December 12. Among the gag gifts presented by co-star Natalie Wood and Bob Wagner, then her husband, was an album of *Christmas Carols* by Elvis Presley.

Kings Go Forth had the makings of a controversial film. The ending made it clear that the white soldier played by Frank would marry the Negro girl played by Natalie. Queried on the set as to how he thought audiences might react, Frank said: 'I think most people who have any kind of common sense and think fairly will not go out of the theatre and start race riots. As for the bigots, they'll scream at anything. But I took this part as a performer, not as a lecturer on racial problems.' When it came to the bigotry, he thought that the intellectual was 'twice as dangerous as the person with no education. The uneducated man can be taught he is wrong. But the intellectual will rationalise.' As to whether his own feelings about intolerance had changed: 'Back then,' Frank replied, 'I used to feel an indignity that shook me up. But I know that you don't lick that sort of thing overnight.'

To demonstrate how his own outlook had developed, Frank told of having a drink 'with some supposedly educated people' in Monterey. 'Some dame with a couple of drinks in her came up and told me that I was very popular with her crowd. "Do you know what we call you?" she asked. "We call you The Wop Singer."

'"Thank you," I said, "that's very sweet." Why, a few years ago, I would have been tempted to bop her in the nose even though she was a mouse. But, luckily, I didn't need to educate her husband. A pretty nice fellow, he apologised for his "educated" wife.'

IMAGE 5

THE SWINGER

In this period, Las Vegas girls, show, sales and serving, reportedly defined a 'square' as a chick who had not slept with Frank Sinatra. He was later to say that if he had had affairs with all the broads rumour paired him with, he would have long been in a jar at Harvard Medical School. But he did have a series of well-publicised 'romances', some short, some extended, with Lauren Bacall, Lady Beatty, Dorothy Provine, Kim Novak, Jill St. John, Juliet Prowse, and *en passant*, with an unidentified list of chorines, counter girls, cashiers, clerks, comediennes, coeds, canaries, hat-chicks, culinary workers, chantoosies and just plain pussycats.

But the image of the swinger had other elements in it than romance and sex. It embraced high spirits, rowdiness, off-colour gags, horse play and highjinks. 'He has an insatiable desire to live every moment to the fullest,' an actor associate has said, 'perhaps because he feels that right around the corner is extinction.'

As The Clan or The Rat Pack (Sinatra's preference when he admitted to its existence) was the embodiment of the Swinging Years, so the so-called Summit Meeting became its most vivid manifestation. The *en masse* appearance of The Clan at an important club engagement of one of its members and the staging of an improvised, unbuttoned show, proved the peak point of night-clubbing for many customers, an offence to some, and a matter for adverse comment by others. But despite criticism, which eventually rocked Sinatra himself, the antics of The Rat Pack fired the public imagination and caught the fancy of magazine editors, some of very sophisticated publications, intrigued at first by what Richard Gehman, in writing of Bogart, described as a 'frig you' attitude. A news magazine referred to this facet in more elegant fashion when it wrote: 'They spit in the face of custom.'

Sinatra's LPs of these years bore titles like *Come Swing With Me*, *Swing Easy* and *Ring-a-ding Ding*. The arrangements by Billy May, Johnny Mandel, later Neal Hefti and Quincy Jones, were jazz-spiced, and the swinging vocals were more and more improvisational in their inflections.

There were also a series of movies, all with numbers in their titles, in which Frank and his buddies gave Technicolor vividness to Clan concepts. Regardless of whether they portrayed wartime buddies bent on a hold-up caper (*Ocean's Eleven*), Indians, troopers and trumpeters (*Sergeants Three*), romping, rival cowboys (*Four for Texas*), or good-hearted Chicago gangsters (*Robin and the Seven Hoods*), Frank and his Clansmen played themselves, projecting an image of an uninhibited, high-living group of nonconformists. In *Come Blow Your Horn*, Frank gave visual embodiment to his own rakish image in the role of a swinging bachelor.

As late as September 1965, shortly before his fiftieth birthday, he was typed 'the senior swinger of the land' and a news magazine wrote: 'Sinatra goes where the action is. And if perchance it isn't, it is after he gets there.' But by then he was just exploding cherry bombs at Jilly's, enjoying horror movies with his guests, and really much more concerned with the growth of a fiduciary octopus known as Sinatra Enterprises. Only his interest in a TV actress, younger than two of his children, served to keep the fading image of the romantic in ambiguous focus.

XX

THE THREE B'S—ON THE DISTAFF

'Sinatra sat before me tensely,' wrote Peer J. Oppenheimer in *Family* magazine late in 1958, 'not like a conqueror on top of the world but like a little guy who finds himself on a smouldering volcano.' Both the number of projects in which Frank involved himself in 1958 and the tensions surrounding them, bear out the impression that his comeback generated not only a feeling of super-confidence but a nagging fear of again toppling from the heights.

The beginning of the year brought no improvement in the reception of his TV series. 'One of the biggest and most expensive disappointments of the current season,' was *TV Guide*'s description in February. Explanations for the failure varied. In actor Ronald Reagan's opinion, the show missed because Frank had 'too much pride specifically to go out and try to be liked'. Eddie Fisher's chief writer argued that the TV screen compelled Frank to be 'a gentle man with no rejoinders', instead of himself, Pal Joey-isms and all. Another analyst contended that producers hurt Sinatra by not letting him come through as the public knew him—a man of character 'but not nice'.

An actor on one of Frank's dramatic shows offered a different explanation 'I've seen him show up for an 11 a.m. rehearsal as late as 4.30 p.m. The other actors work with a stand-in, then Frank comes in at the last minute, races through the scene in one take and that's it.' Contrariwise, a TV executive said: 'He works like a dog. He runs every last phase of the show and he's taking the brickbats. He has yet to put the blame on anyone else.' An agency executive concurred: 'Sinatra has belied his reputation. He was fantastically co-operative, superhuman in his efforts to clear other bookings ... He accepted criticism and sought advice as if he were a newcomer to show business.'

And what advice did Frank receive? The producer of the Danny Thomas show recommended that he play to live audiences. A trade-paper editor proposed that he play himself as he did on a night-club floor and argued that putting on a special TV personality was a mistake. After many conferences, Frank adopted the 'live kinescope technique' employed by Bob Hope and others. The show was pre-recorded but in the presence of a live audience. Since a kinescope could not be announced, 'Live from Hollywood', a jokester suggested 'Dead from Hollywood'. They settled on 'Direct from Hollywood'. But neither Frank's flexibility nor the advice of TV experts helped. By March, when he was playing the Fontainebleau, he was not sure he wanted to continue the show. Chesterfield was not sure it wanted to continue sponsorship. And ABC was not sure what to do about its $3,000,000 investment.

While Frank was at the Fontainebleau, his relationship with Lauren Bacall reached its denouement. Both Frank and Lauren had been scheduled to appear on the Academy Award telecast of March 26. After agreeing to sing one of the five nominated songs—*All the Way* took the Oscar—Frank cancelled out. At about the same time, Bacall indicated that she, too, could not appear. That both were planning to attend the Carmen Basilio–Sugar Ray Robinson fight in Chicago the night before the Oscar presentations seemed too simple an explanation. Encountering Bacall at a party given by Zsa Zsa Gabor, Louella Parsons asked a blunt question about marriage. 'Why don't you ask Frank in Florida?' Lauren replied. I. P. Lazar, the literary agent, who was Bacall's escort, eyed Louella in a way that provoked the columnist to seek him out alone. 'Don't you dare say I told you this,' he allegedly said, 'but since you know, yes, it's true—they'll marry.'

Miss Parsons sprang her exclusive on March 12: 'Sinatra and Bacall to Marry.' If Bacall's purpose in *sic*-ing Parsons on Sinatra had been to discover where she stood, the Parsons item fulfilled the function. In Miami, Frank refused all phone calls, including those of Warren Cowan, his own press agent. Came the Robinson–Basilio fight on the 25th, and Frank appeared without Bacall.

'It was like Gable and that French doll,' a friend said. 'When she told the papers they were gonna be married, pow! She was dead. Not that Bacall ran after Frank. She's too classy a dame.'

'Marry that bum?' Lauren said to a reporter. 'I ought to clobber you!'

'Unwittingly,' Miss Parsons wrote later, 'I caused their romance—if it was that—to break up.'

It was that, as Bacall conceded years later: 'I eventually did get involved with Sinatra on a boy–girl basis. It worked out marvellously for a while until the press went absolutely mad and drove both of us mad.'

To promote *Pal Joey*, playing the country's theatres in winter 1958, Frank prepared what was described as a *Broad Dictionary*. It was quite opportune since 1958 was a big 'broad' year for him. The word 'broad' itself created a problem when his *Come Fly with Me* album was about to be released in England. Frank had made two changes in the lyric of Rudyard Kipling's famous ballad *On the Road to Mandalay*. 'A man can raise a thirst' became 'a cat can raise a thirst' and a 'Burma girl' became 'a Burma broad'. When British Capitol approached the Kipling Estate for clearance, the author's daughter flatly refused to accept the alterations. An offer to send Sinatra's disc for her consideration was likewise curtly rejected. The head of the Estate's literary agency said: 'Mrs. Bainbridge feels that her father knew best how to express the ideas embodied in his poems and that what he created should not be tampered with.' The British publisher added that, while the changed words were the main difficulty, 'another might be Billy May's orchestral accompaniment. It definitely hots it up. After all, his style is JAZZ—isn't it now?'

Attempting to mediate the situation, the *Record Mirror*, a British pop music trade paper, suggested that Frank re-record the song with the original words for British consumption. 'This bit of gallantry to a lady,' it wrote, 'would please the many admirers of Sinatra's vocal artistry in Britain.'

Since Frank did not re-record the song, the English edition of *Come Fly with Me* appeared with *French Foreign Legion* in place of *On the Road to Mandalay*.

By the time Frank closed at the Fontainebleau on March 23,

his gross was so great that *Variety* dubbed him 'the hottest attraction ever to have played the area'. Fourteen nights in a room seating six hundred yielded a whopping $101,000. Closing night, there were more than three times as many reservations as there were seats in La Ronde—and Frank's appearance had to be moved to the Grand Ballroom whose two thousand seats were a sell out.

Walter Winchell, who accompanied Sinatra on the train ride from Miami to Chicago, was agog at the attention Sinatra attracted when they entered the huge stadium for the Basilio–Robinson fight. As they walked down the aisle to their ringside seats, people stood up everywhere to get a look at Frank—and the crowd consisted, as it generally does at fights, mostly of men. Frank had brought along the nine-year-old daughter of a Chicago friend. When a reporter asked the name of his date, he replied: 'Lauren Bacall.'

While Miss Bacall was not in Chicago, Elizabeth Taylor and other Hollywood luminaries were. They had come, not for the middleweight fight, but for the funeral of film producer Mike Todd. So Frank and W.W., who had come for a fight, stayed for a funeral. After spending several days with Sinatra, in New York and Palm Springs, Winchell reported that Frank had notified ABC he was through with his TV series. 'Who needs all that fric frac with the rating stuff,' Frank said. 'I'm going to do a show whenever I feel like it, maybe two a year just for the fun of it.'

On April 9 Frank opened at the Sands in Vegas. That evening Lauren Bacall went to a Dean Martin opening at the Cocoanut Grove in Hollywood. Asked by a reporter about her feelings towards Frank, Bacall responded: 'Do me a favour. Never mention me in the same breath as Frank Sinatra.' Frank had told Winchell that he was leaving on a world tour in May, but that there would be 'no third party'. He was just taking his Japanese butler along.

Between the Fontainebleau and the Sands dates, Frank severed another relationship. Voyle Gilmore, who had been his A & R producer from his first Capitol date in 1953, did his last session with Sinatra on March 3, 1958.

'As a singer, there's no one like him,' Gilmore said in his soft-spoken drawl. 'As a guy, there was no one more difficult to handle. Each time you saw Frank, it was like meeting a different guy. How he treated you depended solely on how he felt at *that* moment and what was bugging him. And, believe me, he has a lot to bug him. Because he's gotta be on the move all the time, he keeps getting involved in more than any human being can handle.

'Also, to prove you were loyal, and loved him, you always had to do the impossible. Like he would call up and say, "Let's record Wednesday!" You'd say, "Frank, all the studios are booked on Wednesday." He'd say, "See if you can't get Wednesday." Well, you knew that unless you made it Wednesday, you'd be marked lousy. But then by the time you succeeded in clearing Wednesday, he might say, "No can do. Make it Tuesday." Then, you'd have to go back and talk with all the people who were upset because they had to give up Wednesday.

'When he dropped me as a producer after five years, his reason was picayune. While he was in Chicago for the Basilio–Robinson fight, he made the rounds of the disc jockeys. Apparently, they hadn't yet received his new record. He phoned Sanicola and told him to get another producer. Sanicola knew I didn't do the shipping, and he refused. So Frank got his attorney to talk to Glenn Wallichs (who was then president of Capitol). Wallichs wouldn't give Frank his own producer, but he offered to substitute Dave Cavanaugh, another Capitol producer, for me. I must admit that when Glenn informed me, I felt only relief. No artist is easy to handle. But when they're as complex as Frank ... Which is not like saying he's a bad guy.

'He can be very considerate. The first Mother's Day after our boy was born, a truck backed into our driveway and delivered some beautiful shrubs. Neither of us had a relative named "Frank", which was the signature on the card. We never thought of Sinatra, but the florist advised that it was he.

'But he could be cruel, too. Once, when Frank was doing a guest shot on the Comedy Hour, the conductor was Frank Black, who started his career way back with the famous quartet, The Revelers. Frank wouldn't make allowances that Black was not Nelson Riddle, who can sense what Sinatra wants before he says it. The rehearsal went so badly that in desperation Black muttered: "What do you want?" Sinatra gave no quarter. "If you haven't figured out by this time," he said, so that everyone heard him. "I can't do anything for you." '

Gilmore added: 'Contrast this with what happened one afternoon when Frank barged in and wanted to hear the preceding evening's takes. Lauren Bacall was with him. A young engineer was so nervous, he just couldn't find the takes. He'd roll past them or start before them. Finally, Frank got up and without saying anything—also without hearing what he came for—he and Bacall left. The engineer was miserable. When Sinatra phoned me the next day, I didn't know what to expect. I started to thank him for having been so nice to the kid. "Forget it," he said, "I could tell the kid was nervous. I'll hear those takes some other time."

'With musicians, he was a prince. He wanted the guys to think well of him. It goes back, perhaps, to his days as a band singer when a vocalist was just another member of the band, not the kingpin he is today. But he'd never take a suggestion in the presence of a musician—or anybody else, for that matter. You'd have to come out of the booth and go into the studio. If you tried talking to him over the speaker system, as you frequently did with other artists, you were dead.

'Once when he was really acting up, I went at him: "I'm trying pretty hard, Frank," I complained, "and all I get is abuse." He broke into a broad smile. "Don't let any artist get your goat," he said, "not even me." He was so appealing at times he could charm butterflies—and then again, so miserable he could bother a snake.'

Dave Cavanaugh, who succeeded Gilmore, supervised Frank's dates from a double session on May 29, 1958, until Sinatra formed his own record label in 1961. 'It was always challenging to work with him,' Cavanaugh said, 'because his musical intuitions were always right.' Cavanaugh was a former tenor saxist. 'But he had his wrinkles, as all artists do. Once when he had a "frog" in his throat, I flipped the talk-back switch and said gently over the mike: "Got a little fuzz there, huh?" He came back like a flash: "Hell, that's sexy." It got a big laugh from the studio audience. And that's really the crux of it. For Sinatra, a recording session is like a nightclub appearance. He has his crowd and he's putting on a show. He gets a kind of vibrancy into his records because he's not just singing. Man, he's acting. And you're not just an A & R producer. You're straight man for his jokes.

'The most dangerous thing was to "yes" him, or to be critical without being able to articulate what you wanted. He'd come at you, and if you backed away he was like a barracuda. He'd eat you alive if he thought you were afraid.

'At record sessions he always kidded with his entourage and joked with the musicians. But he missed nothing that was going on around him. His eyes were constantly roving round the studio. You could tell a lot from those eyes. Occasionally, he'd come to a session—and those baby blues would be positively black. If you were smart, you didn't even say "hello". Anything could cause an explosion. But singing was like a lightning rod, particularly when he was in good voice. It discharged the hostile electricity.'

Amidst false rumours, spread by the tabloids, that he had suffered a throat haemorrhage while at Palm Springs, Frank flew to Europe during the week-end after his first date with Cavanaugh. On his way to Monte Carlo, he paused in London to do the town with Peter Lawford. It was the week that the Earl Beatty was divorcing his wife Adelle, who was to make headlines with Sinatra later in the year.

The Monte Carlo première of *Kings Go Forth* included three days of partying and promotional activities, attended by American newsmen and European royalty. Even though he had done a film with her as Grace Kelly, Frank had to be formally presented to Princess Grace by the Court Chamberlain of Monaco. The following day, he and the Princess appeared before TV cameras for a *Kings Go Forth* plug to be used on the Sullivan Show. The première showing of the film on Saturday, June 14, was followed by a midnight gala at which Noel Coward introduced Sinatra, speaking first in French and then in English. 'Never once a breach of taste,' Coward later said, 'never once a wrong note.' At $50 a head, the evening netted $12,000 for the UN Refugee Fund, a pet Princess Grace charity. When they left the famous gambling Casino at closing time, Sinatra and his party continued festivities in his hotel suite into a sunrise breakfast. Screenwriter-playwright Harry Kurnitz later said: 'Sinatra is the only person who invites you to a black-tie dinner and tells you to bring sunglasses.'

Late one evening during the gala week-end, Art Buchwald, Leonard Lyons and others accompanied Frank to a cellar strip-tease joint, the Ali Baba. Frank gave the pianist 10,000 francs to yield his stool to his own accompanist. Buchwald went upstairs and stood outside the club shouting: 'Extra added attraction tonight! Hear Frank Sinatra sing!' After a half hour of barking, during which no one entered the club, a bewildered Buchwald came downstairs 'They didn't believe me!' The highjinks brought heavy column and news coverage, the quantity, out of proportion to the quality of *Kings Go Forth*.

Returning to Hollywood for Nancy, Jr's, high school graduation, Frank paused in New York to catch Ella Fitzgerald at the Copa. Exhausted by the encores demanded by enthusiastic prom kids, Ella turned to Frank for an easy 'bow-off'. The mention of the Sinatra name electrified the crowd. Responding to their wild applause, he strolled on to the Copa floor and sang a chorus of *Moonlight in Vermont* with Ella. As they were finishing, Vic Damone joined them. Johnny Mathis, who was in the audience, come onstage and sang a number. Ella asked Peter Lawford to take a bow, after which she introduced 'Cliff Montgomery'. It turned out to be Rocky Marciano, who croaked: 'Folks, I can't sing like Sinatra or Damone. But I'll fight anyone in the house.'

Frank was soon back at a Capitol Tower recording mike. He had sought the talents of Gordon Jenkins for the backgrounds of *Only the Lonely* but Jenkins was working in Las Vegas. Nelson Riddle led the string-filled orchestra, conducting with the index finger of his right hand as if he were rhythmically pressing a bell-button. The modal title tune had been written especially for Frank, like many of his LP title tunes, by Cahn and Van Heusen. Frank added a low-down version of *Blues in the Night* and a bar-soaked *One for My Baby*, the latter audaciously recorded only with piano accompaniment. Always a poignant spokesman for the lonely, Frank bought himself the No. 2 best-selling album of 1958. *Only the Lonely* was nosed out for the No. 1 spot by *Come Fly with Me*, another Sinatra LP.

The US première of *Kings Go Forth*, during the July 4 week-end, brought negative notices. The reviewers were more favourably disposed to Frank than the film. While the NY *Times* dismissed it as banal, clichéd, and a 'travesty of the atmosphere of war', Wanda Hale in *The News* announced that Sinatra 'may not be the best actor in the world, but there is none more interesting to watch'. Apart from weaknesses in the script, the involved way in which the film was shot may have contributed to its shortcomings. Two of the principals were so tied up—Curtis with another picture and Natalie Wood with a honeymoon—that only Frank made location shooting in France. Thus, all sea-side scenes shot in Nice and Villefranche, Antibes, were aimed inland, and the reverse angles involving Wood and Curtis were filmed later in Monterey, California.

In view of the interracial love story, Frank wrote an 'as-told-to' article for *Ebony*. In it, he described his debt to various Negro artists. Naming Ella Fitzgerald as 'the greatest of all contemporary jazz singers'—an opinion he later altered—and commenting on how deeply he was moved by Ethel Waters' 'feeling for the blues and great warmth', he reserved his greatest tribute for Billie Holiday: 'With a few exceptions,' he wrote, 'every major pop singer in the US during her generation has been touched in some way by her genius.' As for himself, 'it is Billie Holiday whom I first heard in 52nd Street clubs in the early '30s, who was and still remains the greatest single musical influence on me'. Sinatra could have added that the qualities of intensity and immediacy, self and sex, which became earmarks of pop singing after his emergence, were a blues heritage transmitted via Billie.

The on-location shooting of *Some Came Running* in August brought a new wave of adverse publicity. The first of three films in a new MGM deal, the James Jones story was shot in part at Madison, Indiana, a small Ohio River town. By the time the company had left, the villagers had drawn up an indictment that was aired in the nation's press. Afterwards the NY *Daily News* ran two full-page articles titled *They Raised Hollywood in My Home Town*, in which a reporter who had grown up in Madison, sought to get at the truth of the allegations.

Residents of the town accused Frank of everything from saying, on his first day in town, 'This joint is worse than skid row in Los Angeles,' to drinking on the set. They claimed that Frank had refused to be friendly with townspeople, and that on a Saturday night, instead of favouring a local dance with his presence, he had gone with Dean Martin to a roadhouse crap game in Newport, Kentucky. Shirley MacLaine, who did attend the party, was rapped because she sat playing solitaire and did not dance.

The most serious rap of all, involved a sixty-six-year-old hotel clerk, a former song-and-dance man, who claimed that Martin's manager had yelled at him and that he had been shoved around because of a misunderstanding over an order of hamburgers. Confronted with this accusation, Frank denied that he had threatened or touched the clerk. As to the other items, 'one four-letter word would cover each rap', he said. (The same four-letter word shocked the diners at a Screen Producers Guild social when Eva Marie Saint used it to deflate an overblown introduction of her by Jack Benny.)

Rumours of dissension within the company were denied by the cast. Much was made by columnists of producer Sol Siegel's visit to Madison, ostensibly to make peace between director Vicente Minelli and Sinatra. 'The minute he gets on location,' Minelli complained, 'Sinatra wants to get through and out. But we had two-and-a-half weeks of work there. Frank demanded we cut some of the location shooting. Since we couldn't agree, Sol flew out, we got together, made re-arrangements, and Frank was happy. There's no use kidding yourself. If he's not happy, you don't get the most ... If you can get the company into Frank's fast tempo and enthusiasm and pace, there are fewer shooting days and you spend less money.'

Frank's impatience added tension to a general situation, which Minelli felt was not good. 'We were virtual prisoners in Madison,' he said. 'People came from all over the state. Autograph seekers. Curiosity seekers. We couldn't go to a restaurant. It was a terrible way to live. And Frank was all cooped up in that little bungalow, along with Dean and a couple of characters from Chicago. You know, he attracts characters.'

To which actress Martha Hyer added a postscript: 'Outside Frank's door, there was constantly a crowd of eight hundred people, mostly women. Some had songs they wanted him to listen to. Others had won a beauty contest and were waiting to be discovered...' And Miss Hyer laughed over Frank's use of the word 'broads' to which townspeople had objected. 'Frank did not call me an old broad,' she told Earl Wilson, 'just a broad. He only calls his best friends old broads.'

Though Minelli was critical of Frank's compulsion to move, he praised Sinatra's suggestions for script changes. In the original story, Frank was supposed to be shot at the end. But the ending was altered when he urged that Shirley MacLaine be killed instead, thereby giving her part more importance. Minelli went on to explain that in the final, big scene, Shirley had to fall on Frank when she was hit by a rifle bullet. 'Well, Frank was lying on the pavement,' Minelli laughed, 'and Shirley jumped at him, an eight foot leap. Shirley is a big girl while Frank, well, you know ... When he finally got up, he said, "Whew, I thought that was it!" Then I told him that the take was not as good as it could be. He could have refused to do it over. But the scene was a big moment for Shirley. So he did it over, not once, but four more times.' For Shirley Mac-Laine, *Some Came Running* did prove the beginning of a busy film career.

When the company returned to Hollywood for studio shots, Frank's desire to follow a noon-to-eight work schedule instead of the customary nine-to-five pattern, became an issue. As Hollywood columnists were quick to point out, in the days when Louis B. Mayer (who had died the previous year) ruled MGM, anything so drastic as a change in working hours would have brought a swift cancellation of the picture. But by 1958, TV and independent production had caused a major shift in the balance of power. The day of the big studios was gone. And the name of a super-star like Frank Sinatra on a theatre marquee meant money in the bank. *Some Came Running* was shot on a noon-to-eight schedule, with a break at 4 p.m. for lunch. 'I got the idea for these hours in Europe,' Frank explained. 'Performers work better in the afternoon. The gals look better and they don't run out of gas by five.'

On September 19 Frank was in London, set to emcee the première of Danny Kaye's picture *Me and the Colonel* in a benefit performance for the British Empire Cancer Fund. The première was on the 27th. During his stay, Frank spent some hours with the American-born, English socialite, Lady Beatty —and he was off on a merry-go-round with the British press that paralleled his grotesque encounters with the Spanish and Mexican press during his courtship of Ava! Frank had apparently met the twice-divorced Lady during her California sojourn—her first marriage had been to a deputy Attorney General of the state—and had renewed the acquaintance while he was making *Some Came Running*, at which time she had been in Hollywood.

The day of his arrival in London, British newsmen noted that Frank had lunch and dinner with Lady Beatty, and then took her to a high society party. 'He's so smitten with the beautiful Adelle,' one paper reported, 'he's almost forgotten about spaghetti.' In the London *Daily Mirror*, a columnist wrote: 'Despite his abrupt manners, the petulant Frank Sinatra seems to be *persona grata* in London's high society.' The NY *Post* put it more succinctly: 'Mayfair Flips Its Crumpets Over Frank Sinatra.'

On the 21st, two days after Frank's arrival, the *Daily Mail* announced that Lady Beatty and he were planning to wed and that the only questions open were precisely when and where. To Earl Wilson, who was then in London, Frank stated that the announcement had 'embarrassed the Lady and my children ... I happen to love London more than any city in Europe,' he said, 'but they're going to drive me out of it'. Despite the press, however, Frank continued to escort the Lady through a never-ending round of lunches, dinner parties and night-club dates.

On the seventh evening of his sojourn, the British press noted, Lady Beatty abruptly left Sinatra at a night-club table and took off for Zürich, reportedly to consult her physician. Although papers reported that Frank was in seclusion in his $75-a-day hotel suite—allegedly phoning Zürich all through the day—he actually had flown to Rome just a few hours after the Lady's hasty departure. (His trip to Rome might, in fact, have provoked her flight.) David Hanna, who was then doing publicity on Ava Gardner's film *The Naked Maja*, has reported that Frank had phoned Ava, asking for her as 'Mrs. Sinatra'. She had apparently agreed to see him; but on his arrival from London, she would not accept his calls. Frank kept phoning and Ava reportedly kept instructing her switchboard to say that she was not in.

The following morning, however, she took Rags, the Corgi dog Frank had given her, and went to Frank's hotel. 'Rags was so happy to see him,' she later told Hanna. 'And do you know what I did? I'm so sorry now, I threw my wedding ring at him and came right back home. I told him to give the ring to his English Lady.'

On the evening of the benefit première of *Me and the*

Colonel the traffic around the Odeon Theatre in Leicester Square was tied up for many blocks. When Frank arrived, hundreds of youngsters were chanting, 'We want Frankie! We want Frankie!' Before the showing of the film, he and a long line of celebrities were received by the Queen and the Duke. Later, on stage, before he introduced Danny Kaye and other stars of the film, Frank announced: 'I'm here in London solely for this film, the charity of tonight's showing and to introduce the cast. I did not come here to get married.' It was a curious statement in view of Frank's unremitting effort to separate his professional from his private life. He added: 'Some of your newspapers would have me marry as often as King Farouk, and I'm not even as fat as he is.' It drew a laugh. But, according to the papers, the Queen was not amused.

Although the film première and Sinatra's appearance raised $70,000 for the British Cancer Fund, the English press rapped Frank at every opportunity, castigating him as 'the beatnik with money'. Reporters made much of an exchange between Frank and the Queen, who asked before the showing of the film: 'Are you in this thing?' When Frank replied that he had come over simply to introduce the film's principals, Elizabeth Regina commented: 'Oh, a sort of compère.' And Frank said, 'That's right,' and allegedly had muttered to an aide: 'Wotta hell is a compère?'

Cholly Knickerbocker of the Hearst press chortled because Frank was 'squelched'. But the *Hollywood Reporter* supported Frank. It felt that the British press had been rude and lacking in gratitude, considering that Sinatra had travelled 6,000 miles for a single appearance, and had helped a British fund raise $70,000.

Stopping briefly in New York on his return, Frank dined with several friends at the Harwyn Club. As he came out with model Nan Whitney, actor David Niven and comedian Joe E. Lewis, a *Journal-American* reporter and photographer approached him. He allegedly took umbrage at the former for addressing him as Frank and angrily warned the latter against taking pictures. As he entered his car, according to the *Journal-American*, he exclaimed: 'You newspapermen are a bunch of finks.' Later that morning, the photographer went to the police and charged that he had been struck by Sinatra's car and that the car had sped away, its siren wailing, without stopping to offer aid.

Since the car had no siren, the photographer's story seemed spurious. Moreover, although he claimed that he had been injured, the doorman of the Harwyn reported that he had eaten there immediately after the car had sped away. Nothing came of the photographer's charge, except a flurry of disagreeable headlines. It is not unlikely, however, that the incident, dismissed by many New York reporters as a 'hoax', was partly responsible for the press's treatment of Frank when he went to Miami shortly thereafter for location shooting on *A Hole in the Head*.

In November 1958, *Playboy* was licking its chops at the prospect of Frank, whom it described as a 'hip brand of love god', making a film with Brigitte Bardot. 'What happens when these two volatile substances mingle in the same crucible,' it asked, 'when The Voice meets the Broad of Broads? The concept is enough to make Olympus tremble, the skies darken, the oceans churn, and to knock the whole world flat on its collective clyde.'

All through 1958 the publicity mills churned with stories that Frank and Brigitte would make a film called *Paris By Night*. Bardot's producer, the late Raoul Levy, later reported that negotiations were conducted on a *global* basis over a period of fourteen long months. Levy chased Sinatra from country to country, meeting him in Las Vegas, Rome, London, Monaco (Frank slept through the day while Levy sunned himself on the beach), but could get no final answer or agreement. Finally, in New York, during a ten-day stopover between London and Miami, Frank stated his terms: $250,000 plus 40 per cent of the profits as co-producer plus 6 per cent of the profits as star. Levy balked but did not reject the deal. Suddenly, however, Frank made it clear that he would not make the film in Paris. Levy tried to argue, but Frank said: 'I've had that location bit. There are too many idiots around watching.' *Paris By Night* was never made, despite the protracted, global negotiations.

When Frank arrived in Miami about a week after the Harwyn incident, he was met by a group of newsmen, one of whom wore a baseball catcher's protective head mask. It was the beginning of newspaper heckling that did not let up for the stay of the *Hole in the Head* company. Frank was blamed for an extra's complaints about the pay and food. There were constant digs at his 'bad boyishness'. When he came down with a virus, papers criticised him for preferring parties to work. Differences between Frank and Edward G. Robinson regarding rehearsals were magnified.

Having read how badly Frank was allegedly behaving, Hollywood columnist Joe Hyams went down to see for himself. He found Frank 'in fine good humour and as professional as one could wish'. At that moment, readers of *Playboy* were persuing a lead article in which jazz buff Robert George Reisner described Frank as 'the most potent performer in show business today, the most spectacularly popular singer of songs, the most sought-after movie star, the most successful wooer of women' —a considerable array of 'most's' for presumably the hippiest of hip mags. But the impression that Frank left with Hyams was that of a man who, at the peak of his new-won success, was 'frightened' and 'expecting to be cut down from the heights at any moment'.

'I'm always bucking the American game,' Frank told Hyams. ' "He's on top now. Knock him off." People root for you going up so they can knock you off later.'

The *Hole in the Head* company left Miami more than a week before its schedule provided. Capra and Sinatra explained that a speed-up in completing location sequences had permitted an earlier return to Hollywood. Granting that the news fraternity might, perhaps, have been slightly at fault, a reporter averred that he and his colleagues 'had no reason to apologise to a man of Frank's colossal rudeness'.

Early in 1958, Frank had been saddened by the death of Manie Sachs, his Columbia mentor and loyal friend. Shortly after his return from Miami, a friend and promoter of the newly risen Sinatra died. Years later, Frank noted that he had not had an agent since the Thanksgiving week-end passing of Bert Allenberg of the William Morris agency. 'How I miss that man,' he said. 'Wow, what brains he had. Jesus! He was so much more than an agent to me. He was—a father confessor. He spoke four languages better than any man I ever knew in my life. He was a scholar. The charm of him. A true scholar with a great knowledge of law ... And he played 74 type golf. A sweet, wonderful gentleman, and he had to go. And all the *mothers* that are still left in the world ...'

XXI

TALENT, INC.

In the summer of 1959, 'the love voice of America', as Sid
Skolsky of the NY *Post* christened him, played the 500 Club in
Atlantic City. He had planned to loaf between the shooting of
Never So Few and *Can-Can*. But word came from Skinny
D'Amato, a friend who owned the 500, that the club was in
financial difficulties. On July 25 Frank opened an eight-day
run so spectacular that police had to keep excited fans under
control both at the club and his hotel. During his stay, more
than two hundred women required hospital treatment. Reservations were re-sold at a 1,000 per cent profit. One customer
offered Frank $50 for a butt he was about to discard. At the
height of the engagement, a forty-year-old woman ran in front
of his limousine and as the car screeched to a halt, she pleaded
hysterically: 'Run me over, Frankie! Run me over!'

Frank obviously had no need to be concerned about his
erotic appeal or his standing as a love god. But in 1959 he
began to manifest concern about another type of power. For
years he had been involved in many enterprises. Now, harking
back to an idea of Tommy Dorsey's, he became interested in
Talent as a business and the possibility of the performer
sustaining his career without dependence on existing talent
combines.

That year Hollywood tongues were wagging about Ingrid
Bergman's first visit in years as an invited guest of the Academy and about Elizabeth Taylor's Jewish wedding to the ex-
husband of her former Matron of Honour.

Some Came Running opened late in January to conflicting
reviews. 'An acceptable screen entertainment—but not much
more,' said the *Mirror*'s Justin Gilbert. But to the *World-
Telegram*'s Alton Cook, the film was 'a surefire cinch to become one of the year's biggest hits financially and in artistry'.
Between the two extremes, Bosley Crowther of the NY *Times*,
who regarded the screenplay as 'oddly garbled', said of Sinatra: 'He is downright fascinating—or what the youngsters
would call "cool" . . . He is beautifully casual with a bottle,

bull's-eye sharp with a gag and shockingly frank and impertinent in making passes at dames.' Other reviewer comments on Frank ran to superlatives like 'the finest performance of his acting career' (*Daily Variety*) and 'one of Sinatra's best performances, perhaps his greatest' (LA *Mirror-News*).

In February Frank began hearing rumours that Sammy Davis, Jr., had rapped him in a radio interview. When he asked Davis, Sammy dismissed his remarks as inconsequential ad libs. But Frank was so upset that he went to the trouble of getting a tape of the interview. Appearing on the Jack Eigen Show in Chicago, Davis had said: 'I love Frank but there are many things he does that there is no excuse for . . . I don't care if you are the most talented person in the world. It does not give you a right to step on people and treat them rotten. This is what he does occasionally.' Sammy was then scheduled to appear in *Never So Few*, a film that had been rewritten at Sinatra's request to provide a role for Davis. When Frank verified that Sammy had, indeed, rapped him, the part was again rewritten and the role given to Steve McQueen. It was rumoured that Sammy was also being dropped from Frank's future independent production *Ocean's Eleven*. When Sammy met Frank in Miami shortly thereafter, he was penitent and made overtures to heal the breach. Frank rejected them.

It was not until May that Davis was reinstated in the good graces of The Leader. The reconciliation occurred spontaneously at a party held to raise money for mentally retarded children. Frank and Dino emcee'd the May 14 show at the Moulin Rouge, and as they were ad libbing an introduction for Davis, who was one of the performers, the three made up, contributing an unexpected sentimental note to the proceedings.

1959 was one of Frank's thinnest recording years, yielding only fifteen sides. He was then edging towards a break with Capitol. Although he already had a deal whereby the masters he cut were owned by Essex Productions, one of his own companies, and assigned to Capitol for processing and distribution, he was determined to launch his own record label. When Capitol resisted his efforts to get out of the contract that expired in November 1962, he cut no sides in 1959 after May 14.

Three sessions in March under the subtle baton of Gordon

Jenkins resulted in a pensive, blues-inflected album titled *No One Cares*. Included was *I'll Never Smile Again*, cut by him with Dorsey in May 1940, nineteen years earlier almost to the day. The new version revealed a deepening of voice and a waver in the low notes that was surprising. Jenkins' orchestrations had an almost symphonic quality, with brooding chords and melancholy counter-melodies drawing long, elegiac lines around Frank's vocals. The collection reached sombre depths in the Alec Wilder–Arnold Sundergard composition *Where Do You Go*, which is hardly a pop song but not beyond Sinatra's expressive reach.

'I don't go for the isolation booth bit,' Jenkins said later, 'where I keep aural contact with him through earphones and have to watch his hands for note extensions, changes in tempi, etc. Let the engineers take care of separation and comparative levels electronically. I like to be close enough to Frank to watch his eyes. They're damn expressive.'

The other two May sessions were with Nelson Riddle and were directed at the singles market. Sinatra's aim was bull's eye. Out of the date on May 8 came *High Hopes*, a Cahn–Van Heusen hit written as the theme for Sinatra's film *A Hole in the Head*. The song inescapably recalls the Burke–Van Heusen hit *Swingin' on a Star*, and like the theme of Crosby's film *Going My Way*, the Oscar song of 1944, *High Hopes* won the Academy Award for 1959. *Talk to Me*, recorded a week later, proved less successful but remains one of the more seductive ballads of Frank's record career.

The *Come Dance with Me* album, cut with Billy May and released in February, was certified in 1961 as a Golden Album by the RIAA (Record Industry Association of America). On its release in February of 1959, John S. Wilson in the NY *Times* criticised its 'surefire but bland approach' and argued that Frank's 'cocky assurance' was becoming a bit monotonous. After he launched his own record company, Sinatra conceded that, being then unhappy with Capitol, his work 'lacked some of the spark it might have had'.

Among the new, hot male singers that year were Italian song writer Domenico Modugno and Johnny Mathis, who had a string of hits beginning with *Wonderful, Wonderful* and *It's Not For Me to Say*. Modugno's *Volare* was the runaway song and disc of the year. But Frank pursued it on best-seller charts with *Witchcraft*. And he outran Mathis for the No. 1 spot as

Male Singer in *Down Beat*'s Readers Poll by a margin of 11 to 1. Sinatra won so many other polls, both movie and music, that *Down Beat* found his failure to win a Grammy newsworthy. The Grammy, a miniature replica of an old-fashioned phonograph, was a new prize voted by members of the National Association of Recording Arts and Sciences. Perry Como's *Catch a Falling Star* beat out *Witchcraft* in the balloting for Best Male Vocal Performance while the Grammy for Album of the Year went to Mancini's *Music for Peter Gunn*, not to *Come Fly with Me* or *Only the Lonely*. The latter album did win an award, but it was for its cover, and Frank accepted the Grammy for artist Mario Volpe. 'Sinatra did not conceal his disappointment,' *Down Beat* observed; the awards were a 'bitter defeat for the hottest property in show business'.

That the continuing triumphs of 'the hottest property' did not bring him tranquillity was suggested by a letter that *Down Beat* printed in its succeeding issue. The page-long missive was from Lee Castle, a trumpet player leading the Jimmy Dorsey band, who had been Sinatra's room-mate when Frank had first joined the Tommy Dorsey band. Stating that he was 'tired of all the criticism of Sinatra', Castle defended Frank as 'the most generous guy with time and money'. After his letter appeared, an amazed Castle phoned *Down Beat* to advise that he had been on the air almost every night defending himself for his defence of Sinatra. Frank's career was then booming, but the key-words in three large-circulation magazine articles were 'trouble', 'war' and 'hate'. 'Frank Sinatra's War with the World' was the title of one and 'Why They Hate Me', of another.

When Frank flew to Australia in April for concert appearances, Ava was in Melbourne filming *On the Beach*. Ava had set off on the wrong foot with the Australian press with an unguarded statement on her arrival: 'I'm here to make a film about the end of the world and this sure is the place for it.' According to David Hanna, the film publicist, Ava had been phoning Frank for weeks. The calls could have been motivated by a feeling of remorse over her treatment of him in Rome. Friends felt that she was suffering from some deep-seated emotional crisis and reporters came away from interviews shocked by her debilitated appearance. All through 1959 and 1960, film stars who met or worked with her, felt that she

255

was still very much in love with Frank and was brooding over their broken marriage. Whatever the motivation of her calls, she had come to believe in Frank as a dependable friend. More than a year earlier, when she had been hurt during highjinks in a bull ring, Frank had been one of the first to phone. And when she had developed a laetoma on her cheek, a delicate swelling caused by the breakage of small blood vessels, he had independently checked medical authorities and flown to New York to urge her to undergo an operation. She had agreed, especially since months of massage and heat treatments had not eliminated it. But at the last minute, after Frank had left, she had 'chickened out'.

When Frank arrived, the Australian press and representatives of American papers were out in full force. Anticipating a possible meeting of the divorced couple, they went at Frank with the type of personal questions that invariably infuriated him. And *Truth*, an Australian magazine, reported later that Frank entered the Melbourne Stadium flanked by a retinue of 'tough-looking characters'. Calling newsmen who pressed around him 'slobs', he allegedly said: 'If I see you again you'll never forget it. If you're around later, they'll find you in the gutter.'

Although Ava had not gone to the airport to meet Frank, as her publicist had suggested, she did go to the recital, where she was quickly spotted. When he finished singing, Frank dashed into a rented limousine and sped back to his hotel. There, he and Ava had their reunion. According to Hanna, it lasted thirty minutes. According to *Truth*, it was a 'secret three-hour meeting' in which 'the cranky crooner and his glamorous ex-wife drank wine together'. The Australian magazine advised that the reunion was such a happy one, 'it could mean the flame of love between the pair is rekindling'. However, its final comment on Sinatra was: 'As an ambassador of the US, he failed to spread any good will. At any rate, Melbourne won't miss him.'

The filming of *Can-Can* on a sound stage of Twentieth Century-Fox went off smoothly, except for the period of the World Series when Frank insisted on attending the games played in Hollywood. Typical of his relaxed state of mind was an incident that occurred during the filming of a scene in which Shirley MacLaine comes to kill him. As she opened the door of a closet in which he was hiding, Frank was supposed to exclaim, 'All right, shoot me!' Instead, when she tore the door open, she found him standing with his back to her. Over his shoulder, he muttered: 'Sorry, lady, you're in the men's room.'

When *Can-Can* was released the following spring, John McCarten wrote in *The New Yorker*: 'Duck it! The book becomes stale and foolish, and the Porter tunes are dispensed without any particular verve.' McCarten felt that neither Shirley MacLaine as the Parisian cabaret-owner nor Frank as her carefree barrister 'seemed too excited about the proceedings'. As for the dances, including the can-can which shocked Nikita Khrushchev during a visit to the studio: 'Hermes Pan's efforts would have been utterly wasted if not for a girl named Juliet Prowse.'

'The first time I ever heard about The Clan,' said Milton Berle, who was at times called its Jester, 'was when I read about it in *Life*.' Sinatra also attributed the concoction of the group to the magazine. Although other members of the staff have been given credit for coining it, the phrase first appeared in an article by Paul O'Neil in a special issue on *USA Entertainment* dated December 22, 1958. Hollywood was covered in a picture spread on the 'casual but ebullient' Dean Martin and also in an article listed as *The Hollywood 'Clan', Sinatra's Nonconformist Players*, which also bore the heading *The Clan Is the Most. Led by Sinatra and Martin, It Hoots at Hollywood's Names and old Traditions*.

Paul O'Neil was friendly if not approving in his approach. 'Nonconformity is now the key to social importance,' he wrote, 'and that Angry Middle-Aged Man, Frank Sinatra, is its prophet and reigning social monarch.' In O'Neil's view, the ties that bound the Clan's membership together were that they were all saloon entertainers, owned $250,000 homes, bought their clothes at Sy Devore's on Hollywood and Vine, exchanged expensive gifts, never went to fancy-dress parties, never (?) ate out in public, and owned or planned to own a Dual-Ghia, a luxurious Italian car of which only a hundred were manufactured each year.

O'Neil traced the relationship of The Clan to Bogie's Holmby Hills Rat Pack, noting that Bogart was the first film star to spit in the eye of Hollywood and, because of his remarkable talent, to get away with it. Not surprisingly, Lauren

Bacall was quoted as considering her late husband's group superior to Sinatra's. Known inside The Clan as The Pope, The General or The Dago, Frank personified its basic tenet: public and aggressive indifference to what customers expected of stars and what Hollywood expected of its citizens. According to O'Neil, Clan members died for publicity but distrusted reporters; they lived for applause but bitterly resented the 'rubes', 'jerks' and 'creeps', who stared at them, pawed them and constantly demanded autographed photographs.

Shortly after the appearance of the *Life* article, Sid Skolsky asked Frank about the Clan. 'There's no Clan,' Frank stated. 'How could there be with Sammy Davis, Jr., a member?' But Dean Martin blamed Davis as the source of *Life*'s info while Sammy Cahn, another 'member', thought that Davis might have coined the title 'Clan' itself. Despite Frank's denial, the existence of The Clan had actually been acknowledged in the article Joe Hyams had written during the shooting of *A Hole in the Head*. 'In Hollywood Sinatra lives in a mountain hideout,' Hyams stated in *The Trouble with Being Frank Sinatra*. 'His world is called The Clan. It's peopled by other headliners like himself . . .'

In October 1959, The Clan began to assume a somewhat different meaning, at least for some members of the press. In a twelve-part series on Sinatra in the NY *Post*, Al Aronowitz noted the nonconformist character of the group, but saw The Clan as an economic, and not merely a social entity. Aronowitz contrasted Sinatra's flock with Bogie's Rat Pack in terms of its flamboyance, also its public, rather than private, expressions of rebelliousness. 'To be one of The Clan you have to be kookie,' Aronowitz wrote, 'and you have to be hip in their way of hip, but you have to have talent.' And this was where the economics entered; for The Clan not only played together, it worked together; and the cement that held it together was Sinatra's increasing hold on employment in films as well as at night clubs.

Pursuing this line of thought, Aronowitz made a new, startling charge against the man who had so long fought the battles of the underdog. 'Everybody in Hollywood is afraid of Frank,' he announced. The true rebels in the movie capital were now those who rebelled against Frank, for Sinatra had become— Aronowitz asserted—the new King and Dictator of Hollywood.

It was a characterisation that appeared subsequently in a

number of major publications. One reason was Frank's plan to form a talent agency. The *Hollywood Reporter* of November 30 noted that a group of performers, headed by Sinatra and Dean Martin, was set to open and operate its own artist management corporation. Three men were already active in the administration of the enterprise: Hank Sanicola; Milt Ebbins, Peter Lawford's personal manager; and Nick Sevano, later Jack Jones' manager, who was leaving a small agency to join the new outfit.

To evaluate the daring of Sinatra's move, one must recognise that the multi-billion dollar entertainment industry is controlled by those who represent Talent—performing, writing, acting and directing talent. Although there were scores of small and medium-sized agencies, the industry was then dominated by three giants: GAC (General Artists Corporation), William Morris (Sinatra's agents), and MCA (Music Corporation of America), the giant of giants. The last-mentioned was also rapidly becoming one of the largest producers of TV shows, giving it the strange, dual role of negotiating with itself for talent that it managed—a situation that eventually led to a Justice Department anti-trust suit and forced the dissolution of the agency set-up.[*] (That Sinatra may have moved when he did, in anticipation of this development, is not beyond the reaches of his business sagacity.)

Ever since 1952 when a record company (Columbia), a movie company (MGM) and an agency (MCA), for each of which he had made millions, had seen fit to turn him loose, Frank had been preoccupied with the problem of how to prevent similar setbacks to his career. Step by step, he had moved to own the movies in which he starred, the TV shows on which he performed and the masters he cut for Capitol. The logic of the process called for him to control the talent, his own as well as others, out of which these products all came. If he could yank out of the country's mammoth agencies talents like himself, he could become a formidable power in the entertainment world.

Regardless of the fears he stirred in others, Sinatra's basic motivation may well have been fear itself. In perhaps the first admission that his voice no longer was what it had been, he told a *Redbook* writer in August 1959: 'I ran up against an F sharp the other day and I realised how much I've changed. I'd rather not sing that high note any more. I could but I don't think I should. Back in the old days when I was seventeen or eighteen, I'd wail any note in the book. I was lousy but I was fearless.'

XXII

THE PRESIDENCY AND THE CLAN

In 1960 Frank's public image underwent a significant change. At the Copa, comic Jackie Kannon, speaking of a tune he was about to do, quipped: 'I heard it in a little place Frank Sinatra owns called Hollywood.'

'In Hollywood, the whim of the tough and talented kid from Hoboken is almost law,' wrote John C. Bowes in a February *American Weekly* article, *The Reign of King Frankie*. 'Not since the late thirties when Louis B. Mayer ruled from his Metro throne, has anyone had such power.' Five months later, *Good Housekeeping*'s cover called attention to: *The Disturbing Truth about Sinatra, his changed personality and power*. The article by Richard Gehman warned ominously that Sinatra was not only immensely powerful, 'a law unto himself', but that he had become 'the most feared man in Hollywood'. Urging that Sinatra's expanding power should be of concern to all, Gehman concluded: 'It would be disturbing indeed if this enormous power were in the hands of a completely stable and predictable human being. When it is in the hands of a man torn by emotions that he apparently either cannot or does not care to control, it is something to view with alarm.' (Gehman later claimed that these sentences were added by his editors.)

Yet at the same time that Gehman was researching his alarmist article, Frank was in the throes of a public controversy that far from demonstrated that he was a law unto himself. In fact, Frank's handling of the Albert Maltz affair brought into question, doubtless for the first time in his career, his celebrated independence of mind and his refusal to yield to public and newspaper pressure.

On March 21, the NY *Times* broke the story that Frank had hired one of the so-called Hollywood Ten to write the screenplay of *The Execution of Private Slovik*, a study by William Bradford Huie of the only American soldier executed by the US Army since the Civil War. The assignment was to be novelist Albert Maltz's first screen credit since he had been convicted of contempt of Congress in June 1950. At that time, having declined to answer queries of the House Un-American Activities Committee regarding membership in the Communist Party, Maltz had been fined $1,000 and sentenced to a year in prison. Released in April 1951, he had been unable to secure movie assignments although it was rumoured that he, like Dalton Trumbo and others of the Hollywood Ten, had sold screenplays and their services under noms de plume.

Reached by long-distance phone in Miami, where he was appearing at the Fontainebleau, Frank said that he had not made the assignment public earlier because of incomplete legal negotiations. *Times* Hollywood correspondent Murray Schumach hazarded the opinion that Sinatra wanted to keep the hiring of Maltz secret until after the Democratic National Convention for fear of hurting Senator Kennedy's nomination chances.

News of the Maltz appointment had immediate repercussions. Expressing dismay at Sinatra's act, the Hearst papers suggested that 'the impact of Mr. Sinatra's move may also cause dismay in the campaign camp of Sen. John F. Kennedy'. By contrast, the NY *Post* preferred 'An Oscar!' to Frank: 'He has joined the select company of Hollywood valiants who declared their independence from the Un-American Activities Committee and the American Legion ... In defying the secret blacklist that has terrorised the movie industry for more than a decade, Sinatra—like Stanley Kramer and Otto Preminger before him—has rendered a service to the cause of artistic freedom...'

On the Hollywood scene, actors John Wayne and Ward Bond quickly became a vocal opposition. Referring to Sen. Kennedy as 'a Sinatra crony', Wayne announced that he was curious to know the candidate's feelings regarding the hiring of Maltz. In response, Frank took full-page ads in the Hollywood trade-papers: 'This type of partisan politics is hitting below the belt,' he asserted. As for hiring Maltz 'I spoke to many screenwriters but it was not until I talked to Albert Maltz that I found a writer who saw the screenplay in exactly the terms I wanted. This is, the Army was right. Under our

Bill of Rights, I was taught that no one may prescribe what shall be orthodox in politics, religion or other matters of opinion.' Frank added that as producer and director of the film, 'I and I alone will be responsible for it. I am concerned that the screenplay reflects the true pro-American values of the story.' In closing, he said: 'I am prepared to stand on my principles and to await the verdict of the American people when they see *The Execution of Private Slovik*. I repeat: In my role as a picture-maker, I have—in my opinion—hired the best man to do the job.'

If Frank hoped that his forthright statement would end the attacks, he had misjudged the opposition. On the 29th, the LA *Examiner* began its editorial column with a 'Note to Sinatra'. It argued that in hiring Maltz 'you are not giving employment to a poor little sheep who lost his way...' but are 'making available a story wide open for the Communist line ... Therefore, we suggest you consider thoughtfully the strong request of National Commander Raymond O'Leary of the Catholic War Veterans. Dump Maltz and get yourself a true American.' In the LA *Times* Hedda Hopper opined that *real Americans* could not accept Sinatra's reasons for hiring Maltz. 'If Sinatra loves his country he won't do this,' Miss Hopper wrote. 'He'll write off the cost of the story and forget it. But will he? He's stubborn but not viciously pig-headed. He has a fine family of which he's proud. Will he do this to them?'

When Miss Hopper's comment appeared on April 8, the controversy had been raging for eighteen days. That evening, a statement was released from Frank's home in Palm Springs. 'Due to the reactions,' it read, 'of my family, my friends and the American public, I have instructed my attorneys to make a settlement with Albert Maltz and to inform him he will not write the screenplay for *The Execution of Private Slovik*. I had thought the major consideration was whether or not the resulting script would be in the best interests of the United States. Since my conversation with Mr. Maltz had indicated that he had an affirmative, pro-American approach to the story and since I felt fully capable as producer of enforcing such standards, I have defended my hiring of Mr. Maltz. But the American public has indicated that it feels the morality of hiring Mr. Maltz is the more crucial matter, and I will accept the majority opinion.'

Frank's reversal rated an eight-column streamer, which the

LA *Examiner* ran in red above its own masthead SINATRA OUSTS MALTZ AS WRITER. In a front-page story, Louella Parsons observed: 'Knowing Frank as I do, I am sure that the influence of his ex-wife Nancy and daughter Nancy, Jr., played a big part in his decision. There may have been an influence brought to bear on him from some of his political friends.' Editorially, under an approving head, *Sinatra Sees the Light*, the *Examiner* commended Frank for displaying 'a greater degree of maturity' in firing Maltz than in hiring him. The NY *Post* did not agree. Granting that Sinatra was the first producer to become the subject of continuing assaults by veterans' groups and the Hearst press, the *Post* regretted that only Frank had capitulated 'to the know-nothings of cinema and journalism'. Stanley Kramer had stood firmly on his right to retain scripter Nedrich Young on *Inherit the Wind* and Otto Preminger had kept Dalton Trumbo on *Exodus* despite rebukes by the National Commander of the American Legion. 'Chalk up another victory for lynch-law mentality,' a commentator wrote in *Publishers' Weekly*, to which Sinatra subscribes for advance information on new books.

Frank never made any comment on the Maltz dismissal beyond his public statement firing the writer. But that he was not happy about the situation is suggested by an occurrence at a charity dinner the following month. Frank came face to face with John Wayne, who said a friendly 'Hello.' 'Mr. Sinatra immediately began berating him,' witnesses alleged, 'for publicly opposing the hiring of Maltz.' Belligerent stares did not lead to fisticuffs, but the following day's papers reported: 'Sinatra, John Wayne Tiff Over Maltz at Star Party.'

A friend of Sinatra's, who was not pleased by his conduct, said: 'Maybe he's growing up, like they say. Maybe that's another word for "chicken".' An oft-repeated, though never confirmed, story has it that the elder Kennedy got in touch with Frank and gave him the alternative of dumping Maltz or getting off the JFK bandwagon. Shortly after Frank reversed himself, Bill Slocum revealed in his NY *Mirror* column that Peter Lawford had lost Pontiac as a sponsor for a series called *The Bachelor* in which Sinatra and Clan members were to appear; only when Frank 'had cleansed himself' had sponsors begun falling into line. Frank told writer-friends that he could never have produced the film with Maltz as screenwriter; the banks would not provide the necessary financing.

Walking out of the Share party after his tiff with John Wayne, Frank walked into new headlines. As he crossed the parking lot outside the Moulin Rouge, a car attendant slammed on the brakes to keep from hitting him. Newspapers immediately reported that 'a parking lot attendant was beaten up by a man identified as Mr. Sinatra's bodyguard'. After almost a week of headlines, it was established that the bodyguard was not Sinatra's but Sammy Davis'. By then, so much circulation had been given to the erroneous story that Joe E. Lewis could get a laugh when he announced on a café floor: 'Ladies and Gentlemen! I just got some wonderful news for Frank. Next May 2, there's going to be a nationwide tribute to him. On that day, all the parking lots in the country will be closed.'

During the year, Frank's recording activity suffered, as he manoeuvred to free himself from his Capitol contract. Not a single Sinatra disc was released from September 1959 until May 1960, a long hiatus for any record artist. On April 13, just after he concluded the Maltz business, Frank cut the title tune for the album *Nice 'N' Easy*—Top Ten by September—as well as *It's Over, It's Over, It's Over* and *River Stay 'Way from My Door*.

There was much concern in the control booth, as there was discussion later in the press, about Frank's substitution of the definite article for the possessive pronoun in the *River* standard. 'Wanna tell him, Eddie?' The question was addressed to Eddie Shaw, a short man with close-cropped hair and squinty, corner-creased eyes. 'And give up eating?' Eddie asked; he was one of very few publishers who managed to get Sinatra recordings on his songs. 'How about you, Hank?' Bald, with a few strands of hair lying across a flat, shiny pate, Sanicola turned a pouchy-eyed stare at Eddie Shaw. 'Hank's a worrier,' Shaw said to several entourage faces, 'but he don't show it. He's gotta a lotta grey hair in his stomach.' It was A and R man Dave Cavanaugh, who finally raised the question with Sinatra. 'Frank, are you singing "*the* door" purposely?' he asked over the speaker system. The blue, watchful eyes arrowed across the brightly lit studio towards the thick glass of the darkened control booth. '*The* door is *my* door,' Sinatra said through his mike. '*My* door is *the* door.' The attractive smile full of glistening teeth flashed on. Then, Frank added 'Let's make it a band record. Keep the band as fat as you can with me singing against it.' In the final take, all the possessive pronouns were gone.

In a July column, song-writer, pop-poet, *Mirror* columnist Nick Kenny wrote: 'When The Voice deliberately misinterprets the line from the American classic *River, Stay Away from My Door* and sings it *River, Stay Away from THE Door* instead, it makes us a little sick.' Although the switch stirred considerable comment inside the business, the record enjoyed only limited popularity.

During the year, a twenty-four year old singer who had a hit two years earlier with *Splish Splash,* a novelty he wrote, worked at attracting press attention by hitching on to the Sinatra publicity train. Whenever he talked to interviewers, Bobby Darin both admired and challenged Sinatra's achievement. 'If I want to think about lost love,' he said, 'I listen to Sinatra.' Frank is a singer 'whose throat's been trod on,' he told another interviewer. Frank's comment on a bit of Darin insouciance about surpassing The Voice's accomplishments was: 'I sing in saloons. Bobby Drain does my prom dates.' Jack O'Brian of the NY *Journal-American* observed acidly: 'Darin seems to imitate all the bad details of the Sinatra "image", as the grey-flannels say, without Sinatra's superb musical instincts.'

In March, before the Maltz affair, another idol of the rock generation returned to civilian life from a two-year stint in the army. Except for the Congressional investigation of Payola, which shook up the Top 40 programming format in radio, nothing was so newsworthy to teenagers as the welcome to Elvis Presley. Frank latched on to the event for his fourth and last ABC-TV Special for Timex, a costly group of shows for which he had been signed the previous year, despite his problems with the medium. His third show (in February) had been a Valentine's Day salute to the ladies. It had drawn so-so notices, despite the presence of Juliet Prowse, with whom he was then romantically linked, and a novel appearance by Eleanor Roosevelt, who had recited the lyrics of *High Hopes* to a special setting by Nelson Riddle.

Advance excitement for the 'Welcome Elvis' show started with its taping in March during Sinatra's stand at the Fontainebleau. The atmosphere was highly charged, even before

Presley's entry, because the last three nights of Frank's booking were turned into 'Summit Meetings', as Dean Martin, Sammy Davis, Jr., Joey Bishop and Peter Lawford joined Sinatra for hours of improvised comedy.

'How could anybody pay all you geniuses to work three nights?' Earl Wilson, who came to Miami for the Presley taping, asked Sammy Davis. 'Nobody could and nobody did,' Sammy replied. 'We did it for love of Frank because he asked us to. If you dig Frank, you do things like that.' Elvis' appearance had little to do with love. Sinatra, it was reported, paid Presley $100,000 for a ten-minute stint. 'You should make in a year,' producer Sammy Cahn told a reporter, 'what Frank is losing on this show. But he wants to prove he can go big on TV.'

The 'taped' encounter of 'two generations of idolatry', as a reporter described the excited audience of pedal-pushers and mink-coaters, gave the press a field day. Confusion in the handling of arrangements, the distribution of an excessive number of tickets, an overflow crowd—all contributed tension to excitement. There was no riot and no swooning. But the press noted close parallels between the hysteria of Elvis' followers and the unbuttoned conduct of Sinatra's bobbysoxers eighteen years earlier.

'Ex-bobbysoxers who once risked truancy,' Alan Levy later wrote in *Operation Elvis*, 'to venture within swooning distance of The Voice, will watch their idol nostalgically and view with parental alarm their daughters' rapture over the Pelvis. The men of their houses will gaze at both millionaires and ponder the classic riddle, "What's he got that I haven't".' Levy suggested one answer: beyond such tangibles as talent, they represented the *unlimited dream* come true: from a Memphis housing project, or a Hoboken tenement, to a millionaire's mansion. A major contrast between the generations was that Elvis' fans were richer—average teenage spending had quadrupled—and Presley could come 'into a child's life about the time he or she discovers peanut brittle and pony tails'.

The 'Welcome Elvis' telecast in May garnered tremendous newspaper and magazine coverage, and the ratings were headlined in the *Hollywood Reporter*: SINATRA–ELVIS SPEC RATES 5 YEAR HIGH. Trendex gave the show a whopping 41.5 rating against CBS's 4.2 and NBC's 21.1. Critical reaction did not reflect public interest. The *Reporter* thought the show was 'hastily thrown together' and criticised 'Frank's humble condescension to Elvis'. *Variety* felt that the show 'did not generate a quarter of a million dollars worth of excitement' and that Elvis did not deliver 'the climatic wallop' expected of him. Nor—shades of yesteryear—was it happy about 'the screaming kids in the background'.

Presley continued to figure in Sinatra publicity while Frank was in the Far East, a trip he took with Jimmy Van Heusen and his butler shortly after the parking lot incident. Juliet Prowse, whom he had described as 'the sexiest dancer I ever met', was then occupied in the making of *GI Blues* a film starring Presley. The newspapers and fan magazines, egged on by the Paramount press department, worked at making a triangle of Prowse–Presley–Sinatra. On his return, Frank brought a jade bracelet and a double-string of matched pearls for Juliet, and high praise of Japanese women. 'The chicks don't have nicotine stains on their fingers,' he told reporters. 'They don't wear trousers. And you don't smell of Chanel No. 5 after shaking hands with them.' Dorothy Kilgallen observed that Presley had merely been 'scrap-book fodder' for Prowse and that no one doubted all along that she was 'Sinatra property'.

That Prowse was more than a passing dance partner to Frank became evident in 1961. But in 1960, he seemed more concerned with three other 'P's: politics, power and possessions. He bought co-op apartments both in New York and in Hawaii, the latter for a down payment of $68,000. He tried unsuccessfully to buy Ernie's, one of San Francisco's oldest and most fashionable restaurants. And with Dean Martin, Hank Sanicola and Paul D'Amato, owner of the 500 Club in Atlantic City, he formed a syndicate to buy the Cal-Neva Lodge, the plush gambling casino on Lake Tahoe. His 6 per cent share of the Sands had been so profitable—it was then worth close to $100,000 a point—that he sought 25 per cent of the Cal-Neva stock. Sanicola put up cash for 16 per cent, D'Amato for 13 per cent and Dino for 3 per cent, giving the group a 57 per cent ownership when the Nevada Gaming Control Board eventually okayed their application. At his Copa opening in September, Joe E. Lewis quipped that if Kennedy was elected President, Sinatra would buy a couple of points in the White House.

Frank's major film effort during 1960 was *Ocean's Eleven*, his own Dorchester Production for Warner Bros. A tale of a group of veterans who execute a ten-million dollar raid on five plush gambling casinos, the film was largely shot in Las Vegas during the early months of the year. The hotels co-operated fully, redecorating their façades with reindeer and animated Santa Clauses to accord with the film's time sequence, Christmas to New Year's Eve. And the casinos of five major hotels opened their premises for on location shooting.

In turn, Frank and his cast, which included the 'Summit Meeting' five, treated Las Vegas, and particularly, patrons of the Sands, to a rare round of highjinks. The routine of Sinatra and his 'clansmen' was to work before the cameras during the day and, after relaxing in the Sands steamroom, to put on an evening of ad lib shenanigans. In a lengthy article, *Playboy* presented an almost joke-by-joke description of what went on during the weeks that *Ocean's Eleven* was shooting. It was not simply the simultaneous presence of five big-name personalities that attracted *Playboy*, but the fact that this group was 'in the public eye, *the innest in-group* in the world' and that it had 'a wild iconoclasm that millions envy secretly or even consciously...' The article drew disapproving letters from many readers, who condemned both its 'reverential and admiring tone' and The Clan's potpourri 'of ancient burlesque lines, race-and-religion cracks and high school outhouse humour'. And yet Milton Berle said of the evening when he was present: 'I've seen a lot of wild nights but this was the greatest.'

Regardless of *Playboy* reader reaction to the 'Summit Meetings', on June 15 Warner Bros. announced that *Ocean's Eleven* had garnered more than $1,000,000 in advance bookings. The world première, on August 3 at the Fremont Theatre in Las Vegas, featured a New Year's Eve celebration in mid-summer, which paid off in a jackpot box-office. The opening on Broadway at the Capitol Theatre toppled a record set seven years earlier by *From Here to Eternity*. After the film's initial eighty-five bookings, the *Hollywood Reporter* estimated that its grosses would make it 'one of the five biggest box-office attractions' in Warner Bros.' history, joining the select company of *Giant*, *Sayonara*, *Auntie Mame* and *Mister Roberts*.

As with the 'Welcome Elvis' show, the film's critical reception did not accord with audience interest. 'The picture is very plush,' Archer Winsten observed in the NY *Post*, 'so chromium, so smooth, so much a display of performers who act as if a mere appearance would induce hysteria in the adoring public, that you wonder who's fooling whom.' Alton Cook of the *World-Telegram and Sun* represented a minority point of view, which found the film 'bursting with both laughter and dramatic tension'; he traced the laughter to 'the lack of morals or any shade of respectability'. Precisely this lack of morality outraged Bosley Crowther of the *Times*, who raised an outcry against 'the surprisingly nonchalant and flippant attitude towards crime, an attitude so amoral it roadblocks a lot of valid gags'.

Despite critical brickbats, *Ocean's Eleven* moved Frank up to No. 6 in *Fame*'s annual survey of the screen's *Top Ten*. Above Frank were Rock Hudson, Cary Grant, James Stewart, Doris Day and Debbie Reynolds in that order while below him were Glenn Ford, John Wayne, Jerry Lewis and Susan Hayward.

Frank dedicated a large portion of his time in 1960 to the presidential race. Not since 1944 when he had campaigned vigorously for the election of Roosevelt had he, or Hollywood for that matter, been so deeply embroiled in politics. And he succeeded in involving all his friends in the campaign to elect John Fitzgerald Kennedy President.

At the Democratic Party's July nominating convention in LA, Frank and his buddies were very much in evidence. Armed with stop-watches, he, Lawford and Shirley MacLaine clocked the applause for each nominee. Once Kennedy was nominated, Frank participated both in fund-raising and vote-getting meetings. The climax of his politicking came late in October when he, Tony Curtis, Janet Leigh and Peter Lawford trekked east to New Jersey to attend a monster ball in honour of Governor Meyner and the Democratic national ticket. 'Monster' it was for it drew so many people that police had to bar the doors of the Sussex Armoury in Newark, leaving a crowd of 20,000 milling outside. It was clear that the drawing card was not Adlai Stevenson or the other Hollywood stars who came.

And yet there was a strange imbalance in Frank's relationship to the campaign, and specifically, to the future President. Kennedy had been photographed with Frank on the grounds of the Sands and had attended and been introduced at a Summit shindig. Dean Martin had kidded, after the applause had died down: 'What was the last name?' But shortly after the nominating convention in July, columnists reported that the Kennedy high command had sent an envoy to Las Vegas to pick up all photographs (and negatives) showing Sen. Kennedy at play with Sinatra and his pack.

Late in August, Frank went to the trouble of issuing a statement to the press, objecting to the labelling of his friends as The Clan. 'It's a figment of someone's imagination,' he stated. 'Naturally, people in Hollywood socialise with friends, as they do in any community. But we do not get together in childish fraternities, as some people would like to think.' About ten days earlier, the Sunday *News* had run a two-page spread on Frank's Clan and its relationship to the political campaign. Its opening sentence: 'One question which will be answered once and for all by the 1960 Presidential campaign is: Can a man whose brother-in-law is a member of the Clan be elected President of the United States?' The next sentence made it clear that the writer was not referring to the Ku Klux Klan [sic!] but to a 'gang of Hollywood fun and money seekers'. To Joe Hyams of the *Herald-Tribune*, The Clan was a 'political casualty'. He felt that Sinatra's attempt to dissociate himself and his buddies from the label was based on the warning, presumably communicated by JFK's advisers, that they could work effectively for Kennedy's election only if they were regarded as 'serious citizens'.

In mid-September Dorothy Kilgallen reported that JFK had been protesting column items linking him with Sinatra. Miss Kilgallen gave as a direct quote: 'He's no friend of mine, he's just a friend of Pat (his sister) and Peter Lawford.' 'So what?' Miss Kilgallen asked. 'So last week the Democratic candidate for the presidency was guest of honour at a private little dinner given by Frank. No reason why he shouldn't, of course— but why try to kid the press.'

As the campaign neared its climax, Sammy Davis, Jr., who had been wooing Swedish actress May Britt in a guarded, non-public style, went to Frank to tell him of his impending marriage plans. Frank is 'two people', Sammy wrote in *Yes I Can*. 'One, his public image—the swinger, the legend, the idol, the "ring-a-ding-ding" and "woweewow" guy who says, "Let's get the broads and get the boys and be somebody!" The other is the serious businessman, the father, the friend. The façade of fun, the atmosphere of laughs comes off like a coat . . .

'He was studying me, evaluating, balancing the factors involved, weighing one against the other, understanding as only a friend and another performer—exactly what I stood to gain or possibly lose by such a marriage.

'Finally, he spoke and the words were deliberate. "Yeah. It's a good thing. Do it, Sam . . . Get yourself some happiness." '

And Frank, with whom Sammy was filming *Soldiers Three*, upped his income, and agreed to be best man.

After the invitations went out, the inter-racial character of the marriage began to be used to smear Kennedy. 'Politicos are giggling,' one columnist wrote, 'that the SD, Jr.–May Britt nuptial is really secret Republican strategy.'

Shocked by this development, Davis phoned Sinatra. Pretending that their house would not be ready for occupancy in time, he indicated that he and May were postponing the wedding until November 13. Frank saw through the manoeuvre and tried to remonstrate. Davis told his disappointed bride-to-be 'For almost twenty years Frank has been everything a guy could be to me. There's nothing in the world he wants from me, nothing I can do for him except be his friend. Ninety-nine per cent of the others come and go, and you help them if it's convenient, but Frank is a *friend*! . . . It's got to be the ends of the earth and back for him if he needs it.' Disappointed, May Britt agreed and the following morning, they sent telegrams postponing the wedding until the Sunday after election. To the press, they sent an announcement advising that nuptials had been postponed 'due to a legal technicality in Miss Britt's Mexican divorce from her previous husband'.

Shortly after the election, the White House announced that the show for the Inaugural Gala would be produced by Peter Lawford and Frank Sinatra. Now the opposition press mounted a frontal attack on Frank. On December 5, in a piece on Hollywood, *Time* reported that on election night Frank had tried arrogantly but unsuccessfully to get Nixon on the phone to have him concede the narrow election. And it repeated the gag stories that had been going the rounds: all the Clan members were expecting high posts, Dean Martin as Secretary of Liquor; Sammy Davis, Jr., as Ambassador to Israel, though he was worried that he might be appointed Ambassador to Kenya; and Frank, as Ambassador to Italy or Secretary of

Trouble.

Two weeks later, in a story on the Democrats, *Time* opined that 'some of JFK's biggest headaches may well come from an ardently pro-Kennedy clique that is known variously as the Rat Pack or the Clan...' It thought that the group had been 'wisely' kept pretty much offstage during the campaign and regretted that there now seemed 'less need for discretion and more for money'. It quoted Lawford 'This will be the biggest take in show business history for a one-nighter'; and Frank: 'We expect to raise $1,700,000 for the one night. There's never been anything like it.'

Hearst writer Ruth Montgomery, in a column titled *'Rat Pack' in the White House?*, harked back to the Democratic Nominating Convention when, she claimed, Sinatra, Lawford and their Clan had moved 'uninvited and unwanted into the reserved press seats right under the nominating platform'. It troubled her that the only private soirée attended by JFK during the convention was a birthday party given by Peter Lawford for his wife to which all the Kennedy relatives and all Sinatra's clansmen had been invited. But her major concern, and that of 'some Washington residents', was that 'The Rat Pack may be making a nest for itself in the White House after next January 20'.

As *Ocean's Eleven* opened around the country, Frank returned to Las Vegas but not for his customary night-club appearance. On September 11, his daughter Nancy, turned twenty in June, was married to singer Tommy Sands at the hotel of which Sinatra was part-owner. It was a small, intimate wedding, attended by about forty-six friends and family members. Frank gave the bride away and Sammy Davis, Jr., sang the song long associated with her, *Nancy (With the Laughing Face)*. Later in the year, Nancy was to tell a writer in Redbook: 'My brother and sister and I look up to him, respect him and love him. My mother and father have refused to let their personal differences upset our lives. We're a family and we know it. There is more warmth and understanding among the five of us than I've seen in many homes where there is no divorce. My father may have left home but he never left his family...'

Al Aronowitz of the NY *Post* phoned Las Vegas to round out his story on the nuptials. It was the father of the bride himself who took the call. According to the *Post* reporter, the gist of a twenty-minute conversation was this: 'I just want to know,' Frank allegedly said, 'where you got the — to call me after what you wrote about me (in 1959). I'm not going to tell you a thing. You're a cop and you're a fink and you're a parasite. I've got $3,000,000, Al, and I don't need you. You can bleed, Al, because I'll never tell you anything, you fink.'

On November 1, Frank was the main guest on the Dean Martin Show on NBC-TV, or as Nick Kenny put in the NY *Mirror*: 'The chief disciple made obeisance to The Leader.' After Martin announced that he was presenting *The Frank Sinatra Story*, a spoof of *This Is Your Life*, comic Don Knotts came onstage with the report that Frank was late. 'But Frank's plane landed three hours ago,' Dino protested. 'I know,' Knotts said ruefully, 'but he hasn't come down yet.'

Frank was actually late, returning from Hawaii where he had just finished shooting *The Devil at Four O'Clock*. And so, for the first half hour, Dino sang Frank's songs, Knotts did a well-received take-off, and Dorothy Provine, then a romantic interest of The Leader's, danced an inventive interpretation of The Roaring '20s. Finally, Frank came on to Dino's introduction of a 'man whose outlook is never narrow but who sees everything in terms of the broad'.

The *Hollywood Reporter* felt that the show could have been funnier without so many 'inside buddy ribbings'. This opinion was shared by Jack O'Brian of the NY *Journal-American*, who contended that 'a sick joke or two and an *inside* dirty reference' hurt the tone of the show. 'Such dedication to the morally shabby and the humourlessly disreputable,' O'Brian observed, 'continue to infect the TV activities of the Rat Pack.'

On November 20, when the company of *The Devil at Four O'Clock*, was back shooting in Hollywood, Clark Gable died of a heart attack. Spencer Tracy, a close friend and pallbearer, took a three-day leave of absence. Tracy's absence compelled the company to re-schedule shooting from the Fox ranch in Malibu to the Columbia studios on Sunset Boulevard. When Frank learned of the shift, his emissaries advised that he would not be there 'because Columbia Sunset is a Class B lot and Frank's contract calls for a Class A lot'. To overcome the objection, Columbia agreed to shoot at its Gower Street studios, an A lot. To do this, it had to rebuild an expensive set, a mock-up of an aeroplane. Insiders attributed the 'raucous ruckus', as *Hollywood Reporter* termed it, to tension between the two men on the set.

If there ever was a feud, it was surely short-lived. A story that went the rounds had Frank rousing Tracy one morning at 3 a.m. 'Spence? Ready?' Frank chirped. 'Let's do *Exodus*. You play the father. I do the son bit. How about it, Spence?'

Tracy was silent for a moment, then mentioned the story's climax where the son carries the father. 'I'm overweight now,' Tracy said, 'and I won't drop 25 lb. just to be carried by you.'

'If they don't take you as is, we'll buy out the creeps,' Frank announced. Then he added in more intimate tone: 'Besides, I got a double who's real strong...'

The Devil was still shooting on December 12 when Frank celebrated his forty-fifth birthday. George Sidney, filming on a nearby set, sent over thirty girls with a tag: 'For the Man who has Everything'. *A Hi-Fi Stereo* cover story characterised Frank as 'the most accomplished and influential singer of popular songs of the past two generations'. *Fame* announced that the Film Exhibitors of America had voted him and Elizabeth Taylor the 'Top Box Office Stars of 1960'. And *McCall's* pictured him, along with twenty-three other public figures, as one of the 'Most Attractive Men in the World'.

XXIII

THE INAUGURAL GALA

Frank had scarcely arrived in Washington to stage the Inaugural Gala when the capital press corps began making copy of him. Snide about his references to the President-elect as 'Jack', they stirred up a fracas because he and JFK's brother-in-law, Peter Lawford, were driven from the airport in a GI-chauffeured limousine. In Congress, a Republican representative arose in righteous anger to make an outcry against the misuse of manpower. By vetoing the plan of the American

Newspaper Women's Club to fete gala performers at a champagne party, Sinatra antagonised a number of female reporters. Apparently, the Democratic National Committee had okayed the club's plan and Frank's explanation that he was himself giving a party for the cast did not sit well with the ladies. When reporters inquired the name of the lady he brought to a cook-out—it was the wife of singer Nat 'King' Cole—he snapped: 'Where are you from? Bulgaria?'

The anti-Sinatra murmurings that appeared in newspaper columns took many shapes. Some suggested that he lacked the dignity necessary for the occasion; others argued that he failed to provide 'the proper cultural tone'. When nothing else offered a target, they went to work on his wardrobe, which had been designed by Don Loper of Hollywood. Columnists were quick to capitalise on a quip made by Milton Berle at a testimonial dinner for Gary Cooper, then ill with cancer. 'Sinatra would have been here,' Berle joked, 'but he was trying on his new Don Loper wardrobe and the zipper got caught in the sequins.' Since Loper was known primarily as a designer of women's clothes, the rib opened the door to the obvious innuendoes. 'The wardrobe is classic, correct and legitimate in every detail,' Loper's angry business partner advised the press. 'He's a designer period.' Frank phoned the Hollywood papers to re-assure them that, contrary to rumours, the wardrobe was just what he had ordered. Frank added: 'I never once opened my mouth to anyone. But this is the story of my life. I buy some clothes and it becomes a big crisis.'

Frank did not manifest his growing irritation with newsmen until the dress rehearsal on the afternoon of the gala. Claiming that they had disrupted a practice session the preceding day, he issued an edict barring them. Upset party officials pleaded with him and he finally relented but assigned them to a remote balcony. However, guards were stationed to keep the press out of the Statler-Hilton's South American suite, where he threw a black-tie reception for the cast and the Kennedy and Johnson families before the show. Murray Kempton, columnist on the NY *Post*, who attended the so-called 'disrupted' practice session, reported that it was full of good-natured banter and observed: 'All these people, the Sinatras, Nat Coles, Gene Kellys—the most inescapably valuable collection of flesh this side of the register of maharanis—were sons of immigrants or second-class citizens of not so long ago. They are in their wealth, their authority, their craft, the heirs of the Roosevelt revolution.'

As January 19, the day of the gala, progressed, it began to snow. By nightfall, capital traffic was crippled. The wags called the snow a 'GOP fallout' and comedian Joey Bishop remarked: 'Those Republicans are sure poor losers.' Although many streets were blocked by stalled cars, the President and his wife succeeded in reaching Constitution Hall where half of the hundred-man orchestra, its conductor and soloist were missing. When the concert finally began a half hour late, only sixty musicians were present and most of the audience was not.

At the 12,000 seat National Guard Armoury where Sinatra and his multi-million dollar cast waited anxiously, more than half the seats were empty. Leonard Bernstein, who was to conduct the opening *Fanfare for Inauguration* was marooned with Bette Davis in a stalled car from which they were finally rescued by a White House limousine. Bernstein arrived at the Armoury in a shirt two sizes too big and Bette Davis had to perform in a simple black sheath instead of her special gown. Ethel Merman, also deprived of her wardrobe by the blizzard, appeared in a red-and-black tweed coat, belting out *Everything's Coming Up Roses* as if she had campaigned for Kennedy and not Nixon. Miss Merman's appearance necessitated the one-night closing of the musical *Gypsy*, an unheard-of feat that Sinatra accomplished by agreeing to appear 'for scale' in Leland Hayward's TV production of *The Gershwin Years*.

Although there were rows of empty seats, the gala was a whopping financial success since every bit of available space had been sold and paid for in advance. Close to a million-and-a-half dollars were raised to wipe out the Democratic National Committee's campaign deficit. In *Variety*'s view, it was 'the super-benefit of all time'; it had smooth continuity, was 'adroitly framed' and devoid of 'the bad taste that can torpedo such occasions'. At 1.25 a.m. after enjoying the efforts of Mahalia Jackson, Joey Bishop, Juliet Prowse, Ella Fitzgerald (who had come from Australia), Gene Kelly (who flew in from Switzerland), Nat Cole, Jimmy Durante, Harry Belafonte, Milton Berle and many others, the President-elect arose and said: 'We're all indebted to a great friend, Frank Sinatra. Long before he could sing, he was pulling votes in a New Jersey precinct ... Tonight, we saw excellence.' And Frank told Earl Wilson: 'I only wish my kids could have seen it. I can't find the words...'

Frank's hour of triumph was not over until twenty-four hours later. Then, after Kennedy and Lyndon Johnson had taken their oaths of office and after five Inaugural balls were under way in snow-bound Washington—with 40,000 patrons who paid from $25 to $40—the President made an appearance at a private party given by Frank at the Statler-Hilton. The following day, Frank and the Lawfords breakfasted with Robert F. Kennedy, and after attending his swearing in as Attorney General, flew with the elder Kennedy in the family plane to Palm Beach for sunshine and rest.

A columnist reviewing the Inaugural proceedings suggested that change was the order of the time—for Leonard Bernstein had replaced Lawrence Welk, Stravinsky had superseded Fred Waring and Robert Frost had ousted Tennessee Ernie. Though his tenure seemed unsure, Frank Sinatra had succeeded Robert Montgomery. Sinatra's potential value to the Democratic Party, according to former Ambassador James Gerard, had been sensed by FDR. In his autobiography, Gerard tells of a letter written by the war-time President concerning Frank's widely publicised visit to the White House in 1944. Roosevelt allegedly told his aide, Admiral McIntyre: 'Mac, can you imagine girls swooning over someone like the thin one in our days?' But, Gerard reports, FDR added that while the girls swooned, their pockets could be picked for the Party.

The week-end before the Inaugural Gala, Frank was in New York taping songs for the ninety-minute special *The Gershwin Years* produced by Leland Hayward. It was his payment for Ethel Merman's appearance at the gala. With her, Frank sang *Let's Call the Whole Thing Off*, and by himself, a medley which included *I've Got a Crush on You*, *A Foggy Day* and *Nice Work If You Can Get It*. While he was taping the duet, the show's director urged: 'Frank, you're supposed to be in a happy frame of mind. Think of something funny.' Frank muttered: 'Ha, Nixon!' Dorothy Kilgallen, who viewed the proceedings, reported that Frank 'seemed sleepy—or gloomy', and attributed his depression to the slow sale of tickets for the Carnegie Hall tribute The Clan was paying Martin Luther King. 'Anyone would assume that the Sinatra name would be a guarantee of a packed house,' she observed, 'but apparently it hasn't happened because Sammy Davis, Jr., has been reduced to writing letters to his best friends for help.'

Apparently, Davis was quite effective as a letter-writer. On the night of the 27th, Carnegie Hall was filled to overflowing with an audience that paid as much as $100 a seat. After a parade of all-star entertainers that included Count Basie, Mahalia Jackson and Tony Bennett, the second half of the proceedings were taken over by Sinatra and Co. With Jan Murray substituting for Joey Bishop, Clan members clowned, sang, danced and raised a rumpus for over two hours. 'The combination itself,' *Variety* later commented, 'is one of the greatest ever seen in NY.' As the evening's emotional 'capper', Harry Belafonte introduced Dr. King, who had been freed from a Georgia jail through the intervention of President Kennedy.

Ava Gardner flew from NY to Frank's February opening at the Sands. It was clear that she was not thriving, despite desirable picture commitments and no lack of male admirers. Louella Parsons was not alone in feeling that she was 'one of the more tragic figures in recent Hollywood history'. Apparently, she was much concerned about her looks as she travelled west, for she monopolised the powder room of the plane to a degree that created talk among passengers. Then, in her nervousness, she left her coat aboard. Returning to find it, she missed Frank who had come to the airport to meet her. Came opening night and 'the hottest star in Las Vegas—and probably anywhere else', as *Variety* labelled Sinatra, displayed his skill as 'a powerhouse performer ... combining dramatic sensitivity with overwhelming drive'. Only Ava was not there to savour the show, or to meet Frank afterwards. After her arrival at the hotel, she discovered to her dismay that the first Mrs. Sinatra and daughter Nancy had also come to the Sands for a reunion. So she returned to the airport, flew back to New York and took off for Spain.

By the time he played the Sands again, the press was trying to make a thing of Frank and Marilyn Monroe. She was his date at a wedding anniversary party given by Tony Curtis and Janet Leigh. Then, she showed up at the Sands and sat at the edge of the stage, gazing moon-eyed up at Frank, who entertained her afterwards at his private table. The Hollywood columnists and fan magazines saw the makings of a torrid romance and devised elaborate psychological explanations for one. They reasoned that Frank, hypersensitive about his lack of a male physique, and Marilyn, neurotic about brute male force because of a childhood rape, would be naturally drawn to each other. There was just one thing wrong with all the amateur couch casuistry. As *Photoplay*'s Cal York noted: 'Everybody was so busy trying to make a serious romantic item out of the episodes that other scoops behind their meetings were overlooked. Frank, who always has a keen eye for business, arranged the dates to offer Marilyn a fantastic deal to co-star with him in a film for his own company.' Although it was not made public, the film Frank apparently had in mind was a musical remake of *Born Yesterday*, with Marilyn playing the Judy Holiday role of the 'dumb blonde'. Playwright Garson Kanin heard Frank offer half a million dollars for the screen rights—and then Marilyn died.

In December of the preceding year, Frank and Morris Ostin, by then an executive of the newly formed Reprise Records, were strolling past the newly built Capitol Tower on Vine Street, one of the first completely circular buildings erected in the United States. 'I helped build that,' Frank said. 'Now, let's build one of my own.'

1961 was the first year of Reprise Records, and Frank dedicated much of his time to its operation. Despite trips to different parts of the world—Mexico in April, Europe in the summer, the Orient in December; picture-making which occupied him in January (*The Devil at Four O'Clock*) and in May, June and July (*Sergeants Three*); personal appearances at the Fontainebleau in March and at the Sands in February, June and November; despite this crammed schedule, Frank oversaw every phrase of the company's functioning. He recorded three albums himself, *Ring-a-Ding Ding* (released in April), *Swing Along with Me* (July release) and a sentimental reprise of his days with Dorsey, *I Remember Tommy* (October). And his recording schedule, seventeen dates and sixty-seven titles, also included two albums which he still owed Capitol as a part of his contract 'buy-out'.

In *Ring-a-Ding Ding*, his first Reprise LP, Frank sought to capture the upbeat feeling of a new, exciting adventure. With Nelson Riddle unavailable because of his Capitol contract,

Sinatra chose as his arranger-conductor, Johnny Mandel, who has since collected an Oscar for *The Shadow of Your Smile*. Mandel was then highly regarded as a jazz arranger-composer who had made a potent use of the jazz idiom in his score for Susan Hayward's film *I Want to Live*. On the release of *Ring-a-Ding Ding*, *Playboy* praised Frank's 'jazz-rooted songstering' and 'self-assured vocal swagger'. *Down Beat* applauded Mandel's charts as 'a fine set of no-nonsense big band swingers', hailed Frank for sounding, not as if he was just swinging 'but kicking the band along', and extolled the album as 'vibrantly alive, a punching, shouting delight...' Not so to Doug Watt in *The New Yorker*, who thought that Sinatra has carried his offhand, easy-going approach too far and rejected Mandel's work as 'clatter and percussive effects ... without any fresh ideas'.

Regardless of how Capitol felt about Frank's setting up a rival label—some said Reprise stood for Reprisal—it brought out two new Sinatra albums before Frank had his first album on release—*Swingin' Session* in February and *All the Way* in May. By the time that Reprise had a second LP on the market, music trade papers were front-paging a legal wrangle between the two companies.

Frank called his July Reprise LP *Swing Along with Me* and kicked it off with ads that described him as 'a newer, happier *emancipated* Sinatra ... untrammelled, unfettered, unconfined'. In a lawsuit brought in California Superior Court, Capitol charged the *Swing Along with Me* 'closely resembled in concept, type of repertoire, style, accompaniment and title' the *Come Swing with Me* album that Frank had cut in March for Capitol. In a press statement, Frank replied: 'Album titles are hard to come by, particularly swing albums. The title *Swing Along with Me* is the theme for my recording company, the main line being "Swing Along with Reprise".' The Court sided with Capitol, granted a temporary injunction prohibiting Reprise from selling its LP, and ordered Frank's company to change both its title and cover. A few days later Reprise announced that *Swing Along with Me* would be called *Sinatra Swings*.

Now, the competition between the two companies took an intense merchandising turn. Capitol offered dealers an extra 15 per cent discount on its LP plus 100 per cent exchange up to a hundred LPs. As a counter-offensive, Reprise rushed

Frank's album out three weeks ahead of schedule. When Capitol caught wind of this move, it sent its exploitation force out with advance copies of the LP and promotional literature attacking Sinatra's aggressive activities. Reprise in turn threw a swank party for Hollywood disc jockeys at Romanoff's where Frank personally used his charm on station librarians and platter-spinners.

Title duplication proved a headache to Sinatra in his movie-making as well as recording enterprises. As a follow-up to *Ocean's Eleven*, he embarked on a film which co-starred Clan members and which was called *Badlands* but went into production as *Soldiers Three*. As soon as the new title was announced, MGM descended on Essex Productions with a legal warning that it had been used in a 1953 movie and would have to be dropped. In an attempt to get clearance from Metro, Frank offered to make a *cuffo* (free) cameo appearance in its historical extravaganza *How the West Was Won*. The situation remained unresolved during location shooting in Kanab, Utah, and even after filming was resumed, after a summer hiatus, in Hollywood. Eventually, though, Frank adopted the title under which the picture was released in 1962 —*Sergeants Three*.

Frank's continued preoccupation with his holdings manifested itself in many ways throughout 1961, not the least being two long interviews he gave to his unacknowledged press spokesman, Joe Hyams. The first, which appeared in *Show Business Illustrated* was tilted *Sinatra, Inc.* Enumerating Frank's numerous enterprises, which then totalled 'twenty-five million dollars' worth of investments', Hyams allowed Sinatra to explain his motivation. 'When I think of myself five years hence' (he would then be fifty), Frank said, 'I see myself not so much an entertainer as a high-level executive, interested in business, perhaps in directing and producing films ... The things I'm involved in personally—such as acting and recording—steadily earn less money while the things I have going for me earn most. And that's the way I want it to be.'

The second interview with Hyams led to a cover story in *Cosmopolitan*. The many pictures accompanying *Frank Sinatra's Corporate Image* told the story better than the text. One showed Frank standing at his own United Press International ticker, with the caption: 'Teletype gives Sinatra up-to-the-minute news information needed to run far-flung projects from record distribution in Latin America to benefit in Monaco.' Another photo pictured Frank and Dean Martin in black business suits, the latter pensively picking his teeth: 'Reprise Records President Sinatra and Dean Martin discuss number "Dino" is recording for firm,' the caption read, 'expected to gross $3–4,000,000 in this, its first year.' And spread across two pages was a panoramic view of Frank's office with a so-called Summit-Conference in progress. Only at this Summit meet, there were thirteen men, not cavorting on a stage, but seated on soft office chairs and couches, with papers spilling out of attaché cases. Officers of his film company, attorneys, sales managers, advertising directors, accountants, record executives, and tax lawyers, they were the top echelon of a larger group, comprising thirty-nine men, to whom Frank turned for advice, but all of whom were well aware that Sinatra made the decisions.

Despite Frank's new high-level executive orientation, the year was not without low-level displays of temper and temperament. In a February issue, *Time* reported that 'Sinatra was about to buy a Palm Beach pad and a night club so he could wage war with an established night-club owner who had refused to offer Frankie $5,000 for a one-shot appearance.' Crackling over the Western Union wires came an angry denial: 'I am glad to see that you are still batting a thousand regarding any information concerning me. As usual your information stinks. I need a house and a night club in Palm Beach like you need a tumour.'

Late in September, when Sinatra was in New York, Earl Wilson described one evening's festivities: 'Frank Sinatra and Ava Gardner went on the town with the Porfirio Rubirosas, the George Axelrods, Mrs. Mike Romanoff and some others … A photographer who asked to take a picture of Frank and Ava was told: No they were merely part of a group. There was no incident.' But the photographer, who happened to be on the same paper as Wilson, had a slightly different view and the NY *Post* gave him ample space to present what purported to be a verbatim report of several long, argumentative conversations between him and Sinatra. There was no incident, but there was extended coverage.

Earlier in the month, Frank also traded verbal blows with

TV impresario David Susskind when the latter invited him to participate in an *Open End* discussion of 'Sinatra and The Clan'. By return telegram, Frank advised that his fee was $250,000 an hour. Susskind wired back: 'Presume stipulated fee is for your traditional programme of intramural ring-a-ding dinging with additional fillip of musical lyrics mounted on Tele-Prompter. Please advise price for spontaneous discussion.' Sinatra responded: 'The $250,000 fee is for my usual talent of song and dance. However, now that I understand the picture a little more clearly, I must change it to $750,000 for all parasitical programmes.'

IMAGE 6

IL PADRONE

In the feudal concept that Italian emigrants brought to this country around the turn of the century, Il Padrone was the 'lordly father' whose absolute authority was tempered only by acts of benevolence. As he grew up in Hoboken's Little Italy, Sinatra was sensitised to this concept. By the time he was in his teens and had observed his mother operate in ward politics, he was given to displays of bounty. Through the years, as friends, girl-friends, needy members of show business, and even strangers testify, giving costly gifts has been as constant as manifestations of his supersensitive pride. Friends call him the most generous of men; hostile critics contend that he does things for others as a means of possessing them, or to make himself feel needed.

From the beginning of his career, Sinatra never functioned or moved about without an entourage—in the early days, it was known as The Varsity. Demanding unswerving loyalty from its members, he also inescapably elicited a subservience proper for the man who sat at the head of the table and was known as The Leader, The Pope, or The King of the World. But above loyalty and subservience, Sinatra wanted, like Il Padrone of old, to be a Man of Respect.

The press attack on Clan antics little bothered him until the cooling of White House amity was capped by a Presidential slight. Then came the shattering realisation that The Clan not only had become a detriment to his career, but that it was depriving him of that most treasured of commodities—respect. His pride piqued, he set about separating himself from his troupe of fun-loving swingers. Anxious to divest himself of the playboy image, he embarked on a concert tour that took him through seven countries and yielded a charitable contribution dwarfing all of his eleemosynary gestures. The man who had never forsaken his role as protector of his own children, his parents, and even his ex-wives, donated more than a million dollars to underprivileged youngsters throughout the world.

Now, Il Padrone, who had always been concerned with doing things in style, began to re-define his concept of class. Once, style had been identified in his mind with lavish spending and he had squandered a fortune to prove that he had class. A growing maturity brought the realisation that over and above quantity and size, taste really counted. Soon, he began publicly cultivating the social élite of Hollywood.

At a tribute to the late Cole Porter, he heard lyricist Alan Lerner describe a visit to a hospital where Porter was recuperating from one of his many leg operations and where he was served hot *hors d'œuvres*—Porter had rented an additional hospital room and installed a stove to ensure hot appetisers for his visitors. Il Padrone's excited comment was: 'That's class. That's real class. I like that.'

XXIV

THE YEAR OF THE CLAN

In March 1961 *The New Yorker* ran a cartoon in which a psychiatrist was shown asking a morose businessman: 'What makes you think Frank Sinatra, Dean Martin and all that bunch are so happy?' At about the same time, the peelers at a Hollywood striptease joint, The Pink Pussy Cat, began advertising themselves as Fran Sinatra, Peeler Lawford, Tino Curtis, Samya Davis, Jr., and Deena Martin. These were two of many indications of The Clan's hold on the public.

Its appeal was, perhaps, best analysed by a Hearst columnist, who indicated that, despite occasional lapses in taste, he found nothing objectionable in its 'lusty shenanigans ... exaggerated highjinks'. The late John McLain added: 'They are certainly liberal to a fault, insanely generous and public spirited.' And he concluded, doubtless to the dismay of some of his colleagues on the NY *Journal-American* 'They are a crazy and wonderful part of America.' What McLain and the public found so attractive was soon to be used to destroy The Clan. But if the mischievous and raffish pranks served as the basis of the attack, they were not really the cause of it.

There is no indication that The Clan developed out of anything but the social and psychological needs of its so-called members. The guys who began to cluster around Sinatra included a singer-comic then regarded as the less talented partner of the separated team of Martin (Dean) and Lewis (Jerry); a Negro entertainer, who had converted to Judaism and lost an eye; a shy, introverted comic (Joey Bishop) whose career had been greatly enhanced by Frank's support; an actor (Tony Curtis) who seemed to alienate people by his defensively brash conduct; and others who needed a Leader. As for Sinatra, he had an unrelenting need for people to laugh at his jokes, marvel at his ideas, witness his miseries and acceot his largesse. Clustering was not only a form of psychological refuge; for Hollywood stars, it provided protection from a public that hungered for a glance at, contact with and autographs from movie people.

Regardless of what it represented to its members, The Clan loomed as a powerful entertainment combine to the Hollywood Establishment. At a Copa opening, Sammy Davis, Jr. quipped 'The Clan? Why, that's just a little group of ordinary guys that get together once a year to take over the entire world.' It was no joke to the heads of talent agencies, TV production companies and movie studios. The tough attack came, however, after it injected itself into politics, and the plum and prestige of staging the Inaugural Gala fell into its lap. Then, the Establishment ganged up.

An opening gun in the attack was fired while the gala was still in preparation. The Hearst-owned NY *Mirror* presented a series whose consecutive headlines were: 'Sinatra Doles Out the Cheese'. 'Frankie Cracks the Whip on All', and 'Sinatra: Never a Bore Often a Boor'. The tone of the series was set early by Bill Slocum: '(The Rat Pack) is generally disliked as thoroughly in lush Beverly Hills as it is in grimy hangouts of editors and reporters. But there is one important difference—

in the swank offices and homes the words "The Clan" are spoken with respect and not a little fear. Folks downtown just spit out the words "Rat Pack" contemptuously.'

In May's *TV Guide*, Garry Moore fixed on The Clan to defend his own shows against corniness. 'Who says that?' he asked. 'Guys like Frank Sinatra and his bunch of parasites. Sure, they think I'm square because I rehearse and observe standards of good taste.' Moore continued: 'Sinatra and Dean Martin and the rest of "The Clan" are no credit to the business. They think it's clever to pull off-colour gags on the air ... I'd rather be a cornball than descend to the gutter.' But TV columnist Jack O'Brian, who was hardly a Sinatra partisan, commented: 'Fine. But suppose Sinatra never said Garry is corny?'

In July Frank and Co. paid a visit to the Slate Bros. night club to honour a buddy, Sonny King. News of their impending visit packed the small club on Hollywood's La Cienega Boulevard. But it also led to a column by Sidney Skolsky, who is a Sinatra partisan, and who characterised the evening as a kind of 'college initiation to see if Sonny could get into the fraternity known as The Clan'. Whatever the reaction of the club audience who watched Dino and Frank pour whisky over the comic and wallop his toes—they sat smack against the edge of the stage—newspaper readers were left with a bad taste.

The Clan gathered again for Eddie Fisher's opening at the Cocoanut Grove. July 25 was the first night out for Elizabeth Taylor after her near-death from pneumonia. In the middle of Fisher's rendering of *That Face*, Dean Martin exclaimed loudly: 'If I were you, I wouldn't be working. I'd be home with her.' Eddie smiled and part of the audience broke up. After some more ribbing during Fisher's programme of songs, Frank, Dino, Sammy Davis, Jr., and Joey Bishop charged on stage, liquor glasses in hand. (Peter Lawford who was with them remained in his chair.) For twenty minutes, they recited limericks, did impromptu imitations, indulged in ad lib shenanigans, much in the manner of their so-called Summit Meetings in Las Vegas.

The headlines that greeted them the following day were anything but friendly or appreciative. 'Noisy Rat Pack Takes Over Eddie's Club Act', was typical: and the papers reported that Fisher sat 'forlornly' on the bandstand while the Sinatra Clan carried on. Heddar Hopper commented: 'Frank and his henchmen took over and ruined Eddie's performance.' She heard, she said, Milton Berle snort: 'This was a disgusting display of ego.' *Variety* supported Miss Hopper's position: what was presumably meant to be sophisticated humour 'came off with a thud. The audience was not amused ... (by) The Clan's sophomore pranks.' Even Sidney Skolsky tilted his subsequent column in *Motion Picture* magazine: 'Has the Clan Gone Too Far?' Skolsky wrote: 'You sensed a feeling of audience resentment ... This was the first time The Clan played to a hostile audience; the first time they received unfavourable comment in the press.' Editorially, the magazine answered Skolsky's title query: 'The Clan has got to calm down—or go ... They offended a lot of people that night.'

However, Earl Wilson reported after a long-distance chat with Fisher, that Eddie 'felt honoured, pleased and grateful that Frank and Dean and the rest of The Group heckled him at his Cocoanut Grove opening. "I like to be heckled by them and the audience was hysterical—it was marvellous," said Eddie.' And Sidney Skolsky felt called upon to report, not without some bewilderment, that Eddie Fisher and Liz Taylor were at Frank's home the night after the opening, watching a screening of *The Devil at Four O'Clock*, 'as if nothing had happened the previous night at the Grove'. The late Ernie Kovacs, who attended the opening, made the explanation: 'Eddie did his complete show.' Despite references like 'the Desert Mafia's bust-up of his opener', The Clan had, in fact, come onstage only after Fisher had extended an invitation: 'Okay, fellows, now it's yours.' And there were reviewers, as in the *Hollywood Reporter*, who stated that the Summit Session had 'delighted the majority of pewholders despite some lapses into questionable taste'.

Nevertheless, press comment on The Clan grew acrid. Dorothy Kilgallen quoted William Holden as saying: 'When I first started in pictures I hoped to retire at thirty. What happened? The war came—and when I came out I had three children and I owed a fortune in back taxes. It was fine for Sinatra and others who never shouldered a rifle. They kept on making money throughout the war ...' From the former Mrs. Humphrey Bogart, by then Mrs. Jason Robards, the NY *Post* elicited a put-down: 'The Rat Pack automatically dissolved in 1956. I don't recognise the present group at all ... I think their pleasures are rather simple—simple minded. Any colour

they might have escapes me because I think it's pretty manufactured stuff.'

The interesting fact is that this was not the first time that
The Clan had 'taken over' during an Eddie Fisher performance. About a month earlier, they had held a series of Summit
meetings, all on the same evening, at three different clubs. Vic
Damone was appearing at one. Danny Thomas at another, and
Eddie Fisher at the third. At that time, Frank had said: 'We
never hurt anybody and we don't plan to ... I've never yet
seen an audience dislike what we do. Like for instance the
other night ... what we did to Eddie Fisher. It was beautiful.
When we jumped on stage, he broke up and couldn't sing any
more. I never saw a reaction from a crowd like we saw that
night—I swear it was like New Year's Eve ... What we do is a
rib—a good-natured kind of rib. Really we rib ourselves.'
Frank's comment notwithstanding, the fact is that the outcry
against The Clan came only after the second Eddie Fisher
meet, not the first. Why? The answer seems unavoidable. The
first occurred in Las Vegas, the second at the Hotel Ambassador in Los Angeles. One took place in the free-wheeling
world of one-arm bandits and whirling roulette wheels; the
other, in a fashionable hotel of the movie Establishment.

In the midst of the rumpus over the Fisher opening, another
situation came to a boil in the papers. It involved a Mediterranean cruise and a visit that Frank, Dean Martin, Janet Leigh
and others, were planning to pay the President's father on the
Riviera. Announcement was at first made that the group had
been invited by the elder Kennedy for a ten-day stay at his
villa at Cap d'Antibes, near Nice. But on August 3, an AP
dispatch from Nice advised: 'Joe Kennedy Tells Clan: No
Boarders' (NY *Post* headline). The former Ambassador to the
Court of St. James was quoted as saying: 'I know they are
coming to the Cote d'Azur. Certainly, they will come to visit
me and I'll be happy to see them. But they will have to go to a
hotel because I just don't have the room at my place to put
them up.'

On his arrival at Nice, the press met Sammy Davis, Jr. It
noted that, unlike the rest of The Clan, he had come to work
as the top-billed performer at an August 11 gala at Monaco.
After putting on an impromptu show for the airport press
corps, Davis informed newsmen that Sinatra and Martin were

definitely not coming to Riviera. 'I saw them last night in London,' Davis said, 'and they told me that they had to get back to the States right away. I don't know why.'

Frank and Dino had gone to London to perform cameo roles in *Road to Hong Kong*, staring Crosby and Hope. They played two astronauts in space suits. On August 23, they did return to the United States without visiting the President's father, also without making a planned Mediterranean cruise for which Texas oilman, Bob Neal, had chartered a yacht. There was much speculation as to why the pair had skipped the cruise after chipping in for its cost. In a statement attributed to Neal, Louella Parsons gave 'the real reason': 'Frank felt that he would be embarrassing his friend President Kennedy by being part of such an excursion when the world is in such a state of tension over Berlin.' But columnist Mike Connolly of the *Hollywood Reporter* wrote: 'The real dope: Frank ferreted out the fact that thirty photogs had hired a boat to follow him and his pals as they cruised the Mediterranean.'

Frank was a guest of President Kennedy later in the year. But it was at the Compound in Hyannis Port in October. In answer to a *US News and World Report* article attacking the President for his association with the Hollywood set, Pierre Salinger explained that Frank was conferring with the elder Kennedy regarding 'a souvenir recording of the Inaugural Gala to be used as a Democratic Party money-raiser'.

Not too long afterwards Dean Martin said: 'It's silly to call it anything like The Clan or The Group. If anything, it's more like the PTA—a Perfect Togetherness Association.' And Sid Skolsky predicted: 'Call it what you will—clan, group, PTA, or what have you—the summit meeting boys are going to dissolve slowly. The Clan will be no more because that's what the leader wants.' The following month, Peter Lawford was quoted as saying: 'Now look—that Clan business—I mean that's hokey. I mean it makes us sound like children—like we all wore sweat shirts that said, "The Clan" ... We're just a lot of people on the same wave-length. We like each other. What's wrong with that?' Admitting that he was asked about the group wherever he went, he told of his arrival in France: 'This French reporter comes up to me and says, "Etes vous un rat?" ... She's asking me about the Rat Pack. But there's no word in French for Rat Pack, you dig?'

So intense was interest in The Clan that a paperback publisher printed a full-length study *Sinatra and His Rat Pack* by Richard Gehman who said he loved Bogart but feared Sinatra. Gehman's tome was in a third edition when David Susskind latched on to the subject for his opening show of the autumn season. Inviting Gehman and writer Marya Mannes to represent the opposition, Susskind assembled a panel that included restaurateur Toots Shor, actress Lenore Lemmon, and comics Joe E. Lewis, Ernie Kovacs and Jackie Gleason. If Susskind hoped for fireworks, he was doomed to disappointment, as were the millions of viewers whose curiosity was peaked by one of the biggest press build-ups that a TV discussion show has ever had. Fork-tongued Marya Mannes tried to stir controversy by accusing the Rat pack of lacking decency and gallantry, and abounding in brashness and arrogance. Jackie Gleason, who locked horns with Miss Mannes, argued that Frank was entertaining as a frivolous image of our time. When they were not telling jokes, the other comics made comments about Sinatra that provoked Susskind to exclaim: 'Gentlemen, you make him sound like Albert Schweitzer!' As the discussion progressed, it appeared to some observers that the teapot from which refreshment was being poured contained something stronger than tea.

Public interest in The Clan continued unabated through the year. Shortly after the Susskind firecracker fizzled, TV producer Al Morgan, in a review of Bill Davidson's book on Hollywood, observed: 'Sinatra and his Brat Pack emerge as a show business auxiliary of the Mafia.' Dorothy Kilgallen, taking off from Sid Skolsky's prediction that The Clan was dissolving, commented: 'Reports elsewhere that the Frank Sinatra Clan has disbanded, or is coming apart at the seams, are far from factual. It's still a tightly knit organisation, even if some members had to pretend to go "underground" for obvious reasons.' At the end of the year fan magazine covers, carrying article titles like 'Did Jackie Kennedy Give the Order: Drop Sinatra?' and 'Is Sinatra's Clan a Menace to Hollywood?', reflected both the continuing curiosity of the public and the film capital's concern about The Clan.

'Clan, Clan, Clan,' Joey Bishop said. 'I'm sick and tired of hearing things about The Clan—just because a few of us guys get together once a week with sheets over our heads!'

1961 witnessed no diminution in Sinatra's dedication as a recording artist. During March, when he cut one of the LPs he still owed Capitol, he also recorded seven sides for an *I Remember Tommy* album on his own label. Although he was anxious to create new product for his fledgling company, he was not satisfied with the results and went back into the studio in May to re-record all seven sides. (Released in October, *I Remember Tommy* became a Top Ten best-selling LP by December.) Actually Frank rejected more masters in 1961 than in any other year of his recording career. All told, there were thirty-two unreleased sides, or five times as many as in 1946–47, the years of his decline. The rejects included the efforts of a gruelling set of sessions on November 5 when he cut eighteen sides for the first time, and the last, with the leader of the band at the Sands in Las Vegas.

The nostalgia of using Sy Oliver as arranger-conductor on the *Tommy* album led Frank, perhaps, to revive another relationship of the Dorsey days. For the last album he owed Capitol (*Point of No Return*), he employed Axel Stordahl, his arranger-conductor of the Columbia era. However, his main collaborator of a swinging year of recording was Billy May, who accounted for almost half of the year's seventeen sessions. Sinatra also used Don Costa, an arranger-conductor who had worked mostly with Steve Lawrence and Eydie Gorme, and who had brought Trini Lopez to Frank's label. The resulting LP, *Sinatra and Strings*, was a lovely change-of-pace album that emphasised mood ballads. The treatment of *Star Dust*, released also as a single, was a surprise, since it was wholly limited to the standard's rarely heard verse. *Night and Day*, recorded twice before by Frank, emerged as one of the most perfect of Sinatra discs. Impressionistic scoring by Costa and impassioned singing by Frank combined to produce a disc of unsurpassed beauty.

To celebrate his acquisition of a new $740,000 plane, a Martin 404 reconverted into a music man's den in the sky, Sinatra flew fourteen friends to Las Vegas. As they left the plane, each passenger received a memento of the trip—a keychain with a gold clown's head attached. Something of the inner man also came to light in a project he discussed with Carl Sandburg. Encountering the famous poet and biographer of Lincoln on the Twentieth Century-Fox lot, he proposed that they form an American Association of Illiterate European Peasants. Originating in the circumstance that the grand-fathers of both men used an X for their signatures, the organisation would demonstrate that people who are illiterate are not necessarily stupid.

One night at the Stork Club, Frank spotted a woman columnist who was generally unfriendly to him. She was wearing sunglasses. Frank arose from his table and walking past hers, dropped a dollar bill into her coffee cup. 'I always figured she was blind,' he told startled friends.

xxv

'THAT DAME FROM SOUTH AFRICA'

In August 1959 Frank was driving to the set of *Can-Can* in his custom-built Dual-Ghia. It was almost noon, and as he approached the Twentieth Century-Fox studios, he passed a tall, leggy redhead striding vigorously along. Walking is such a rare exertion in Hollywood that Sinatra pulled over to the kerb.

'Car break down?' he asked for starters.

'Haven't got a car,' the redhead replied. She measured 39 in. from toe to hip, more than half of her 5 ft. 7 in. frame.

'Hop in,' Frank said, 'I'm going to the studio.'

'I'm not,' she said. 'I'm going to lunch. I've been rehearsing all morning.'

Frank's curiosity was piqued. On the *Can-Can* lot, he had not been unaware of Juliet Prowse's attractive legs. But he had never really spoken to her. Inquiry elicited the information that she had, indeed, been rehearsing dance routines all morning, that she really did not have a car and that she was making a paltry $300 a week. (Sinatra was receiving $200,000 plus 25 per cent of the gross profits.) He also learned that she was twenty-five, had been born in Bombay and reared near Johannesburg, and that when she arrived, a stranger in Hollywood, no one from the studio had bothered to meet her or help her get settled.

Admiring her moxie, he invited her to a party at his mountain-top home and sent his chauffeur to fetch her. Although she later admitted that she had been terrified by him 'I was nothing ... he, one of the biggest names'), she had not shown it. If she was impressed by his lavish style of living, she did not say so. If she was anxious for other invitations, she made no play for them. (Girls frequently called Frank after a date, instead of vice-versa.) And if after a number of invitations, she knew that he liked her, she made no display of personal intimacy on the set.

During the filming of *Can-Can*, Barrie Chase, Fred Astaire's protégé, staged a sit-down because one of her dances was assigned to Shirley MacLaine. When choreographer Hermes Pan confessed that she was intractable, producer Jack Cummings allowed Astaire's prodigy to release herself from her contract. With Sinatra's blessing, Pan, who had hired Prowse after seeing her dance in Madrid, gave her Chase's routines. By December Sinatra had arranged to present Prowse on his ABC television show and was tipping columnists: 'The kid's got it. She's the sexiest dancer I have ever seen.'

Through the following year, Frank took Juliet to movie premières, brought her to record sessions and had her act as hostess at his parties. Remembering his experiences with the press in the Ava, Bacall and Lady Beatty periods, he confided his dating to private places. But on occasion, Prowse did not balk at travelling to spots where he was shooting a picture, or making a personal appearance. When a reporter tried to make something of a visit she was planning, she easily blunted the probe: 'Why, I'm going to make some home-cooked meals for him.' Her candour, lack of pretence and natural gutsiness prevented the press from making either a big romance or a back-street affair of their relationship.

If the press found it difficult to upset Juliet, Sinatra found it equally difficult to keep from getting more involved. He liked the fact that she was neither possessive nor neurotic about their relationship, and yet it apparently bothered him that she seemed to feel as free as he did. She made no secret, after a time, that she was in love with him. And Sinatra, the price of whose friendship generally included not talking about him to reporters, did not seem to mind when Juliet talked openly about him, and about them.

All of Frank's friends knew that a new marriage did not figure in his plans. And yet after his daughter Nancy was married in October 1960, he did something which it was not easy to reconcile with his interest in bachelorhood. At Christmas time, he allowed Juliet to bring her family—mother, step-father and brother—to a party at his home. Nevertheless, during 1961, except for a period when Paramount Picture publicists tried to construct a Presley–Prowse–Sinatra triangle, Frank was linked mostly with other girls. The most publicised of these was Dorothy Provine, whom he took for a jaunt through the Orient around Christmas 1961. And there was Princess Soraya, who was his New Year's Eve date when he flew friends in his private plane from Palm Springs to Las Vegas.

In fact, by the autumn of 1961, the rumour was that Frank and Juliet had had a falling out. Friends believed that she may have hinted that it was time 'to knit or split'. And she did tell a reporter that her seeing Frank was 'serious inasmuch as I was very fond of him and still am. But how long can something go on without any ultimate goal?' Her comment at the time of the split, however, was a simple, 'I go my way and he goes his. I have my life to lead and I'm not going to sit around. If I want to go out with someone else, I go out. No strings.'

At this time, Prowse's behaviour proved an enigma to Frank. He was accustomed to being pursued when he dropped a girl. But there were no phone calls from Juliet, and she did not accidentally happen to be where he was. Before long, a young agent, Eddie Goldstone, left his father's talent agency to become, not only Juliet's personal manager but a constant companion as well. While her film career marked time—she turned down a second Presley picture—Goldstone arranged for her to play the lead in a Las Vegas production of the Broadway hit musical *Irma La Douce*. By then, it was known that Goldstone's frequent trips to the gambling city and, at New Year's to New York when he got her a $10,000 guest shot on the Como show, were not purely professional.

It was while she was rehearsing for the Como show in New York that Frank returned from the Far East with Provine. He later said that he had endured 'agonising loneliness' on the trip and had spent days in his own room brooding. When Juliet stepped off the plane from NY, Frank was at the LA airport to greet her. The following evening, as they were dining at Romanoff's, he proposed. He also proposed that she give up her career as a dancer. Instead of saying 'yes' immediately to the man who was one of the love-gods of our time and a multi-millionaire, Juliet said she would like to think it over.

That evening they drove to Palm Springs where they apparently reached a compromise. Prowse agreed to give up show business and Frank agreed that she could do a film or two and an occasional TV shot. At Romanoff's the next evening, Frank proferred a diamond engagement ring and Juliet accepted.

When the newspapers of January 10 carried the announcement of Sinatra's engagement to Prowse, Sammy Davis, Jr., who was apparently taken by surprise, asked his Copa audience to observe a moment of silence 'for our leader who is leaving us'. In Washington where Congress had convened that day, senators and representatives scanning the papers to see how they had been mentioned, were amazed to find that the cocky Hoboken entertainer had pushed them off the front pages of most magazines and out of many of the columns. Among New York papers, the betrothal received front-page coverage in two of the four morning papers and in all three afternoon papers.

'You really shook us up,' said a reporter, who found Frank finishing a round of golf at Hillcrest Country Club. Frank replied: 'I'm a little shook up myself. I'm forty-six now. It's time I settled down.' Asked when the wedding would occur, Frank stated 'Probably not for some time. I'll let her call all the shots—that's the way it's done. I know she wants to have her parents over from South Africa and I want them here, too.'

The announcement caught not only Hollywood gossips by surprise, but also members of the so-called Clan. Peter Lawford, who reportedly learned of the engagement in a long-distance call from a friend, would not believe it until he received a wired confirmation from Frank. The surprise was shared by song-writer Jimmy Van Heusen, Sinatra's closest pal, who had said not too long before the betrothal: 'I don't think Frank will ever get noosed again.' Apparently, Frank had given advance notice of the engagement only to his daughter Nancy.

Shortly after the betrothal was announced, Juliet left for Johannesburg to discuss wedding plans with her family. Frank went to New York to continue filming his independent production of *The Manchurian Candidate* and to attend the première of *Sergeants Three* at the Capitol. Before Juliet left the States, she adverted to continuing differences regarding her career. 'He doesn't want me to work. But I do,' she said. 'After working this long and this hard for a career, I hate to give it up.' Eddie Goldstone, Juliet's manager and interim boy-friend, confirmed: 'Juliet hasn't yet told me to stop with her career so we're going right ahead with plans.' He was, in fact, seeking to negotiate a new contract for her with Twentieth Century-Fox.

About a week later, while he was shooting a scene for *The Manchurian Candidate* at Madison Square Garden, Frank told Earl Wilson: 'Irresponsible people are saying those things. She's not going to do any work. I'd rather not have it.' Wilson noted that Frank was acting the role of an engaged man, travelling only with guys and daily phoning Juliet in South Africa. 'She's committed to do a TV show for Arthur Freed,' Frank said. 'That's probably going to be the end of it. Her contract with Twentieth Century-Fox? Even though it has several years to go, she'll probably just walk away from that.'

On Valentine's Day, Mike and Gloria Romanoff threw an engagement party for Juliet and Frank. A few days later, it was announced that Joe Williams had, through Sammy Davis, Jr., been invited to sing at the wedding. Louella Parsons commented: 'All those who bet the marriage wouldn't take place are beginning to renege on their bets and now believe that Frank means it when he says he wants to settle down.'

Then, on the birthday of the father of our country, Frank suddenly announced that he was giving up the pleasure of being the father of Juliet's children. Viewers of late TV news shows that night heard a terse release put out by Sinatra's Essex Productions: 'Juliet Prowse and Frank Sinatra today disclosed that they have called off their wedding plans. The pair in a joint statement said: "A conflict in career interests led us to make this decision. We both felt it wiser to make this move now rather than later."' A columnist observed: 'Talk about short engagements, Frank has had longer engagements at Las Vegas.' The betrothal had actually lasted six weeks and one day. There were 'no tears' on Juliet's part, a spokesman at NBC's Burbank Studios reported, when she refused to see newsmen during the taping of a show. 'Why should she cry?' a friend said. 'Her asking price at Las Vegas jumped from $500 a week to $17,500.'

According to Sidney Skolsky, Frank, who had returned to his Palm Springs home, was devastated. 'The trouble is with Miss Prowse's career,' Skolsky wrote. 'It leaped higher than a vaulter with a fibreglass pole after the engagement was announced.' The Flamingo in Las Vegas had immediately grabbed her for a date; she had been signed for an NBC-TV special; and Twentieth Century-Fox had picked up her option.

During the engagement, Sheilah Graham had reported that she could not get over Frank's 'beaming friendliness' ... 'which even includes me! He shook my hands a few days ago and I think our feud is over. Love is a glorious thing.' Now, Miss Graham observed: 'At no time had Frankie been making like a man in love—something he does very well when he feels it—nor had Juliet exactly been acting like the one courted by Romeo.' Not to be outdone, Louella Parsons announced that she had known that the engagement would be broken even before the prepared statement had been given to the press: she had received word that Juliet had cancelled the order for her wedding gown.

Dorothy Kilgallen indulged in a series of speculations. On the 26th, she wrote: 'There were many sceptics who didn't for a minute believe Sinatra would marry Prowse, but the girl most "in the know" must have been Dorothy Provine. The lovely Dorothy has been receiving all kinds of expensive presents from Frank and thinks he's marvellous—but isn't likely to marry him because she's deeply religious and her religion would forbid marriage to a divorced man ...' A few days later Miss Kilgallen appended another juicy bit: 'Frank Sinatra's "broken engagement" to Juliet Prowse could have been forecast by his friends last time he was in New York ... Ask actor Richard Conte; he was one of the pals who noted that Frank wasn't behaving like a fiancé whose one and only love was miles away ...' Whom did Earl Wilson consult when he made precisely the opposite observation on Frank's conduct?

Dean Martin suggested that no one really had the truth about the bust-up: 'Juliet wanted Frank to give up *his* career.'

Some months later, Juliet told a NY reporter: 'Frank wanted me just to be his wife, to travel with him, to be with him constantly.' But as she confirmed that her career desires had disrupted their relationship, she added some new details: 'I would have married Frank,' she said enigmatically, 'but I've always been a little too difficult for him.' No less surprising, but more understandable was her assertion that Frank might have been flexible but grew more adamant about her career as he discovered that his children were opposed to the marriage.

At the same time that others were explaining why Sinatra did not marry Prowse, Sidney Skolsky tried to explain 'Why Sinatra Must Marry Juliet': 'For one thing, he is forty-six. His life has been changing. He is no longer Frank Sinatra, but Sinatra, Inc. The Clan has disintegrated. It exists in name only. On any night, when the laughs get sleepy, and there's no more booze and there are no more hours, Dean goes home to his wife, Lawford goes home to his, Sammy to his. But Frank just goes home.'

In April 1962, just after he returned from charity appearances in Mexico City and on the eve of his departure for similar appearances abroad, Frank cut a new album. Neal Hefti, former Count Basie arranger who served as arranger-conductor, suggested the title *The Thin One and Hefti* but Frank chose *Sinatra and Swingin' Brass,* presumably as a follow-up to *Sinatra and Strings.* Although the schedule called for three successive nights of recording, Frank was in such good voice that the LP was completed in two. After the first session on April 10, when Frank did six songs instead of four, Hefti never went home but holed up in a Hollywood hotel to rush his scores.

After hearing playbacks of *I Get a Kick Out of You* and *They Can't Take That Away from Me,* the musicians broke into applause—a rare sound in a recording studio. But Sinatra is still one of the few singers who is held in awe by recording musicians, an in-group of overworked gentlemen who are not easily moved, but many of whom will drop other dates to record with Frank. When he interrupted a take of *Serenade in Blue* with the comment, 'I *blue* that one,' it got a laugh. So did his spoken words at the end of *Goody Goody*: 'You got yours, lady.' But despite the relaxed atmosphere he sought to create, he worked with a perfectionist's drive during the six hours and fifty minutes of the two sessions. In *Pick Yourself Up* he insisted on another take because of a popping P—the letter registers with a thud unless a singer turns his head slightly away from the microphone. A film director present at the session commented: 'Just try and get him to re-do scenes before the camera! He's a genius at thinking up ways of making cuts and insertions—anything to avoid a re-take.'

After the second session, a small crowd followed him out of United Recorders studio on Sunset and watched him as he crossed the dark Boulevard, thin-legged and broad-shouldered. As he raced off alone in his Dual-Ghia to his mountain-top home at the summit of Coldwater Canyon, one of the older women in the crowd exclaimed: 'What a sad, lonely, little man!' The girls were still feeling motherly towards the *mother*, in his lingo, of American entertainers.

XXVI

RELATIONS ON THE ROCKS

During the colouring book craze of 1962, *The JFK Colouring Book* became almost as sensational a seller as Vaughn Meader's famous satirical record on *The First Family*. Among the outlines to be crayoned was a group of five figures; the legend read, 'They are friends of the family/They are always at our home/Colour them important/I know almost everybody here/Just that skinny one in the middle/I wonder who he is?' The skinny one was, of course, Sinatra, and the figures around him were Lyndon Johnson, Harry Truman, Mrs. Roosevelt and Adlai Stevenson. Pertinent as an observation concerning Frank's standing in presidential circles during the Inaugural year, it was out-of-date at its appearance. A cold wind was blowing from the White House, fanned, many believe, by Mrs. Jacqueline Kennedy. Rumours emanating from Hollywood had linked both the President and Attorney General Robert Kennedy with unbuttoned Clan parties. Many Washington denizens felt that the dignity and prestige of the Presidency were being damaged by the link with The Clan or Rat Pack.

The White House chill troubled Frank. Though he resented authority, he still had the awe of the self-educated Hoboken boy for his head of State. Too loyal to give up his friendship with Dino, Sammy and the rest, he set about changing his public image. Perhaps, even the marriage that never occurred was a move to persuade the public and the President's associates that he was more mature in outlook than slanted publicity suggested.

In the meantime, as a result of the White House's cooling demeanour, there was an estrangement between Frank and Peter Lawford. Hearst social columnist Suzy had predicted at the time of the Inaugural Gala that 'Peter Lawford is going to ease away from the Hollywood buddies as per request. No clean break, mind you, just an inch at a time.' In December 1961 Lawford and Sinatra had dissolved an enterprise in which they had been partners for a number of years, selling the jointly owned Puccini restaurant to a Chicago syndicate. In a May item, Walter Winchell inquired: 'Are JFK and FS having a diff of opinion over something? Insiders suspect so. Blame it on Peter Lawford over some pic deal.' The film deal was apparently not a cause, but an effect. Frank reportedly asked a prohibitively large sum to appear in *The Great Train Robbery*, a film Lawford was producing. By October, Winchell wrote: 'Jackie, insiders suspect, broke up JFK's romance with that Sinful Set.'

Earlier in the year, the President had personally requested Frank to entertain at a Miami dinner honouring Florida Senator George Smathers. 'As the President himself intends to be there,' Louella Parsons wrote, 'you just know that the matter of making a movie wouldn't stop Frankie from showing up. Sinatra is not only a Democrat, he's an all-out Kennedy man.' Frank did, in fact, arrange for the shooting schedule of *The Manchurian Candidate* to be switched so that he could fly out on Thursday and sing in Miami on Saturday. Just two days before the March 10 dinner, however, an announcement came from the Sinatra office to the effect that laryngitis would prevent him from appearing at the Smathers shindig.

At the time, anticipating a California visit by JFK, Frank was adding a five-room guest house to his Palm Springs home. But JFK did not elect to avail himself of this Presidential Wing, which included a dining room seating forty. Instead, he stayed at Bing Crosby's home and used the neighbouring house of Bill Morrow as his telephone exchange. It was a shattering blow to Frank who left town when the Presidential visit occurred. Later, Eddie Fisher cracked that Frank's home had a sign in front: 'JFK Almost Slept Here.' Actually, there is a bedroom door in Frank's home that bears the plaque:

John F. Kennedy
SLEPT HERE
November 6th and 7th 1960

It refers to the two days before JFK's election. There is also a red telephone in the study, cherished because JFK used it for calls to Washington.

In April 1962, the entertainment world was in a dither over the decision of MCA, then under investigation as a monopoly, to go out of the talent business and concentrate on production. The scramble for its clients, numbering almost a hundred of the biggest names in films, TV and recording, did not come to a head until mid-July when MCA formally went out of the agency business. But the manoeuvring of agents, managers, smaller agencies and stars was in full swing in the spring. Had Frank persisted in the agency business he had launched late in 1959, when he had, perhaps, anticipated MCA's exit from the agency field, he could have reaped a bonanza. But the talent firm he had started, despite continuing rumours and approaches from managers and talks with various artists, came to naught. It was columnist Bill Slocum who hazarded the opinion early in 1961 that Sinatra would never organise his own agency because 'major talent agencies have a long and mutually agreeable relationship with the hoodlum empire'. Whatever the reasons for his decision to stay out of the agency business, it was a fortunate one considering the problems he faced in 1962 because of his newly established record company.

If the snub by JFK did nothing else, it surely convinced Frank that The Clan had not only outlived its usefulness as a publicity gimmick, but had become a liability. And yet the charity tour on which he embarked in April was hardly a spur-of-the-moment idea. He had talked about it as early as 1955, shortly after the rebirth of his career. It was not until the spring of 1961 that he was able to take a first step. Flying Nelson Riddle and his orchestra down to Mexico City at his own expense, he played a series of benefits from May 5 to May 7 for the Rehabilitation Institute of MC. Out of the venture came a charitable contribution of $50,000. Rep. James Roosevelt had inserted a tribute in the *Congressional Record*, which read in part: 'Sinatra's humane contribution entitles him to applause beyond that given a great entertainer.'

For a time in September 1961, Frank had contemplated doing a series of charity benefits in ballparks throughout the United States. But having completed the shooting of *The Manchurian Candidate*, he made a second trip to Mexico City and contributed $25,000 to charity on behalf of underprivileged children. Then, in mid-April 1962, he embarked on a two-month international good-will and charity tour, which he hoped would temper the image of the flip playboy.

It was a different Sinatra who greeted newsmen at LA's International airport as he embarked on his global charity trip. Joking with reporters, he denied that he was older but accepted the epithet 'mellower'. Before he returned in mid-June Frank was scheduled to do thirty concerts, which meant one every night. Except for necessary local expenses—Frank himself footed the travelling and living expenses of his musicians and entourage—the intake of all thirty performances went to children's charities. In Tokyo, where he became the first non-military American to receive the key to the city, $28,000 was raised for sixty Orphanages for Eurasian children. In Israel, his next stop, the gross of two weeks of giving concerts went to an International Friendship Youth House, which was to be named after him. In Rome and Milan, Frank sang for the benefit of Boys Town. In Great Britain over $80,000 was raised for the Invalid Children's Aid Association, a Princess Margaret charity. All told, the total sum contributed by Frank from concerts that took him also to Greece, France and Monaco, was in excess of a million dollars. The cost of the trip to him was reportedly $200,000. On May 14, Sheilah Graham commented: 'Now, hear this. Frank Sinatra, who has made a couple of pictures currently on the screens of Europe, including his unexpectedly successful *Sergeants Three*, has categorically rejected any publicity in this trip—for his pictures or his records. "That's not what I'm here for," says Frankie.'

From Paris where he encountered Sinatra, *Variety* editor Abel Green cabled a front-page story: 'The "new" Sinatra, from the press viewpoint, is his general affability and availability...' Green added: 'The singer's genuine all-out work for children's hospitals ... was globally approved.' But the approvers did not include the editors of *Time*, who snidely described Sinatra's manner as 'a winning confection of goodwill and grandeur—like a maharajah on a mahout outing'. Nor did they include the Arab League, which banned Sinatra's films and records because of his concerts in Israel.

On May 18, when *Time*, tongue-in-cheek, dealt with Frank as a 'prince of charity, prophet of peace and generous, sober, chaste diplomat', it felt completely at ease in announcing the demise of The Clan. 'Only Dean Martin and Mike Romanoff remain. Peter Lawford (whom Sinatra now snubs) is in a dark sulk. Sammy Davis is a family man ... At forty-six Sinatra is more alone than since the days before his *From Here to Eternity* success ...'

Shortly after he returned from his triumphal charity tour, Frank found himself in open combat again with the record company for which he had cut discs from 1953 through 1961. In an all-out advertising campaign, Capitol Records offered twenty-one Sinatra LPs at a bargain Two-fer rate. It was a giant business manoeuvre, not calculated to build up Frank (which it in fact did), but to shake up Frank's infant record company. In its first year of operation, Reprise Records had produced only three best-sellers, all of them Sinatra's albums: *Ring-a-Ding Ding, I Remember Tommy*, and *Sinatra Swings*.

In an attempt to halt the manoeuvre, Frank filed a million-dollar lawsuit against Capitol. Alleging restraint of trade and violation of the Robinson–Patman Price Discrimination Act, Reprise requested a court injunction. Capitol's drastic slashes, not only injured Reprise's ability to compete, but jeopardised its very existence. The price-cutting had already bought dealer demands that Reprise adjust its prices to the level 'fixed by the defendant', resulting in damages totalling $1,050,000.

In August, in a counter-move, Reprise launched a Bonanza campaign, offering dealers an increased 10 per cent discount over normal wholesale prices on ten selected new releases and a graduated scale of 15 per cent on others. By September, Reprise had lost its first round in the courts when its suit on price discrimination was dismissed. In October Sinatra's company initiated a new lawsuit, again requesting an injunction and seeking damages of $850,000. Undaunted, Capitol made a new move, which *Variety* headlined: 'Dustoff of Old Sinatra Discs Needles Him Anew.' The new move consisted in the release of an anthology of twelve Rodgers and Hart tunes and a giant three-disc package titled *The Great Years*.

In a liner note, whose approach *Billboard* characterised as a 'let-the-chips-fall style of liner writing', Capitol emphasised that Sinatra had been given a second chance in 1953 after other record labels had shown 'little interest in the spent

Hoboken baritone'. It pointed out that while he had earned $11,000,000 in the crooning years from 1941 through 1946, he had grossed more than $30,000,000 from 1953 through 1960. Harking back to an August Reprise ad in which Sinatra had written, 'In my opinion (and who knows better), if it's on Reprise, it's fresh ... it's new ... it's my very best!'—Capitol observed of its three record package *The Great Years*, 'Were better records by a singer ever made?'

Bitter though the feud became, its results could not have been other than satisfying to Sinatra as well as Capitol. Late in August, *Billboard* reported: 'Sinatra Two-fer Deal Shoots Capitol to Top of Album Heap.' Sinatra was then represented on best-seller charts by no less than fourteen albums, two of them on Reprise. In the course of the year, three Capitol albums (*Come Dance with Me, Songs for Swingin' Lovers, This is Sinatra*) and one Reprise album (*I Remember Tommy*) passed the half-million mark in sales. Sinatra had an extraordinary total of twelve album releases in the one year, with Reprise trying hard to hold its own against its giant competitor, by releasing four new albums. It was unquestionably the biggest sales period for Sinatra LPs in his entire recording career. (Before the onset of hostilities, Frank had also realised a capital gains on his Capitol recordings, for the label had purchased from his Essex Productions the rights to 635 masters cut by him from December 1955 on.)

Despite his drive to develop a new public image of maturity, Sinatra made headlines as the result of an altercation with a photographer. At the new Facks club in San Francisco a cameraman snapped a picture without asking Frank's okay. At the moment, two unidentified blondes, by accident or design, were leaning over his shoulder. A columnist of a local San Francisco newspaper reported that Frank 'leaped for the photographer's throat and wrestled him to the floor' and that club employees 'hustled Sinatra off to a cloak room to allow him to cool off'. A member of the Mary Kaye Trio performing in the club, claimed that Frank was polite until he was 'goaded into anger by the cameraman'. Approached by a UPI correspondent, the photographer characterised the columnist's report as untrue and stated that he was grabbed 'by some guy in the Sinatra party—I don't know who', and that the exposed film was removed from the camera. 'That's all there was to it,'

Jimmy Jaye said. 'I talked to Sinatra later and he said he was sorry.'

But that was not all there was to it. Two days later, Mr. Jaye filed a lawsuit against Sinatra, demanding $275,390 in damages. Now, he claimed that Frank had seized him by the necktie and tried to choke him. The suit never came to trial.

August also saw the opening of the newly renovated Cal-Neva Lodge in whose swimming pool one could cross the border from California to Nevada. Managed by Skinny D'Amato, owner of the 500 Club in Atlantic City, the Lodge was to bring a number of crucial changes in Sinatra's affairs. For its reopening he was himself on stage, and ex-fiancée Juliet Prowse was part of a group that flew in for the event in Frank's private plane.

During Frank's absence abroad, Juliet had frequently dated Eddie Fisher. While the papers tried hard to see romance in the meetings, Fisher and Prowse both kept insisting that they were just friends; they did not indicate that they were really discussing a forthcoming NY Fisher appearance which was to co-star Prowse. Frank paid no mind to the press, and when he developed laryngitis, it was to Eddie Fisher (and Joey Bishop) that he turned for substitutes during the first week of the Lodge's reopening. As the year wore on, the press turned from Fisher back to Sinatra, and tried hard to discover a renewed romance in Frank's dates with Juliet. Even Sidney Skolsky concluded a column: 'She might marry Sinatra yet—don't bet against it.' After the October opening of 'Eddie Fisher at the Winter Garden'—Prowse was the featured dancer—a critic gave Skolsky's thought a bright turn: 'Aside from getting "A" for anatomy and "E" for effrontery, Miss Prowse should do herself a favour: forget her career and take Sinatra up on his marriage proposal.'

The Cal-Neva reopening, reopened not only the question of Sinatra's relationship with Juliet, but brought into question a relationship that was of infinitely longer standing. By 1962 Sinatra and Hank Sanicola had been associated for more than a quarter of a century. On September 17, Sanicola said: 'We had one of our little beefs—about the operation of Cal-Neva ... It could be okay tomorrow. It's happened before,' and he mused: 'I guess I'm the only guy who will disagree with Frank once in a while.' Reached on the set of *Come Blow Your*

Horn, Sinatra said: 'That's nobody's business.' The coolness between the two continued so that by the beginning of November columnist Louis Sobol was at ease in stating that the rift had widened and that 'their business alliance is coming to an end'.

In November, too, Frank journeyed eastward for an appearance at the Villa Venice, a club reactivated in a suburb north of Chicago. For several years, it had functioned as a banquet hall for conventions and weddings. Eddie Fisher headed the bill that reopened the sprawling mansion. After ten days Sammy Davis, Jr., took over. He was joined on November 26 by Sinatra and Dean Martin.

Fisher opened to reviews that characterised his show as 'potent, electric and superbly staged'. *Variety* thought that the cover charge of $5 per person with a minimum of $7.50 was 'the biggest per head charge in recent history, excluding New Year's Eve parties'. Three days after the 'summit troika', Sinatra/Martin/Davis, Jr., opened, the cover charge and minimum were raised to $10 and $10. However, Dinah Shore, who was to follow, suddenly postponed her engagement, forcing the management to scramble for a name replacement. 'More mystery at Chicago's Villa Venice,' Dorothy Kilgallen observed.

Delving into the 'mystery', *Variety* featured the answers in a front-page story: *Chi Spotlight on Floating Dice Game Situated Near the Villa Venice*. 'The mystery of why a long-dormant and remotely located suburban night-club reopened with top-name headliners for only a month, began to unravel last week when it was revealed that a big-money floating crap game had set up shop in a plushly outfitted quonset hut less than a quarter-mile away.' State's Attorney Daniel Ward said that the game had folded just before a scheduled raid had taken place. Noting that his investigators had observed nationally prominent gang figures going in and out of the quonset hut, he told *Variety* that he did not feel that the entertainers at the Villa Venice were aware of the crap game. To which *Variety* appended the comment that tradesters were puzzled by the club's reactivation: 'Treatment of the press was indifferent and long-range information from the registered owner was vague.' Just as the reason for Dinah Shore's bow-out remained unstated, so other mysteries surrounding the Villa Venice remained unanswered.

In February, *Sergeants Three*, described by *Variety* as a

'warmed-over Gunga Din', took a beating in the press. *Time* said: 'Sinatra and his cub scout troupe are pioneering in a new art form: the $4,000,000 home movie.' But the reaction to *The Manchurian Candidate*, released in October, was in marked contrast. Frank dubbed it 'the best picture I've made since *The Man with the Golden Arm*'. And *Variety* found it that rare film that works in all departments—'top performances', 'a literally stunning climax' 'topical excitement' and 'sheer bravado of narrative and photographic style'. Of Frank it wrote: 'After several pix in which he appeared to be sleep-walking, Sinatra is again a wide-awake pro creating a straight, quietly humorus character of some sensitivity.' While the general press was less than unanimous in its praise, the film drew rave reviews like *The New Yorker*'s: 'Many loud hurrahs for *The Manchurian Candidate*, a thriller guaranteed to raise all but the limpest hair ... Sinatra in his usual uncanny fashion, is simply terrific.'

If the tensions of Frank's relations with the President of the United States, Peter Lawford, Juliet Prowse and Hank Sanicola contributed to repeats bouts with his psychosomatic ailment (laryngitis), his position in the 1962 world of pop music should have prompted quick recovery. Promoted or accidental, the procedure of NY Station WINS in programming only Sinatra records for several days was both startling and revealing. 'Startling' in that the station had been pursuing a policy known as 'Top 40' programming, which involved ad nauseam plays of the best-selling rock 'n' roll discs. 'Revealing' in that Frank's continuing hold on record-buyers, despite the teenage slant of pop music, was fully demonstrated. By the time the station received an appreciative call from Frank and began adding discs by other artists to its programmes, a total of sixty-six Sinatra hours had passed.

Waxing cynical about the occurrence, *Billboard* suggested that, if Sinatra publicists had not proposed the idea, the heavy press coverage was surely well-timed for the opening of *Sergeants Three*, then premièring on Broadway—also for WINS, which had apparently planned to switch from the Big Beat to the Beautiful Ballads. Nevertheless, news of the Sinatra-thon girdled the globe, stirring comment even in Moscow where *Pravda* congratulated WINS for dropping 'That contaminator of American youth', rock 'n' roll. Within days of the WINS manoeuvre, WITH of Baltimore announced a Sinatra Marathon while WIBG of Philadelphia made February 17 a 'Frank Sinatra Day'. The following month, KRAK of Sacramento launched a Sinatra-thon. And so it went—spontaneous developments that seemed to coincide with openings of *Sergeants Three* around the country.

1962 brought the death of a number of people linked with Frank's career: press agent Mack Millar, who had worked for Frank in the days of Ava; Barney Ruditsky, the detective who had led the 'wrong door raid' on Marilyn Monroe; and Marilyn herself. Frank's name was repeatedly dragged into the so-called mystery surrounding her suicide. Under a six-column headline, Dorothy Kilgallen urged a wider probe of MM's mysterious death and cited three facts that ostensibly needed investigation: '1. That when Marilyn visited the Cal-Neva Lodge (shortly before her suicide) a maid found her unconscious on the floor of her room—from pills, not from liquor. 2. That she was revived, but that night drank too much and passed out cold, in full view of several hundred guests. 3. That she was then carried out and flown to San Francisco in Frank Sinatra's private plane.' Nothing came of Miss Kilgallen's needling. But it stirs the afterthought that her own premature death was the result of the same alcohol–barbiturate combination that killed Marilyn.

IMAGE 7

THE CHAIRMAN OF THE BOARD

'Chairman of the Board', the nickname give to Sinatra by disc jockey William B. Williams as an accolade for his vocal authority, acquired new meaning after Frank turned forty-five. Before then, he had begun developing his own production companies, seeking to transform recording, acting and TV talent into capital gains, not just fees or royalties. He had also been investing in non-creative enterprises that made him a restaurant owner, radio station executive, hotel keeper, gambling casino proprietor, etc.

But in 1960 he launched his own record company and began

to move aggressively in the field of film production. In 1960, working within the walls of Warner Bros., he defiantly signed an escalated contract with the Screen Actors Guild that the parent company would not accept for itself. It was an indication that power in the movie industry had shifted from the major studios to the many independent producers, and particularly to companies headed by super stars like Sinatra. Regardless of what The Clan meant to his ego, for his buddies or as a symbol of fun-loving non-conformism, to many in Hollywood it represented a powerful, and potentially dangerous, concentration of show business talent.

American Weekly sounded the alarm in an article provocatively titled *The Reign of King Frankie*. Sinatra and his publicists took steps to give the new image a positive cast. In a major article, Joe Hyams emphasised the stern demands made upon Sinatra by his burgeoning enterprises, while in another, on Frank's *New Corporate Image*, Hyams added the tantalising thought that Sinatra's millions had 'not brought him emotional security'. Nevertheless, the troubadour's vast expansion as a tycoon continued to be a troubling thought. A writer in *Esquire* observed without humour: 'With a cold he can in a small way send vibrations through the entertainment industry and beyond as surely as a President of the United States, suddenly sick, can shake the national economy . . .'

As he celebrated his fiftieth birthday in 1965, the era of capital expansion seemed just to have begun. The entertainer was becoming increasingly an entrepreneur and the actor was moving in the direction of producing and directing. Long the appealing symbol of the American Romantic, Sinatra was now Sinatra, Inc. Soon he would marry, climb into the higher social reaches of The Establishment—and The Chairman of the Broads, as someone had accidentally called him, would, indeed, become The Chairman of the Board.

XXVII

JUNIOR BLOWS HIS HORN

On the evening of September 9, 1963, the Royal Box of the Americana Hotel in Manhattan reopened for the autumn season. Other hotel rooms featured established name performers like Sheilah and Gordon MacRae (Waldorf), Peter Duchin (St. Regis) and Xavier Cugat and Abbe Lane (Plaza). The Royal Box was presenting a newcomer, but there was no question that the eyes of the entertainment world were fixed on it and that it had the heaviest table reservations, despite a cover of $6.00 per person. *Variety* called the booking 'boffo showmanship', for it brought together two names that nostalgically harked back to the 1940s. Backed by the Tommy Dorsey band, Frank Sinatra, Jr., was making his début in the big time.

It was roughly a year since Sinatra *fils* had given evidence that he wanted to try walking in the giant tracks of Sinatra *père*. Junior's first appearance had occurred in July of 1962 at Disneyland in California. It was an unbilled guest shot, ostensibly solicited by the eighteen-year old. 'A few days ago,' bandleader Bill Elliott told an AP reporter, 'young Sinatra came up and said he would like to sing with us on Saturday night when we did Dorsey.' The Elliott Bros. band regularly did take-offs on name bands of the forties. 'With a name like that, I didn't ask if he could sing—I just answered yes.' The 'yes' led to an AP wire story that apprised readers throughout the country: 'Frank Jr., Has Old Sinatra Touch—Bewitches Bobby Soxers.' Elliott was quoted as saying: 'The kid's good ... I'd sign him permanently even if his name were Joe Smith.' Junior was described as 'not yet officially embarked' on a professional career, but the guest appearance did not quite come off as an accident. Junior was later to say: 'I don't make a move without his (Sr.'s) OK.'

In the thirteen months between Disneyland and the Royal Box the build-up of young Sinatra proceeded slowly. Early in October, he appeared in a song-and-skit take off on rock 'n' roll on the Jack Benny Show. After that, Junior, who was a music major at the University of Southern California, returned to his classes. Personal appearances in May 1963 in Dallas and at the Wagon Train in Lake Tahoe eventually led to an 'offer' from the Dorsey band. After a seven-week road tour, Junior made an appearance in August at the Flamingo Lounge in Las Vegas. The verdict of *Variety*'s reviewer: 'He may not now have the tonal texture of his father; he may not now generate excitement; however, he has the stuff which can build into another Sinatra legend: excellent voice ... in tune ... proper intonation plus imaginative phrasing; he's a very handsome youngster with humility, who shows poise and assurance.'

Now, the Sinatra public relations battery went into high gear. Three weeks before the Royal Box opening, Sinatra, Sr., *sans toupé*, and Frank, Jr., appeared on the cover of *Life* magazine. Inside, three large pages of photos and friendly text set the stage for Junior's début. 'He set off an uproar by simply walking on stage. The new Sinatra sound is an eerie, incredible exact echo of Frank, Sr.'s, singing.' Reporting that Junior played drums, flute and piano, and had composed a piano concerto, *Life* noted that he warmed up his voice by singing along with his father's recordings. 'I think the kid has a future,' Pop predicted, 'but he needs experience.... I mean he's got to learn to drink, carouse and stay up all night.'

The *Life* article included 'Advice to his boy from the master': 'Singing is almost like reading prose or poetry to a musical background.' 'Being nervous before a show never stops. I still am ... That's why this going on the road, singing every night, all kinds of songs, to all kinds of audiences is the best thing.' 'You must pace yourself even when you feel strong ... I'm always worried about Sammy Davis, who never gives his throat a rest.' On handling the press, Senior observed: 'This will get a lot of laughs but I really mean it: be honest and courteous and fair and hope the press reciprocates ... In spite of my so-called problems, I've had a damned good press ...'

In *Variety*'s view, Junior was 'handicapped as much as helped by his heritage' in his Royal Box début. But editor Abel Green's verdict was: '*Thumbs Up*.' 'Frank, Jr., clicked.' Packing his twenty-minute stint 'with commendable professionalism', he reeled off five numbers, including such Sinatra perennials as *Night and Day* and *I'll Never Smile Again*. Contributing to the excitement was the presence of an unexpectedly large number of entertainment luminaries, friends of Sinatra *père.* According to Earl Wilson, Jackie Gleason was 'ringleader in a sentimental session'; *Newsweek* reported that he helped 'the slobs slobber'. Gleason's determination to protect his pal's son proved a trial to some reporters, if not to Junior himself. In an intermission interview, Atra Baer of the NY *Journal-American* found young Sinatra 'pleasant, personable, polite and no dope'. The interview was proceeding smoothly when Jackie, by then well-lubricated, intervened to insist that no unfavourable quotes appear in her article. Young Sinatra exchanged an understanding glance with Miss Baer, who reported: 'One guess—who wound up "protecting" whom that night?'

What added most to the evening's tension was not the presence of so many Sinatra cronies, but the conspicuous absence of Senior himself, who was known to be in New York. 'I spoke to Dad on the phone,' Junior told reporters, 'and he was coughing. He was very tired. He'd been working all afternoon on his record business. He thought he'd stay home until he felt better.' One of the reporters who had no compunction about putting a nineteen-year-old on the spot, asked: 'Did your father stay away because of the Nevada situation?' Junior surprised the newsmen with his control: 'I've discussed it with my father,' he replied, 'and he said when he's ready, he'll make a statement.'

'The Nevada situation' was not then public knowledge. But some reporters were aware of a development that became official two days after the Royal Box opening. On September 11, the Nevada Gaming Control Board, watchdog of the State's lucrative gambling industry, moved to revoke Sinatra's ten-year-old gaming licence. The grounds: that he had played host to a notorious underworld figure, one of eleven hoods whose names were listed in the *Black Book* issued by the State Gaming Commission and whose mere presence in any Nevada gambling casino constituted sufficient cause for licence revocation. The mobster, described in the complaint as 'one of the twelve overlords in the organisation known as Cosa Nostra, sometimes known as the Mafia', was Sam (Momo) Giancana, fifty-four, of Chicago.

The Nevada Gaming Board claimed that Sinatra had received Giancana as a red-carpet guest at his Cal-Neva Lodge from July 17 to July 28, 1963, where he had occupied Chalet No. 50, 'registered to a female performer then appearing at the

Lodge'. The performer was Phyllis McGuire of the well-known McGuire Sisters to whom Giancana was rumoured to be married. Amother item in the Board's complaint concerned a phone conversation on August 31 between the Chairman of the Board and Frank. Chairman Edward Olsen claimed that Sinatra used language and a tone 'designed to intimidate and coerce the chairman and members of the State Gaming Control Board to drop the investigation'. A further allegation involved an alleged act of attempted bribery of two board auditors by Paul D'Amato, listed on the Lodge's payroll as an advisor. The Board maintained that Sinatra had not only 'continued social association with Sam Giancana while knowing his unsavoury and notorious reputation', but that he had 'openly stated that he intends to continue such association in defiance' of Nevada Gaming Laws.

Ensconced in his elegant New York duplex, Frank could not be reached for comment for several days. But on September 12, the third night after his son's début, he visited the Royal Box. The papers quoted him as saying: 'The kid sings better than I did at that age.' He thought that his son was 'way ahead of me because he's a studied musician, which I am not'. Later, Junior revealed that Senior's visit to his dressing room had not been without sparks. 'I'm going to kick you right in your Francis,' Sinatra *père* yelled. 'Don't ever let me catch you singing like that again, without enthusiasm.'

'I'm upset over something,' Sinatra *fils* tried to explain. Fencing with the press over his father's Nevada situation and facing the tough Americana crowd were obviously trying the young man's nerves. The overawing presence of his father could also have been a disturbing factor. ('Until September 1958 when I was put into a college preparatory school,' Junior has said, 'my life with the family was very, very normal. Once outside the inner circle, my position within was never re-established . . .')

'Get lost!' the father shouted. 'No matter what your name is, you're nothing if you aren't excited about what you're doing.'

Junior commented later 'I was hurt to have him scold me like that. After thirty years of singing, you'd think *he'd* have lost some of his enthusiasm . . . I asked him how to fight depression . . . "Concentrate," he said. "Concentrate on the music, on the people around you. Every song holds a special

313

meaning for someone and you can't think of yourself." '

That Junior venerated Sinatra the singer is as clear as the reservations he voiced not too long ago about Sinatra the man. Commenting on what he called 'the press-release Sinatra', who had been depicted during the first flush of fame as *super-normal* and set apart from other men, the son said: 'Here is the great fallacy ... the great bullshit, for Frank Sinatra *is* normal, *is* the guy you'd meet on a street corner. But this other thing, the supernormal guise, has affected Frank Sinatra as much as anybody...'

Queried at the Royal Box about the charges that he had entertained a 'Black Book' Mafia chieftain at his Lake Tahoe resort, Senior replied: 'There's nothing I can say. I won't know anything until I get back to Los Angeles and talk to my lawyer.' But he announced: 'We'll fight this.' Two days later, Frank appeared at the General Assembly Hall of the United Nations where he emceed a show for UN staff members. After being introduced by Sec. Gen. U Thant as 'the great uplifter of spirit', he asked, 'Do you mind if I smoke?' As he lit a cigarette, he said: 'It's essential to relax—with the hot spots around the world ... Vietnam ... Congo...' he paused for an instant—'and Lake Tahoe.' While the audience was still laughing, he asked in a stage whisper: 'Anybody want to buy a gambling casino?' If his gaming licence was revoked, he would be compelled to dispose of his interest in the Sands as well as the Cal-Neva Lodge.

In the fifteen days allotted to Sinatra to answer the charges of the Gaming Board, the issues were extensively reviewed in the nation's press. Louis Sobol, a Sinatra rooter, contended that the Gaming Board was making a scapegoat of Frank: 'What the local gambling fraternity can't understand,' he wrote, 'is all this fuss about Sam Giancana's stay at the Cal-Neva Lodge when it is no secret that he has financial interests in several casinos in Nevada and has occasionally lodged in Las Vegas hotels.' Attorney Greg Bautzer commented: 'I don't think it should be possible that an individual can lose a property right by virtue of having a friend.'

On October 7, hours before the postponed deadline for Sinatra's reply to the Gaming Board's charges, Frank announced that he had decided not to contest the Board's attempt to revoke his licence. It was a startling statement that he handed to reporters. In bars throughout the country, and wherever gambling and fighting men assembled, you could hear the snorts as they read: 'No useful purpose would be served by my devoting my time and energies convincing the Nevada gaming officials that I should be part of their industry.' Frank expressed the hope that the industry would continue to grow and prosper since casinos provide 'wonderful opportunities for established and new performers to present their talents to the public'. He was planning to divest himself of his Nevada holdings and to devote all his time and efforts to the entertainment industry, more specifically, to the fulfilment of new administrative responsibilities he had undertaken at Warner Bros.

The closing chapter came on October 22 when the Nevada Gaming Control Board did vote at a Carson City meeting to revoke Frank's gambling licence. Claiming that he had brought discredit to the legalised gambling industry, the commission gave him until January 5, 1964, to cash in his chips on both his Las Vegas and Lake Tahoe holdings. It was a 'kick in the head', in Frank's lingo, but despite the sinister aura with which some columnists surrounded the incident, it apparently had no effect on Sinatra's popularity.

As surprising as Sinatra's submissive statement was a November postscript written by Robert Ruark, the Scripps-Howard columnist who had blasted Frank for his Havana contact with Lucky Luciano. Admitting that he had been 'unduly severe', he explained that Sinatra had been 'a pigeon at the time because he was serving as a model for the nation's youth'. As for Frank's treatment by the Nevada Gaming Commission, Ruark was emphatic that he had received 'a bum rattle'. In a paragraph full of moral indignation and rambling rhetoric, he wrote: 'For Nevada—by God, Nevada!—to go high and mighty and bust The Voice's licence ... is the absolute Chinese end. There isn't enough real morality in Nevada to make a louse blink if it was all in his eye. Any state that lives off big gambling and its by-products—and I should not like to mention a high order of harlotry—and which has paid court to the likes of Bugsy and Mickey Cohen, living in the glassiest of parlour houses.'

In February 1963 *Playboy* magazine ran a long interview with 'the acknowledged king of showbiz'. Considering the Gaming Board's denunciation of Frank's use of 'vile, obscene and indecent language'—he told Earl Wilson he merely said, 'You're a bunch of bums!'—Sinatra's informed and elegantly phrased replies to searching questions seem strangely incongruous. Of religion, he said: 'I'm for anything that gets you through the night, be it prayer, tranquillisers or a bottle of Jack Daniels. But to me religion is a deeply personal thing in which man and God go it alone together without the witch doctor in the middle ... You can find him anyplace. And if that sounds heretical, my source is pretty good: *Matthew*, 5 to 7. *The Sermon on the Mount* ... Remember, they were men of God who destroyed the educational treasures of Alexandria, who perpetrated the Inquisition in Spain, who burned the witches at Salem ... I'm for decency—period. I'm for anything and everything that bodes love and consideration for my fellow men. But when lip service to some mysterious deity permits bestiality on Wednesday and absolution on Sunday—cash me out ...'

Revealing a wide range of reading, Frank discoursed analytically on topical matters: 'Continuation of cold war preparedness might be more effective to maintain the peace than the dewy-eyed notion of total disarmament' ... 'Our concern with a Sovietised Cuba ninety miles from Key West must be equated with Russian concern over our missile bases surrounding them' ... 'Stop worrying about communism; just get rid of the conditions that nurture it' ... 'A lot of us consider the UN a private club—ours ... I don't happen to think you can kick eight hundred million Chinese under the rug ...' It was clear that the man was conversant with the major socio-political problems of our time, and deeply concerned with questions of morality, decency and the well-being of his fellowmen. One could readily accept Junior's statement, made at the height of the Nevada Gaming Board controversy: 'What I've learned from my father is to abhor prejudice, to respect the other fellow, to be honest and uncompromising with principle. When it comes to principle, my father never wavers.'

Reader reaction to the *Playboy* interview varied from a surprise, 'Is he that intelligent?' to unrestrained admiration of his candour. One reader took his remarks as 'a parody of the banal Liberal' while a Presbyterian minister challenged him to use his $25,000,000 fortune to better the conditions that bred communism. At one point, the *Playboy* interviewer asked: 'Shall we cut this off now, erase the tape and start over?' Frank replied: 'No ... I've thought this way for years, ached to say these things ... I don't want to chicken out ...'

Sinatra was profoundly probing in his comments about the singer's art. Asked as to how he communicated the mood of a song, he replied: 'It's because I get an audience involved, personally involved in a song—because I'm involved myself ... Being an eighteen-carat manic-depressive and having lived a life of violent emotional contradictions, I have an over-acute capacity for sadness as well as elation ... Whatever else has been said about me personally is unimportant. When I sing, I believe. I'm honest ... You can be the most artistically perfect performer in the world, but an audience is like a broad—if you're indifferent, endsville.'

Like many singers of his generation, in 1962–63 Sinatra found himself in a *cul de sac*. He was unable to identify with the songs that communicated to the new generation of record-buyers, and he found that the sound of the forties commanded only a limited audience. Accordingly, he moved in the only direction left open to a singer of his rare reach and vintage. He cut an album of songs with one of the jazz greats, Count Basie.

Musically speaking, the pace and the drive were not new. Sinatra had achieved both in recordings with Nelson Riddle and Billy May. It was an improvisational quality that gave the collaboration a fresh sound. In his search for expressiveness, he had always subordinated other elements to communication and involvement. But he had not had the Basie piano and band, or Sonny Payne's drumming to react to. For the first time, Frank sang as if he were another instrument in a swinging band. He employed all the devices that improvising instrumentalists use to freshen a melody: rhythmic variation, melodic invention, and extensive pitch alteration, like his 'I' in *I Won't Dance* and his 'please' in *Please Be Kind*. Although singing was 'talking words expressively to a background of music'—as he had always said—he was now manipulating melody. It made the difference between pop and jazz singing.

The 'charts' for the sessions were prepared by Neal Hefti, and ex-Basie arranger and the composer of Basie perennials like *Li'l Darlin'*. Recorded in October of 1962 and released early in the following year, the *Sinatra–Basie* album marked the beginning of a collaboration that lasted into 1966.

In addition to the buoyant Basie album, Reprise released two other Sinatra LPs during 1963. *The Concert Sinatra* in June and *Sinatra's Sinatra* in September marked the resumption of a recording partnership, which had been interrupted when Capitol, to which Nelson Riddle was contracted, would not permit him to record with Sinatra. Before the expiration of Riddle's Capitol deal, Sinatra had used six other arrangers: Johnny Mandel, Billy May, Sy Oliver, Don Costa, Neal Hefti and Gordon Jenkins.

The Concert Sinatra, the first Sinatra–Riddle record collaboration since September 1960, was in the nature of a departure for both. Instead of working with the usual swing-string band of twenty to thirty men, Riddle scored for a semi-symphonic instrumentation of fifty. The technical problems of recording the ponderous orchestra may have accounted for the draggy tempi. Although the eight selections were great show tunes, the album was reminiscent in its lack of fire and warmth of *Close To You*, a Capitol album that Frank had made with the Hollywood String Quartet.

Sinatra's Sinatra, the second Riddle collaboration, included eight songs (of twelve) that Frank had previously recorded for Capitol. Record people felt that the contents represented a calculated attempt by Frank to give Reprise buyers what they could until then, get only on Capitol. A triumph commercially, *Sinatra's Sinatra* remained on best-seller charts for almost a year. But a comparison of the original Capitol versions with the Reprise treatments reveals that most of them are done in lower keys. The tempi are brighter, shortening the duration of sustained notes. The orchestra is larger and the arrangements are fuller and adorned with sweeping counter-melodies. Like the man, the voice ages—the breath shortens, the pitch becomes lower, the texture thinner and the vibrato wider. But what disappoints in comparing the new with the old versions is the difference in mood and expressiveness. When they were first sung, *In the Wee Small Hours of the Morning* and *All the Way* et al., expressed intensely experienced feelings. Unless anger and resentment against a business competitor are to be regarded as personal emotions, the songs were external to Sinatra's emotions. Now, Frank was giving a peformance. Good performances they are. But uninvolved they also are.

In May 1963 Clifford Odets, author of *Golden Boy* and

other successful plays, filed a suit asking $752,500 in damages from Sinatra and two of his film production companies. Odets claimed that in May of 1962, he had reached an understanding with MGM on a story, *The Actor*, whereby he was to write the screenplay for $200,000 plus a percentage. In July, when contract terms were to be confirmed in writing, MGM suddenly terminated the deal. Odets held Sinatra responsible. It was his contention that Frank had asked the studio to relinquish its hold on *The Actor* so that he could acquire it and then re-sell it, along with his services, to MGM. Odets had apparently entered into an oral agreement with Frank in October 1962, whereby he would write the screenplay for $75,000 and jointly produce the film with Sinatra. According to Odets, *The Actor* was only one item in an overall package that Sinatra was trying to sell MGM and that was to include other films, a motel and miscellaneous properties. When MGM turned down the package deal, Frank allegedly breached his oral agreement with Odets, causing him to lose out completely on *The Actor*.

The package Frank had been trying to sell MGM, and perhaps Twentieth Century-Fox as well—he had been meeting frequently with Darryl Zanuck—went instead to Warner Bros. The August 1963 deal with Warners was far-reaching and embraced three major items. The first was a merger of Sinatra's Reprise Records with Warner Bros. Records, a venture that left Frank with a third ownership but brought him a sum of money reported to be between one and three million dollars. (For a week or more, Sinatra carried around the advance payment, refusing to deposit it. 'This is what I call real pocket money,' he would say, holding up a Warner Bros. certified cheque. 'I always wanted to have a million bucks in my pocket.') Part two of the deal involved Sinatra as a movie and TV consultant, who would work on package deals under Jack Warner's guidance. The third facet, then still under discussion, was a deal with Sinatra Enterprises to produce feature films, financed and distributed by Warners. The arrangements were to be similar to those governing *Four For Texas*, a joint venture just completed—'Should be re-titled *Four For Iowa*, it's so corny,' a critic wrote later—and *Robin and the Seven Hoods*, slated to roll in October as a joint enterprise of Warner Bros., Sinatra Enterprises, and Claude Productions (Dean Martin). Columnist Louis Sobol, disputing the figures cited by others, claimed that the entire deal involved 'the staggering sum of approximately $10,000,000'.

In October 1963, in the midst of his difficulties with the Nevada Gaming Commission, Sinatra was named a special assistant to President Jack L. Warner. *Variety* used the development as a peg for a front-page headline on 'Capitalists in Greasepaint'. Noting that star-dominated production harked back to the twenties when Douglas Fairbanks, Charles Chaplin, Mary Pickford and others, had founded United Artists, it pointed to Jerry Lewis, Doris Day, Marlon Brando, among other new super stars, who dictated many aspects of film production. Motivation of such power expansion was, of course, fear of confiscation by taxation and the desire to convert productive years into retainable and future-maturing income. In the Sinatra–Warner Bros. development, *Variety* saw 'a further breakthrough whereby key talent may actually dominate the studios'.

In February, after helping his parents celebrate their fiftieth wedding anniversary in New Jersey, Frank flew west to host a pre-press showing of his picture *Come Blow Your Horn* at Palm Springs. The benefit première netted the City of Hope Hospital $15,000. The press première occurred in May, with Paramount flying a hundred reviewers and columnists to Las Vegas from both coasts. An elaborate ritual of news conference, reception, buffet dinner and midnight show, all hosted by Sinatra, was performed to stir critical excitement. The world première at the Radio City Music Hall in June yielded better trade reactions than critical reviews.

'Art it ain't, fun it is,' *Variety* opined. 'It's a gas for the mass, shop-worn and predictable ... but crammed with gags, spiced with sex and played with style and gusto by an attractive cast. For exhibs and Paramount, a promising "horn" of plenty.' The reviews in all the NY papers were adverse, with critics using epithets like 'over blown' (*Journal-American*), 'cinematically elegant pandering' (*Post*), 'Gaseous gags, banal situations and scenic digressions' (*Herald-Tribune*), 'Everything is a stereotype' (*World-Telegram*). The sharpest barbs came from the NY *Times*' Bosley Crowther, who experienced 'a feeling of vapid boredom', felt that 'the extravagant decor matched the utter vulgarity of the clothes' worn by the girls, and smeared the film with the phrase 'bad taste'. Crowther digressed to suggest that bad taste 'seems to be a fault endemic to Mr. Sinatra's films'. Of Frank's performance, he wrote: 'He appears so indifferent and coolly self-satisfied that he moves and talks in the manner of a well-greased mechanical man.' (*Variety* had written: 'Sinatra's jaunty performance is his best in some time. The role is perfectly suited to his rakish image.')

Frank came east for the Radio City première and attended a midnight party in Toots Shor's basement. When he elbowed up to the bar, three matrons swarmed over him. Columnist Frank Farrell reported that 'one grabbed Frankie in a Stanislaus Zybysko headlock' and announced that she had to *hug* him so she could tell her daughter. Another squealed, 'I've been promising myself this for years,' and proceeded to kiss him.

Earl Wilson claimed that it was neither the première nor the party that brought Frank east, but beautiful Jill St. John. Earl maintained that he had heard Frank refer to her 'a couple of times as "my girl"' and that they were 'mutually possessive at Jilly's bar'. Still legally Mrs. Lance Reventlow, Miss St. John told Wilson that one of Sinatra's great charms was his intelligence. Despite the rumours—typical of much film publicity— Jill was the *Come Blow Your Horn* girl as Kim Novak had been *The Man with The Golden Arm* girl, and Juliet Prowse, the *Can-Can* chick.

1963 saw the bust-up of several of Sinatra's close personal relationships. The permanent 'amicable' split between Frank and his longtime partner-manager Hank Sanicola, was followed by a temporary break with Joey Bishop. Presumably, Bishop had made some adverse remark about service at the Cal-Neva Lodge. But it apparently cost him a co-starring role in *Robin and the Seven Hoods*, which began shooting early in 1964. This film brought an estrangement between Sinatra and a man who had been a helpful associate during his early days in Hollywood and who had remained a friend through the years. After being named producer of *Robin*, Gene Kelly entered into pre-production discussions with Sinatra. Kelly thought that there were too many musical numbers. Frank did not agree. Shortly after a long-distance phone conversation in which Kelly felt impelled to suggest that Frank stick to acting and let him stick to producing, a spokesman for Sinatra Productions announced that the two had 'agreed to disagree'. Kelly said: 'I wasn't making any decisions. I was taking orders. Quietly, I like the boys, but friendship isn't always everything in this business.' Sinatra served as producer as well as star of *Robin*.

Two Carnegie Hall charity concerts with Lena Horne led to a breach of relationship. According to musicians, differences developed over who was to appear in the second half of the programme, naturally the more important half. Since the advance announcement indicated that both would appear 'in both portions of the programme', Lena also felt that they should do some duets. Sinatra ruled out duets on the ground that there was not adequate time for rehearsals. Eventually, after some words, it was arranged that Miss Horne would appear alone in Act I and, after a fifteen-minute intermission, Sinatra would solo in Act II. Lena had her revenge, or at least, gave vent to her resentment, when she refused to appear for curtain calls at the end of each evening. Sinatra was obviously troubled because he remained at the microphone calling her name and importuning her to appear. More than a year later, when Frank discussed various singers in *Life*, he referred to Miss Horne as '. . . really a mechanical singer. She gimmicks up a song, makes it too pat.'

Frank was on Stage 22 of the Warner Bros. lot when John Fitzgerald Kennedy was assassinated in Dallas. Some days later, as they were about to film a courtroom scene in *Robin and the Seven Hoods*, Frank rapped for order. 'I have heard some unfortunate remarks on this set about Texas,' he said, over the speaker system. 'This indicates that we are still not unified, despite the terrible happenings of the past week. I beg of you not to generalise about people, or make jokes about anyone from Texas. Or say anything that will keep us divided by malice or hatred. Now is the time for all of us to work together with understanding and temperance—and not do or say anything that will prevent that . . .' The startled silence was followed by applause that echoed in Hollywood newspaper columns.

1963 came to a harrowing close for Frank with an occurrence that claimed the front-page headlines of papers from coast to coast. On a December evening, shortly before he was to go on stage at a Lake Tahoe resort, Frank, Jr., was kidnapped at gunpoint.

XXVIII

'THE WORLD FOR MY SON!'

December 8, 1963, was a Sunday night. About two hours before show-time at Harrah's Lake Tahoe Casino, Frank Sinatra, Jr., sat eating dinner in his motel room with John Foss, a musician associate. Half an hour later, or about 9.30 p.m., there was a knock at Junior's door. 'Room service,' a voice outside said. When Foss opened the door, a man in a brown jacket entered and placed a box on the table. When he turned, there was a blue-steel revolver in his hand. He motioned Junior and Foss to the floor. A second man entered the room, bound Foss' wrists behind his back and gagged him with adhesive tape.

'Get some clothes on!' the gunman ordered Sinatra. Junior donned a blue overcoat over a white T shirt and grey slacks. He was wearing moccasins and was not given time to put on socks. As they were leaving with Junior, who had been blindfolded, one of the desperadoes shouted to Foss: 'Keep your trap shut for ten minutes or we'll kill your friend. If we don't make Sacramento, your pal is dead.' He ripped the phone cord from the wall connection. Foss thought he heard a third man outside say, 'Okay, let's make Sacramento!' Then he heard the clank of auto-tyre chains as the getaway car raced over snow that had been falling steadily for seven hours. After he managed to free his wrists, Foss raced downstairs to the motel switchboard. Officers from a sheriff sub-station at Zephyr Cove, five miles away, were at the motel within minutes. Since kidnapping is a federal offence, the FBI at Reno was advised within an hour of the abduction.

Sinatra, Sr., received the terrifying news of his son's kidnapping at his home in Palm Springs. The phone call came from Tino Barzie, the boy's manager who occupied the room next door at the motel. 'I'll be there as fast as I can fly!' Frank announced. But there were no scheduled flights and the nearest landing strip, at Reno, was sixty miles away over winding mountain roads. Since Frank's private plane was unavailable, a charter had to be arranged. On his arrival at Reno, Frank and an old friend, Washoe County DA William Raggio, immediately took off for Zephyr Cove. But icy mountain roads was impassable, and the car had to turn back. The owner of the Mapes Hotel in Reno made his private suite available for Sinatra's use. Distraught, Frank began the desperate wait for a phone contact with the kidnappers.

In the long, front-page, banner-headline stories and picture-filled pages that greeted newspaper readers on December 9, there was wide speculation as to the motives for the abduction. Apart from the demand for a high cash ransom, the press saw revenge. Columnist Frank Farrell conjectured that it was the result of a desire to hurt Sinatra 'emotionally and financially for some past difference of opinion'. Another writer thought it might be 'an obscure underworld reaction to the Giancana episode, possibly involving an effort to discredit Harrah's, the chief nearby rival to Cal-Neva Lodge for gambling customers'.

'He's been sitting right at the phone for the last sixteen hours, sleepless,' Jim Mahoney, Frank's press agent, reported the next day. 'He jumps when the phone rings.' By then twenty-six FBI men were on the scene to supplement the search efforts of almost a hundred local police. 'You know how emotional he is,' Mahoney said. 'I finally got him to force down some food ... He just sits there looking at the phone. The newsmen here sympathise and they aren't bugging Frank.'

Two other people sat glued to phones. In Beverly Hills, Junior's mother, guarded by FBI agents, waited for a possible call, while at the scene of the snatch, the boy's manager, Tino Barzie, also waited for a possible contact. 'Sinatra is willing to make a deal with the kidnappers,' Mahoney reported, 'and no questions asked.' The direct quote from Sinatra was: 'I'd give the world for my son.'

Frank first heard from the kidnappers on Monday afternoon, nineteen hours after the abduction. A curt call to the Mapes advised him that his son was alive. The following morning, at 9.30 a.m., the abductors put Junior on the phone. Three hours later, Frank was told by 'a firm voice between baritone and tenor' to go to a service station in Carson City, thirty miles south of Reno. By then, several suspects, including two escaped convicts, had been seized. But since John Foss, who had witnessed the abduction, could not identify any of the men, they were absolved of complicity.

Using a basement exit to avoid reporters, Frank drove to

Carson City as instructed. At Ron's Gas Station, a surprised attendant said: 'Someone's been phoning you here. I thought it was a gag.' When Frank finally received the call, he was instructed to go to another gas station. The phone conversation here dealt with the ransom. Frank was also told to go to his ex-wife's Bel-Air home and await further instructions. Returning to Reno, he made arrangements to fly to Los Angeles. To keep the press off his trail, Charles Entratter, a friend who ran the Sands in Las Vegas, called a conference for 8 p.m. that evening at the Mapes. At the conference, Entratter explained that Sinatra had left for LA to comfort his distraught daughter Christina and would return late that night or early the next morning.

By the time Frank arrived at his ex-wife's home, the agreed-upon ransom was ready for delivery. A friend, Alfred Hart, President of the National City Bank of Beverly Hills, had prepared $240,000 in cash. At 9.26 p.m. that night, the phone rang and Sinatra was told to bring the money in an attaché case to a phone booth at LA International Airport. He was instructed to identify himself as 'Patrick Henry' when his caller announced himself as 'John Adams'. The call to a booth in the Western Airlines terminal came at 11.10 p.m. Frank was directed to a service station eight miles away in west LA. At midnight, a third call sent him to a Texaco station, two miles to the north, where he was instructed to leave the attaché case between two parked school buses. The drop was actually made by a Federal agent, Jerome Crowe. The time was 12.30 a.m., Wednesday, December 11. On instructions from 'John Adams', Crowe then went to the airport Marina Hotel and registered as 'Arthur Martell'. Junior was to be released three hours later and given dimes to phone Martell.

Back at Nancy's home, a phone call—apparently not that of 'John Adams'—advised that Junior would be left at an overpass at Mulholland and the San Diego Freeway. Speeding away from the house with the lights of his car out, Frank quickly left pursuing reporters' cars behind. But he was back in thirty-five minutes, despondent and worried that the ransom had been paid in vain. He and the Federal agents with him had not found any trace of Junior. It was then 2.35 a.m. and 'Arthur Martell' still waited at the airport motel.

Not too long after Frank returned to the house from the fruitless search, a private policeman driving along Roscomare

Road in the Bel-Air area heard somebody yell, 'Hey!' Halting his patrol car, he studied the figure of a boy about six feet tall in his rear-view mirror. The youngster was in a topcoat but seemed to be wearing moccasins. Backing his car, the policeman noticed a Halloween-like blindfold dangling around the boy's neck. When the youngster asked to driven to 700 Nimes Road—Nancy Sinatra was a customer of the Bel-Air patrol— the private policeman recognised Junior. Frank's son explained that he had persuaded his guard to release him while the other kidnappers were away picking up the ransom money. He had been dropped, as the call to his mother's home had advised, at Mulholland and the San Diego Freeway. He had walked the two miles to Roscomare Road, hiding in the bushes each time a car approached, for fear that the kidnapper might have had a change of heart and was cruising around looking for him.

Aware of the crowd of reporters camped outside Nancy Sinatra's home, Patrolman Jones took Junior to patrol headquarters. There it was decided to bring him to the house in the boot of the car. When Junior stepped out unharmed, he embraced his mother and urged her not to cry: 'I'm all right.' To his father, he said sheepishly, 'I'm sorry.' Sinatra exclaimed: 'Sorry? Sorry for what?' The time was 3.10 a.m., and young Sinatra had been in captivity for thirty-four hours, virtually all of it in blindfold.

Sinatra, Sr.'s, December 12 birthday party became a celebration of Jr.'s unharmed return. Held at the home of ex-wife Nancy, it brought Nancy, Jr., from New Orleans where Tommy Sands, her husband, was singing. 'Despite the divorce,' Hollywood columnist Mike Connolly commented, 'the Sinatras are the most loyal family I know in a town where loyalty rides a mean seesaw.' The day of the party, the private cop who brought Junior home, was invited to Nancy's house and presented with an envelope containing ten crisp $100 bills by a Sinatra aide.

Behind the scenes, the FBI was feverishly at work. And the surprise break in the case came less than a week after the kidnapping. On Saturday, December 14, three men were arrested and each held in $50,000 bail. FBI director Edgar Hoover announced that the suspects were John W. Irwin, forty-two, a Hollywood house-painter apprehended as he was about to cross the border from Imperial Beach into Tiajuana; Joseph Clyde Amsler, twenty-three, an abalone fisherman of

Plaza del Rey, Calif., picked up in Culver City; and Barry W. Keenan, twenty-three, unemployed, arrested in La Canada, a suburb of LA. In Irwin's possession, police found a ring bearing the initials FS and bills amounting to $47,938. Amsler had $168,927 in his possession, leaving only $23,135 unaccounted for. All three suspects had arrest records but no prison records. It was confirmed that a house in Conoga Park, fewer than twenty miles from Beverly Hills, was where Junior had been held captive. When Sinatra was advised of the arrests, he said 'Thank God, it's over. I'm gonna sleep for a week.'

Newspapers of December 16 reported that young Frank, guarded by the FBI, had moved back to his own apartment. A very mellow Sinatra, Sr., who had returned to the filming of *Robin and the Seven Hoods*, attended the eleventh anniversary celebration of the Sands, accompanied by Jill St. John, whom he had brought in his own plane. 'People have attached too much importance to our dating,' the beauteous Jill avered. 'I adore going out with Frank but I'm not in love with him. He is anything but a wolf. He is a charmer, a ladies' man.' Reporters commented on Sinatra's courteous demeanour at the Sands towards strangers who approached him to congratulate him on his good fortune. Sidney Skolsky noted: 'For years, Frank has staged a running battle with members of the press, photographers and television men. Yet none covering the (kidnap) story would go beyond the facts and propriety to jeopardise the safety of Frank, Jr.' Murray Schumach, the NY *Times*' Hollywood correspondent, thought that Frank had been so badly hurt by the publicity attending the surrender of his Nevada gambling licence that he 'needed the public sympathy aroused by the abduction of his son'. On his return to Harrah's, young Sinatra's name, originally at the bottom of the list of performers, was moved way up on the marquee, directly under the top-billed Dorsey band.

The trial of the kidnappers in US District Court of LA began on February 10 and went to the jury on March 6, 1964. In opening statements and through nearly four weeks of testimony, the attorneys for the defence tried to establish that the kidnapping was engineered for publicity purposes. Irwin's counsel characterised the abduction as 'an advertising scheme', conceived by young Sinatra so that 'he might make the ladies swoon like papa'. Amsler's attorney pointed to a vacant seat in the courtroom and claimed that it was reserved for 'the financier who financed this whole thing'. Counsel for Barry Keenan, who later admitted that the scheme was his, contended that young Sinatra 'co-operated or consented to his taking away', and argued that the issue is 'not who committed the crime but was a crime committed?'

Self-possessed in two appearances on the witness stand, Junior admitted to specific acts of co-operation. Yes, he had told his abductors that he would help them through the road-block and he had reclined in the back seat as if he had passed out from too much partying. Yes, he had suggested the removal of the signet ring bearing his initials; this was found on Irwin. Yes, he had made no move to escape even though he was not bound. Yes, he had guided captor Irwin, who was very kind to him, to the spot where he was dropped. But he denied firmly that the kidnapping was a publicity stunt or hoax. Asked why he had co-operated, he said : 'I didn't want to get killed.'

Apparently, Junior's cool common sense had been helpful to the FBI. Although he had been blindfolded throughout the ordeal, he had occasionally seen things through a small opening at the bottom of the blindfold. As he was being fed a hamburger, he had spotted the name and address of a diner on a wrapper. With this information, which he had memorised, the FBI had been able to pinpoint within blocks the house where he had been held captive.

Reporters who had hoped for fireworks when Frank, Sr., appeared on the stand, were largely disappointed. Although Mrs. Gladys T. Roote, Irwin's attorney, made a special point of needling Sinatra and used finger-prodding routines, Frank contained himself. The most that Mrs. Roote could elicit with her demands that he answer 'Yes or no' was a strained, caustic : 'No, dear !'

The prosecution produced a number of valuable witnesses. One was a rock 'n' roll singer, Dennis Torrence, described as Irwin's best friend, who at first denied knowing of the plot, but later returned to confess that he had had advance knowledge of the kidnap scheme. Torrence stated that he had received, but had returned, $25,000 of the ransom money. Ronald T. Bray, Jr., twenty-one, a friend of Barry Keenan, testified that the latter had on three occasions, beginning in October 1961, tried to draw him into the plot. A third corroboration came from a couple who were friends of both Amsler and Keenan. The husband, Dennis Gray, testified that the two kidnappers had played football with the ransom money in his home, and, as a gag, had walked through it in their bare feet. Mrs. Theresa Gray confirmed her husband's damaging testimony, punctuating her replies with giggles which, she explained, she was powerless to prevent when she became nervous. A letter written by Barry Keenan to his family was a telling piece of evidence: he wanted them to know of the plan to kidnap Junior for ransom in case he was captured or killed.

Convicted of the kidnapping, the trio were sentenced on Friday, March 13: Amsler and Keenan to life imprisonment plus seventy-five years; Irwin, who had been kind to Junior, to sixteen years and eight months. Irwin was in effect eligible for immediate parole. The sentences of the other two technically set the stage for psychiatric analysis and reduced terms. On July 17, in what was termed 'a sentence of hope', Federal District Judge William Este reduced the prison terms of Amsler and Keenan to twenty-four years and five months, making them likewise eligible for immediate parole. US attorney Sheridan argued against the drastic reduction, not only because of the crime itself, but because of 'the crime of the trial: that for the rest of a young man's life, Sinatra, Jr., will have the shadow over him that he really pulled off a publicity hoax'. The judge was apparently swayed, however, by the return, unharmed, of young Sinatra and of almost all of the ransom money.

A British judge later displayed great concern over the possible injury suffered by young Sinatra. Ruling on a libel suit brought by Jr. and Sr. against a TV panel show, where it had been claimed that the kidnapping was a publicity stunt, High Court Judge Sir Frederick Lawton awarded large damages 'to mark the gravity of the libel'. Frank announced that the money would go to the Great Britain Sunshine Home for Blind Babies.

Late in January, the Bing Crosby Golf Tourney at Pebble Beach witnessed some unexpected 'entertainment'. On a Saturday morning, Frank and Dean Martin entered the Lodge in search of food. A clerk explained that the kitchen did not open until later. At Frank's insistence, the President of Del

Monte properties was hurriedly summoned. Richard Osborne arrived with a bottle of champagne. Later, nursing a cut over one eye, Osborne said with a smile: 'I guess I over-estimated Sinatra's sense of humour.'

In mid-February, Frank allowed George Jessell to use his luxurious NY apartment, including his ample stock of liquor, staff, chauffeured limousine, and Sherle Wagner 'status' bathroom with the $250 taps. After Jessel was comfortably settled, Frank received a wire: 'What about spending money?'

By then, Frank was on his way to Tokyo to interview Oriental actors for *None But the Brave*, a film he was producing as well as directing. 'My desire to direct became acute about five years ago,' he said. When the film was completed, he observed: 'Directing's my favourite medium. It keeps me busier and I like that. I also like the sense of responsibility.' And he told of how he found himself working out problems even in his sleep. *Time* found 'the careless carouser and muscular seducer' a changed man. It noted that The Clan was dispersed and even the vocabulary had changed. Gone were 'dullsville' and 'cloudsville' and other *ville*s, and even the all-purpose 'clyde' had been superseded by an all-purpose 'bird.'

By the end of April, Sinatra was in Kauai, one of the smaller Hawaiian islands, shooting the film which, a wag suggested, in view of Sinatra's penchant for number titles—*Ocean's Eleven, Sergeants Three, Four for Texas, Robin and the Seven Hoods* —should be spelled *O But the Brave.* During the shooting, he occupied a $2,000 a month, beachfront house, redecorated by the owner in Frank's favourite colour, orange. On May 10 he was wading in the surf of Wailua Bay, together with the wife of his executive producer and two friends, when a giant wave suddenly welled up and engulfed all four. In a matter of seconds, the riptide had dragged Mrs. Howard Koch about fifty yards and Sinatra about a hundred yards from shore. While one friend fought his way back through the surf and ran for help, the other, actor Brad Dexter, swam out to Frank. 'I can hear you,' Frank cried, who was by then suffering from anoxia, 'but I can't see you.' As a beachfront neighbour, who had heard the cries for help, plunged into the sea with a surfboard, guests of the nearby Coco Palms Hotel summoned the local fire department. Mrs. Koch was quickly pulled in. But Frank was close to losing his battle against the powerful currents when County Supervisor Louis Gonsalves, who swam out, helped him on to the neighbour's surfboard. The ordeal was not yet over. The men and the surfboard continued to be dragged out to sea until a rope was thrown to them. After he received artificial respiration, Frank was carted to his cottage on a stretcher.

'Another couple of minutes,' he said, 'and I wouldn't have made it.' Later he chirped: 'Just got a little water on my bird.' Joey Bishop telegraphed: 'You must have forgotten who you are. You could have walked out on those waves.'

Before he left Kauai, Frank donated a fifteen-foot motorboat to the county for use in rescue work. The following year, Brad Dexter the actor credited with risking his life to save Sinatra, was appointed by Frank to an executive post in his film production set-up at Warner Bros.

With the editing of *None But the Brave* completed in July, Frank headed for Tel-Aviv, Paris and Stockholm. It was the Floyd Patterson–Eddie Machen heavyweight bout that attracted him to Sweden's capital city. But Frank never made the fight. Although he had apparently been in good health during a New York stopover, he collapsed in Stockholm. 'Overstrain' was the explanation of surprised members of his entourage. Dorothy Kilgallen cannily attributed his sudden incapacity to a statement made by Juliet Prowse. According to Miss Kilgallen, the leggy Juliet had said in an interview: 'I still love Frank Sinatra. But I love him as a widow loves her husband. Sinatra is dead, a closed chapter in my life.' Kilgallen observed: 'That's enough to depress even a less sensitive soul than Frank.'

From Stockholm Frank went to Tel-Aviv for the dedication of the Frank Sinatra Youth Centre at Nazareth. The building cost over $150,000 and was intended as an intercommunity home for Jewish and Arab youth. Most of the money had been contributed by Frank two years earlier during his tour for the world's underprivileged children.

Arriving in Paris in a playful mood, Frank upset the cosmopolitan city with his antics. It was too early for Bastille Day (July 14) and too late for Independence Day. But as Frank and entourage went night-clubbing, they exploded cherry-bombs in gay abandon. One French newswoman asked: 'Is that a sport for middle-aged men?' The Paris papers reported that he was in the city with a gang of 'Chicago gorillas'.

Unpublicised in the USA until after the well-publicised cruise with Mia Farrow was a nautical 'adventure' off the shores of Monaco. The scene was a rented yacht, the *Trenora*. One night when a Sinatra shindig was in full swing, a mock battle broke out on the floodlit quarterdeck. Guests used food, glassware and crockery as ammunition. Occupants of neighbouring yachts who protested at the noise were at first appeased with gifts of champagne but later subjected to the same brickbats, as the high-spirited revellers on the *Trenora*. Since bizarre cut-ups of the European jet set are hardly a novelty on the Cote d'Azur, the all-night throwing party drew only limited press attention. It was recalled, however, after Sinatra's New England cruise because *beano*, or throwing things, had caught on and was then the widely-touted, new in-game.

The shooting of *Von Ryan's Express*, which took Frank to Rome for August and September, was uneventful except for minor brushes with Italian freelance photographers. In fact, when he first arrived in the Italian capital, Frank allowed the *papparazzi* to take all the shots they wanted. But then he retired with his thirty-two pieces of luggage, four bodyguards and entourage to an eighteen-room villa rented for him by Twentieth Century-Fox. The villa grounds included ten fountains, stables, indoor and outdoor swimming pools, landing strip for helicopter and most important of all, a ten-foot wall. Before his arrival, columnists tried to make something out of the presence in Rome of Ava Gardner. According to a story that went the rounds, the photographers made a collective offer of 160,000 lire if Frank would pose with her; Frank reportedly made a counter offer: double the money for free swings at several of the *papparazzi*.

En route to Rome, Frank had stopped in NY for the première of *Robin and the Seven Hoods*. Bosley Crowther performed his customary surgery, starting with the title, which he thought 'just too cunning'. Characterising it as a 'minor musical whimsey', he found it 'an artless and obvious film' with some 'mildly amusing by-play' and 'a few songs of no distinction'. Of Frank's performance, he wrote: 'The usual Sinatra arrogance is subdued. It is about as humble and harmless as a romp with the Keystone Cops.' The music trade-papers, however, found the Cahn–Van Heusen score exciting and heard a top song in *Chicago—My Kind of Town*. It not only proved one of Frank's most fetching numbers at Newport in 1965, but yielded a hit disc for Jack Jones.

Columnist Bill Slocum of the NY *Journal-American*, who ran into Frank at Toots Shor's, noted that Sinatra had lost his lean and hungry look by a full 15 pounds—Von Ryan's uniform did bulge at the midriff—and his curly locks by a full $33\frac{1}{3}$ per cent. As for his fatal charm, Slocum told of two sweet things who spotted Frank. 'My lord, honey,' one erupted, 'isn't that Frank Sinatra?' Her companion nodded: 'Yes, and isn't he sure bald.' The first girl, lost in her dream world, sighed: 'Yeah. He's bald. But ain't it gorgeous on him!'

At Jilly's afterwards, comic Marty Allen sneaked up behind Frank and dropped a tray full of crockery. As Sinatra half-jumped out of his chair, Allen demanded: 'Now, do I get a role in your next film?' Frank was seated in a blue armchair, which was removed immediately after The King, as owner Jilly Rizzo called him, left town; the chair was stored in the basement until Frank returned to use it. 'To have him in the room,' Jilly told an *Esquire* writer, 'you know, like you say a person purifies the room, you know what I mean? So I say to him, "Frank, you purify the goddam room!"'

In early September, Frank was in Spain shooting *Von Ryan's Express*. One day, he paused in Torremolinos, some distance from Madrid, for some food. While he was eating, a photographer from a Madrid paper asked him to sit for some pictures with a Cuban actress. Frank declined. An argument ensued. The girl later claimed that Frank pushed her. She threw her drink at him, cutting him slightly on the face. Employees of the hotel-restaurant intervened. The photographer ran to the police, allegedly pursued by a member of Frank's entourage. Later that day, the police came to Frank's hotel and invited him to appear at Malaga, the provincial capital ten miles away, to make a statement. He declined, explaining that shooting cost $25,000 a day. The police seized a member of the cast, and allegedly held him incommunicado for hours without food or drink. Several dozen police soon appeared in Frank's hotel lobby, where they remained presumably to prevent his sudden departure. After several conversations with US Ambassador Robert F. Woodward, Frank reluctantly went to the Malaga police station. After a long wait, he was told that the charges were disturbing the peace and disobeying police orders. There was no hearing or trial. Rather than become involved in lengthy proceedings, he paid the fine of 25,000 pesetas, or $416.

In 1964 Frank's recording activities (forty-three songs in a dozen sessions) became less a personal expression than a re-action to professional and business demands. At midyear he cut an album of songs from *Robin and the Seven Hoods*. Later, he participated in sessions of a Repertory Theatre Series, launched by him to add *Guys and Dolls*, *Kiss Me Kate* and other show scores to the Reprise catalogue; also to make use of artists on the label, who were unable to penetrate the singles market. At the end of the year, he put together a best-selling Christmas package, in which he, Crosby and Fred Waring re-corded the best-loved songs of the Yuletide season.

Frank also experimented with a more commercial approach to the singles market. His magnificent ballad recording *Softly As I Leave You*, which had delicate rock 'n' roll triplets in the background, climbed on best-seller charts, but only into the low 20s. When Dean Martin came up with a No. 1 record in *Everybody Loves Somebody*, Frank tried with *Somewhere in Your Heart*, a disc that embodied the sing-a-long, country sound cum heavy afterbeat of Dino's hit. It was neither good Sinatra nor a good market item.

More typical of the mature Sinatra was a second LP he recorded with the Count Basie band. The arrangements for *It Might As Well Be Swing* were the work of Quincy Jones, who thereafter frequently conducted for Frank in personal appear-ances. Jones had first met Sinatra casually at a benefit gala in Monte Carlo in 1958. Six years later, on a May Day in NY, Jones, who had meanwhile become an A & R executive at Mercury Records, received a call from Hawaii. Sinatra, who was then directing *None But the Brave*, came on the phone with a casual, 'Come on over here.' Quincy picked up Bill Miller, Frank's accompanist, in Hollywood, and the two flew to Kauai to plan the new LP. The decision to add strings to the Basie band was made in Hollywood, where the second meeting of the giants became record history on June 8 and 9. Even though it became a Spotlight Pick in *Billboard* and the trade-paper review characterised it as 'a gasser ... with Sinatra swinging at his best', the LP seems to lack the fire and hip beat of the first meeting of Frank and Splank, as Basie is known among musicians. Whether the addition of strings diminished the Basie drive, or Frank was just too tired—recording as he did after full days on a movie stage—*It Might As Well Be Swing* just doesn't swing. Nevertheless, by October it had climbed into the No. 13 slot on best-seller charts, after which it gently drifted downward.

Not too long afterwards, Frank tried the first of what developed into a two-year series of personal appearances with the Basie band. On Thanksgiving night, the night before the black-tie opening at the Sands, the general public was excluded as Sinatra and Basie tried their new act on an invitation audience of celebrities and press people. Frank concluded the introduction of luminaries by turning to a ringside table at which Frank, Jr., Nancy, Jr. and Sr. sat—'And now, the mother of my three children, Mrs. Nancy Sinatra.'

Columbus Day of October 1964 was a significant anniversary for Frank. Twenty years earlier, he had made his most riotous stand at the NY Paramount. Two months short of the anniversary, a hand-printed note appeared on the glass doors of the famous theatre. It read: 'Paramount Theatre/ Closed/ Till Further Notice.' The entertainment landmark was entangled in the snarled, financial affairs of a bankrupt real estate firm. But actually the passing of the Paramount had been foreshadowed by the closing of other giant movie palaces of the '30s, by the conversion of several midtown Loew's movie houses into hotels, and by the transformation of many, smaller Manhattan movie theatres and some legitimate theatres into TV studios. Although the Paramount had abandoned regular stage shows in 1952, Sinatra and Dorsey had played a brief, nostalgic reunion at the theatre in 1956. The following year, a Rock 'n' Roll Show, emcee'd by the high priest of the movement, disc jockey Alan Freed, proved as riotous as the mêlées of Frank's early days. But the days of the Paramount, which had been to the Big Band and Big Ballad eras what the Palace had once been to vaudeville, were inescapably numbered. Its shuttering in 1964 was a reminder of the many changes in public taste that Sinatra had survived, and a silent testimonial to his power as a showman.

Early in November, a columnist on the LA *Herald-Examiner* phoned a young actress of the night-time TV soap-opera *Peyton Place* to inquire about rumours of a romance with Sinatra. 'I've been out with Frank a few times,' Mia Farrow told Harrison Carrol, 'but the rumours are silly. We are discussing the possibility of my playing a role in his picture *Community Property*. If I do, I'll play his daughter.'

As the year of *Goldfinger* came to a close, Sheilah Graham advised her readers that Mia would not play the daughter in *Community Property*, later re-titled *Marriage on the Rocks* 'So this would eliminate the word "business" from Mia's dates with Frank,' Sheilah wrote. 'At least everyone now knows where they stand.'

XXIX

SEPTEMBER OF MY YEARS

Of Sinatra's massive press in 1965, a *New Yorker* writer, in an unrelated article on golf, was moved to comment: 'The numerous newspaper and magazine stories about Frank Sinatra this past summer, both before and after the famous cruise (with Miss Farrow), informed us that the singer-actor was enjoying not merely a mild renaissance as a public idol but a degree of popularity that was actually higher than at any previous stage of his career.' 1965, a year of turnabouts and achievements in areas where success had eluded him previously, marked Frank's fiftieth birthday and his twenty-fifth year in show business.

A major source of the year's heavy press was, of course, his courtship of Mia Farrow. He had met the young actress on the Twentieth Century-Fox lot in October 1964. She was working in the TV serial *Peyton Place* and he was acting in *Von Ryan's Express* on a neighbouring set. One day, she came over to the *Express* set to see John Leyton, a young English actor with whom she was then romantically linked. Recently, she has described the meeting as follows: 'I had some time off, and I was fooling around the *Von Ryan's* set, climbing up in the rafters. I remember that Edward Mulhare was there, and Frank was climbing out of one of the freight cars ... I was embarrassed and wanted to get out of their way ... But they didn't say anything. I had a friend on the set, and he'd let me ride the motorcycles and little cars. I saw Frank again, and it got to "Hello, Mr. Sinatra" ... He asked me to a screening of one of his pictures, and of course I went. I liked him instantly. He rings true. He is what he is...'

It was Sheilah Graham who first apprised the public of a burgeoning romance. On November 30, the night after Miss Graham had watched the shooting of a *Peyton Place* segment, she disclosed that Miss Farrow had received a call on the set from Mr. Sinatra. Although Frank's interest in the young actress was dismissed by his office as talk about a picture, the talks lengthened into weekends at his Palm Springs hacienda. While they dined at Ruby's during their desert weekends, they made their first public appearance in Hollywood at a Share charity luncheon in the spring of 1965. When Maureen O'Sullivan, Mia's mother, was first interviewed regarding rumours of a possible merger, she said impulsively: 'Marry Mia? It would make better sense if he married me.' Joe E. Lewis quipped: 'Frank's going with a girl of nineteen. I couldn't marry such a young girl. I'd want somebody very mature ... a girl of twenty-two or twenty-three.' Comic Jack E. Leonard praised Sinatra's choice of Mia because she didn't drink or smoke. 'She's still teething,' he explained. Dean Martin phoned Frank to deny that he had sent a wire bearing his signature, which read: 'I have a case of Scotch in the house that's older than Mia Farrow.'

Earl Wilson first advised the public that Miss Farrow was to be Sinatra's companion on a month-long cruise, chaperoned by such solid members of the Hollywood Establishment as Roz Russell and husband, Claudette Colbert and husband and producer Bill Goetz and wife. The July 31 pre-sailing party at Voisin in NY for crew and chaperones was only a column item, as was the decision of the producer of TV's *Peyton Place* to put Allison Mackenzie, the character played by Miss Farrow, in a coma for six weeks.

But on August 5 when the *Southern Breeze*, the 168-ft. yacht chartered by Sinatra at $2,000 a day, sailed from Newport, RI, the NY papers erupted with front-page headlines: SINATRA AND MIA SAILING TO ALTAR? (*Daily News*) ARE THEY OR AREN'T THEY? (*Journal-American*). The following day, Frank advised that he had had a slew of horror films sent to the yacht since their movements on shore at Edgartown, Mass., had caused such a furore.

On Saturday, August 7, the *Southern Breeze* was anchored off Hyannis Port. Accompanied by Miss Russell and Miss Colbert, Sinatra paid a visit to ailing former Ambassador Joseph P. Kennedy. The press gave scant notice to this call. But late that afternoon, an unidentified woman boarded the Sinatra yacht, clad in white sneakers, white pants, black sweater and white kerchief. The following day's papers carried both pictures and headlines: JACKIE SEES FRANKIE AND HIS DREAMBOAT (*Daily News*). The immediate public reaction was disbelief and shock. It did not seem possible that the widow of the country's President had lent her presence to the sensation-soaked Cape Cod romance. The denials and retractions came quickly. While readers were still studying photographs in August 9's morning papers, the NY *World-Telegram* announced in an early afternoon edition: IT'S ALL A MISTAKE JACKIE KENNEDY DENIES VISITING SINATRA YACHT. 'I looked right in her face,' said the AP photographer who had taken shots from a press launch, 'and (through the binoculars) I thought it was Jackie.' Voicing regret for the mistaken identification, papers speculated that the visitor had probably been Pat Lawford.

The worst of the over-extended coverage came the following day through a mishap, not a mistake. In the pre-dawn hours of Tuesday, August 10, two crewmen who had spent the evening on shore and missed the last launch, tried to return to the yacht in a dinghy. Too small to accommodate the crewmen and their two waitress companions, the dinghy capsized in the choppy, fog-shrouded waters. Strong, sea-going currents made it easier to swim to the yacht than to transact the four hundred yards to shore. When the two girls reached the *Southern Breeze*, a launch returned immediately to the capsized dinghy. Only one man was found bobbing in the water. An instant alarm brought out a Coast Guard Cutter, two patrol boats, a helicopter and an amphibious plane. It was to no avail. The other man could not be found.

Tuesday's papers blazoned the accident across their front pages. The drowned seaman was identified as third-mate Robert Goldfarb, twenty-three, of New Rochelle, NY. As the two girls disclosed that Goldfarb had sacrificed his life by giving the only preserver to his fellow crew-member who could not swim, the *Journal-American* focused on the collapse and bitterness of the widow, Goldfarb's bride of less than a year, and on the anger of his father, both of whom claimed that they had first heard the shocking news on a radio broadcast. 'The tragic accident cast a pall of gloom,' other papers reported, 'over what had been a gay cruise.' By mid-afternoon, the *Southern Breeze* was steaming back towards Long Island, as an upset Sinatra called the sail off. Only after the yacht was anchored in the Hudson River did a reporter elicit from Frank the definite statement that he was 'still single'.

On Friday, August 13, as The Beatles were boisterously welcomed in NY and Negro comedian Dick Gregory was shot during the rioting of Watts ghetto Negroes in Los Angeles, the papers gave the SINATRA MYSTERY, in the *Journal-American*'s phrase, another front-page blast. A visit paid by the drowned man's family to the *Southern Breeze* was used by the press to stir sympathy for the family at Sinatra's expense.

On Saturday, nine days after the torrent of printer's ink had begun gushing, the press was silent about the Sinatra–Farrow idyll. Though Frank had employed bodyguards and at one point stationed private policemen in boats to keep newsmen and sightseers away from the yacht, the cruise had been, in *Time*'s words, 'probably the most closely watched since Cleopatra floated down the Nile to meet Mark Antony'.

Running through the river of print were references to sundry professional endeavours, not only of the principals, but even of secondary figures. *The Subject Was Roses*, the Broadway play in which Maureen O'Sullivan was replacing the female lead, received its share of coverage. *Marriage on the Rocks*, completed by Sinatra before the boat-ride, attracted much attention because of a curious parallel between the film and the real-life romance: when Deborah Kerr, Sinatra's ex-wife in the movie, meets a young dancer, whom he is romancing, she tells the girl, 'Okay, I'll buy you wedding presents—a crib for you, an oxygen tent for him.' Sinatra's forthcoming film *Assault on a Queen* came in for frequent mentions, since producer Bill Goetz was on board and the picture dealt with the hi-jacking of a ship in mid-ocean. *Von Ryan's Express*, then in its première run, became a high-flyer with the flood of publicity. Had a group of press agents put their heads together to find a peg for publicising various clients and their vehicles, they could hardly have devised a more glamorous gimmick than the cruise of the *Southern Breeze*. Of course, it was young

Miss Farrow who reaped the windfall. In October she was on the cover of *Look*, and by the end of the year, her asking price for film work had zoomed to $100,000 a picture.

Renewed coverage of Frank and Mia began after only three days of quiet. On Monday night, August 16, they went to see *The Roar of Greasepaint—The Smell of the Crowd*. At the intermission, they left, ostensibly because they were bothered by an aggressive group of inquiring photographers. Assisted by bodyguards, they forced their way out to a private chauffeured limousine. The small incident rated large pictures and space in three afternoon papers.

Early in September, after Frank took Mia for a home-cooked meal to his parents' home in Fort Lee, NJ, Dorothy Kilgallen wrote: 'The most cynical sideliners in Frank Sinatra's NY camp are beginning to admit "there may be something after all" to his romance with Mia Farrow. They think "the kid" gets along well with him, better than any girl he's dated in the last twenty years...' The following day, in the same paper, Walter Winchell began his column: 'Frank Sinatra's inner circle now will bet that he has no plans (and never did have) to marry Mia Farrow. "This whole thing was manufactured by newspaper people!"' In December, Jack O'Brian, who had succeeded the recently demised Miss Kilgallen as the *Voice of Broadway*, announced that the guessing game was still on.

Three Sinatra films had their premières during 1965. In February it was *None But the Brave*, directed by Frank, who also was its star and producer. Granting that the story was competently filmed, Rose Pelswick of the NY *Journal-American* voiced a majority opinion that 'so many of the customary Hollywood war film clichés turn up in the acting and handling that the result is routine and predictable'. Kevin Thomas, who shared the enthusiasm of most critics for Sinatra's maiden directorial effort, was unenthusiastic about some members of the cast. 'It's too bad,' he wrote in the LA *Times*, 'that Sinatra didn't avoid nepotism ... Son-in-law Tommy Sands is hopelessly hammy as a greenhorn lieutenant'. Nine months after his putdown appeared, Thomas was attacked in his office by Sands and suffered a bloody nose and bruised jaw. By then, Sands was four-months divorced from Nancy Sinatra. Asked why Sands had waited from February to November to vent his anger, Thomas mused: 'I guess he's a slow reader.'

Sinatra spoke of directing shortly after the release of *None But the Brave*: 'I found out that it was in some ways tougher than I had thought. The director has so many things to worry about—pace, wardrobe, the performances ... Next time I won't try to perform when I direct...' To Peter Bart, the NY *Times*' Hollywood correspondent, he confided that 'Sinatra the star will become Sinatra the picture-maker'. Confessing that he was 'well aware of the shortcomings of some of my recent pictures,' he added, 'I guess the trouble has been that at the time, nothing better seemed to be available. It all boils down to material.'

Von Ryan's Express, another World War II film and Sinatra's second release of the year, fared better. Rose Pelswick's verdict that it was exciting melodrama, replete with action and suspense, was seconded by most reviewers. When the well-directed Mark Robson production was released late in June, the popular guessing game among columnists was whether Frank would bring Mia or his leading lady to the première. Frank brought neither. Instead, he attended in the company of his daughters, Tina and Nancy. 'Say what you will—and think what you will about this man Sinatra,' columnist Louis Sobol wrote, 'but his name has become the magic box-office lure. The fact that he was to attend last night's première made tickets to the event the hottest item on the market—just as the fact that he was to be on the Soupy Sales TV session Tuesday night brought such a demand for seats that the producers decided to close the session to the public altogether...'

Of Frank's three film releases in 1965, *Marriage on the Rocks* fared best at the box-office and worst with the press. Opening in New York during a newspaper strike, the domestic comedy of mixed-up divorces was panned by the only two reviewers in action. Archer Winsten of the NY *Post* found it 'well below the best Sinatra–Martin movie levels and almost out of sight of Deborah Kerr's best'. And the NY *Herald-Tribune*'s Judith Crist characterised the Cy Howard script as 'a fumbling attempt at risqué sophistication', and observed that what looked like a sparkling cocktail came up 'flat, insipid and watery'—a 'mediocrity-on-the-rocks'. A few days later, *The New Yorker* admired Sinatra's playing of his 'uncannily confident self' but dismissed the film as a 'long, coarse and nearly always unfunny comedy'. (A weird aftermath of the picture occurred early in 1966 when Sinatra, who had bought a home in Acapulco and had contributed immensely to Mexican children's charities, was suddenly barred from visiting the country. The authorities were apparently offended by the role of a comical divorce judge played by Cesar Romero, although some columnists claimed that they were troubled by Frank's gambling interests.)

By year end, Sinatra was at work on a new film, the plot of which emphasised a recurrent motif in his movie-making. In *Ocean's Eleven* he had, with a group of war buddies, held up five Las Vegas casinos. In *Robin and the Seven Hoods*, he had led a gang of Chicago crooks, albeit humanitarian crooks. And in *Von Ryan's Express*, he had directed the theft of a railroad train. Now, in *Assault on a Queen* he was to stage a hold-up of the ocean-going liner, *Queen Mary* from a submarine. An old friend of Sinatra's commented: 'You know Frank is acting out all the frustrations of his Hoboken youth when he wanted to be a hood, and couldn't make it or was stymied by his smart parents. He's gone from casinos to ocean liners? What's he gonna steal next?'

Sinatra's public appearances in 1965 were remarkably successful, even considering the fantastic aspects of his career. Almost at the very moment that he was giving interviews about phasing out his work as a performer, he embarked on a singing tour with Count Basie that took him through six major cities. It was the first time in twenty years that he had gone out with a band. Try-out for the run was at the Kiel Opera House in St. Louis in a benefit for a convict rehabilitation centre. Frank brought along Sammy Davis, Trini Lopez, Dean Martin and Johnny Carson, as well as the Basie Band, and drew a capacity crowd that contributed more than $300,000 to the charity. The first non-charity performance of the tour came at the Newport Jazz Festival.

I have attended these annual July 4 leviathan presentations since their inception in 1955. There have been many memorable moments like the 'discovery' of trumpeter Miles Davis in 1955 and the first appearance of Dave Brubeck in 1958. No one individual so electrified and literally possessed the Festival as did Sinatra in 1965.

Producer George Wein's booking of Frank did not win unqualified approval. Long and loud were the discussions among jazz purists before and after Sinatra's appearance as to whether he really was a jazz singer. Whitney Balliett of *The New Yorker*, who felt that the festival's jazz orientation was growing thin in several areas, voiced the attitude of the opposition. 'Sunday evening was a circus,' he wrote. 'After a dozen desultory Count Basie numbers, Sinatra paraded onstage with his own drummer, his own trumpet player—Harry (One-Note) Edison—and his own arrangements. Basie put on a pair of businessman's glasses and started reading his part, and Sinatra sang *Get Me to the Church on Time*. Seven or eight vocals later Sinatra paused, got himself a cup of tea from the piano, and sipping it stage centre, delivered a monologue made up of Bob Hope gags larded with plugs for a Las Vegas hotel that Sinatra has an interest in, recent and forthcoming Sinatra movies and Dean Martin and Sammy Davis. Then he replaced his teacup, sang ten more songs and waved good-bye. He was airborne (he had also arrived by helicopter) before the Basie band, struggling to regain its soul, had finished a concluding *One O'Clock Jump*.'

Variety, on the other hand, termed the 1965 Newport bash 'Sinatra's festival', characterised his appearance as an 'overpowering hour-long vocal assault', and noted that he had left to 'the biggest ovation'. Conceding that what he offered might not have been jazz, it contended that he had added a new dimension to the festival by supplying something no other artist could offer: 'Glamour showmanship—his own brand of casual hipness.' In *Variety*'s view, the $40,000 or so which he earned for an hour of vocalising 'was worth every penny'. The management kept $38,952 over and above his take, and the overall attendance at the festival, which had been slipping, rose to 40,000, an increase of 6,000 over the previous year.

While Sinatra's appearance helped build an audience for the purer jazz performers at the four-day fete, he was the conversation piece of the entire proceedings. At previous festivals, the last evening had always been the least attended. Frank's Sunday night concert was not only the best attended, but it was the first sell-out of the fete.

From Newport, Frank went to Forest Hills for his first major appearance in NY since 1952, and packed the West Side Tennis Club Stadium for three sell-out nights. The audience was made up mostly of middle-aged matrons whose reactions were almost as voluble as their teenage daughters' at a Beatles' concert. The three performances hit a record gross of $271,886. Next stop was Cobo Hall in Detroit for a one-night gate of $74,580. In Baltimore, the cash register of the Civic Auditorium rang up $78,094, and two shows at McCormick Place in Chicago registered $79,359. All told, the Sinatra–Basie box-office showed a whopping gross of $582,871, or an average of $72,859 per hour of singing.

Regardless of purist questioning of Sinatra's status as a jazz singer, his 'dazzling concert tour with the Basie Band', as *Playboy* characterised it, must have figured in the minds of its readers. Sinatra was not only chose Male Vocalist in its regular poll, as he had been annually from 1959 on, but in its newly-established Playboy Jazz Hall of Fame, he became one of the three initial occupants. His vote was greater than that of pianist Dave Brubeck and second only to pioneer jazz show-man Louis Armstrong.

Musically, 1965 continued as a year of bushy-headed teen-agers, with the mop-haired Beatles still setting the pace in a singles record market full of Rolling Stones, Animals and Byrds. The airwaves vibrated not only with the *Liverpool Sound*, and *Mersey Beat* (British derivative of Negro rhythm and blues), but the *Detroit Sound* (Negro gospel and blues in a white, pop frame). Bob Dylan, recognised as the gifted originator of a new type of song known as *folk rock* or protest rock, was booed at the Newport Folk Festival by folk purists, outraged because he added electric guitars, a screaming electric organ and a thumping, electric Fender bass to his folk ruminations: nevertheless, the amalgam yielded his biggest seller in *Like a Rolling Stone*. Meanwhile, Sonny and Cher, new American teenage idols, whose clothes on and offstage consisted of bell-bottom slacks with bright, wide, horizontal stripes (Sonny wore a shaggy bobcat-and-possum fur vest), were ejected from an LA restaurant when their appearance disturbed customers.

It was not a musical scene to warm the heart of a middle-aged ballad singer. But Sinatra stuck to his traditional style in three of four new albums. In the fourth, titled *Sinatra '65, the Singer Today*, he attempted an approach to the singles market in several numbers. Employing a new (for Sinatra) arranger, Ernie Freeman, he was accompanied by a guitar-dominated rhythm section that produced a big-band afterbeat, and by a large vocal group that provided a sing-a-long quality. *Somewhere in Your Heart*, in this genre, was hardly as successful as a more typical Sinatra side *It Was a Very Good Year*.

The latter came from what was easily his most personal collection since the best of the Capitol LPs and the first *Ring-a-ding* Reprise album. *September of My Years* was the self-analytical study of a romantic of fifty looking backward. Song titles like *How Old Am I?*, *It Gets Lonely Early*, *The Man in the Looking Glass*, *September Song* prompted *Hi Fi/Stereo Review* to remark that 'Sinatra now sings with more depth and insight than ever.' Perhaps the most remarkable development was that out of this frankly non-commercial group of literate songs, this brooding, my-hair-is-turning-grey musical approach came one of Sinatra's first hit singles in a number of years. *It Was a Very Good Year*, in fact, proved the beginning of a new cycle of single, Top Ten best-sellers that included *Strangers in the Night*, *That's Life* and *Something Stupid*, all of which climbed fantastically to No. 1.

Frank's interest in autobiography, now that he was approaching fifty, manifested itself in areas other than the recording sphere. Early in the year, he made a startling about-face and permitted *Life*, with whose management he had occasionally been at odds, to pay *A Visit to His Private World*—as it was blazoned on an over-sized, pull-out cover of the magazine. *Life* also offered *The Secrets of My Success* by Frank Sinatra himself. All told, eighteen pages of text and giant pictures were dedicated to the man whom the editors described as 'the most controversial, powerful and surprising entertainer around ... the first living singer of popular songs, an astonishingly good actor, ambitious director, a shrewd business-man.'

While the visit to Frank's private world was tepid, non-revealing stuff, his own article on singing was a gem. It was technically informative: 'Many singers never understood, and still don't, that a microphone is their instrument ... Instead of playing a saxophone, they're playing a microphone.' It was frank in confessing errors: he had turned down *Mona Lisa* ('pretentious') and *Love Is a Many-Splendoured Thing* ('over-arranged'). He was opinionated: 'Actual jazz, really good jazz, the jazz that we think is fine jazz, good-music, is dead.' He praised: 'Tony Bennett is the best singer in the business'—and he panned: Vic Damone has 'better pipes than anybody but lacks the know-how'; Lena Horne, 'a beautiful lady but really a mechanical singer'; Judy Garland and Ella Fitzgerald, 'technically two of the worst singers in the business'. The April 23 issue of *Life* proved a national sell-out, the first since the issue devoted to the assassination of President Kennedy.

Also in the realm of autobiography was a CBS-TV documentary presented on November 16. Here, Frank went through a double gambit, co-operating initially with the network news staff, then threatening to sue if some of the footage was telecast. Although Sinatra was genuinely concerned about the contents, he once again had given the country's publicists a lesson in how to build audience through controversy.

'But why was Sinatra incensed?' Al Salerno asked in a NY *World-Telegram* headline. 'Tough it wasn't.' Bob Williams wrote in the NY *Post*. 'Searching it certainly wasn't either.' And *Variety* damned the show as 'an unmitigated rave for Frankie Goodfellow, star performer, tycoon with heart of gold, family man (yet), and all-around ball-haver'.

Virtually all reviewers commented on one fleeting scene where Nancy, Jr.'s, voice was heard over the din of late-hour partying at Jilly's 'You want a daddy to be a daddy all the time ... Sometimes when he's with his friends, they carry on like a bunch of kids ... And it's great ... they're having a marvellous time ... But that bothers me a little...' Jack O'Brian's comment in the NY *Journal-American* was representative: 'His daughter Nancy's low-keyed whimper seemed somewhat embarrassing, plaintive, even poignant.'

In *Variety*'s opinion, the programme was 'remiss in not making clear the kind of childishness or cynicism, which prompted the fifty-year-old terrible infant to threaten the network'. Kay Gardella of the *Daily News* thought that interviewer Walter Cronkite's more probing questions 'were edited down to appease the temperamental star', while Jack O'Brian complained that 'they seemed gentlemanly and restrained in areas from romance (not a question about Mia Farrow) to hoodlums ... CBS didn't pinpoint the names of gangsters and others whose personalities, characters or lack of same have touched the life of this gifted, superb-singing sorehead'.

The ultimate verdict? Jack Gould of the NY *Times* said: 'Sinatra wasn't authorised but it could have been.' John Horn concluded: 'CBS and the public had been had. The programme was an institutional advertisement ... for the public image—the dedicated singer, the generous benefactor, the deep thinker, the happy comrade, the film executive, the devoted parent ...' Columnist Robert Sylvester quipped: 'the programme should have been sponsored by Humble Oil.'

And what of Sinatra's reaction? When Jim Mahoney, his press agent, advised that Don Hewitt, producer of the special, had called, Frank bristled. 'Shall I call him?' Mahoney asked, and Sinatra replied: 'How do you transmit a rap in the mouth?' However, through Mahoney, Frank released an about-face statement: 'I enjoyed watching the programme tremendously and was most satisfied the network had honoured its original representation to us regarding the programme's content. I was both pleased and honoured ...' CBS-TV should have been too, for the programme garnered a higher audience rating than NBC's *Tuesday Night at the Movies* and ABC's *The Fugitive,* two shows that consistently commanded high ratings.

Sinatra's protest, in which he involved his buddies who were also interviewed, was unquestionably an enormous audience-builder, whether he intended it as a publicity stunt or not. But at least three matters could have been of genuine concern to Frank. Item 1: he had refused to answer some of Cronkite's queries; it is likely that he did not want either the questions or his evasions telecast. Item 2: a beer company had put up $500,000 for Frank to sing on a rival network a week later; Frank's action in withdrawing permission for the telecast could have mollified executives, displeased, perhaps, that they were shelling out heavy coin for something that someone else got for free. Item 3: one New York newspaper noted that Frank pronounced the word 'scandalous' as if it were spelled 'scandulous'. Sinatra was also, perhaps, sensitive to the occasionally awkward character of his speech. Regardless of suspicions and criticisms, reviewers of the CBS profile had no reservations about the quality of his singing.

With *Sinatra/A Man and His Music*, the NBC Special sponsored by Budweiser Beer, the huzzas over his vocals swelled to a hullabaloo of acclaim. Since the Thanksgiving eve programme consisted entirely of songs, with only a thin rivulet of the spoken word, it came off as a 'gasser' (Al Salerno's epithet), and 'the television musical of the season' (John Horn's phrase). The sole new song in a sequence of seventeen standards, and the stunner', as Horn typed it, was *It Was a Very Good Year*—

347

the usual recording of the song had been presented on the CBS profile. Between stanzas of the song, focusing on the key years of a man's life. Frank interpolated old favourites: 'when I was seventeeen' led to *Young at Heart*; 'when I was twenty-one' segued to *The Girl Next Door*; and 'when I was thirty-five', underscored by brooding celli and basses, prompted *When We Were Young Last Night*. Dorothy Manners, who had succeeded ailing Louella Parsons as Motion Picture Editor of the Hearst chain, voiced the feeling of most TV editors: 'The class—and the best musical TV hour of the year ... A shining hour on the tube...'

News of Dorothy Kilgallen's accidental death reached the coast on the November morning when Frank began taping his NBC Special. He had a cold but was trying, unsuccessfully as it proved, to tape some segments for the Thanksgiving eve telecast. While on the set, Frank was told of the columnist's demise by his press agent. For years he had been making satiric cracks about her in his night-club appearances. 'Kilgallen's dead,' he reportedly mused. 'Guess I'll have to change my night-club routines.'

Unforgiving in his hates, Frank could be as unyielding in his arrogance. A story that went the rounds at the time, and later appeared in *Esquire*, involved an encounter between Sinatra and Harlan Ellison, who wrote the screenplay for *The Oscar*. The confrontation was in a private Beverly Hills club where Frank took a dislike to the country-type sports clothes that Ellison was wearing. Although he had never met the screenwriter, who was quietly watching a game of pool, Frank informed him: 'I don't like the way you're dressed.' Annoyed, Ellison stood his ground even when Frank approached him belligerently. As uncomplimentary remarks passed between the two, friends of Sinatra's intervened, and the threatened explosion never came. But it was reported that the manager of the club left for home as soon as he learned of the incident. An assistant was told by Sinatra: 'I don't want anybody in here without coats and ties.'

The hoopla over his fiftieth birthday on December 12 was to Frank an exciting memorial. But it was also a means. In a front-page *Billboard* advertisement, Reprise Records announced: 'This is the Month of Sinatra ... a sledgehammer trade and consumer promotional effort of unprecedented intensity to highlight—and sell—the most memorable anniversary in music history.' *It Was A Very Good Year* won Grammies for Frank (Best Male Vocal Performance) and for arranger-conductor Gordon Jenkins (Best Accompaniment Arrangement). A new LP of show tunes, *My Kind of Broadway*, leaped quickly on to best-seller lists while *A Man and His Music*, a two-record LP issued in three elegant editions with a special retrospective brochure and discography, became Top Ten. The earlier autobiographical album *September of My Years*, Top Ten at the same time, also copped a Grammy as Album of the Year. By February of 1966, both albums had grossed over $1,000,000 on the manufacturer's level and were certified as Gold Records.

In the middle of Reprise's monster promotion, Frank went to a swank party at the Trianon Room of the Beverly Wilshire Hotel. It was a Sunday evening, exactly fifty years to the day of Frank's birth, and the party was planned and hosted by the mother of Sinatra's children. According to the society editor of the NY *Journal-American*, the invited guests constituted 'the veritable cream of Hollywood society ... emphatically A and not B group people'. With Milton Berle as MC, the after-dinner show included Sammy Davis jack-in-the-boxing out of a six feet tall cardboard birthday cake to sing a parody, *My Kind of Man, Sinatra Is*. The laugh highlight of the evening was an interview assembled by Jack Haley, Jr., in which the replies came in the form of clips from Sinatra films. The answer to, 'How is the food in the restaurant of which you are part-owner?' showed Frank in a convulsion scene from *The Man with the Golden Arm*. In Dorothy Manners's view, the star of the evening was Nancy Sinatra, Sr., 'beautiful glowing and gracious, who worked for weeks to make this an unforgettable night for Frank'.

But the very column in which Miss Manners gave starring honours to Nancy, bore an eight-column head: 'Did Mia Farrow Clip Her Hair to Clip Her TV Role?' Salvador Dali called Mia's shearing of her tresses 'mythical suicide' while most columnists termed it pique at not being invited to Frank's birthday party. 'That wasn't it at all,' Mia later said. 'I just got tired of fooling with it.' Dorothy Manners' conjecture had its logic since the boyish bob gave Mia a hard look that was hardly in keeping with the guileless, girlish character of

Peyton Place's Allison Mackenzie; also, Mia was seeing Frank immediately after his party finished and was soon the recipient of two gifts, a white horse and a diamond bracelet. 'Just a little old diamond bracelet,' in Dorothy Manners' words, 'big enough to use as a shield if somebody were throwing darts at her.' Whatever the explanation, Miss Farrow's hair-bob attracted so much notice that several columnists picked it as the most memorable scissoring since Samson's locks were shorn. No one bothered to observe that Miss Farrow had succeeded in drawing attention to herself at a time when Sinatra's *fiftieth* was garnering peak coverage. It could be that, despite her youth, Mia's publicity sense was more than a match for the master.

'Mia has an uncanny sensitivity about people,' her childhood friend Liza Minnelli has said. 'She's so wise it's spooky ... There is something so open and tender about her that people are always trying to protect her, but she is stronger than all of us.' Sinatra himself was later to call Mia his 'twenty-two-year-old wife with the forty-five-year-old mind,' while some of her detractors claim, as UPI Hollywood correspondent Vernon Scott reported, that 'she deliberately creates headlines, then feigns surprise at them'.

As he left his birthday party to celebrate more privately with Mia, Frank had countless reasons to feel satisfied. In New York, the marquee of Basin Street East read 'FRANK SINATRA JR. SHOW featuring the Pied Pipers, Charlie Shavers, Sam Donahue Ork'—the Dorsey name was no longer needed to carry the bill—and it was just weeks before another Sinatra, Nancy, Jr., was to have the No. 1 hit record in Great Britain as well as the USA. Looking backward down the long, winding road his boots had trod from Hoboken to Hollywood in twenty-five years, he could glory in the continuing upward tilt of the many-laned highway of his career.

In the course of the year, apart from his tremendous success on TV and on records, he had captured the covers of three of the country's biggest news magazines, *Life* in April, *Newsweek* in September and *Look* in November. (In May 1967 Mia, then Mrs. Sinatra, was on the covers of *Life*, *McCall's* and *Ladies Home Journal*.) According to Publimetrix Poll, a service that tabulates printed mentions of celebrities, Rex Harrison had been the most publicised star early in the year. But by October, Harrison had dropped to No. 10, with Bob Hope No.

5, Patricia Neal No. 4, Elizabeth Taylor No. 3, John Wayne (partly because of his battle against cancer) No. 2, and leading the list, Frank Sinatra—which was the way he finished his twenty-fifth year in show business.

In the words of the song that helped make his fiftieth birthday exciting ... *it was a very good year* ...

CODA: RETREAT OF THE ROMANTIC

Reviewers of recent Sinatra films have noted the marked resemblance of Tony Rome to Sam Spade. Were it not for Sinatra's longtime pairing of cops with reporters and 'finks', his copout would occasion little surprise. A great bond existed between Bogey and Frank, and, as we know, Bogart's Rat Pack modulated, after Spade's passing, into Sinatra's Clan. The polarity of the two groups, despite their nonconformist, anti-Establishment orientation, was expressive of the contrasting personalities of their leaders. As Bogart was cool, imperturbable, so Sinatra has been intense, rash, unpredictable, romantic.

A review of the seven images he has presented to the public reveals that the composite is not a face of composure. Dean Martin, Andy Williams and Perry Como are all public images of the relaxed performer. Sinatra is at the other end of the emotional spectrum, a figure of tension, turbulence, and most of all, of provocative contradictions.

Through the years, Sinatra has manoeuvred to be all over the newspapers, but he has constantly been at odds, and not unproductively, with columnists and reporters, who could be helpful. In 1968, after a 25-year old friendship, he barred Earl Wilson from his opening at the Fontainebleau in Miami Beach. Last year he reportedly prompted Caesars Palace, where he was appearing, to pull its advertising from the *Las Vegas Review-Journal* with whose editor he was feuding. When the paper attacked him in an editorial, such a flood of mail poured into its office that it felt compelled to devote an entire page to the controversy—thereby giving Sinatra more attention than any paid ad would have secured.

Sinatra wants to be the last word in charm but he has been unable to restrain unattractive manifestations of a violent temper. He prides himself on his exquisite taste but he has used his fists and four-letter words in public. He wants to move gracefully among the cultured and social elite—and he has—but he has associated with pugs and hoods.

The ambivalence runs deeper. He has despised and resented authority, but woe to him who questions his word. He has always had a fine feeling for the underdog but has been known to run roughshod over the underdogs around him. He has mocked and challenged the Establishment but has worked strenuously to amass the goods and status that make the Establishment what it is. Nevertheless, he took chances, he fought for the things he believed in, and he had the courage to face the world with his complexities, ambiguities and limitations. Allowing his emotions, his appetites and his sensitivities to endanger his career, he became an appealing symbol of the twentieth-century American romantic.

But there was a turning point. In fact, there were two major crises. The more remote came in the dark days just before he captured the award-winning role in *From Here to Eternity* that sent his career rocketing to new heights. It involved the agency that had been booking him from the days of his buyout from his Tommy Dorsey contract. He was not too upset when, in 1952, Columbia Records failed to renew his contract. He was more troubled that he could not then get film roles of any consequence. But he was flabbergasted, shocked and irreparably hurt when MCA dropped him. Unquestionably, there crystallised in him at that moment the determination never to be again in a position where he could not control his own artistic and financial destiny.

An even ruder awakening, perhaps, occurred in 1961, long after he had built an impregnable position as a singer, actor and entrepreneur. It is interesting that just as one President of the United States (FDR) brought out Sinatra's liberal tendencies, so another (JFK) was pivotal in the transformation of the romantic. At the height of the campaign to elect John Fitzgerald Kennedy, Sinatra faced the troubling choice of getting off the political bandwagon or firing a left-wing writer he had retained as a scripter. For the first time in a life of cocky, arrogant and controversial behaviour, he made a major compromise. In backing down, he had to face demeaning comparisons with other producers who had stood pat when they were attacked for employing blacklisted writers.

352

Having made the aggravating compromise, he then had to endure an even more upsetting turn of events. Not even the celebrated, fund-raising Inaugural Gala which he staged for the Democratic Party helped. Suddenly, there was a cold wind blowing from the White House. And when JFK came to Palm Springs, Sinatra, who had made elaborate plans to entertain the President, found that JFK elected to stay instead at the home of Bing Crosby.

For the man who had been supersensitive to slights from his boyhood, and who had wanted even his enemies to treat him as a man of respect, the Kennedy rejection was the snub of snubs. It is from this time forward that Sinatra worked systematically, not only to erase his playboy image, but to establish himself on a high level of the Establishment itself. When his Nevada gambling licence became an issue, a public that had relied on him not to back away from a fight, was amazed to find him strangely conciliatory. Instead of 'frig you!' so sorry. Instead of belligerent headlines, quiet acquiescence. No one questions whether this was not wise conduct. But in earlier years, when compromise also seemed the more practical course, he had invariably stood his ground. Now, the dissonances of the controversial years were to resolve themselves into predictable diatonics. Sinatra became even more deeply immersed in the quest for money and status.

The new Sinatra showed himself in October 1966, when he spent $25,000 to give Rosalind Russell an elegant and memorable 25th wedding anniversary party. It landed him on the cover of ... *Ladies' Home Journal*. The posed, high-society photographs, released by news services with whom he had occasionally tangled, were an appropriate accompaniment to a special boxed listing of 'Who Was There' as well as 'Who Couldn't Make It'—two lists that did not include a single former member of the Clan.

On TV Sinatra has recently appeared on a number of magical, prize-winning hours of 'A Man and His Music'. But he has also become a television pitchman for Budweiser Beer, an undertaking that has garnered a group of his associates the wholesale franchise for Annheuser–Busch in Long Beach, California.

On the movie screen, where he once assayed challenging roles like Private Maggio, a Presidential assassin (*Suddenly*), a heel of a song-and-dance man (*Pal Joey*), a would-be drummer and narcotics addict (*Man with the Golden Arm*)—all unforgettable portrayals—he now appears content to sail through cliche roles in suspense films and whodunits.

Only in the area of songs and singing, despite the inevitable ageing of his vocal chords, do we still find signs of the adventuring spirit that marked Sinatra's artistry. His willingness to assay material he once eschewed—a rock 'n' roller like *That's Life*—bespeaks his determination to maintain contact with new audiences. He is not content to be known as 'Nancy's father' to today's teenagers, some of whom first discovered him through the father–daughter duet on *Something Stupid*. His receptivity to new things led him to a fresh harvest of superbly attractive ballads—*Cycles* by Gayle Caldwell, *Little Green Apples* by Bobby Russell, *From Both Sides, Now* by Joni Mitchell, *Didn't We* by Jimmy Webb and *Gentle on My Mind* by John Hartford. And his still-potent power as a pop meister-singer demonstrated itself when youthful Paul Anka provided him with a gem of a lyric to a stirring French melody. As autobiographical as any ballad he had ever sung, *My Way* was a dramatic reminder of the unremitting individualist that Sinatra had once been.

The romantic singer was still a seeker. That he should have inspired Rod McKuen to compose a brace of special songs was as inevitable as his recording an album by the best-selling American 'poet' of all time. *A Man Alone* seemed a natural sounding of a theme implicit in the biographies of both men. But the romanticism of the album is in the soaring arrangements of the melodies by Don Costa. The frequently prosaic words are full of self-pity and occasionally of a bitterness that once had no place in Sinatra's outlook as a romantic. 'Someone might be kind,' he sings at the close of the album, 'and muddle up your mind...' Perhaps it is too late in time as well as in Sinatra's own biography.

How does a man in his fifties capture the romantic rapture of the days when he and the world were young? If the marriage to 21-year old Mia Farrow suggested that he was still in pursuit of the love of his life, his manner of handling their bustup was not. Once when a love affair had caused him great anguish, he had worn his suffering on his sleeve and made the public witness to his agonies over Ava Gardner. His approach to Mia was that of a mature, practical man. He had wanted a companion and an intimate relationship. When it became clear that Mia would not fill either need, he took the initiative of announcing their separation. The public was then reading a cover story in *Look* in which the marriage was depicted in idyllic terms and in which Sinatra was quoted as saying of The Beatles: 'No, I could never sing *with* them. I wouldn't know how. They have completely different interpretations. I'm an optimist and a romantic. Yes, a romantic.'

It was a defensive stand in an area where the public that grew up with him would like him to remain. But 'Frankie Boy', who had once raised his fists to slug somebody for a racial slur, had just had two front caps broken over a gambling debt. Once, he wanted to be more than the man in charge. Once, it appeared that he might go beyond protest to comment. Instead, the noncomformist is more and more donning the conservative clothes of the Establishment. (In the 1968 Democratic primaries, instead of riding the dark horse or administrative challenger, he threw his support to the regular party plug-horse.) Once challenger as well as champion, he now appears content to be Il Padrone or, as his friend Jilly persists in calling him, the King of the World.

Now that the great romantic of our time is in retreat, what does he leave the little people who have lionised him, the women who have idolised him from near and afar, the young who have admired his moxie—what is left except a foggy day in London town . . . a paper moon . . . and the wee, small hours of the morning . . .

CHRONOLOGY

12/12/15	Born in coldwater flat, 415 Monroe Street, Hoboken, NJ
28/1/31	Graduated from David E. Rue Junior High School of Hoboken
8/9/35	The Hoboken Four, including Sinatra, wins 1st Prize, Major Bowes Amateur Hour
Autumn 1935	Vaudeville Tour, Hoboken Four, as part of Major Bowes Unit
1937-8	Sings at Rustic Cabin on route 9-W, Alpine, NJ
4/2/39	Weds Nancy Barbato at Lady of Sorrows Church, Jersey City
June 1939	Joins Harry James Band as male vocalist
13/7/39	First record sessions with James Band. First side: *From the Bottom of My Heart*
25/1/40	Starts with Tommy Dorsey Band
1/2/40	First record session with Dorsey Band. First side: *The Sky Fell Down*
8/6/40	Nancy Sandra, first child, born at Margaret Hague Hospital, Jersey City
19/1/42	First solo record session. First side: *The Night We Called It a Day*
30/12/42	First solo appearance at NY Paramount. Billed as 'Extra Added Attraction'
6/2/43	Male Vocalist, 'Your Hit Parade', coast-to-coast radio show
17/3/43	First major nightclub engagement, Riobamba, Manhattan
7/6/43	First Columbia Records session. First side: *Close to You*
14/8/43	First appearance, Hollywood Bowl. Work on *Higher and Higher* first starring film
12/10/44	Appearance at NY Paramount causes Columbus Day bobbysox riot
10/11/44	Franklin Wayne, second child, born at Margaret Hague Hospital, Jersey City

April 1946	Special Academy Award citation for film short *The House I Live In*
7/10/46	Separates from Nancy. Reconciled sixteen days later
13/10/47	'Frank Sinatra Day' celebrated in Hoboken, NJ
20/6/48	Christina, third child, born at Cedars of Lebanon Hospital, Hollywood
14/2/50	Nancy announces separation
July 1950	First appearance, London Palladium
7/10/50	TV debut over CBS
30/10/50	Nancy secures interlocutory decree of divorce
7/11/51	Weds Ava Gardner, Philadelphia, Pa.
9/1/53	Signed for role of Maggio in *From Here to Eternity*
2/4/53	First session at Capitol Records. First side: *Lean Baby*
27/10/53	MGM announces separation of Frank and Ava
April 1954	Academy Award, 'Best Supporting Male Performance of 1953'
1956	Produces first independent film and stars in *Johnny Concho*
5/7/57	Divorced from Ava Gardner
19/12/60	First session at Reprise Records, his own label. First side: *Ring-a-ding Ding*
January 1961	Stages Inaugural Gala, JFK's Inauguration as President
9/1/62	Announces engagement to Juliet Prowse. Engagement broken 22/2/62
August 1963	Sells Reprise Records to Warner Bros. and settles on lot
11/12/63	Arranges for release of kidnapped son, paying $240,000 ransom later recovered
1964	Directs his first film and stars in *None But the Brave*
July 1965	First appearance, Newport Jazz Festival
24/11/65	NBC telecast *Sinatra: A Man and His Music*, winner of Emmy, Peabody and Edison awards
12/12/65	Fiftieth birthday party, Beverly Wilshire Hotel
June 1966	*Strangers in the Night*, first No. 1 disc in USA
19/7/66	TV actress Mia Farrow becomes Mrs. Frank Sinatra No. 3

2

SINATRA FILMS

1935 Major Bowes Amateur Hour short. Sang with Hoboken Four.

1941 *Las Vegas Nights* (Par.) With Tommy Dorsey Orchestra. Musical. Sang *I'll Never Smile Again* et al.

1942 *Ship Ahoy* (Loew's) With Tommy Dorsey Orchestra. Musical. Soloed and sang with The Pied Pipers.

1943 *Reveille with Beverly* (Col.) Ann Miller, William Wright, Dick Purcell. Bands of Duke Ellington, Count Basie, Bob Crosby and Freddie Slack. Musical. No billing.

1944 *Higher and Higher* (RKO) Michelle Morgan, Jack Haley, FS. Musical. Speaking and singing role. Songs by Jimmy McHugh and Harold Adamson.
 Step Lively (RKO) FS, George Murphy, Adolph Menjou, Gloria DeHaven. Musical. Starred. Songs by Jule Styne and Sammy Cahn.

1945 *Anchors Aweigh* (MGM) FS, Kathryn Grayson, Gene Kelly. Musical. Sang and danced. Songs by Jule Styne and Sammy Cahn.
 The House I Live In (RKO) FS. Short on racial intolerance. Special Academy Award.

1946 *Till the Clouds Roll By* (MGM) June Allyson, Lucille Bremer, Judy Garland. Jerome Kern biopic. Singers: Lena Horne, Dinah Shore, Kathryn Grayson, FS.

1947 *It Happened in Brooklyn* (MGM) FS, Kathryn Grayson, Jimmy Durante, Peter Lawford. Musical. Songs by Jule Styne and Sammy Cahn.

1948 *The Miracle of the Bells* (RKO) Fred MacMurray, Valli, FS, Lee J. Cobb. First dramatic role. Played town priest.
 The Kissing Bandit (MGM) FS, Kathryn Grayson, J. Carroll Naish. Musical. Songs by Nacio Herb Brown and Eddie Heyman.

1949 *Take Me Out to the Ball Game* (MGM) FS, Esther Williams, Gene Kelly. Musical. Songs by Roger Edens, Betty Comden and Adolph Green.

On the Town (MGM) Gene Kelly, FS, Betty Garrett. Musical. Songs by Leonard Bernstein, Betty Comden and Adolph Green.

1951 *Double Dynamite* (RKO) FS, Jane Russell, Groucho Marx, Don McGuire. Bank clerk. Songs by Jule Styne and Sammy Cahn.

1952 *Meet Danny Wilson* (UI) FS, Shelly Winters, Alex Nichol, Raymond Burr. Night-club performer.

1953 **From Here to Eternity* (Col.) Burt Lancaster, Montgomery Clift, Deborah Kerr, FS. Private Maggio. Academy Award as Supporting Player.

1954 *Suddenly* (UA) FS, Sterling Hayden, James Gleason. Presidential assassin.

1955 *Young at Heart* (WB) Doris Day, FS, Gig Young, Ethel Barrymore. Misfit piano player. Sings title song, standards and duet with Doris Day.

*Not as a Stranger (UA) Olivia de Havilland, Robert Mitchum, FS, Gloria Grahame. Young, money-hungry doctor.

The Tender Trap (MGM) FS, Debbie Reynolds, David Wayne, Celeste Holm. Swinging Bachelor. Hit title song by James Van Heusen and Sammy Cahn.

*Guys and Dolls (GOLDWYN) Marlon Brando, Jean Simmons, FS, Vivian Blaine. Singing gambler. Songs by Frank Loesser.

1956 **The Man with the Golden Arm* (UA) FS, Eleanor Parker, Kim Novak, Arnold Stang. Card dealer, jazz drummer and junky.

Johnny Concho (UA) FS, Keenan Wynn, William Conrad, Phyllis Kirk. Produced and starred as cowboy coward.

*High Society (MGM) Bing Crosby, Grace Kelly, FS, Celeste Holm. Newspaper reporter. Sings songs by Cole Porter.

1957 **The Pride and the Passion* (UA) Cary Grant, FS, Sophia Loren, Theodore Bikel. Spanish guerrilla fighter.

The Joker is Wild (Par.) FS, Mitzi Gaynor, Jeanne Crain, Eddie Albert. Joe E. Lewis biopic. Sings Academy Award song *All the Way* by James Van Heusen and Sammy Cahn.

*Pal Joey (Col.) Rita Hayworth, FS, Kim Novak. Night-club singer. Songs by Rodgers and Hart.

1958   *Kings Go Forth* (UA) FS, Tony Curtis, Natalie Wood. Soldier boy in a story touching mixed marriage problem.

1959   *Some Came Running (MGM) FS, Dean Martin, Shirley MacLaine. Writer and army vet.

       *A Hole in the Head (UA) FS, Edward G. Robinson, Eleanor Parker, Carolyn Jones. Ne'er-do-well father. Comedy. Co-producer.

       Never so Few (MGM) FS, Gina Lollobrigida, Peter Lawford, Steve McQueen. American soldier in Burma.

1960   *Can-Can (Twentieth Century-Fox) FS, Shirley MacLaine, Maurice Chevalier, Louis Jourdan, Juliet Prowse. Parisian lawyer. Songs by Cole Porter.

       *Ocean's Eleven (WB) FS, Dean Martin, Sammy Davis, Jr., Peter Lawford. Vet in a scheme to hold up five Las Vegas casinos.

1961   The Devil at 4 O'clock (Col.) Spencer Tracy, FS, Kerwin Matthews. Noble-hearted convict.

1962   *Sergeants Three (UA) FS, Dean Martin, Sammy Davis, Jr., Peter Lawford, Joey Bishop. Army trooper in Western re-make of Gunga Din.

1962   The Manchurian Candidate (UA) FS, Laurence Harvey, Janet Leigh, Angela Lansbury. Army intelligence officer.

1963   *Come Blow Your Horn (Par.) FS, Lee J. Cobb, Molly Picon, Barbara Rush. Swinging bachelor.

       Four for Texas (WB) FS, Dean Martin, Anita Ekberg, Ursula Andress. Cowboy in a comedy Western.

1964   *Robin and the Seven Hoods (WB) FS, Dean Martin, Sammy Davis, Jr., Peter Falk. Spoof of Robin Hood in Chicago setting. Songs by James Van Heusen and Sammy Cahn.

1965   None but the Brave (WB) FS, Clint Walker, Tommy Sands, Brad Dexter, Tony Bill. American Marine on South Pacific island. Directed and produced by FS.

       *Von Ryan's Express (WB) FS, Trevor Howard. US Army Colonel.

       Marriage on the Rocks (WB) FS, Deborah Kerr, Dean Martin. Married business tycoon.

1966   Assault on a Queen (Par.) FS, Virna Lisi, Tony Franciosa, Richard Conte, Alf Kjellin. Sea diver.

1967   The Naked Runner (WB) FS, Peter Vaughan, Derren Nesbitt, Nadia Gray. London business man.

Tony Rome (Twentieth Century-Fox) FS, Jill St. John, Richard Conte, Gena Rowlands. Tough private eye.

Cameo appearances in *Around the World in Eighty Days, Road to Hong Kong, The List of Adrian Messenger* and *Cast A Giant Shadow*.

An asterisk* preceding film title denotes an 'All-time Box-office Champ', which, in *Variety*'s compilation, signifies a film that has paid the distributor at least $4,000,000 in US–Canada rentals.

3

A SINATRA GLOSSARY

Sinatra, not unlike Crosby, has always had an intuitive feeling for language, something that directors of his pictures as well as critics of his records have always sensed. That he developed a lingo of his own is hardly surprising. A mixture of music biz, baseball and hip colloquialisms, it is infused with his sensitivity to the rhythm of language. It most assuredly is not, as some critics claimed, mainly a system of 'coded obscenities' although it contains the normal complement of biological and sexual allusions to be found in male conversation.

broad—a girl but, more specifically, a girl with sex appeal
barn burner—a 'broad' with real polish and class
beard—a cover, a blind, a guy who comes along when you're dating a married broad or someone you don't want to be connected with
beetle—a flashy 'broad', sharp clothes and all
big-leaguer—a guy who can handle any situation, who can hit the ball out of the park
bag—style, groove, interest
bird—a suitcase word that has succeeded 'clyde' in Sinatra's private vocabulary
bombsville—it missed, it failed, it's a bust. See *ville*
bunter—a sad sack, a guy who can't get to first base, a sorry soul who will 'step with both feet in the cement up to his neck'
Charley—a ready handle. 'It saves remembering names. You can always catch a waiter's attention by calling him Charley or Sam. Even a girl turns 'round if you call, "Hey, Charley!"'
chick—a girl
The Chinaman—Yul Brynner
clyde—a general utility word, acquiring definition from each situation or intonation. 'Let's give it another clyde' at a gambling table, clyde=spin. 'Let's get some clyde as soon as

you get off your clyde' = 'Let's go get some broads, pizza or liquor as soon as you can get off your ass.' 'He's a real clyde' meant 'He doesn't belong'

creep—a guy you would like to squash, a worm

crumb—a guy for whom you have no respect

Dag—Dean Martin

dame—a broad who lacks sex appeal

endsville—it's over. See *ville*

feelsville—let's give it a run-through. See *ville*

fink—a guy without loyalties. On the Hoboken docks, it referred to a strike-breaker; there had been one named Fink whose disloyalty during a strike resulted in a friend's death

gas—the end, the greatest, like 'a gas of an evening'

gasser—a great guy or a 'broad' who's a knockout

gasoline—liquor, more specifically, Jack Daniels bourbon

go-fer—a guy who runs errands, goes for coffee, etc.

Good night, all—drop it, forget it. Like if a guy comes in with a 'broad' and someone says: 'Is that his wife?'

Harve or Harvey—a square or a typical tourist. Like a guy who goes into a French restaurant and asks, 'What's ready?'

Hello!—an alert signal, an exclamation of pleasure. Like when a gas of a broad appears

hunker—a general utility man, a 'go-fer'

'I think it's going to rain'—Let's move, let's go. Like if you're at a dull party

jokes—his lines in a movie script

locked-up—unavailable, engaged

loser—a guy who's loused up, drinks too much, makes enemies easily

mish-mash—a broad who's all mixed-up

mother—a Negro and jazz colloquialism, both a commendation and a knock. The greatest and the worst. Derived from Negro slang, *mother fucker*

mouse—a cuddly 'broad'

(the) odds aren't right—'Let's not go, accept or buy'

original Major Bowes Amateur Hour loser—a no-talent guy or chick

player—a guy who tries, takes chances, makes friends

The Pope—Sinatra to the members of his entourage

quin—an easy pick-up

Smokey—Sammy Davis, Jr.

tomato—a dame ripe for marriage

twist and twirl—a 'broad' who likes to dance

ville—a suffix combining form that originated in music biz and transformed states of mind and situations into places. See *bombsville, endsville,* etc., above. The origin of the device, as I suggested in a booklet on the *Lingo of Tin Pan Alley,* could well be the red-light district in New Orleans known as Storyville and named after the alderman who caused it to be legalised. By creating employment opportunities for New Orleans musicians, Storyville helped give the Delta City its crucial role in the development of jazz. *Ville* is, of course, the French word for town or city

4

SINATRA AS A RECORDING ARTIST

If the vocal chords of Frank Sinatra have not yielded the most highly orchestrated financial complex in entertainment business, they surely are among the most recorded in all of popular music. In a singing career that spans more than a quarter of a century, he has participated in over three-hundred record sessions, cut more than a thousand sides and currently is represented by sixty active LPs. Both Columbia and Capitol, with whom he has not been associated for years, continue to release new albums by re-packaging old masters. The years of his heaviest recording were 1940, the first in his tenure with Tommy Dorsey (twenty-one sessions); 1947 when he kept twenty-five dates at Columbia and recorded seventy-two sides; and 1956, when his busy Capitol schedule included nineteen record sessions.

Although his name is to be found on as many as ten different labels, the bulk of his recording is on only four. His earliest discs, with the Harry James band, were on Columbia. When he went with Dorsey, his voice was to be heard on RCA Victor and, for four solo sides, on Bluebird, a Victor subsidiary. His first record contract, after he left the Big Bands and became a solo 'bedroom singer', was with Columbia. A two-year deal dated June 1, 1943, it was re-dated November 11, 1944 because of the record ban and renewed once. Before it expired on November 10, 1948, it was re-negotiated for a five-year term commencing January 1, 1948 and terminating December 31, 1952. Columbia's failure to renew in 1952 led to his affiliation with Capitol Records for whom he cut his first session in April 1953 and his last in September 1960. He began recording for his own label in December 1960 and his first Reprise discs appeared in the spring of 1961. Less than three years later, in August 1963, he sold his label for over a million dollars to Warner Bros., part of a deal that involved his services on the movie lot. Nevertheless, his discs continue to appear under the Reprise emblem.

Sinatra's loyalties to songs and song-writers are no less

fervent than his feelings for friends. Of more than eight-hundred songs, he has cut over one hundred and fifty more than once. A smaller group of thirty-eight odd has gone into the studio with him three times or more. But of this select company, only eighteen have actually been triple releases. This count is based on original releases, not re-packaged items. It should be borne in mind that virtually all record contracts bind an artist not to record a song for another label before five years have elapsed. The favoured baker's dozen, arranged on the basis of their earliest recording, are as follows:

1 ALL OR NOTHING AT ALL   39/61/66
2 FOOLS RUSH IN   40/47/65
3 I'LL NEVER SMILE AGAIN   40/59/65
4 NIGHT AND DAY   42/56/61
5 THE SONG IS YOU   42/47/58
6 WHITE CHRISTMAS   44/47*/54
7 PUT YOUR DREAMS AWAY   45/57/63
8 HAVE YOURSELF A MERRY LITTLE CHRISTMAS   45/57/63
9 THE MOON WAS YELLOW   45/58/61/66
10 ALL OF ME   46*/47/54/66
11 SEPTEMBER SONG   46/61/65
12 SOLILOQUY from *Carousel*   46/46/55/63
13 I LOVE YOU   46/53/62
14 ONE FOR MY BABY   47/58/66
15 I'VE GOT A CRUSH ON YOU   47/60/66
16 LONDON BY NIGHT   50/57/62
17 YOU MAKE ME FEEL SO YOUNG   56/61/66
18 I'VE GOT YOU UNDER MY SKIN   56/63/66

Other songs have been recorded by Sinatra at least three times, but dissatisfaction with the masters has not led to three releases. These tunes are:

19 IMAGINATION   40/40/61/61/61
20 POLKA DOTS AND MOONBEAMS   40/61/61
21 I'LL BE SEEING YOU   40/61/61/61/61
22 THE ONE I LOVE BELONGS TO SOMEBODY ELSE   40/59/61/61
23 VIOLETS FOR YOUR FURS   41/41/53
24 WITHOUT A SONG   41/61/61/61

* Not released in USA.

25 THERE ARE SUCH THINGS 42/61/61
26 TAKE ME 42/61/61
27 THE MUSIC STOPPED 43/46/47
28 NANCY 44/45/63
29 WHERE OR WHEN 45/58/66
30 ALWAYS 46/47/60
31 APRIL IN PARIS 46/47/60
32 NONE BUT THE LONELY HEART 46/46/47
33 DON'T CRY JOE 49/61/61/61
34 IT ALL DEPENDS ON YOU 49/58/60
35 YOUNG AT HEART 53/61/63
36 WITCHCRAFT 57/61/63
37 SECOND TIME AROUND 60/61/63
38 YOU'RE NOBODY TILL SOMEBODY LOVES YOU 61/61/61

The foregoing list suggests that Sinatra has been a meticulous craftsman through the years, frequently rejecting masters and, regardless of cost and time, re-recording them until he achieved a desired result. During the Columbia period, 1946 and 1947 were the years of the largest number of rejects (six each). Six masters were also rejected in 1958 during his Capitol contract. The year that brought the greatest number of unreleased sides was 1961 when, recording for his own company, he turned down thirty-two Reprise masters.

During his days as a band vocalist, Sinatra's favourite songwriters were the team of Burke and Van Heusen, who had been responsible for many of Crosby's biggest hits. Close seconds during those years (1939–43) were Irving Berlin and Frank Loesser. After he embarked on his solo career and became the bobby-sox idol, his preference was for the songs of Cahn and Styne, with Richard Rodgers running second, and Van Heusen, Berlin and Porter being favoured in that order on his Columbia discs (1944–52). The shift to Capitol brought a new team into favour, Cahn and Van Heusen, a creative marriage that resulted from the break-ups of Burke and Van Heusen and Cahn and Styne. Cole Porter and Richard Rodgers moved up to the number two and three positions, suggesting an increasing interest in show tunes. During the Capitol years (1953–60), the next most-favoured songwriters were the Gershwins, Johnny Mercer and Jule Styne, all of whom underline Sinatra's feeling for show material. Both Mercer and Styne had by then given up Hollywood and Vine for Shubert Alley.

Between 1960 and the present, the same group of song-writers maintained their hold on his recording sessions. Cahn and Van Heusen continued to lead by a wide margin on his Reprise discs, followed by Berlin, Rodgers and Hammerstein, Cole Porter and lyric writer Johnny Mercer. Carolyn Leigh, the lyricist responsible for *Young at Heart* and *Witchcraft*, also figured in the favoured group, as did composer Jerome Kern.

A preference for the work of given songwriters has not deterred Sinatra from reacting sensitively to shifts in public taste. His career as a recording star divides itself naturally into, not the three B's, but five. There is, first, the *Big Band* Sinatra, encompassing the years with James and Dorsey, when the dance tempo and bouncing gusto of the swing era determined his singing style. With the former, he participated in only five sessions, recording only ten tunes between July 13, and November 8, 1939. One of these was *All or Nothing at All*, cut on August 31, whose release during the recording ban of 1943–4, sent Sinatra's solo career spinning merrily. With Dorsey, he participated in forty record sessions, the first on February 1, 1940 and the last on July 30, 1942, cutting ninety sides. During this two-and-a-half-year period, he did one solo session—the first of his career—recording four sides on January 19, 1942 with Axel Stordahl as arranger-conductor. For more than two years after he stepped forth as a soloist, The Voice was prevented from making records by the strike of the Musicians Union against the record companies. The only break in this hiatus was a series of *a capella* sessions executed with the Ken Lane Singers between July 6 and November 10, 1943, and productive of five Hit Parade songs.

Two days after the strike was settled in November 1944, Sinatra was in a Columbia studio cutting new discs. Now, we have the emergence of the *Big Ballad* Sinatra, with ex-Dorsey arranger Axel Stordahl creating the velvet background sound of swirling strings, heady woodwinds and soft rhythm. The best-selling discs of the Columbia era were *You'll Never Know*, *People Will Say We're in Love*, *Sunday, Mondays or Always* (all issued in 1943), and *Five Minutes More* (1946).

As his sales began to slump in the late '40s and complications in his personal life led to the *Big Bust* Sinatra (it only appeared that way because of his meteoric rise and the previous phenomenal popularity), he began to experiment with arrangers other than Stordahl. He had previously made occasional sides with Xavier Cugat, The Charioteers and Mitch Miller. In December 1946, he had recorded two songs with Page Cavanaugh; in September 1947, he had done one tune with Alvy West and the Little Band; and in April 1948, he had cut with the Jeff Alexander Choir. But a more determined effort to arrive at a new, and perhaps more saleable sound, occurred in December 1948 when Sinatra recorded with Mitchell Ayres (later Perry Como's arranger-conductor) and with the Phil Moore Four.

Between July and October 1949, the tempo of the search increased, as he cut four tunes with Hugo Winterhalter (later Eddie Fisher's arranger-conductor), three with Jeff Alexander, and three with Morris Stoloff. In March 1950 he recorded three sides with Mitch Miller, who had by then succeeded Manie Sachs as head of Columbia's A and R department. Before the end of 1950, Frank also cut seven sides with one of his radio arrangers, George Siravo. But none of these experimental dates halted the downward dip of his sales, a development resulting in part from the rise of new record idols like Frankie Laine, Nat 'King' Cole and Perry Como. The final session at Columbia came on September 17, 1952 when Percy Faith, then of the A and R department, arranged and conducted a single side that was to serve as backing for a Faith-scored tune cut in 1950.

Regardless of the different arrangers whom Sinatra tried between 1945 and 1952, the sound of his Columbia discs was created by Axel Stordahl. In an overall survey, Stordahl arranged and scored two hundred and twenty-odd discs against forty-six by all other arranger-conductors.

It was a different singer that record-buyers heard after Sinatra switched to Capitol Records. Stordahl handled his first date on the new label. But a new record star, Eddie Fisher, with a big TV show beckoned just as Sinatra was set to try Billy May and ex-Dorsey arranger Nelson Riddle. Although two of the four sides cut on April 30, 1953 are credited to Billy May, all four were scored by Riddle, who became the major sound architect of the Buoyant Sinatra. The voice was deeper, the delivery had greater rhythmic thrust and the feeling for contrasting textures was more pronounced. *Young at Heart*, the first Sinatra–Riddle hit and his first big seller on Capitol, was in the can by December 9, 1953, little more than seven months after their first date together.

During the Capitol years (1953–61), Sinatra used a number of other arranger conductors: trumpeter Ray Anthony (two sides in 1954); Dave Cavanaugh of the Capitol A and R department (two sides in 1955); composer Gordon Jenkins (twenty-four sides in 1957 and eleven in 1959); and Billy May (twelve sides in 1957 and fifteen in 1958). But the swinging brass-and-string sound on Capitol was the creation of Riddle as the dulcet string-and-woodwind Columbia sound was the work of Stordahl.

After he founded his own label in 1961, Frank moved further in the direction of a jazz-oriented style, giving us a singer whom we may characterise as the *Basie* Sinatra. Johnny Mandel, one of several arranger-conductors who emerged during the era of so-called West Coast Jazz, scored the songs in his first Reprise album *Ring-a-ding Ding*! Billy May arranged and conducted the second. Former Dorsey arranger Sy Oliver handled the third. Former Basie arranger Neal Hefti scored the fifth, as well as the first album Sinatra made with the Basie band itself. Quincy Jones arranged and conducted the second Basie–Sinatra collaboration, serving in the same capacity during personal appearances of the two.

As soon as contractual commitments to Capitol permitted, Nelson Riddle began recording again with Sinatra. The renewal of their association in 1963 resulted in *The Concert Sinatra*, a plodding LP, *Academy Award Songs*, and *Sinatra's Sinatra*, a re-recording of a number of tunes on which they had collaborated during the Capitol era. Another arranger of this era, Gordon Jenkins, to whom Sinatra turned for introspective backgrounds, backed Sinatra on two LP's, *All Alone* and *September of My Years*, both in a more reflective mood than most of the albums of the ebullient Basie years.

While jazz buffs do not regard Sinatra as a jazz singer and the purists were not too happy about his record-breaking appearance at the Newport Jazz Festival in 1965, students of pop singing have always been aware of his concern with intensity, immediacy and involvement, all earmarks of jazz singing. But Sinatra is too much of a perfectionist to explore extensively the techniques of improvisation. His feeling for Billie Holiday's soulful, blues styling has led down the years to collaborations with jazz artists like Bobby Hackett, Billy Butterfield, Pearl Bailey and recently with Ella Fitzgerald and

Duke Ellington, and to the use of jazzmen like trumpeter Harry Edison, trombonist Juan Tizol, bassist Arvell Shaw, saxist Ben Webster, among others. With Sinatra, words like 'swinging' and 'swinger' have never merely referred to a hip search for 'where the action is' but, musically, to where the rhythm and beat are.

Yet Sinatra had no use for the Big Beat of rock 'n' roll, and like Mitch Miller, whom he blamed for his decline in the 1940's, and other ballad singers of his generation, tried to sit out the trend. Despite his outspoken antagonism, in July 1964, he recorded for the first time with an accomplished rhythm-and-blues arranger, Ernie Freeman. *Softly As I Leave You*, the best number of the session, did not quite make it, nor was it an out-and-out rock disc. After he went to the top of the singles charts with a movie ballad *Strangers in the Night*— it was his first Gold Record in years and, curiously, the first of his recording career—he tackled a hard rocking blues in *That's Life*. It, too, went to Number 1, as did *Something Stupid*, a duet with daughter Nancy, who had become a teenage favourite with *These Boots Are Made for Walking*. (By then he was venerated by even the youngest record-buyers as 'Nancy's Pop'.) Having surprisingly demonstrated that he could still be a force in a singles market dominated by rock and rock groups, he went on to explore Bossa Nova in a gentle, tender LP with Brazilian composer-guitarist Antonio Carlos Jobim. This album swiftly climbed bestseller charts.

Where he goes from here on records poses a difficult question —for Sinatra has always been an autobiographical and internalised singer. The watermark of his style, regardless of changes in technique, material, backgrounds and public taste, has been sincerity. Clearly, his vocal powers even today when he has long passed the prime of most pop singers, are great enough to encompass almost anything he cares to tackle. But where will he find the material expressive of his outlook and attractive to the record-buying public? Some will regard his recent turn towards rock as compromise. Others will see it as the ceaseless adventuring of the greatest pop singer of our time.

Sometime in the early 1960s, he indicated that he was planning to taper off his personal appearances and, as befitted a middle-aged multi-millionaire, become more and more involved in the private activities of an entertainment entrepreneur. But in 1967, he embarked on a record-breaking, mid-summer swing of personals with the Buddy Rich band, as he had the previous summer sung to SRO audiences with the Basie band. There are no signs of a let-up or slowdown in the café appearances in Miami and Las Vegas. Despite his status as a film Super-Star and as 'the most powerful American of Italian descent', as he was described recently in *The New York Times*, singing remains his unassailable first love—and entering a recording studio is always for him like coming home.

DISCOGRAPHY

SINATRA'S SWINGIN' SESSION (Capitol W1491, SW1491)

When You're Smiling; Blue Moon; S'posin'; It All Depends On You; It's Only a Paper Moon; My Blue Heaven; Should I; September in the Rain; Always; I Can't Believe That You're in Love with Me; I Concentrate on You; You Do Something to Me.

COME SWING WITH ME (Capitol W1594, SW1594)

Day by Day; Sentimental Journey; Almost Like Being in Love; Five Minutes More; American Beauty Rose; Yes, Indeed!; On the Sunny Side of the Street; Don't Take Your Love From Me; That Old Black Magic; Lover; Paper Doll; I've Heard That Song Before.

COME FLY WITH ME (Capitol LCT6154, SLCT6154)

Come Fly With Me; Around the World; Isle of Capri; Moonlight in Vermont; Autumn in New York; French Foreign Legion; Let's Get Away From it All; April in Paris; London by Night; Brazil; Blue Hawaii; It's Nice to Go Trav'ling.

POINT OF NO RETURN (Capitol W1676, SW1676)

(Ah, the Apple Trees) When the World Was Young; I'll Remember April; September Song; A Million Dreams Ago; I'll See You Again; There Will Never Be Another You; Somewhere Along the Way; It's a Blue World; These Foolish Things; As Time Goes By; I'll Be Seeing You; Memories of You.

THE CONCERT SINATRA (Reprise R1009, R9–1009)

I Have Dreamed; My Heart Stood Still; Lost in the Stars; Ol'

Man River; You'll Never Walk Alone; Bewitched; This Nearly
Was Mine; Soliloquy.

SINATRA'S SINATRA (Reprise R1010, R9–1010)

I've Got You Under My Skin; In the Wee Small Hours; The
Second Time Around; Nancy (with the Laughing Face); Witch-
craft; Young at Heart; All the Way; How Little We Know;
Pocketful of Miracles; Oh, What It Seemed to Be; Call Me
Irresponsible; Put Your Dreams Away.

MY FUNNY VALENTINE (Capitol T20577)

My Funny Valentine; My One and Only Love; You Go To
My Head; The Nearness of You; You're Sensational; You, My
Love; To Love and Be Loved; You'll Always Be the One I
Love; Love Looks So Well on You; All My Tomorrows; When
I Stop Loving You; Sleep Warm.

SINATRA SINGS DAYS OF WINE AND ROSES, MOON RIVER AND OTHER ACADEMY AWARD WINNERS (Reprise R1011, R9–1011)

Days of Wine and Roses; Moon River; The Way You Look
Tonight; Three Coins in the Fountain; In the Cool, Cool, Cool
of the Evening; Secret Love; Swinging on a Star; It Might As
Well be Spring; The Continental; Love is a Many-Splendoured
Thing; All the Way.

IT MIGHT AS WELL BE SWING (Reprise R1012)

In Other Words (Fly Me to the Moon); I Wish You Love; I
Believe in You; More (Mondo Cane theme); I Can't Stop Lov-
ing You; Hello Dolly; I Wanna Be Around; The Best Is Yet to
Come; The Good Life; Wives and Lovers.

SEPTEMBER OF MY YEARS (Reprise R1014)

The September of My Years; How Old Am I?; Don't Wait
Too Long; This Is All I Ask; Last Night When We Were
Young; The Man In the Looking Glass; It Was A Very Good
Year; When the Wind Was Green; Hello, Young Lovers; I See
it Now; Once Upon A Time; September Song.

THE CONNOISSEUR'S SINATRA (Capitol T20734)

Memories of You; I'll Be Around; Guess I'll Hang My Tears
Out to Dry; This Love of Mine; Taking a Chance on Love;
Moonlight in Vermont; September in the Rain; Day In, Day

Out; That Old Feeling; Here's That Rainy Day; Someone to Watch Over Me; Wrap Your Troubles in Dreams; Young at Heart.

A MAN AND HIS MUSIC (Two-record set, Reprise R1016 (a & b), R9–1016 (a & b))

Put Your Dreams Away; All or Nothing At All; I'll Never Smile Again; There Are Such Things; I'll Be Seeing You; The One I Love Belongs to Somebody Else; Polka Dots and Moonbeams; Night and Day; Oh, What It Seemed to Be; Soliloquy; Nancy (with the Laughing Face); The House I Live In.

Come Fly With Me; (How Little It Matters) How Little We Know; In the Wee Small Hours of the Morning; Young at Heart; Witchcraft; All the Way; Love and Marriage; I've Got You Under My Skin; Ring-a-Ding-Ding; The Second Time Around; The Summit; The Oldest Established; Luck Be A Lady; Call Me Irresponsible; Fly Me to the Moon; Softly As I Leave You; My Kind of Town; The September of My Years.

THAT'S LIFE (Reprise RLP1020, RSLP1020)

That's Life; I Will Wait for You; Somewhere My Love; Sand and Sea; What Now My Love; Winchester Cathedral; Give Her Love; Tell Her; Impossible Dream; You're Gonna Hear From Me.

SINATRA FOR THE SOPHISTICATED (Capitol T20757)

I Get A Kick Out of You; Brazil; Always; Too Close for Comfort; I've Heard That Song Before; Oh Look At Me Now; I Concentrate on You; That Old Black Magic; Baubles, Bangles and Beads; I Love Paris; Just One of Those Things; Day by Day; Lady is a Tramp; Let's Get Away From It All.

STRANGERS IN THE NIGHT (Reprise R1017, R9–1017)

Strangers in the Night; Summer Wind; All or Nothing At All; Call Me; You're Driving Me Crazy; On a Clear Day You Can See Forever; My Baby Just Cares For Me; Downtown; Yes Sir, That's My Baby; Most Beautiful Girl in the World.

IN CONCERT, SINATRA AT THE SANDS WITH COUNT BASIE AND THE ORCHESTRA (Reprise RLP1019, RSLP1019—2 LP's).

Come Fly With Me; I've Got a Crush on You; I've Got You Under My Skin; Shadow of Your Smile; Street of Dreams; One for My Baby; Fly Me to the Moon; One O'Clock Jump; Frank Sinatra monologue; You Make Me Feel So Young.

All of Me; September of My Years; Get Me to the Church on Time; Don't Worry 'Bout Me; Makin' Whoopee!; Where or When; Angel Eyes; My Kind of Town; Sinatra closing monologue; My Kind of Town.

FRANCIS ALBERT SINATRA AND ANTONIO CARLOS JOBIM (Reprise RLP1021, RSLP1021)

Girl from Ipanema; Dindi; Change Partners; Quiet Night of Quiet Stars; Meditation; If You Never Come to Me; How Insensitive; I Concentrate on You; Baubles, Bangles and Beads; Once I Loved.

FRANK SINATRA'S GREATEST HITS—THE EARLY YEARS (C.B.S. BPG66201—2 LP's)

Put Your Dreams Away; Dream; Girl That I Marry; Sunday, Monday and Always; House I Love In; Nancy; Saturday Night; Coffee Song; I Have But One Heart; I'm A Fool to Want You; Day by Day.

Five Minutes More; If You Are But A Dream; I've Got a Crush on You; September Song; I Couldn't Sleep a Wink Last Night; People Will Say We're in Love; Full Moon and Empty Arms; Time After Time; Moon Was Yellow; Mean to Me; Ol' Man River.

SONGS FOR SWINGIN' LOVERS (Capitol LCT6106)

You Make Me Feel So Young; It Happened in Monterey; You're Getting To Be a Habit With Me; You Brought A New Kind of Love to Me; Too Marvellous For Words; Old Devil Moon; Pennies From Heaven; Love Is Here to Stay; I've Got You Under My Skin; I Thought About You; We'll Be Together Again; Makin' Whoopee!; Swingin' Down the Lane; Anything Goes; How About You.

HIGH SOCIETY (Soundtrack) (Capitol LCT6116)

High Society; High Society Calypso; Little One; Who Wants To Be a Millionaire*; True Love; You're Sensational; I Love You Samantha; Now You Has Jazz; Well Did You Ever?*; Mind If I Make Love To You*.

(*Featuring Frank Sinatra)

THIS IS SINATRA (Capitol LCT6123)

I've Got the World on a String; Three Coins in the Fountain; Love and Marriage; From Here to Eternity; South of the Border; Rain; The Gal That Got Away; Young at Heart; Learnin' The Blues; My One and Only Love; The Tender Trap; Don't Worry 'Bout Me.

A SWINGIN' AFFAIR (Capitol LCT6135)

Night and Day; I Wish I Were In Love Again; I Got Plenty of Nuttin'; I Guess I'll Have To Change My Plan; Nice Work If You Can Get It; Stars Fell on Alabama; No One Ever Tells You; I Won't Dance; The Lonesome Road; At Long Last, Love; You'd Be So Nice To Come Home To; I Got It Bad And That Ain't Good; From This Moment On; If I Had You; Oh—Look at Me Now.

A JOLLY CHRISTMAS FROM FRANK SINATRA (Capitol LCT6144)

Jingle Bells; The Christmas Song; Mistletoe and Holly; I'll Be Home For Christmas; The Christmas Waltz; Have Yourself A Merry Little Christmas; The First Noel; Hark, The Herald Angels Sing; O Little Town of Bethlehem; Adeste Fideles; It Came Upon A Midnight Clear; Silent Night.

FRANK SINATRA SINGS FOR ONLY THE LONELY (Capitol LCT6168)

Only The Lonely; Angel Eyes; What's New; It's A Lonesome Old Town; Willow Weep For Me; Good-bye; Blues In the Night; Guess I'll Hang My Tears Out To Dry; Ebb Tide; Spring Is Here; Gone with The Wind; One For My Baby.

COME DANCE WITH ME (Capitol LCT6179)

Come Dance With Me; Something's Gotta Give; Just in Time; Dancing In The Dark; Too Close For Comfort; I Could Have Danced All Night; Saturday Night; Day In, Day Out; Cheek To Cheek; Baubles, Bangles and Beads; The Song Is You; The Last Dance.

NICE 'N' EASY (Capitol SW1417)

Nice 'N' Easy; That Old Feeling; How Deep Is the Ocean; I've Got a Crush on You; You Go To My Head; Fools Rush In; Nevertheless (I'm In Love With You); She's Funny That

Way; Try A Little Tenderness; Embraceable You; Mam'selle; Dream.

FRANK SINATRA SINGS THE SELECT COLE PORTER (Capitol SRS 5009)

I've Got You Under My Skin; I Concentrate On You; What Is This Thing Called Love?; You Do Something To Me; At Long Last, Love; Anything Goes; Night and Day; Just One of Those Things; I Get A Kick Out of You; You'd Be So Nice To Come Home To; I Love Paris; From This Moment On.

THE ESSENTIAL FRANK SINATRA, VOL. I (C.B.S. M63172)

From the Bottom of My Heart; Melancholy Mood; My Buddy; Here Comes the Night; Close To You; There's No You; The Charm of You; When Your Lover Has Gone; I Should Care; A Friend of Yours; My Shawl; Nancy; You Are Too Beautiful; Why Shouldn't I?; One Love; Something Old, Something New.

THE ESSENTIAL FRANK SINATRA, VOL II (C.B.S. M63173)

Blue Skies; Guess I'll Hang My Tears Out To Dry; Why Shouldn't It Happen To Us?; It's The Same Old Dream; You Can Take My Word For It, Baby; Sweet Lorraine; My Romance; One For My Baby; It All Came True; Poinciana; Body and Soul; I Went Down to Virginia; If Only I Had A Match; Everybody Loves Somebody; Comme Ci, Comme Ca; If You Stub Your Toe on the Moon.

THE ESSENTIAL FRANK SINATRA, VOL. III (C.B.S. M63174)

The Right Girl For Me; The Huckle Buck; If I Ever Love Again; Why Remind Me?; Sunshine Cake; It's Only a Paper Moon; My Blue Heaven; Nevertheless; You're the One; Love Me; I'm A Fool To Want You; The Birth of the Blues; Walkin' In the Sunshine; Azure-Te; Why Try To Change Me Now.

FRANK SINATRA (Reprise RLP1022)

The World We Knew; Something Stupid; This Is My Love; Born Free; Don't Sleep In The Subway; This Town; This Is My Song; You Are There; Drinking Again; Some Enchanted Evening.

FRANK SINATRA'S GREATEST HITS! (Reprise RSLP1025)

Strangers In The Night; That's Life; It Was A Very Good Year; Something Stupid; Somewhere In Your Heart; The World We Knew; Softly As I Leave You; Summer Wind; This Town; Tell Her (You Love Her Each Day); When Somebody Loves You; Forget Domani.

THE SINATRA FAMILY WISH YOU A MERRY CHRISTMAS (Reprise RSLP1026)

I Wouldn't Trade Christmas; It's Such A Lonely Time of Year; Some Children See Him; O Bambino (One Cold and Blessed Winter); The Bells of Christmas; Whatever Happened to Christmas?; Santa Claus Is Coming to Town; Kids; The Christmas Waltz; The Twelve Days of Christmas.

CYCLES (Reprise RLP1027)

Rain In My Heart; From Both Sides Now; Little Green Apples; Pretty Colours; Cycles; Wandering; By The Time I Get To Phoenix; Moody River; My Way of Life; Gentle On My Mind.

MY WAY (Reprise RLP1029)

Mrs. Robinson; Yesterday; For Once In My Life; Hallelujah, I Love Her So; Watch What Happens; If You Go Away; Didn't We; All My Tomorrows; A Day In The Life of a Fool; My Way.

A MAN ALONE (Reprise RSLP1030)

A Man Alone; Night; I've Been to Town; From Promise to Promise; The Single Man; The Beautiful Strangers; Lonesome Cities; Love's Been Good To Me; Empty Is; Out Beyond the Window; Some Travelling Music; A Man Alone.

THE SUMMIT (WITH DEAN MARTIN, BING CROSBY AND SAMMY DAVIS, JR.) (Reprise R5031)

Style; We Open in Venice; Guys and Dolls; Sam's Song; The One I Love Belongs to Somebody Else; Fugue for Tinhorns; Me and My Shadow; The Summit; The Oldest Established; Go Tell It On The Mountain; River Stay 'Way From My Door; Don't Be A Do-Badder; Mr. Booze.

THE MOVIE SONGS (Capitol ST2700)

Young at Heart; Tender Trap; To Love and Be Loved; C'Est Magnifique; They Came To Cordura; All My Tomorrows; All The Way; Monique; High Hopes; It's All Right With Me; Three Coins In the Fountain; Chicago.

THE BEST OF FRANK SINATRA (Capitol T21140)

Young At Heart; Hey! Jealous Lover; All The Way; Witchcraft; Chicago; Only The Lonely; Come Dance With Me; High Hopes; Nice 'N' Easy; Put Your Dreams Away; I've Got The World On A String; South of the Border; From Here to Eternity; In The Wee Small Hours of the Morning.

ROMANTIC SONGS FROM THE EARLY YEARS (Hallmark HM500)

Laura; Spring Is Here; Paradise; I Fall In Love Too Easily; Mam'selle; Over the Rainbow; If I had You; Music Stopped; Try A Little Tenderness; That Old Feeling.

HAVE YOURSELF A MERRY LITTLE CHRISTMAS (Hallmark HM521)

White Christmas; Jingle Bells; O Little Town of Bethlehem; Have Yourself A Merry Little Christmas; Christmas Dreaming; Silent Night, Holy Night; It Came Upon A Midnight Clear; Adeste Fideles (O Come All Ye Faithful); Santa Claus Is Coming To Town.

SUNDAY AND EVERY DAY WITH FRANK SINATRA (Music for Pleasure MFP1324)

Sunday; I'll Never Be The Same; Tell Her You Love Her; Close To You; River, Stay 'Way From My Door; I'm A Fool To Want You; How About You?; I Got It Bad and That Ain't Good; Your Love For Me; If I had You; Laura; Impatient Years.

SINATRA SINGS MUSIC FOR PLEASURE (Music for Pleasure MFP1120)

Same Old Saturday Night; Look To Your Heart; From the Bottom to the Top; It Worries Me; Two Hearts Two Kisses Make One Love; If I Had Three Wishes; Take A Chance; I Could Have Told You; Fairy Tale; You'll Get Yours; Flowers Mean Forgiveness; There's No You.

SOMEONE TO WATCH OVER ME (Hallmark HM592)

Someone to Watch Over Me; None But the Lonely Heart; Always; Stella by Starlight; The Nearness of You; Among My Souvenirs; All of Me; Luna Rosa; I Love You; When The Sun Goes Down.

SINATRA SINGS OF LOVE AND THINGS (World Record Club ST706)

The Nearness of You; Hidden Persuasion; The Moon Was Yellow; I Love Paris; Monique; Love Looks So Well On You; Sentimental Baby; Mr. Success; They Came to Cordura; I Gotta Right To Sing The Blues; Something Wonderful Happens in Summer; Chicago.

WATERTOWN (Reprise RSLP1031)

Watertown; Goodbye (She Quietly Says); For A While; Michael and Peter; I Would Be In Love (Anyway); Elizabeth; What A Funny Girl (You Used To Be); What's Now Is Now; She Says; The Train.

FRANCIS A. SINATRA AND EDWARD K. ELLINGTON (Reprise RLP1024, RSLP1024)

Follow Me; Sunny; All I Need Is The Girl; Indian Summer; I Like The Sunrise; Yellow Days; Poor Butterfly; Come Back To Me.

THE LADY IS A TRAMP (Capitol EAP1013)

The Lady Is A Tramp; Witchcraft; Come Fly With Me; Tell Her You Love Her.